In Glory's Shadow

Shannon Faulkner, The Citadel
and a Changing America

Catherine S. Manegold

ALFRED A. KNOPF

New York   2000

THIS IS A BORZOI BOOK
PUBLISHED BY ALFRED A. KNOPF

Copyright © 1999 by Catherine S. Manegold
Maps copyright © 1999 by David Lindroth, Inc.
All rights reserved under International and Pan-American Copyright
Conventions. Published in the United States by Alfred A. Knopf,
a division of Random House, Inc., New York,
and simultaneously in Canada by Random House of Canada
Limited, Toronto. Distributed by Random House, Inc., New York.
www.randomhouse.com

Knopf, Borzoi Books, and the colophon are registered
trademarks of Random House, Inc.

A portion of this work was originally published in *Interview* magazine.

Library of Congress Cataloging-in-Publication Data
Manegold, Catherine S.
In glory's shadow : Shannon Faulkner, the Citadel and a
changing America / by Catherine S. Manegold. — 1st ed.
p.   cm.
Includes index.
ISBN 0-679-44635-4 (alk. paper)
1. Citadel, the Military College of South Carolina—Trials, litigation, etc.
2. Faulkner, Shannon—Trials, litigation, etc.
3. Sex discrimination in higher education—Law and legislation—United States.
4. Sex discrimination against women—Law and legislation—United States.
5. Sex discrimination in higher education—South Carolina—Charleston.
I. Title.
KF228.C53M36   1999
344.73'0798—dc21   99-18919
CIP

Manufactured in the United States of America
First Edition

For my three sisters,
Nina, Deborah and Elizabeth.
Each with her own journey.

There are no magics, no elves,
No timely godmothers to guide us.
We are lost, must wizard a track
Through our own screaming weed.

—Gwendolyn Brooks,
"A Street in Bronzeville"

Contents

ix

Illustrations follow page 116.

In Glory's Shadow

Prologue:
An Awkward Question

O NCE WE HAD GOD and our fathers and everything seemed to fall quite naturally from that. We were a new nation in a dangerous wilderness, and we needed something just that simple. Far into the trace of human history, powerful political structures were being roughly questioned and then rudely pushed aside. With the hubris of the newly free, we cavalierly challenged monarchies and dynasties and every manner of assumed authority. We dumped tea into our harbors and took up arms against a distant king. We would be our own masters, we decreed. Yet in the chaos and excitement of settling a virgin land and inventing a new body politic, certain domestic absolutes prevailed. With public life in flux, we needed the rigid lines of private life to draw an unknown landscape into a shape we recognized. We needed rules and an internal sense of order. We found both inside our families. Europeans found us quaint—and laughably provincial. We didn't care. We had traded kings and fiefdoms for something far more intimate: the primacy of family. We called it a democracy. Here, a man's home was his castle and there would be no other. Church provided welcome redundancies. Its rule of thumb comfortably reflected what we already knew and most revered. At the altar, all power emanated from the Father and his Son. In our living rooms only the letters changed, dropping down to lowercase, to the father and his sons. Busy as we were challenging authority, we seldom questioned that.

When Europeans cast aside ruling elites they shook their heads with existential pain, deprived of an ancient sense of order. We were slow to feel that loss. For most Americans, the world's natural shape survived world wars and the awful crash of royal dynasties elsewhere. While change roiled all of Europe and ran across her distant colonies, we could still outline our natural order atop the dinner table: father at the head, mother across the way, the children arrayed along both sides, their own pecking order clear among themselves, just like the Cartwrights in *Bonanza,* every member fixed in the irreversible moment of a birth or marriage. To generations of Americans, the child's question "Why?" had always had an easy answer. "Because I am your father. . . . Because I am your mother. . . . Because I am older. . . . Because you're just a girl. . . . That's why." We anchored our lives in simple expectations. For all our famous freedoms, we had our absolutes as well. We held them tight because they gave us purpose and a frame.

As a young nation we might not have known what lay over the next mountain, beyond the next streambed or across those glowing plains of grass, but we did know—and for the most part we did honor and obey—rather puritanical restraints on our relationships. Perhaps it was precisely our rigidity at home that allowed us to tolerate the frightening confusion just outside of it. Home and hearth meant protection against the elements and safety from the hostile tribes whose land we had invaded and whose customs we disparaged. In those early households, meaning and survival lay within four walls. In a frontier land in which telephones were nonexistent and neighbors sometimes miles away, life was organized with rare simplicity around an ancient theme. In this lonely and uncertain experiment in human growth, we were contained within the cocoon of a neat system. In that we balanced the intoxicating freedom of cowboys and pioneers with an innate need for sanctuary. Constrictive family expectations helped us tolerate our limitless horizons without succumbing to the overwhelming terror that we all were simply lost. Anarchy was held at bay. Father, son, mother, daughter; in that we found our way.

For two centuries that balance held. Then, gradually, the wilderness was tamed, the borders closed. Under Theodore Roosevelt, a vast system of national parks and forests grew to remind us of where we had been. But those open fields and ragged mountains, those valleys gold with wild grass were a museum, not the ground that we called home. The world had pulled in tight. Without new landscapes to explore and immense new territories to traverse, we—the proud descendants of restless seekers—turned our questions backwards on ourselves. And what we found was troubling. Our revolution was unfinished. Its elegant ideas still had the power to transform. Now, we challenged the very institutions we had made. The same provocative taunts our forefathers once thrust at rulers whom they fled became the questions that were asked of *our* leaders and at home. Old questions reflected back. What gives you the right? This time, even the dinner table was not spared.

If the war against British rule was a political explosion, then this was social implosion. Our ideas, already old and sanctified in careful marble etchings in the nation's capital, gained sudden new intensity. The catalyst was clear. Not only were our boundaries fixed, but our faith in ourselves, once automatic, was badly shaken. It vaporized in an atomic flash. The depth and importance of that shift came clear to us only slowly. At first, our habits of implicit trust were so well etched that we could "duck and cover" without embarrassment while contemplating the notion of imminent nuclear attack. In time, of course, that silly fallacy disintegrated. Reality was simpler and considerably more stark: Duck and die. It was an undeniable home truth that left us all with nervous questions. Who deserved such terrible authority? Whom could we trust with it? "God is dead!" the posters chided. We had taken too much power for ourselves. At last, our easy faith was crumbling.

We did not see it quickly, but our long childhood was lost. We had always assumed that only other nations abused power or held so much of it as to pose a worldwide threat. Our nation was founded on the shared if somewhat self-serving presumption that we would always do God's will. That was our Manifest Destiny—to lead much of the world and lead it wisely. Danger lay outside our borders, not here among our brethren. We held that credo closely for well over a century. But by the time America waged war in Vietnam, a new cynicism was taking hold. A generation of Americans now read our history differently and was unwilling to march. For many young men then, it was not enough that someone simply told them they should go. A bumper sticker captured the rough anthem of the time: "Question Authority," it goaded. And so a generation did. Only now, it questioned everything, including God and father. A wild cacophony of voices quickly joined. Old questions gained new force.

In time, the splendid notion that "all men are created equal" (so willfully ignored throughout the time of slavery and later in Jim Crow laws) belatedly unfolded to embrace blacks and women, Hispanics, Asian-Americans, Native Americans, homosexuals, new immigrants and everyone else who called this ground their own. The force of great ideas overwhelmed us. And now, much to our surprise, we faced those challenges from the vantage point not of a young nation starting out and fumbling with new theories but of a culture with vested powers firmly in their place. We still thought of ourselves as courageous pioneers on the world stage. But the fact was that we had grown. Politically and socially, we were not innocents anymore, struggling for our footing in a dangerous, wild place. Instead, by the 1960s, we were a bit hidebound ourselves, with institutions of influence and wealth and careful traditions crafted to preserve them. We had built an enormous military, a healthy stock market, a network of elite private schools, some of the world's most powerful universities and a nuclear arsenal sufficient to blow it all to bits in easy multiplications. In a blink of history we had become the kind of power that we once so despised. Soon, we tore along familiar lines: Those without a say in leadership challenged the minority that assumed it as their right. Male, female. White, black. Old balances began to tip. The revolution had come home.

Battlegrounds always seem to have a central logic of their own. Looked at in retrospect, they often contain sparks of predetermination, as though their history were written on the ground before a single shot was fired. Military historians pore over regional topographies, searching for their clues. A hill here, a stand of trees, a granite slope, the rugged curve of a deep river can make the difference between victory and loss. Such are the limitations of our weaponry and perhaps even sometimes of our will to fight. Military experts send satellites aloft to track and trace terrain and try to find advantage. Swagger sticks, aptly named, imply an officer's relationship to maps, not men. Dense jungles can defeat us. An open desert provides easy targets. Sometimes the very ground of war can tell its story best.

Battlegrounds in social conflict have an inner logic, too. There are towns and cities in the United States that are unlikely to catch fire even in the face of the most awkward upheavals. They are too homogeneous or too remote to get involved, too preoccupied with their own affairs, or simply unmindful of their own potential place in history. They look to other cities for great changes when they come. Then they quietly adapt, putting new laws in place and changing with the times, getting on with business.

Charleston, South Carolina, beautiful and sure, was not like that. Even in the worst of times it held a deep conviction of its place in history. Proud of its difficult past, convinced of its grand destiny, birthplace of the Civil War and still utterly enamored of its crusty old hierarchies, it was comfortable in its haughtiness and always loved a fight. So convinced were its people of the honor of dispute that once two gentlemen bored with an old rivalry settled their affairs by simply dueling through their open windows—*bang, bang*—across a quiet street. Better that than seem a coward or somehow lacking in convictions.

In a city still married to the social formulas of a far distant past, the future had come slowly and always with resistance. On that musty, fertile ground, old monarchies still held allure. The best living rooms fairly dripped with regal colors and bright gilt. Major families could trace rootstock directly to old Europe. Some had set their seed well before our revolution. That history had a tendency to modulate their views. In modern times the standing joke enjoyed by all residents was that the oldest houses emulated royalty, were given to ancestor worship and were doused in enough alcohol to keep reality at bay. Given all that, Charleston was no less a part of us than any other place. Indeed, in many ways the city could claim a deeper grip on our hearts and history than most. It had been around nearly three centuries when our nation shot off fireworks for its bicentennial. And in a country best known for its hastily built high-rises, redundant fast-food sprawl and ugly, nondescript developments, Charleston remained largely unchanged, an architectural jewel celebrated for her grace, her manners and long tending to tradition. She made a rare temptation; small enough to be negotiable on foot and perched with a view out to the glinting sea. By the end of the twentieth century she nestled happily among the top tourist destinations in the United States and attracted roughly $1.5 billion a year in expenditures by visitors. Oh, she was envied and admired. We had become a people deeply nostalgic for our past. Indeed, we had become, finally, a people *with* a past. And there it was, orderly and inviting, dripping with Spanish moss, freshly restored after a bruising hurricane and now bursting with new hotels. What a sumptuous seduction. What better ground for a last stand?

New York was its perfect foil. The epicenter of wealth, power, influence and social experimentation, it had an equally invincible sense of self. Somehow from one era to the next it pulled off the impossible, managing to preserve the status quo—and its own position of intellectual and financial predominance—while simultaneously courting endless challenges to its shape. While Charleston kept busy meticulously caring for its history, New York fed on the messy future, inventing new forms and figures for the rest of us to take or leave. Mostly, in time and with resistance, we took them. Though visitors might dismiss Manhattan as a "foreign country" to be examined mostly at a distance with intimidation and delight, that noisy Babylon of clashing styles and high-tuned sensibilities was no less a part of our national psyche, a left hand to Charleston's right.

It could be said, of course, that neither community represents the "real" America. New York City is brash and oversized, so big that it could fit the entire population of South Carolina inside its noisy sprawl twice over with apartment space to spare. Charleston—at least the part of it that draws so many visitors—is really only a handsome collection of exquisite buildings populated by barely two thousand souls. There, the only people with real clout have always lived "south of Broad," as the prestigious neighborhood near the Battery has long been known. Isolated and quite content to rest forever in the backwash of their history, that minuscule (and once walled-off) elite sets the tone of things and keeps the clocks turned back. So no, in the broader context of national life, neither city seems to fit. Yet wars, defining though they are, are not started or won by the meek or the banal or even by the representative mass. They are instead the bloody work of zealots and of visionaries who have the arrogance to presume that they can guide the rest of us toward a future that they seek or a past they wish they could preserve. In that way, Charleston and New York were perfectly matched as dueling partners in a modern conflict over culture. Each possessed a certain arrogance and the willingness to fight. The rest of us could only watch and marvel.

In the early 1990s, they fought over a girl. She was a modern girl raised in a changing South who dared to ask a simple question: What gives you the right? She asked it of The Citadel, a state-funded, all-male military college born of the threat of slave revolt, bred on pomp and circumstance and devoted to a noble image it had painted of itself. On the face of it, hers was a simple question. The school was public. Yet it only accepted men. Why couldn't she march, too? But the battle was not simple, and little about The Citadel was really as that painting seemed. Despite the heady rhetoric that would flow so easily in court, no person and certainly no institution had escaped the torque of social change from the 1960s forward. Surely, despite all outward appearances to the contrary, The Citadel had not. Yet Citadel men took up the challenge as though the world itself might tip. An odd truth lay hidden deep within their rage. Their passion and their persistence grew not from what they wanted to preserve but from what they knew they had already lost. They had lost, forever, a time in America when such a question could not even form. They had lost their righteous sense of place and the guarantee that it was theirs alone, and not for sharing. Their world had tipped already. They were marching in a gyroscope, confined to a rare atmosphere. From that unsteady vantage point, they rallied in defiance.

Shannon Faulkner's challenge to The Citadel would become one of the most expensive civil rights cases ever to drag through the nation's courts. When all was said and won, her New York lawyers would ask for $6.15 million in litigation fees and costs. In a largely rural state that was known for its poor schools and modest cost of living, the price tag for merely preparing the bill was equal to the cost of a small house, $90,000. Lawyers for The Citadel sought an additional $3.8 million from South Carolina's taxpayers. In fact, they worked just as hard and just as long (logging more than twenty-five thousand hours on the case over five years) yet were paid on a more modest scale. Inside The Citadel, other monies hemorrhaged, too. Once, in a forty-five-minute conference call among the school's most powerful, Citadel officials agreed to spend $5 million from college coffers to help create a "separate but equal" program at a private women's college upstate. That expensive ploy died quickly in the federal court. But the money was nonrefundable, and the new women's leadership program sputtered on with minimal enrollment on a campus bristling not with cannons and jet fighters but with ersatz Greek statuary, crystal chandeliers, silk flowers, ubiquitous pianos, and oil portraits of southern women dressed in white, cradling frilly parasols.

What a fight it was. "We argued over every grain of sand," said one lawyer from the Faulkner side. Yet perhaps to many of those not involved, the case seemed quite clear from the start and all the battling not much more than a toxic combination of lawyers' greed and southern bluff. As a woman from Texas said with some contempt while visiting The Citadel's stark, close-shaved campus once, "Well, if it's a public school, then whatever's the fuss?" Indeed. Putting its enormous expense aside, the battle at The Citadel was a backwater business that would at best affect the few. Full of small-town enmities, ugly gossip and empty threats, the battle was petty and it was mean, just gritty hometown stuff. Though the matter wound its way to the U.S. Supreme Court, it did not fundamentally redefine the law. For a while, though, the ugly face-off that Shannon Faulkner's lawsuit spurred captured our own confusion well, boiling with a welter of nostalgia, anger, fear and hope. No one who got near it could easily resist that pull. In its own overdrawn way it said something fundamental about all of us, asking complicated questions with a simple thrust: What can we keep of who we've been? What must we now relinquish? Who will we be once we are done?

Once, we challenged distant rulers. We made a new democracy faithful to some old assumptions. Then we broke the template of our own invention. God and father faltered. To forge a statecraft between anarchy and tyranny, black and white were turned to gray. Having tamed the wild, cast aside our idols and challenged our defining social absolutes, we faced, at last, the wilderness within. The rare conglomerate that we had built demanded nuance and complexity. We are not a homogeneous and easily led people. We are who we set out to be, an amalgam of rebels and idealists, individualistic, opinionated, demanding and almost always full of hope. But now, we had no ready formulas to frame our aspirations. Our innocence no longer served. On the eve of a millennium, from the shards of what we shattered, we were asked to build a new mosaic. It is not finished. Perhaps it never can be. Ideas will not tame. They challenge smooth complacencies. We inherit what we are and, to a large extent, what we aspire to become. It is easy to set patterns. To break them takes an act of will and rare determination. It takes an awkward question. Shannon Faulkner learned that lesson young. In a small, proud city deeply wedded to its past, she stirred the rage of loss. It was a lark at first. She wanted most to make a point. At its end the battle scarred her deeply. A girl stood up to some old men. What gives you the right? she asked. It was a simple question. But the answer proved impossibly complex. To grasp that awful paradox is to know the sharp terrain of our most modern battlefields.

PART I

Battleground

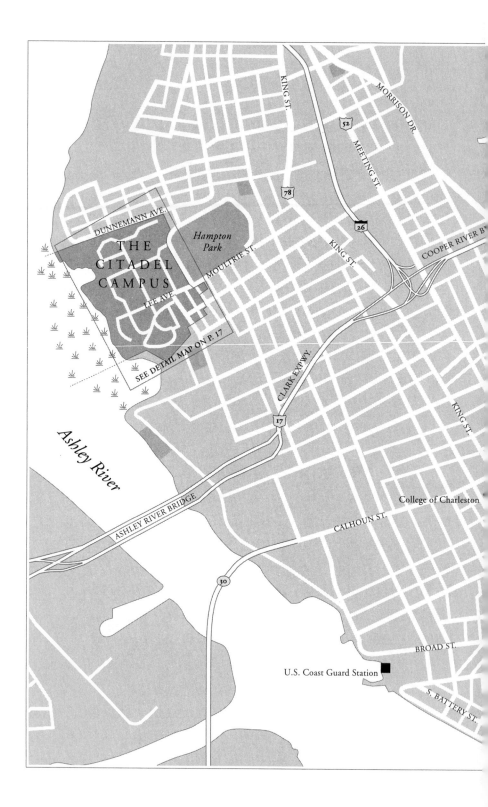

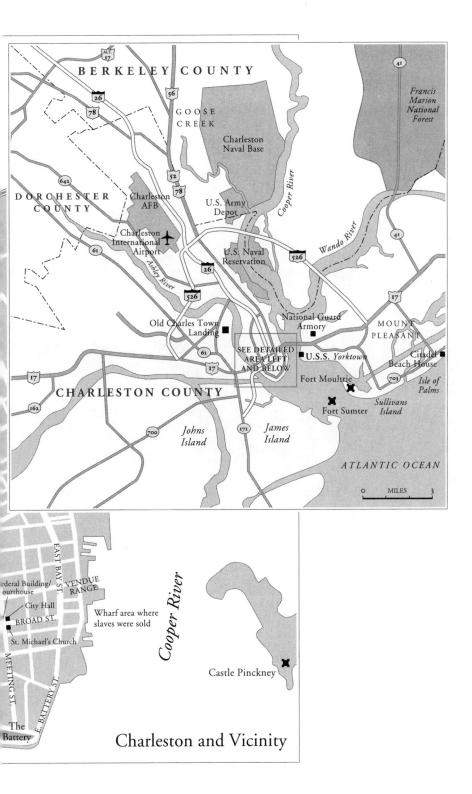

BERKELEY COUNTY

GOOSE CREEK

DORCHESTER COUNTY

Charleston AFB

Charleston Naval Base

U.S. Army Depot

Charleston International Airport

Cooper River

Wando River

Francis Marion National Forest

U.S. Naval Reservation

Ashley River

Old Charles Town Landing

National Guard Armory

SEE DETAILED AREA LEFT AND BELOW

U.S.S. *Yorktown*

MOUNT PLEASANT

Citadel Beach House

Isle of Palms

Fort Moultrie

CHARLESTON COUNTY

Johns Island

James Island

Fort Sumter

Sullivans Island

ATLANTIC OCEAN

0   MILES   3

EAST BAY ST.

VENDUE RANGE

Federal Building/ Courthouse

City Hall

BROAD ST.

St. Michael's Church

MEETING ST.

E. BATTERY ST.

The Battery

Wharf area where slaves were sold

Cooper River

Castle Pinckney

Charleston and Vicinity

Pioneer

You CAN GO to a city thinking that it is a small thing, that it will not dominate or change you; but that was not how she went there. She went hoping for a shape to mold her life against, to push and twist until the contours matched. She was nineteen then. And she went away from home the way so many others had, to Charleston, all full of hope, seduced by the city and its Citadel, that long history, the mildew and magnolias, the fierce old loyalties and that unarticulated sense of something stronger than the mere ephemera of modern lives spent on the move. Like every man who had gone before, she went because she wanted to be tested, because she had the dream of finding some place to belong. Despite The Citadel's famous deprivations, she found the school's hard-burnished promise sweet: Those who wore the ring were guaranteed, among their own, both recognition and respect. But she was first in a new line, not last in an old one, and no one really wanted her.

For all the similarities that had borne her to those gates—and there were many—that one difference was defining. She was an optimistic pioneer in a world quietly dying. Still, she persisted. She broke the privacy of that slow death and brought its grasping rage upon her. It was an adolescent challenge she took up without much thought. But with one step across that old divide she was pulled into the vortex of a battle long since joined. She would be shaped by it completely, though not as she expected. At the beginning, she had no notion what she had touched. By the end, she bore its scar. The contours never matched.

On August 12, 1995, the first day of a hot fall season that would see the induction of the class of 1999, Shannon Richey Faulkner signed in to The Citadel as its first female cadet. Always before, in a 153-year history broken only by the Civil War and Reconstruction, men alone had marched. Indeed, even on that August day the court case hung unfinished, still subject to appeals. Citadel officials had worked furiously in that last week to try to block her way. Arcane academic arguments were no longer of much use to them. Instead, The Citadel's lead lawyer, Dawes Cooke, the boyish, sweet-faced son of a Marine, now pleaded with the judge that Shannon was too fat to march. His arguments fell flat. Judge C. Weston Houck, trying hard to hide his irritation, waved off those final overtures. By then, the federal judge could see no reason why Shannon should be deprived of The Citadel's full experience. As the school's lone day student, she had studied in cadet classes for more than a year but been barred from most other college activities. Since the school's famous barracks system was deemed key to its identity and method of training, Judge Houck believed that awkward compromise left Shannon at a disadvantage. Now, with a final legal resolution pending but a string of interim victories already on her side, every door would finally open. And so on that hot August weekend, though Shannon Faulkner, now twenty, had the college credits and demeanor of an older student, she entered The Citadel as a "knob," arriving early with the freshman class for the rigors of indoctrination.

Because of her singular relationship with that old school, Shannon experienced no sense of initial shock as her parents' van eased past a guard post at the campus gate. Though freshmen reeled and sighed, to her it was familiar ground. Waved through by a white-gloved cadet who scowled equally at every car that passed, the Faulkners moved into a scene designed and scripted to impress. A huge white wall rose high along the edge of Hampton Park, blocking students from the hum of daily life. To the southwest, the Ashley River, rolling languidly behind a wide expanse of marsh, provided a more natural barrier. Everywhere, the school's perimeter was clearly marked and firmly closed. Inside it, the Military College of South Carolina provided students with a stage set from another time and place. Around the green and closely trimmed central expanse of Summerall Field rose Moorish castles painted white. Those buildings, gleaming in a neat array, gave the seventy-three-year-old campus the aspect of an ancient relic transplanted from the dunes.

At the head of the school's central parade field, Bond Hall, the home of college administrators, bristled with turrets and the shining spikes of several flagpoles. To its right, Stevens Barracks (better known by its fond sobriquet, "the Zoo") began a run of four similar buildings that lined the field's southwest flank, their backs facing to the marsh. After the Zoo came Law Barracks, where Shannon was to stay. Next was Padgett-

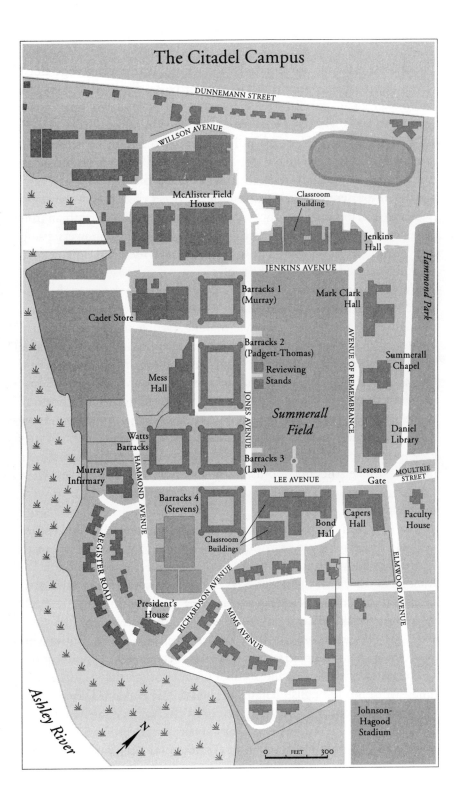

The Citadel Campus

DUNNEMANN STREET

WILLSON AVENUE

McAlister Field House

Classroom Building

Jenkins Hall

Hammond Park

JENKINS AVENUE

Cadet Store

Barracks 1 (Murray)

Mark Clark Hall

Mess Hall

Barracks 2 (Padgett-Thomas)

Reviewing Stands

Summerall Chapel

AVENUE OF REMEMBRANCE

JONES AVENUE

Summerall Field

Daniel Library

Watts Barracks

Barracks 3 (Law)

Lesesne Gate

MOULTRIE STREET

Murray Infirmary

LEE AVENUE

HAMMOND AVENUE

Barracks 4 (Stevens)

Classroom Buildings

Bond Hall

Capers Hall

Faculty House

REGISTER ROAD

ELMWOOD AVENUE

President's House

RICHARDSON AVENUE

MIMS AVENUE

Ashley River

N

Johnson-Hagood Stadium

0   FEET   300

Thomas Barracks, an oversized building finished off with a huge clock tower, flags snapping smartly at its highest point. Situated just behind Summerall Field's metal reviewing stand, Padgett-Thomas housed the corps of cadets' regimental staff as well as several hundred other boys. Of all the buildings on the campus, it was by far the most commanding, implying in its very architecture that students held the upper hand upon that ground. At the end stood Murray Barracks, the first built and now scheduled for demolition, a pattern for the other three. From the street it appeared as imposing as it was plain, a four-story fortress with an iron gate swung heavily across its sally port, short octagonal towers rising stubbily above the stairwells at each corner and medieval crenelations marking a jagged edge along the roof.

The quadrangle of every barracks was an oversized concrete checkerboard neatly painted red and white. Above, smooth white stucco arches rose and fell in even undulations, making each floor's gallery an airy breezeway that gave out onto the central square. Like prison catwalks towering above a constant churn of uniforms, those open hallways lent a forbidding air to the barracks' interior design. The architecture concentrated attention—and focused noise—on the central courtyards in which cadets gathered for instruction, for punishment and, grouped tightly in small companies, in neat, impatient lines just prior to parades. No privacy was possible inside those walls. Even stairwells were exposed. Other than inside the students' rooms, none of which had locks, cadets were subject to relentless scrutiny and constant reprimand. Their lives were not their own.

For four years, everything about a cadet's life would fit into strict devices of hierarchy and control. That was true, to some extent, everywhere they moved on campus; but it was most true in the barracks, where older boys held younger boys to exacting standards of their own invention. Discipline was dealt out in the rhetoric of high ideals. Each yawning barracks' entryway greeted students with reminders of stern absolutes. "A cadet does not lie, cheat, or steal, nor tolerate those who do," came one warning lifted from the honor code. "Duty," said a quote taken from Robert E. Lee and printed up in polished brass, "is the sublimest word in the English language." Upstairs in Padgett-Thomas Barracks, in the carpeted private quarters of the soft-spoken regimental commander, a chalk message on a blackboard put the theme a bit more ominously: "We are not hurting boys, we are disciplining men" came the bleak reassurance to cadets who wore the stripes and studs of ranking officers.

At the foot of the parade field, Jenkins Hall (known in some eras as "the tool shed" for its role in housing cadet rifles), was the home of the college's military staff. Crowded with the uniforms of the Army, Navy, Air Force and Marines, it was home to the commandant and his staff as well as to faculty who served on active duty while teaching ROTC classes to cadets. Next to it stood several other buildings that gazed out across the grass, southeast, toward administrators in Bond Hall, making bookends of adult authority. Along the field's fourth side, directly opposite the barracks, stood the Daniel Library, Summerall Chapel and Mark Clark Hall: the brain, the soul and the heart of the place, respectively.

Set back and off that center stage were a dozen or so other edifices constructed with considerably less medieval zeal but holding just as much importance in each student's life. Among them were the field hall, the new mess hall, the much-visited infirmary and an odd assortment of other structures used to keep the campus running. A large laundry freshened cadet uniforms, and a cadet store kept boys furnished with everything from books to the insignia that might someday denote their rank. Between Law Barracks and the infirmary, a new barracks—Watts—was under construction. Though mimicking the form of the buildings that lay near it, Watts was to be equipped with air-conditioning, an innovation that scandalized Citadel faithful who thought that suffocating heat and swarms of biting gnats were part of the institution's very soul. Faculty and administration housing lay above and behind Bond Hall, out of sight and mostly out of earshot. The president's house, then occupied by a towering, sallow-skinned Air Force lieutenant general named Bud Watts, was a low dwelling built at the head of a sweeping drive. Tucked back behind the school's newly resurfaced tennis courts, the residence had the modestly distinguished look of a house a diplomat might occupy in some small outpost in the tropics.

Situated in Charleston's northwest and occupying what served as the heel of the city's pointed, foot-shaped peninsula, The Citadel's main campus covered only a relatively modest plot of land and was far enough off the beaten path to be hard to find for idle tourists. There, it proved so self-contained that it even had its own postmark. Mail stamped on the campus was identified as coming not from Charleston (though it lay well within the city's bounds) but from "Citadel Station, SC." Cadets, in fact, would soon discover that the college could provide almost everything that they might need. It was a world unto itself, tightly closed and strictly regulated, complete and all-consuming.

To cadets and visitors alike, the parade field and the few buildings situated around it captured the school's central themes of God and country, might and purpose. Idled tanks and jets stood sentry. An enormous cannon loomed below Bond Hall. A cross rose prominently above the arching crowns of gnarly trees outside the chapel. At the parade field's head, an oversized American flag flapped huge and lazy in the humid air. Though cadets arrived on their first day as nervous adolescents barely starting out in life, not one would leave that ground an innocent. Succeed or fail, thrive or falter, they would learn life's hardest lessons there. That was the school's promise. That was its oldest threat. Those few acres would reshape their lives and redefine their destinies. That was what they came for. That was what they most desired.

Shannon Faulkner, a tall, large-boned teenager with a quick wit and extraordinary self-confidence, had hardly paid the school any mind while she was growing up in a rural enclave outside Greenville, South Carolina. No one in her family had ever studied there. But her brother joined the Navy after high school, and Shannon was impressed by the changes it had worked in him. She hoped The Citadel might give her the same discipline and drive. And she was tantalized by the thought of taking that old institution on. So, early in 1993, she applied. Her application was accepted by a college official who mistook her for a boy. Then she was rejected. After that, she sued.

The woman who showed up on The Citadel's campus for knob training in 1995 had changed in the several years that her court case had dragged on. Long-haired and relatively slender in high school, she had cut her smooth chestnut locks to shoulder length and gained some weight and had taken on a certain toughness in the long battle that ensued. Never given to stereotypical feminine charms (she laughingly called herself "Hostesszilla" while at one restaurant job), she did not tolerate fools with grace or ever sweeten what she had to say. Instead, she faced the world with an unvarnished bluntness. It was a trait that could either charm or shock, depending on her audience. Her humor was sharp, her opinions pointed. Her ire was equal-opportunity. Though teams of lawyers sweated on her behalf, convinced her suit had overarching merit, Shannon never lost sight of one simple fact that lay at the litigation's core. "They work for me," she said without self-consciousness.

When she did not like their work, she fired them with neither hesitation nor remorse. She was an unsentimental rebel in that way, a girl caught in an awkward chasm between her disappearing childhood and the nation's own difficult coming of age. Puckish and determined and certainly a bit naive, she was a modern teenager who did not believe in rote obedience yet chose to pit herself against an institution that taught it as a religion. The fireworks she sparked burned and showered from the start.

For nearly three years as Shannon's lawsuit against The Citadel moved through the court system, she was threatened, intimidated, vilified and humiliated. The Scarlet Pimpernel, an anonymous columnist writing in the school's newspaper, the *Brigadier,* dubbed her "the divine bovine," leading some cadets to moo whenever she appeared. ("Who will be the first to mount the cow?" the Scarlet Pimpernel once mused.) Her parents' house in Powdersville was sabotaged and sprayed with obscene epithets. "Bitch." "Dyke." "Whore." Death threats came by telephone. Hate mail raged with no return address. Still, she won her legal battles. But even after the latest court victories her medical records were subpoenaed, and her weight was leaked to local newspapers. That fall, pink bumper stickers reported her arrival, perhaps aptly, as a birth: "IT'S A GIRL! 186 POUNDS, 6 OUNCES." Sharper sentiments showed up as well. "Die Shannon," other messages taunted, echoing a sentiment once printed on a highway billboard to cast an even darker spell.

Some alumni found themselves amused by all those threats. "Die Shannon"? Well, that would stop her, they said laughing. Couldn't everybody see that it was all a joke? Cadets always poked fun. Now they merely aimed their fun at her. What did she expect? She asked for it, students agreed. What did she want with them, anyway? Was she a lesbian? An Amazon? A nymphomaniac? A fool? She did not fit their neat conceptions.

Furor over the case gripped many across the state. On Charleston's streets, Shannon was sometimes applauded. More often she was jeered or coldly snubbed. Her face was known to everyone, and everyone had an opinion. On the radio, disc jockeys spun a country tune with Shannon's court case as its theme. Callers sometimes requested it with raspy cackles of delight. The song never made it to the national airwaves. But at The Citadel demand for "It Don't Make Her a Bulldog" grew so intense that a sports booster organization called the Brigadier Club sold cassettes out of a bottom drawer to anyone who knew enough to ask. For a time, at least, the tune became a noisy anthem for the school. In it,

Shannon was a "bitch" caught in the thrall of liberal New York lawyers. The "Bulldogs," as cadets were known, were set to keep tradition strong. The lyrics made it clear which side should win. Over the twang of a steel guitar songwriters warned: "There's two thousand boys on the coast fired up, and they ain't backing down, and they'll never give up!"

That atmosphere had worn on Shannon's nerves. If she was cocky and self-confident at the fight's start, she was less so three years later when the time finally came to live as one woman among almost two thousand men. Her distress showed up in minor ways. In the weeks preceding that fall term she asked her mother to make her an appointment with a gynecologist. Her mother, Sandy, agreed, without asking any questions. The Faulkners had a pattern that allowed the kids a certain measure of responsibility over their own lives. It was Sandy's thinking that the best support any mother could provide was to make her own opinions crystal clear, then fade back and leave her door wide open. So she kept quiet until Shannon herself demanded: "Well, aren't you going to ask me why, Mom?"

Sandy nodded warily. "Okay, why?" she prompted, swallowing.

"If I get raped," Shannon answered coldly, "I don't want to have a child."

Val Vojdik, Shannon's lead lawyer, rolled her eyes with disgust when confronted with the uglier aspects of the case. Her anger and contempt had only grown from year to year. But by that Saturday in August when Shannon finally arrived to don a cadet's uniform, Vojdik's distress was tempered by the knowledge that her side was close to victory. Dressed conservatively, her gold-brown, blunt-cropped hair straggling in a gentle wind, she rocked and swayed, too excited to stay still. In her early thirties then and sitting on the greatest masterpiece of her career, she smiled broadly at a colleague and raised her eyebrows wordlessly in cheerful signals of delight. Though she had left her law firm for a teaching job while that long case stretched out, she maintained good relations with former colleagues and stood side by side with Henry Weisburg on that day. Taller and grayer (yet dressed more casually in khakis and a baseball cap for the occasion), Weisburg was more used to billion-dollar deals. As a partner at the giant firm of Shearman & Sterling in New York, he often juggled matters that affected affairs of state. But he grinned broadly, too, down by the Ashley River. Swept up in the mood of it, he swayed and bobbed alongside his former colleague in unmindful syncopation.

Standing on a slope of grass outside the music hall, those lawyers made a happy tableau while Shannon swept through a last-minute try-out with the band. Even that detail had been before the judge. Shannon's attorneys hoped to leave Charleston confident that their client was safely ensconced in one of the school's less ferocious companies. Yet Shannon failed her first attempt to tote a musical instrument and not a gun during parades. Citadel officials argued she should not have a second try. Vojdik's entreaties to the judge prevailed, and Shannon's performance went well enough for Herb Day, the flat-topped former Marine in charge of the band, to welcome Shannon then and there. He did not do so. College administrators required more formal procedures of him on that day. The bandleader took it as an insult, but stayed quiet and did as he was told. Even so, as Shannon headed off to Law Barracks she did so with new confidence. She knew her playing had gone well and hoped to soon be out of India Company. It was a minor shift, but an important one. Room 3344 in "the Thundering Third Herd" meant running up and down three flights of stairs on a bad knee every time an upperclassman barked. By contrast, a slot in the band meant a gruff protector in Herb Day and a ground-floor room with no stairwell to navigate as upperclassmen hovered close. After the tryout, Vojdik grinned and administered a friendly pat. They would get it solved, she said.

Elsewhere that morning, Dawes Cooke, shaggy haired and dressed in a dark suit and cheerful tie as was his habit, tended to some last details. He knew the fight was far from over. Though the U.S. Supreme Court had declined to grant an emergency stay, and Judge Houck had dealt the school a rapid sequence of disappointments, Cooke was confident that further struggle lay ahead. The men who paid his bills were hardly ready to give up. In Bond Hall, from his post in the president's chair, Bud Watts had vowed to fight until the end. Several doors away, his former roommate, Lewis Spearman, a Georgia divorce lawyer who by his own count had handled thirteen hundred marriage breakups before he let his bar credentials lapse, was more adamant, still. Their old friend Jimmie Jones, the smooth-coiffed, smooth-spoken head of the board of visitors, was plainly with them, too.

Those men were nothing if not like-minded. No only did each among them wear the school's gold band, but they were classmates and old friends, South Carolinians who had marched together with the class of 1958. Born on the cusp of World War II and weaned on the harsh rhetoric of the Cold War, they came of age in a segregated South under the guidance of General Mark Wayne Clark, a man so deeply averse to social change that he considered the fledgling civil rights movement and moves to racially integrate the United States Armed Forces not only an assault on his sovereignty as a white male but, indeed, a communist design to poison his great country from within. The general retired before the first black ever donned a Citadel uniform. Now, faced with an equally provocative challenge, his former students recycled some old fears. Dogged to the end, they kept their sights on victory even as Shannon opened her few boxes and unpacked.

Several doors down from Watts's office on that morning, Terry Leedom, the school's new head of public relations, fielded calls from around the world. In conversation after conversation he proved monotonously upbeat. Yes, he said blandly into the telephone, the school's first female cadet was now on campus. Yes, he added smoothly, pulling at the sleeves of his mint-green college-issue uniform, students would do all they could to make the system work. Leedom had been severely chastised in recent days. Though normally outspoken and quick to go off the record with insinuations, gossip, and acidic asides, he stayed on his best behavior. He had good reason to. After Shannon's weight appeared in news reports and in a spate of newly minted memorabilia, Vojdik urged Judge Houck to cite the school's public relations representative for contempt for disseminating information then held under a court seal. With Judge Houck clearly angered and an FBI investigation under way, Leedom moved gingerly that morning. If there was trouble, it surely would not come from him.

In fact, there would be no trouble on that day. Everything was battened down. Federal marshals moved across the campus to ensure that all went well. Outside Shannon's room, video cameras with interlocking views of the open gallery outside her door beamed live images to a guardhouse near the college gate. Venetian blinds had been installed inside her room to ensure a veil of privacy. A women's bathroom, the barracks' first, was situated down the hall. In the cool and humming recesses of Bond Hall, Leedom repeated the school's new mantra time and time again. "We have great hopes," he said, defying years of bitter volleys in and out of court. "So far, everything is going well."

On that first morning, someone sent her roses. As Shannon quietly unpacked her things, their delivery sparked a minor drama at the gate. Students at the sally port passed those flowers hand to hand like primed grenades. A note was tucked beside one stem. A tall, hard-faced sophomore opened it and read the message with disdain, then made a face confirming every worst assumption they all shared. The card contained a simple token of good tidings. "Shannon! Best of Luck! This is one giant step for womankind. Think of yourself as a modern day Scarlett. All good wishes from the mother and sister of Citadel graduates!" No signature was scrawled on that small square, not even in a florist's hand. It was an anonymous cheer from women somewhere back behind the scenes. And it made those cadets crazy with contempt. A cluster of uniformed boys shook their heads and scowled, unsure of what to do. Then one among them took control and barked an order sending those flowers back to the main office. "Roses!" he scoffed in a sour whisper of despair. "Shit."

Three floors above, Shannon tied her sneakers tight and touched a tiny charm she had attached discreetly to one lace. In her white shorts and pink T-shirt, her hair pinned neatly back and a silver angel coasting silently above one crumpled sock for luck, she was ready to begin.

"Pretty in pink," hissed an upperclassman as soon as she appeared. Shannon frowned and moved away. She did not see the long-stemmed roses that had come, nor hear, until much later, the good wishes they conveyed. Indeed, those wishes did not take. For in about the time it took those rose petals to fade, Shannon would be gone as well, her life misshapen and her optimism spent.

PART II

A Dance Among the Cannons

Once There Was a Grand Celestial Map

I N OLD CHARLESTON it was sometimes said that the city could sense the arrival of a slave ship well before she docked. More likely, the townspeople could smell it. With a prevailing wind, the awful odor of slavery often reached the shore before its vessels did. No amount of steaming vinegar could rid those galleons of their stench. But slaves had made the city rich, and each new shipment was welcomed with an air of festival. Few white Charlestonians questioned the morality of such trade. Rather, they saw in it a preordained, even heavenly, world order. So fixed was their celestial landscape (and so sure were they of their own high place in it) that alabaster-skinned northerners were themselves occasionally dismissed as of inferior stock. "The Cavaliers, Jacobites, and Huguenots, who settled the South, naturally hate, contemn and despise the Puritans who settled the North," a prominent southern editor once proclaimed. "The former are a master race—the latter a slave race, the descendants of Saxon serfs."

In a world so exquisitely constructed, everybody had his place. And the theme of slaves and masters made for a frame within which much of life was set. Convictions about social dominance were fixed, and crucial to the elite. That was true in every nuance and every corner of society but most crucial in relations between whites and blacks. Simple demographics made for stark imperatives. In 1790, when the federal government took its first census, Charleston County counted three blacks to every one of its white residents. In later years, that imbalance persisted. It made for a fragile and sometimes dangerous mix of souls, especially once the world began to turn away from the assumption that men could buy and sell their brethren.

At home, the rules of dominance were just as rigidly maintained. That was true in all the colonies; but in the South, the map of authority outlined atop the dinner table had an ominous shadow at its back. Some white plantation owners used female servants to find sexual release. Around those dinner tables, meals were sometimes served to white men by sexual partners whom they owned and children whom the master sired but never recognized. It was a fact of life that blurred the lines between domestic life and servitude. A frightful metaphor was close at hand. Its lesson was clear, if only implied. White men were in control in more than just an economic sense, and subtle reminders of their power were available at every turn. At a time when corporal punishment was both common and approved, the punishment of a white child or a case of wife beating was not so very different from the whipping of a slave. White women and white children closely observed that truth. Indeed, they were surrounded by it. But that uncomfortable reality was willfully ignored within most households. A form of denial took firm hold. "Any lady is ready to tell you who is the father of all the mulatto children in everybody's household but her own," wrote Mary Boykin Chesnut, a bitter social critic in private but a charming socialite in her more public life. "Those, she seems to think drop from the clouds." To less iconoclastic souls it simply was God's will that women and children should submit. The southern woman, wrote Daniel R. Hundley, "faithfully labors on in the humble sphere allotted her of heaven." That psychology sat deep. Yet times were changing, and new pressures were at hand.

In 1808, Congress prohibited the further importation of African slaves. The action followed a boom time in the South. Charleston's slave trade had sputtered and soared at various times. It was choked off by an act of the South Carolina legislature from 1792 to 1803. But it opened again on December 17, 1803, and operated until the national ban went into effect. During that time a kind of gleeful excess took hold along the streets of Charleston. In that short span, nearly 40,000 black men, women and children stood upon the streets for sale. Boats packed tight with human flesh dumped their disoriented cargo amid shouting, joking crowds. Great fortunes were made and then expanded in that trade.

In Charleston, the sale of slaves was woven into daily life. There, slaves were auctioned along back streets near the docks, down Vendue Range and other unkempt alleys behind the formidable Exchange building on ground made of pressed dirt and rounded stones. Young and old, frail and hearty, that hobbled merchandise was herded into a world of anxious buyers. Plantation owners always looked for clues to character and type. They liked their workers strong and passive. Gambian slaves were thought to be among the most obedient. Angolans were quite popular as well. New shipments brought a throng to watch. Fueled with rum and grog, the crowds were loud and raucous. Heavy coins soon clinked and rose in piles. Some buyers mortgaged land for flesh— risking everything they had to make their holdings larger. Rice and cotton were the engines of great wealth. Both needed dexterous hands to turn those harvests into gold.

Yet as those fortunes swelled, the city found itself divided. Power and its perquisites were closely held among the "potent few." Only those with land and property could hold a public office. Inequities glared from every mansion's smug exterior. A sense of nervousness prevailed. Poor whites were often lawless. News sheets cautioned readers to remain alert both day and night. Huge homes were robbed of silver, linen and expensive jewelry. Drunken men with knives demanded money. Poor immigrants were restless for their share of Charleston's bounty. Some did not wait to earn it.

Slaves grew restive, too. Once the trade with Africa was closed, they sensed a subtle shift in mood. Some, inspired perhaps by rumors of revolt elsewhere, began to ponder freedom. It was a time of tumult all across the hemisphere. In Santo Domingo slaves rose up against the French in 1791. Then violent upheavals gripped Latin America as distant colonies threw off the rule of Spain. All about, old orders were collapsing. From London to New York, abolitionist fever spread. In Charleston, meanwhile, old notions were retraced and resolutely underscored. Nervous and outnumbered, whites of influence became convinced that the city's African Methodist Episcopal Church was a home for subversive ideologues busy teaching blacks to read and write. Magistrates ordered the enormous church to close. Three thousand worshipers dispersed. The city fathers nodded and approved. Their vulnerabilities were all too clear.

By the early 1820s, Charleston's heyday had already come and gone. Cotton, indigo and rice had earned her leading families extraordinary fortunes and set deep a taste for luxury. But that wealth was reliant on good weather and favorable economic tides. By the turn of the century, the indigo trade was all but lost to India. Soon, the cotton and rice trades would falter, too. In 1818, South Carolina earned $11 million in exports, mostly through the port of Charleston. One year later the world market in cotton collapsed and with it, several king-sized Charleston fortunes. The westward expansion of the American South and improvements in transportation had meant a flood of cheap raw goods in the world marketplace. But increasingly, those products flowed through other ports. Steam engines, developed in Europe in 1800, released ships' captains from the long tyranny of trade winds. Yet those new, deep-drawing vessels found it hard to pick their way through Charleston's shallow waterways. True, the wind was still at the city's back. But her citizens could no longer count upon its blessings. Instead, Charlestonians watched with mounting dismay as their port lost its footing as the anointed point of commerce on the coast. Meanwhile, New York, Philadelphia, Baltimore and Boston surged ahead in prominence. In the South, New Orleans, Mobile and Savannah pushed forward with new energy, exploiting convenient land and river links to growing inland enterprises. Charleston's easy dominance was at an end. And as her feisty new competitors began to grow, some among them drew away philosophically as well, challenging antique maxims and tinkering with old laws.

In New York City, great floods of immigrants created a swirl of differing opinions and demands. If America would be a melting pot, then its flame burned brightest there. In 1821, New York abolished land ownership as a necessary qualification for a citizen's right to vote. Almost imperceptibly, old lines of power had begun to shift. A day's trip up the Hudson River, one of the country's first women's secondary schools, the Troy Female Seminary, was started by Emma Willard. Perhaps education and a political voice should not be linked directly to the accidents of gender and inherited wealth. With such ideas in the air, the full clap of the abolitionist movement would not be far behind. In Charleston, talk of an end to slavery administered a ghastly shock. City fathers knew how quickly they could fall. They lived with simple mathematics. If the majority should rise, their world would tear apart.

In 1822, on a rather temperate day in May, a flash point was finally reached. Down by the fish market where muddy streets were strewn with garbage, two slaves whispered of an uprising. William Paul and Peter Desverneys shared the details of a grand conspiracy. Slaves would rise and fight. Owners and their families would be slaughtered while they slept. Paul and Desverneys talked of secret meetings, weapons caches and thousands of black men ready to quit their servitude and find revenge. The plot was well along, and the rebels' intentions brutal. Desverneys that night replayed the conversation to a mulatto slave owner, William Penceel, who ordered him to go back home to tell his master.

Desverneys's owner, Colonel James C. Prioleau, was alarmed but grateful. He told the city magistrate, who soon threw Paul into the workhouse, a building famous for its instruments of torture and frequent night escapes. Paul at first was silent. The pressure was increased. At last he started talking. Over the next weeks, from various sources, city officials learned of a slave named Mingo Harth and another, Peter Poyas, who helped hatch the rebellion. Gullah Jack, a witch doctor from Angola, would aid the rebels with black magic. On the morning of the uprising, slaves and free blacks sympathetic to the cause were to eat a secret mixture and clamp a crab claw firmly between their teeth. Thousands of men were just waiting for a signal. As tensions in the city increased, the revolt was hastily moved forward. On June 16, black men would move at midnight and gather up by tribe. The Ibo and Mandingos would share a single cause. A verse from Joshua would spur them on: "And they utterly destroyed all that was in the city, both man and woman, young and old, and ox, and sheep, and ass, with the edge of the sword." They planned to take no prisoners. They left no room for God's forgiveness.

Tales of that conspiracy wound like kite string up the coast. On the day named for the revolt, 2,500 armed whites were on patrol. In Charleston, the clop of horses sounded in the muffling heat. Hushed voices echoed house to house. Most residents stayed up until dawn, exploring their worst terrors in a mix of heat and paranoia. Every leaf that rustled sounded like a knife blade's deadly twist. Every twig that broke became a musket shot, each gecko's chirp an interrupted cry, an arson's match, the start of something none of them could stop. At last the sun came up and burned their fears away. No throat was cut, no gunshot fired. There was no revolution.

Soon, the workhouse grew crowded with new prisoners. Terrified slaves appeared in court, took their oaths and testified. The courtroom doors stayed closed despite the heat. Appalling rumors swept the lowcountry. Distant cousins and plantation overseers galloped urgently down rural carriageways with news. Charleston's ladies, strolling through formal gardens green with olive trees, capers, limes and ginger, shared their disbelief. Fear metastasized at dusk. Men with everything at stake bent over wine and beef and turtle soup while slaves who feared for their lives huddled in lightless quarters. As the trial dragged on, men of means demanded action.

One by one, frightened witnesses described a plot that no white Charlestonian would soon forget. Then the hangings started. Of 131 blacks arrested in the course of trials, 35 were sentenced to death. Thirty-one were driven out of town. The rest were allowed to go back home. But who had organized the scheme? Since it was intolerable to think that such an uprising could happen on its own—spontaneous combustion in the souls of men—a single villain was required. This man must be a man of some intelligence and stature. Blame must burn upon that man. Only then could Charleston rest.

The "intended insurrection" was examined and exposed. In the end, one man, Denmark Vesey, a free man of some wealth and position in the black community, was blamed. He had come to Charleston by a circuitous route. As a boy in the Caribbean he was sold at market, then taken on by a ship's captain. It was said that he was a special boy, wrote John Peyre Thomas, "of about fourteen years of age, whose beauty, alertness, and intelligence attracted attention." Joseph Vesey, the ship's captain, gave the boy some clothes and a new name, Telemaque. For two years that handsome slave worked on Vesey's slave ship. For seventeen more he did the trader's bidding on dry land, in Charleston. Perhaps it was a gentler fate than toiling in the fields. But it meant that for much of his adult life, "Denmark," as he came to be called, was a slave who helped to turn the wheel of slavery. Then, by fluke, he gained his freedom. In 1799, he bought a ticket in the East Bay Street lottery and won. His $1,500 windfall was a fortune for those times. He used it in two ways. Six hundred dollars bought his freedom. The rest he used to start a business. A gifted carpenter, he prospered and allowed himself some noteworthy indulgences. He bought a house on Bull Street and married several wives. Well-dressed and well-spoken, he was successful enough and sophisticated enough to put many whites to shame.

In court, his fate was quickly sealed. Authorities held the power of execution in such cases. It was imposed without remorse. Soon, Vesey's lifeless body swung from a rope. Peter Poyas, identified as a lieutenant in the plot, was hanged beside him. "Do not open your lips!" Poyas cried before his hanging. "Die silent, as you shall see me do!" Gullah Jack, the Angolan witch doctor, twisted limply at his side. The city rested easy in

God's judgment. "With little fear and nothing to reproach ourselves, we may, without shrinking, submit our conduct to the awards of posterity," a report on the matter concluded.

Several people prospered from the crisis. Peter Desverneys, the ebony-skinned slave who first brought the plot to light, was cleared of any charges and released. Indeed, the city council thanked him for his loyalty by granting him his freedom and a fifty-dollar pension. Later, he would marry a wealthy mulatto freewoman and become a slave owner himself. William Penceel, the mulatto to whom Desverneys first brought his news, was showered with praise and given a perpetual tax break on every slave he owned. And when he went to see his banker late that summer he carried in his sack a thousand-dollar reward.

Still, Charleston's elite was not appeased. A dire plot had been exposed and rapidly extinguished. But who could say the trouble would end there? For weeks the city lived inside a thick miasma of its dread. Then new actions were taken. In August, the pastor of Denmark Vesey's congregation was given fifteen days to quit the town. Once he was gone, the city razed his church. A new time of repression had begun. In a mood of hate and rising fear, the few controlled the many by any means it could. At the workhouse, a treadmill was installed. Now plantation owners—for a fee—could bring recalcitrant slaves to be lashed to an overhead pole and forced to run along a turning wheel while "drivers" whipped and pushed them on. So long as a man or woman kept the pace, the pain was not so bad. But once a person's legs gave out, those wooden steps slapped hard into bare flesh while strips of cowhide tore and snapped.

Life for free blacks would soon become more difficult as well. Distressed to think that Vesey might have been inspired by news of upheavals abroad, the city council moved to choke off information drifting in from foreign ports. It was a hard task in a busy shipping capital. But the council struck upon a simple solution. Black sailors who arrived in town were confined to jail while in the city. Jailers imposed a fee for room and board, and any ship's captain who refused to settle up did not get his sailors back. Hapless men whose ships left town without them were sold directly into slavery.

Something more was needed, city councilmen agreed. They should build a citadel to guard their interests and estates. In December, with the city in a festive mood, lawmakers approached the state legislature with a plea for funding and support. To protect Charleston's citizenry, it was decided, the city must create a new protective force. The motion was approved. One hundred fifty men would serve. An old tobacco inspection warehouse was provided for their use. In an atmosphere of slave revolt a fortress was conceived. A private army would now form to guard the white elite. In that narrow yet important role, its members—poor boys from the country mostly—could feel the pull of riches and respect. On the day that they arrived, they entered a new world.

For many of those first cadets, social service with a sword opened up new avenues of hope—for it was not just Africans who held no status on that ground. Impoverished whites were bound to unforgiving hierarchies themselves. Ironically, among the "potent few," poor whites were in fact considered more of a nuisance than the slaves. Far from obedient and rarely deferential, those impoverished newcomers were eager to compete in business and had the irritating characteristic—which slaves lacked—of falling under the protective netting of the law. "I almost wish we might have a war with the Yankees," an exasperated Charlestonian once wistfully observed. "We should get some of them killed off, then!" In reality, only the most resourceful offspring of poor families could dodge a life of hardship and contempt. Cadets proved just such men. They used their soldiers' stripes to slash away the bonds of birth, gaining status by protecting that of others who held more. In that, a deep and twining history would find its seed.

In truth, Charleston's elite would need more than loyal soldiers to preserve the life they then enjoyed. Good times for wealthy plantation owners were quickly drawing to a close. Not only had the city lost the easy dominance of its great port, but rapid industrialization meant new empire building to the north. Charleston turned its back on that transition and paid the price in further hardship. In another decade, visitors would dismiss it as a city of the past. Yet while her fortunes dwindled, The Citadel's would thrive. "The nature of our institutions of domestic slavery and its exposure of us to hostile machinations . . . [compel us] to cherish a military spirit," one resident dryly observed. And so a complex dance began. Like lovers through a clouded glass, the two grew close without quite touching. Each admired the other. But the distance would not close. Instead, it was breached only in the most structured of circumstances at grand military balls, which became occasions of considerable talk and celebration. On those nights, the valley between rich and poor would briefly close. All the world seemed of a piece. While a band played and yards of silk rustled softly in the night, cadets in formal dress with brass buttons and swords escaped their humble origins. In a haze of pomp and chivalry, each man and woman knew what steps to take and when a bow or curtsy was required. It was a fleeting thing, but fine, a glimpse into an ordered world, a world of rules and elegance, a night of dancing among cannons. Most participants never dared to hope for more.

Although peninsular in its geography, Charleston clearly would have rather been an island than a mere appendage to a larger land mass. It had deep instincts of containment. Most citizens found no glory in the heaving confusions of nation building. City fathers had their patterns set and sought only to preserve them. To many in the aristocracy a moat had long seemed quite appropriate. Early in its history, Charleston nearly built one. In 1755, amid bristling threats of war, the Charles Town Assembly pondered digging a deep channel to link the Ashley and the Cooper Rivers. Combined with a mighty *Citadelle* it was designed to keep marauders safely at bay. The proposal was a fairy tale complete with alligators swimming fat in those lush marshes. But it was too expensive to pursue, and like most fairy tales, it never came to pass. City leaders instead put their energies and money into a land-based system of fortifications. But always, the impulse to stand tall behind a drawbridge lingered. In Charleston, the instinct to withdraw—then fight—was old. And it would often replay.

The first years of The Citadel's existence came at a messy time in a young democracy. The doors of theory had swung wide, and now the wind blew in. Andrew Jackson's inauguration showed as much. In the spirit of populism, he welcomed the public to the White House and then watched in horror as rowdy mobs came and trashed the rugs, scratched the furniture, scuffed the marble floors and devoured everything available. In Charleston, reports of that wild party left an afterimage of a world gone mad. The drawbridge was pulled up. Instead of joining the raucous national debate over what new shape America might take, city fathers huddled haughtily behind their ramparts and linked arms. In that environment, The Citadel gained new importance. Soon, it would boast new quarters, too, as well as a new mission.

On December 20, 1842, by an order of the state legislature, The Citadel was reinvented as a school. Now, in a large two-story building on Marion Square, boys would find careful balance in a symbiotic world. In return for keeping free blacks and slaves "compleatly subordinate," as local ordinances required, students would receive a free educa-

tion and habits of courtesy and self-discipline that would be their keys
to a new life. Whoever they might have been, however rough-edged and
rebellious on the day of their arrival, they left those boys behind. Once
tucked away in Marion Square a new life started and a new identity took
shape. Each student paid his price. That sharp rebirth was earned
through pain. But once earned, it proved immutable.

For twenty years, that pattern held. Then war came, and all the South
convulsed. Cadets forever afterward would lay proud claim to the first
shots.

In January 1861, a small group of uniformed students from the Military College of South Carolina gathered in the dunes of Morris Island.
Their eyes were to the sea; their attention focused on a ship then drifting
in the half-light before dawn. Moving slowly, making depth soundings
as she came, the *Star of the West*, a huge side-wheeler from New York,
was carrying vital supplies to Union soldiers at Fort Sumter. Talk of war
was everywhere by then, and on that morning it ignited more than bar-
room passions. Out on Morris Island, off to Charleston's southeast, a
stiff command was shouted. Cadet G. E. Haynesworth set to work and
sent a shower of sparks into the air. His was a harmless warning shot.
But the ship did not turn back, and soon a second cannon fired in a haze
of smoke. The *Star of the West* took a glancing blow across her stern. She
shuddered with the impact. More shots poured out in quick succession.
With no large arms on board and no covering fire from the nearby fort,
the ship's captain turned and headed back to sea. The war, though near,
had not begun. No answering fire was heard. And yet in Charleston a note
of victory was sounded.

"The expulsion of the steamer Star of the West from the Charleston
harbor yesterday morning was the opening of the ball of the Revolution," the *Charleston Mercury* crowed. "We would not exchange or recall
that blow for millions! It has wiped out half a century of scorn and outrage. . . . We are proud that our harbor has been so honored." Following
South Carolina's lead, Mississippi voted to secede. Florida followed suit,
then Alabama. The barometer was falling. A terrible storm was on its
way.

By late March, conditions inside Fort Sumter had deteriorated considerably. Union troops were hungry and alone. Having taken the city's
best military prize by stealth just before Christmas, the Union major in
charge now found himself isolated with a band of half-starved troops. As
he scanned the low horizon to each side, he could see large guns trained

on his position from several nearby points. He did not relish fighting. He did not want a war. A southerner himself, he was a former slave owner who understood the Confederate cause but could not bear to desert the Union army that he served. As days and weeks ticked by, he sank into depression.

In Charleston, meanwhile, a keen air of festivity prevailed. Everywhere, talk of war dominated the spring season. Uniformed officers mixed easily with the elite. They were wined and dined and entertained at formal balls that made the season sparkle. Women flirted and hung close. How could those brave young soldiers lose, they prodded, when God himself was on their side? Newspaper editors begged for action. The city was ready. Her forts were busy and well stocked. Let it begin, they urged. Secession was the only way. "Border southern states will never join us until we have indicated our power to free ourselves," the *Mercury* goaded. "The fate of the Southern Confederacy hangs by the ensign halliards of Fort Sumter." At last, the haze of waiting ended. As thousands of well-dressed Charlestonians crowded along the Battery, first shots were fired and returned. In more than a day of shelling amid a fireworks display the likes of which that city had never seen, Fort Sumter's four-story brick edifice was shattered. After a thirty-three-hour attack, the Union major dropped his flag. A Confederate banner soon waved proudly in its place. Crowds cheered along the Battery and fired up a party that lasted several days.

In 1865, when General William Tecumseh Sherman burned his way across the South to victory, he selected South Carolina for the history books. "The hellhole of secession," Sherman called it. Charleston missed most of that last violence. Sherman swept inland instead and reduced Columbia to ashes. Even so, down on the coast, Charleston's once gracious streets and mansions lay in ruin. The city was a broken husk. Fire had swept through its streets, hunger through its populace. Great families were destroyed. The social order was upended.

In that first tide of victory, Union troops used The Citadel as their headquarters. When they left town, the school stayed closed to all but several ragtag squatters. For seventeen years its commanding hulk remained an ugly reminder of losses in the war. Then, its fate would shift again. After briefly debating a proposal to make the institution into a school for recently emancipated blacks, state legislators bowed to pressure from low-country members and voted instead to reopen the school much as it was before the war, serving poor white boys from around the state. Though slavery was done and The Citadel's first purpose obsolete, the occasion stirred both pride and hope in that much battered city. "One of Charleston's brightest aspirations will be realized when the cadet reveille is heard once again in the center of our city," the mayor announced. A palmetto flag against its ground of blue rose high above those walls. Soon, 185 boys, "poor and deserving," would arrive.

As The Citadel reopened, Manhattan was busy with a bridge. In 1883, it was christened with tremendous fanfare in a surge of city pride. The Brooklyn Bridge with all its massive arcs of steel transformed that rocky island into a grand peninsula. Watery boundaries were overcome. The city's door lay open. Soon, a monument would mark that same instinct of welcome. In 1886, it rose above the New York harbor, torch in hand.

A Game of Slave and Master

IN THE YEARS THAT The Citadel stayed closed, Charleston experienced chaotic spasms of great change. The rich were poor. The powerful were hobbled. The once-enslaved were free. Poisonings, sabotage and theft were commonplace. Everyone could feel that edge. The war was over, but it still held the capacity to transform. White Charlestonians who had fled the city for safe havens elsewhere returned in many cases to find their elegant old mansions occupied by former slaves. City streets were filled with blacks who no longer gave way to former masters but bumped them roughly as they passed. One utterly disgusted matron informed a friend that a band of Africans had moved into her home. Her elegant Charleston mansion was filled now with pigs and poultry and a crowd of dark-skinned strangers. Field hands and housemaids were cooking in her drawing room, she sputtered. Nothing was as it had been.

Accustomed to a careful world of absolutes, most members of the elite could not imagine either a meritocracy or a nuanced era of shared power. Instead, they thought in terms of a reversal. "The Negroes are evidently aiming at supremacy," snapped one rattled Charleston socialite. Gone was the time when the city council could rage openly against—and seek legislation barring—the elegant attire preferred by free blacks of means on the grounds that such dress proved "subversive of that subordination which policy requires." Now, the whip was in the other hand. "So far the poor wretches have behaved better than might be expected," Harriott Middleton wrote dourly in the summer of 1865. "That is, they have not attempted to cut our throats as yet."

Stripped, for the time being, of central distinctions between class and race, whites sought new ways to keep those lines intact. Though blacks demanded equal access in a culture that had long reviled them, whites recoiled at the sight of dark-skinned crowds along the Battery or strolling, in their finery, into the town's best theaters where they might rub against the palest skin of Charleston's daughters. To most whites, despite the roving evidence of miscegenation, integration was inconceivable. No grand decrees or constitutional amendments would suffice to make them change their minds. Power seesawed wildly in those first hectic years.

Shortly after the war's end, the all-white South Carolina state legislature passed a Black Code that institutionalized racial inequality before the law. Blacks were free, after a fashion, but they would not be equal. Congress moved to intercede. In Washington, the country's first Civil Rights Act was passed and almost immediately followed by the Fourteenth Amendment, making blacks full citizens and equal under state and federal laws. In the chaotic days of Reconstruction, under the watchful eyes of Union soldiers, South Carolina's Black Code was reversed. Then it was reinstated by other means.

In many regards, the country was still at war. Slavery was finished. But the attitudes it fostered and the assumptions it gave rise to were harder to expel. Now, the two sides clashed inside the courts and at the ballot box. Shortly after the war, Congress granted all black men the right to vote. At the same time it stripped the right from those whites who sided with the Confederacy. Across the South, one-fourth of all white men were abruptly disfranchised. A sudden inversion occurred. Blacks commanded a clear voting majority in South Carolina, Mississippi, Louisiana, Alabama and Florida. In Charleston, the effect was profound—more blacks than whites held public office—but brief. Soon, whites regained control. The seesaw tipped again.

By the end of Reconstruction, Charleston's oldest families were busy building up new fortunes on a growing trade in phosphate. Soon, they translated their revived economic clout into political hegemony as well. With Union troops gone and the blinding light of national scrutiny turned off, Charleston's "potent few" slammed shut the window of black rule. No longer could the city boast a private guard to keep the racial balance fixed; The Citadel was closed and quiet. Yet during its long sleep, its function was restored. Across the low country, white men still imposed their will. They moved with guns and whips in a murky world outside the law. More formal mechanisms followed.

In Columbia in 1882, state legislators approved the Eight Box Law, a voting process so complex that few poor whites or uneducated blacks had any hope of casting ballots. Combined with coarser tactics, it proved devastatingly effective. From 1883 until 1967—a period of eighty-four years—not a single black was elected to the Charleston City Council. In the state capital, the whiteout was almost as complete. "Gerrymandering by the state legislature, complicated voting procedures, intimidation, and fraud" were the tools of the new leadership, said Charleston historian Walter J. Fraser. The white elite would use those techniques to extraordinary effect. The fleeting period of black rule—seven years in all—was finished. In its place, a deep nostalgia took firm root. Among prominent whites, rebel soldiers became the stuff of legend and deep longing. Public speakers and prominent essayists extolled the virtues of the prewar South. Slavery's horrors were downplayed. The old hierarchy was in its throne, and, buoyed by a gentle reading of the past, it was busy celebrating. It was in that heady atmosphere that The Citadel reopened.

In 1882, the sons of the Civil War arrived in Charleston. Born during the conflict between North and South and raised in the season of bitterness that followed it, poor boys who had always made up The Citadel's ranks were joined now by scions of the elite who enrolled for nostalgia's sake or, more pragmatically, because some of them were poor themselves. In some ways, the initial function of educating "poor but deserving" boys of the state was again fulfilled: Sixty-eight boys—two from every county in the state—came as "beneficiary cadets" endowed with scholarships. But scores of paying cadets arrived as well, sending administrators scrambling to find more beds. The reopening proved a huge success. On that ground, grit and a passion for the antebellum South were all a boy would need to make his mark. Inside those walls gray uniforms obscured dividing lines of wealth and class. A farm kid from upstate might bunk next to the son of a former magnate. It was a rare thing, and memorable. Men talked of it until they died.

At The Citadel that fall, former Confederate soldiers mourned the past while boys struggled to adapt to the misty vision of their elders. The tone was set and the nostalgia deep. The textbook was John C. Calhoun's. Thirty years after his death, the man who once defended slavery as a "positive good" and "the most safe and stable basis for free institutions in the world," seemed a living presence in the town. As the class of 1886 graduated, his likeness was installed outside their walls on Marion Square. Perched atop a pedestal, his frown fixed for all posterity, that elder statesman stood with his shoulders in the sky. Years later, that pedestal was raised to a fantastic height, as though no post was of sufficient loftiness for that great man and his philosophy.

It was natural, inevitable, that in the aftermath of slavery a fascination with it would persist. No institution so powerful or way of life so deeply rooted could simply vanish in the smoke of war. Instead, the lure of unquestioned mastery, suddenly rendered quite abstract, was perhaps more seductive than ever to boys who had lost their chance at it for good. For most whites, times were worse than ever. A generation came of age knowing that and longing for another time. Enthralled with loss and inspired by their own approaching manhood, teenage boys used The Citadel's "mansion strongly fortified" to reinvent the world their fathers lost. Let other boys play cowboy. Behind their own closed gates the game of slave and master thrived. To many adolescents, it was too delicious to resist. Formulas of domination were boisterously made new. Every boy who suffered would some day rise to hold the whip. It was an intoxicating transition that none among them would forget. Soon familiar patterns formed. Inside a two-story building modeled after the Charleston workhouse, older students trained the new boys in the ways of abject subservience. For them, the lessons of the past had not been lost.

At the turn of the century, new recruits, called "rats," were assigned to older boys and made to serve their every need and minor whim without complaint. "How we trembled at the sight of an old cadet," a student recalled. The threat of pain was always near. It merged with the promise of power. The treadmill no longer turned in town. But its sharp lessons lingered. "Hydrick wanted to know how long it would be before we would get our stripes; and was told by an unsympathizing corporal that he would get his that very night. History says that the promise was held sacred." In fact, initiation rights were little more than stylized beatings. Boys who cried out suffered more. Like the slaves whose lot they copied, new boys learned quickly that compliance was the key. Complaint just drew the lash.

Though built to roughly resemble the Charleston workhouse (a likeness that would be enhanced in later years) and situated in a location intended to send a subliminal warning to all blacks, the school's grim aspect now gave white students the chills. New recruits quaked before the "impenetrable darkness of its massive entrance," wrote an awe-inspired senior from the class of 1904. Subsequent events soon underscored their sense of panic. In short order, new boys were stripped of their names, their clothes and little keepsakes from their mothers. Every link with childhood was eradicated with a sudden shock. Life as a slave began the minute a cadet unpacked. "At his first contact with the Corps he is no longer a 'boy' but in one moment of time and as if by the touch of a magic wand, he loses his conceit and becomes a simple insignificant 'rat,'" explained a cadet who identified himself only as "X" in an account printed in an early edition of the college yearbook. "This is a critical period at the Academy, for trials await the 'rat' never dreamed of in his philosophy." Many of those trials were simple humiliations that amounted to little more than humbling reprimands relating to style of dress and discipline. But some came with a blow. Boys invariably dodged "ear boxings, hair brushes, T-squares and bayonets" as older boys imposed their will. "Who best bear his mild yoke," reminded X in that early edition of the *Sphinx*, "they serve Him best."

"Do others," came another admonition elsewhere in those pages, "or they'll do you."

Low as they were, however, rats could always find some solace in taking digs at those yet lower on the social scale. Blacks and women fit that role.

"What is the feminine of chairman?" came a popular barracks question of the time.

"Chambermaid," rats answered cheerfully.

Many boys enjoyed a certain gallows humor in that world. A club called the Midnight Bed Turner's Association was memorialized as possessing a motto: *All that goes up has to come down;* a purpose: *The Discomfiture of Rats;* a color code: *T.M. Blacking and Patent Leather Polish;* and a meeting place: *On Galleries.* For the most part, the worst that rats got then was merely a rude awakening when their mattresses were unexpectedly upended, and a face black with boot polish, a sticky, laughable reminder of their low station at the school. Rougher jokes came with the snap of paddles. One yearbook illustration from the *Sphinx* showed a freshman kneeling on the ground, his back arched and his body pitching forward while an upperclassman readied for a strike. A second boy stood ready with a riding crop. Four more lounged nearby, laughing and approving. There was no choice but to submit.

For many young cadets, hazings proved little more than mean, self-serving nudges to show a younger boy that his elders held all power. Indeed, by then a given routine prevailed and was carefully outlined in the college yearbooks. First, wrote one class historian, older boys stole any sweets and trinkets that anxious mothers had tucked away for sons gone off to college. Then rats were made to form a train and paddled each in turn as they crawled about the floor. "Remonstrance is of no avail," reported X. Those with power abused it—and then demanded loyalty and service in return.

In that era, a three-month period of servitude was deemed sufficient for a boy's remaking. Then the "rats" became cadets. On "Recognition Day" each boy received his freedom and the right to be called by his real name. Even there, the analogy to slavery held. Recognition was what freed blacks most desired. In the heady time right after the Civil War, forty-five black leaders gathered at a Charleston church. After meetings lasting several days they emerged with modest requests. They wanted equal protections under the law and one thing more: "We simply desire that we be recognized as men."

Cadets, so recognized, found that pomp and promise beckoned. After turning through that gate they were allowed "the glory of full dress" and bathed in warm approval. "Bright faces greet him at every turn, handkerchiefs wave, flowers are recklessly cast by fair hands," a yearbook writer cheerfully explained. Each year, the metamorphosis was faithfully replayed. Freshmen became sophomores. Servants now were masters. The wheel turned. "We feared no one," boasted X.

Once outside those gates, graduates emerged into a world much like that inhabited by their grandparents. In it, prestigious old families and poor farm boys did not mix. Freed slaves, though graced with citizenship, found it hard to exercise their right to vote. And they no longer sat with whites in Charleston's theaters or in the city's restaurants. Segregation was the rule, and freshly painted signs were in place around the city. Tacked up over drinking fountains and hammered on the doors of public restrooms and in the lobbies of the city's best hotels, they pulled the quilt of race apart: *Whites Only.* In Washington, the Supreme Court supported segregation. The Fourteenth and Fifteenth Amendments to the Constitution—sweeping in scope but lacking in specifics—were methodically undermined. True, the justices agreed, states could not discriminate against blacks because of race, but private institutions were welcome to do so. A welter of new laws quickly took advantage of the ruling. They would keep whites and blacks apart for half a century. The Supreme Court allowed that separate could be equal. Soon separate was the norm.

Though glaring old imbalances persisted, The Citadel's function had changed. Its antique *quid pro quo* no longer held. After the war, cadets (though never allowed any authority over whites) could no longer impose their rule over black men and women. They had lost their role as racial guards and thus their automatic place in the weave of that society. Now, to keep their toehold in the realm of power, they had to pay a far more subtle price. In a new nostalgic era, The Citadel's "citizen soldiers" swore their fealty not to local ordinances so much as to an antique culture, its mores, its traditions and its still-surviving structure. In short, they pledged to keep the world intact. To fill that pledge they needed more than mere book learning. If they wanted access to a web of power they had to live and learn its hardest lessons first. And so they re-created ancient formulas of submission back behind those towering walls. New boys flinched and yelped and learned their place. A simple aphorism drove them on. If they ever were to lead, generations of young boys were told, first they had to follow. Some barracks tricks were more show than savagery. Others proved quite brutal. Those who could not bear it left.

Theirs was a theater of violence and subordination that threatened nothing back outside the gates. Poor boys who walked away returned to small towns and few prospects. They lost their chance at a leg up in a mostly closed society. Boys from the elite, by contrast, their place in life already assured, lost nothing. "If the pampered son of wealthy parents found the discipline too irksome—as was often the case—he could get an honorable discharge," wrote Oliver J. Bond in his history of the institution. That was not so bad. Rich boys had no need for the school's mysterious rebirth and all the ceremony that attended it. The world that they returned to had recognized them from the womb.

School officials, meanwhile, used high attrition rates as a badge of honor, not an indication of internal problems. Though educators around the state did not put The Citadel on a par with other colleges in academic merit, Citadel officials claimed the high ground. High rates of attrition and expulsion, school boosters reassured, were a signal of the institution's standards, *not* its failures. "The difficulty of completing the course of instruction, and the large number of dismissals in this institution," the board of visitors puffed, "are, in the opinion of the Board, not the least cause of its excellence." Those who stayed, those board members believed, learned something more important than what other colleges were offering. They learned to walk the road to power.

A South Carolina politician once described the process with some humor. A prodigal son raised in The Citadel's traditions would be different from most college graduates, he said in a lecture to appreciative cadets. When his funds were exhausted and his prospects hit rock bottom, no man who wore the ring would go back home to admit failure. Never! No, the man barked, a Citadel man would kill the fattest hog that he could find, gorge on spareribs and backbone, and "with all the graces born in the City by the Sea have fascinated and married the old man's daughter. . . . Then with plenty of leisure, he would have entered politics [and] gone to Congress." His audience howled with pleasure. He had spoken to their hearts.

Of course, not everyone could stand the price. Successful as the school's reopening was, its rigors overwhelmed all but the most stoic. Oliver Bond described the first decade after The Citadel's restart as a grim time made of "political antagonism of the most serious kind, grave problems of interior discipline, dire poverty, and lesser calamities from the forces of nature, cyclone, earthquake and fire." Many freshmen never made it. Fewer and fewer bothered even to try. In 1901, nineteen years after the school's auspicious reopening, only forty-four freshmen showed up for class. "From the beginning," wrote one among them, "we had to bear untold miseries." Classwork was the least of a boy's problems. Instead, danger lay with upperclassmen and their constant reprimands. By Christmas, the class historian noted in the *Sphinx,* "one and all turned our faces homeward, forty-four beaming countenances not the least betraying the wounded spirits that lay hidden beneath our glittering uniforms." Only eighteen would stay to earn their rings.

In time, those few passed their training down, dealing freshmen the same blows that they themselves had endured. "With loving hands we brought them up in the way that they should go," wrote the class historian. "We taught them that the way of the transgressor is truly hard, and though it gave us much pain, yet we could not spare the rod." "Sun spots" applied by paddles were the norm. "I must admit," concluded a graduating senior from the class of 1905, "we gave most of our time to the subject of [that] Art; we all became so versed in this science that there was not a single one of us who could not change a green recruit into a blue pygmy in less time than it takes to tell."

Those who stayed were proud and uncomplaining members of a hard-tested elite. Men who wore the ring often signed up sons at birth, assuring them a place and taking part in a tradition that would last to modern times. Perhaps one day their daughters might march, too. The *Sphinx* of 1905 included a wistful portrait of "The New Cadet Girl" in her uniform. Drawn in pen and ink by a woman named Lila Johnson, it was an appealing depiction of a self-possessed young lady dressed in a flowing, ankle-length skirt and simple jacket, a narrow tie closed at her neck and a shako with its floppy plume perched at a jaunty angle on her curls. For ninety years it would not be. Instead, the hardships of the boys increased, and women were kept out. A time of war was soon to start, and it would transform everything.

When War Became Familiar

I T WAS NEVER JUST old soldiers and the "potent few" who saw the world in terms of natural groupings among men. Nor was it only cadets who thought in terms of domination and control. If anything, as a nation, we tended to share such views; and by the early 1900s, we looked outside our borders to trace a map of dominance. We were by then a wealthy state that could extend its reach across the seas. But we needed a strong military to make our presence felt. Soon we had one. In just fifty years our military grew from a haphazard, poorly equipped force trained for battling Indians in the wild into a superpower capable of obliterating the entire human race. War was the language we all spoke. At first, we hardly realized it.

The Spanish War came first. "A splendid little war" of only four months, it was sparked by the sinking of the *Maine*. The ship's loss in Havana harbor in 1898 was probably caused by spontaneous combustion in a coal bin onboard ship. But the possibility of an accidental explosion was not offered at the time. Instead, Spanish forces in Cuba were blamed. We were a nation hungry for new conquests. Spain offered them with little pain. Only 460 American soldiers died in combat in that war. Emboldened, we pushed on and won control of the Philippines ("our little brown brothers"), Puerto Rico and Guam. For the first time, we were widely recognized as a world power. "Remember the *Maine*" became our call to arms. It was answered quickly on a massive scale.

The creation of the modern military was supervised by a corporate lawyer from New York, Elihu Root, who applied business thinking to the structure and organization of soldiers, ships and weaponry. Assigned as secretary of war, Root from 1900 to 1903 built a unified system of defense, a force of one hundred thousand troops that would soon find purpose in minor conflicts and, greatly expanded, in world war. By

1906, we ranked as a naval power only Britain could match. With it and our new army, we consolidated our strength in the Philippines and extended our power to Hawaii and Alaska. We looked south as well. Between 1895 and 1915, the United States sent troops to Mexico, Cuba, Haiti, Nicaragua and Honduras. We had new interests to protect and broad investments to maintain. We liked the role of leader. And we were getting used to men in uniform. The first breeze of a new century had carried with it the strong smell of blood. Soon war became familiar.

At The Citadel, that transition breathed new life into a struggling institution. Strict notions of duty, service and discipline that had once served Charleston's elite were easily transferred onto a broader frame. As the deep imprint of slavery faded, its lessons were translated into the vocabulary of world affairs. Cadets now brightened with fresh purpose and marched with flourish as proud patriots. Protecting private interests and established patterns of authority had always been the institution's function. Four years of stringent training drummed strict imperatives into boys' hearts. Earliest cadets not only imposed their rule over slaves and free blacks while they were marching but often extended the role of guard long afterwards, joining the city's police force after donning their gold rings. In the mid-1850s, when William Porcher Miles became the mayor of Charleston, he named a West Point colonel as the city's first chief of police. Eight officers acted as Miles's lieutenants; of them, six came from The Citadel. "Paddy Miles' Bull Dogs" provided The Citadel with a mascot that would endure and a channel for employment that would last to modern times. Reuben M. Greenberg, Charleston's police chief in 1995, counted forty Citadel men among his 320 officers. They were patriots and men of values, the chief reported proudly. They served their city, state and nation well.

When America entered "the Great War" in April 1917, The Citadel responded with a show of unequivocal commitment. All thirty-three in that year's class went off to fight. So many Citadel men were commissioned in the Marines, in fact, that a congressional inquiry was established to determine whether the institution was being given some unusual advantage over other southern colleges. It was not. Citadel men were simply toughened up and ready to go when Uncle Sam came calling. In 1917, 259 boys arrived at the barracks at Marion Square. That night a Diamond Jubilee celebration marked the institution's seventy-fifth anniversary. Two hundred and ten alumni were off serving the armed forces then. A flag sewn with a star for every one was paraded with great fanfare among cadets and ladies in their flowing gowns. "Alma Mater—congratulations!" cheered a graduate who communicated his enthusiasm by telegram. "May your thousandth birthday find you sending out such sons as you are today." Now, a whole nation cheered them on. These were soldiers for victory. It was our time for heroes.

What terrible excitement lay in that great tragedy. World War I "took a little fellow from a little town, gave him an air and swagger," Willa Cather wrote. Everyone felt part of it. But the war those troops encountered was one of unprecedented brutality. Off on distant shores, Citadel men fought their way through poison gas and sniper fire and volleys of machine gun lead. Along the brown and battered Western Front they fell in heaps among their brethren, as vulnerable to mortar fire and mustard gas as anyone. American losses mounted rapidly. Tens of thousands died. Yet frightful as that tally was, it was nothing to compare to the nine million lost to European nations. Back home, we could hardly comprehend the scope of it. Yet President Woodrow Wilson stirred the people with his rhetoric. One nation, under God, indivisible and young, we would "make the world safe for democracy," he thundered over the crackling static of early radios. Our boys could turn the tide.

We loved this role as heroes. It suited our bright image of ourselves. In Charleston, where civilians had battled a deadly scourge of Spanish influenza and long years of humbling poverty before it, returning soldiers were embraced and folded back into the city's weave. Favorite sons, a harbinger of better times, they made for sweet redemption. In March 1917 officials at the War Department called on Charleston to act as headquarters for the Southeastern Military District. The Holy City (so named for its many towering church spires) happily agreed. All of Charleston hummed with war. The money poured. A 2,840-foot dock was constructed at the Navy Yard in Berkeley County. A massive Army Port Terminal was built. Civilian jobs were opening too. Everything was energized. Once written off as a "buzzard town" starved amid its fading grandeur, that majestic dowager had stirred herself at last and now looked toward Washington for a new era of prosperity. New dependencies began to form. The knot they made would only tighten.

In 1941, with world war once again at hand, defense contracts sent torrents of new money Charleston's way. Twelve destroyers were commissioned. Weekly payrolls jumped. Shipyards and airfields were upgraded. Charleston incomes grew to be the highest in the state, and income from defense spending surpassed tourism as the low country's largest industry. Up North, meanwhile, a wily advocate fought on the region's behalf. L. Mendel Rivers, a Berkeley County native and long-time Charleston resident, had been elected to Congress in 1940. Voters returned him to the nation's capital sixteen times. He returned the favor by gaining control over the House Armed Services Committee and seeing to it that his loyal constituency won vast federal largesse.

In the Holy City, honor and capitalism now were sublimely merged. A ring of support industries sprang up across the low country. From the start, Charleston officials showed their gratitude. They showered it upon cadets, drawing tighter a tie that bound the city and her Citadel. Though expanded in 1908 with a gift of Charleston's old police station, The Citadel, during World War I, outgrew its first headquarters. An additional story was added to the building at Marion Square. But even that was not enough. In 1918, the city gave the school a plot of land out on the edge of town to build a "Greater Citadel." Four years later, cadets started classes on a new campus. A barracks to house 450 cadets rose up beside the Ashley River. There, on ground that once was used for dueling, the school would quickly find its stride. New buildings were copied from old blueprints. The grim visage of the workhouse was preserved. By then it was an honored trademark.

The class of 1922 would be the largest in the institution's history to that time. But it was nothing compared to what would follow. By 1927 the pace of growth was so intense that another barracks was needed. In 1924, 313 boys unpacked beside the Ashley. Three years later, in 1927, the number had more than doubled—to 722. Meanwhile, increased emphasis was placed on academics, and soon the college grew in stature as much as in enrollment. By World War II, Citadel cadets considered themselves proud students of "the West Point of the South" (a claim made just as vigorously by the Virginia Military Institute). Though no match for West Point in academics, aggressive and gung ho Citadel cadets epitomized the nation's fighting spirit. And soon they put that spirit to good use. World War II consumed one boy after the next. One entire class had no time for graduation; its students marched away before their books were closed. Meanwhile, Citadel officials would proudly claim that all but forty-nine of the school's 2,976 living graduates had served the country bearing arms.

Much of the credit for the institution's growing reputation belonged at the feet of one man, an old soldier who strutted about the campus with an air of dignity and purpose. Charles P. Summerall arrived in Charleston in the fall of 1931 and left only reluctantly after a reign of more than twenty years. A hero of the Boxer Rebellion of 1900 and a driven troop commander during World War I, Summerall, after retiring as the Army's chief of staff, laid his mark on that old school, helping it out of a chronic financial crisis and steering boys along their way. His authority among cadets was enormous. In his uniform, his posture always tall and tight, he cut a classic figure of command. The reverence and fear that he inspired stayed with most students always.

Inside the barracks, Summerall's grand manner meshed well with student life. Boys loved his drama and self-confidence. Yet there were frictions, too. Paradoxically, they arose out of a game long played upon that ground. Seventy years after the Civil War, Summerall was shocked to find that boys were whipped and made to serve upperclassmen as their slaves. In some cases, barracks violence was so severe that cadets were beaten senseless. Brutal indoctrinations known as "ass inspections" left boys black and blue and sometimes bloody. After particularly hard sessions in the gym, freshmen could barely take their seats in class. At night, more trials likely waited. In the barracks after lights went out an arsenal of metal coat hangers, broomsticks, palmetto branches, transom rods and riding switches was employed.

By the early 1940s, the "detail system," as it was known, had evolved to the extent that every junior had one freshman at his beck and call and every senior, two. For freshmen, survival meant accommodating every whim, demand, impulse and unreasonable request that a master might impose. Courtesy, respect, speed and an uncomplaining attitude were paramount. Even a sly glance of resentment could bring punishment. Sometimes the whip was brought out for no reason at all. Yet if a freshman could hold out, basic math worked in his favor. New boys invested one year of service, then earned two as a reward.

When the system worked well, upperclassmen made reasonable demands and protected and even mentored boys under their control. Some upperclassmen helped freshmen with their studies or whispered crucial advice at difficult junctures. In such cases, lifelong friendships formed, and the give-and-take made sense. But when the system failed, as it had by the time Summerall took charge, it often turned quite brutal. In those cases, freshmen had two options. They could either suffer constant punishment throughout the year (and call their silence strength) or they could quit, knowing that quitters were reviled.

The tensions of that interplay often found inventive outlets. Some students blew off steam by playing elaborate practical jokes upon their tormentors, filling rooms with frogs or cockroaches and vanishing into the tropical haze of Charleston nights, secure in their revenge. Occasionally, however, communal uprisings occurred. By the time that Summerall took over, a long catalog of riots, mutinies, food fights and other acts of mass outrage dotted the school's history. Early in the school's existence, one whole class walked out, never to return. At other times, the corps simply seemed to go collectively berserk, abruptly dissolving all strict rules of discipline in favor of a free-for-all. Shortly before he took control, Summerall had his first taste of just such mayhem. It started with a game of basketball. After a four-point loss to the College of Charleston, Citadel cadets began a brawl. The ensuing postgame violence injured five firefighters and several civilians. In the end, two fire trucks and the police reserves were required to quell it. The local newspaper screamed riot. But Citadel officials were more circumspect. They preferred to think of it as a virulent and somewhat premature condition of spring fever. Nor did they suspect that a more serious uprising was on its way. It started when the school's new president abolished slavery in the corps.

Several years after Summerall took over, and just five years after adults (the tactical officers known as "tacs") were removed from a thin supervisory role inside the barracks, distressed parents began complaining of severe cases of student violence. They did not feel their boys were safe. Summerall listened, then investigated. What he found was that a combination of barracks ritual and school tradition lay behind much of the abuse. He summoned a top cadet to his office and ordered that the detail system end. "Yes, sir," came the response.

"As soon as CPS found out about the system," a cadet of that era recalled, "it became history. Hence, we were slaves for half our freshman year; then our investment got wiped out." Back inside the barracks, a slow fuse began to burn. Older students felt deprived. They taunted freshmen, calling them sissies and tattletales and accusing them of running to Bond Hall to find protection. Seniors mocked and ridiculed and said those boys were weak. Freshmen wailed in self-defense. They were as tough as anyone, they countered. They did not want the system stopped. They could prove that they were men. For months, subtle hostilities and petty conflicts percolated in the ranks. Morale slipped. Students complied with the president's orders, but compliance brought resentment, and then resentment turned to rage. On March 15, seniors tore the place apart.

"The Rebellion of 1938" began quietly at lunch. In the mess hall, students slipped bottles of ketchup, pieces of fruit, hard rolls, and kitchen implements inside their deep gray pockets. In the barracks, they added to their arsenal using "trash cans, powder cans, toilet paper, shaving lotion, buckets of water, bottles, many other items of glass, fireworks, and various other things that could be thrown onto the quadrangle from the galleries," according to an account by school historian D. D. Nicholson. For an hour, at least, a queer silence hung above the campus. Then someone tossed a trash can, and one building after another exploded in a deafening roar. Boys surged about smashing furniture and raising hell. Desks and chairs hurtled dangerously down narrow stairwells. Trash cans fell from upper floors to clatter on concrete and spill their contents on all sides. Cherry bombs exploded. Firecrackers hissed and snapped. Inside the quadrangles piles of trash and shattered debris rose in a sloppy mess. With each new reprimand from an adult, the mutiny only gained intensity. For nearly two days, no one could control the place. In town, rumors of the uprising were traded over scotch and fine wines in Charleston mansions. Nothing serious, school officials said when they were asked. Just a minor problem with cadets. At last, exhausted and relieved, the students put their weapons down.

Punishment was swift. Seniors were given a vicious tongue-lashing, stripped of rank and warned that any further disobedience would result in mass dismissals. The younger boys looked on and kept their faces cold as stone. But when the humbled senior class walked into the mess hall that evening the other students stood, then banged their metal trays and grinned.

Two weeks later, the president typed up a lengthy report. "Disorders of a riotous and mutinous nature occurred," Summerall said. Efforts to train those boys as gentlemen were wasted. Student complaints that they were being subjected to excessive supervision were "preposterous and insincere," he scoffed. The boys were merely acting out their rage at losing privilege. Their outburst was childish and undisciplined, unworthy of the school, he said. The reason was quite simple. "Resentment over the discontinuance of the detail system contributed to disloyalty on the part of certain members of the senior class," Summerall concluded. "Their standard of values appears to be too low for them to understand the evil to the college of an outmoded and vicious system." Members of the Artillery Battalion were singled out for censure. That group, the president said, had proved to be "without discipline, loyalty, morale, self-respect or respect for any authority."

In fact, the artillery boys had been a campus problem for some time. Rowdy and aggressive, they kept the campus in a constant state of siege. Immersed in tales of war and surrounded now by soldiers who wore the scars of World War I, they added a new game to their dark repertoire. Like boys from generations past, they internalized the war their fathers fought and molded it to their own ends. War was now the game they played and their most consuming passion. Though their rifles were unloaded and their bombs were made of smoke, the war became their world. Inside those campus walls, they focused on vague heroics, secret missions and stunning victory. Lessons about air assaults, flanking movements, sniper fire and enemy infiltrations became their food and drink. Catapults were rigged with long elastic bands and aimed at enemy positions. At night, explosive charges soared over college parapets and landed with cascades of sparks. The Padgett-Thomas Barracks made a perfect mark for air assaults. Long and wide, its quadrangle proved an easy hit from nearby buildings. With just the right speed and angle, a cherry bomb could burst dead center with a boom. Adults came running. No one was stirring. It was hard to pin the blame. When the adults left, new volleys of "torpedo bombs" sailed across the skies. Explosions sent boys scattering and drove the adults into fits.

Cadets of that era perfected their assaults and passed their training down. On the eve of World War II, the artillery boys ran noisy blitzkriegs overhead. Down below, boys sneaked from room to room with water bombs. Snipers shot off rubber bands and threw small smoke bombs at the feet of unsuspecting victims. Constant vigilance was key. Mass assaults were planned, guerrilla movements learned and silent reconnaissance performed. Old soldiers on that ground, men who had lost brothers and comrades in distant battlefields, looked on and shook their heads. Let them have their games, they said. If war came around again— as then seemed likely—those boyish stunts would end. Until then, adults on campus winked off such misbehavior. "If diversity, imagination, and daring can enrich the educational experience," wrote Nicholson, "these years could not have been more rewarding. They were the pre-war years with respect to World War II, but, in some respects, aggressive cadet behavior and other challenges to the administration warrant their being characterized as *the* war years." In those barracks games, the key to victory was not merely a successful hit. Instead, in a world largely defined by punishment and its escape, the sweetest triumphs included misplaced blame. Twice victorious, the victimizers ruled.

World War II, when it came, brought a new tone of sobriety. The mood inside the campus changed. Newsreels brought home death and devastation. There were new horrors now, rumors of concentration camps and people herded about like animals, packed in showers and then gassed. The film stock cadets saw showed dirty soldiers smoking cigarettes and fighting across open fields. Narrators spoke of blood and glory and of loyal soldiers dying. Yet government officials heavily controlled the news. They did not want nervous mothers keeping boys out of the fray. And so the stirring sounds of patriotism were played at a high volume. On campus, boys bent to their studies and marched crisply with unloaded rifles. Summerall kept a constant watch. His boys marched sharp and looked ahead with all the faith and hope of teenagers.

In 1942, 208 men slipped on their gold rings. The war was young, and they were full of optimism. America seemed to move with single-minded purpose. Citadel men moved in step with it, dedicated and intense. Among their ranks, in time, their class would count at least three generals, a nuclear physicist with the Manhattan Project, a U.S. senator (Ernest F. "Fritz" Hollings), two governors and the head of a major newspaper chain. A pinnacle was reached. No later class would match it. Under Summerall's stewardship the school eventually tripled in size and steadily grew in reputation. But finally, reluctantly, at the age of eighty-six, ill and no longer able to manage so complex an institution, he was forced into retirement.

In 1954, a new general arrived, more famous than the last. A hero during World War II and personal friend of such men as Franklin Roosevelt, Harry Truman and Dwight Eisenhower, General Mark Wayne Clark needed little introduction. Winston Churchill, with a smoky chuckle, called him by a private nickname. To that great British statesman, The Citadel's eleventh president was "the American Eagle," the very embodiment of America's brash confidence. It was a name that stuck, and one the general loved, a coy salute that captured both Clark's hawkishness and almost fanatical patriotism.

The class of 1958 arrived on campus with him. They would be Mark Clark's boys, cold warriors one and all, and they revered him. In the

Sphinx upon their graduation, they wrote in gold lettering with stiff formality: "Your Plebes Graduate, Sir!" It was the new president to whom they granted an adoring dedication in their senior year: "Soldier . . . Leader . . . Inspirer . . . Friend . . . Classmate," they called him. They could only hope that he would be as proud of them, in time, as they had been of him.

Flags waved and swing bands played. Theirs was a mild age. Photographs from that time show boys relaxing with their companies in V-necked sweaters, smoking jackets and the occasional beret. They puffed at pipes and wore broad smiles. They were proud southerners training for success. At college "hops" the boys danced with their mothers and with girls wearing white gloves. Freshmen were no longer "rats," but "dumbsmacks" now, "dumbheads" and "squats" whose worst worries came in tandem with exams. Hazing was more or less controlled. There was no terrifying undertow of violence. The rigors of that training—muted by Summerall's persistent reforms—were painful and demanding, still, but the school's rough regimen, its so-called "fourth class system," was made more bearable with "a four-star general for a classmate."

Clark moved quickly to inspire those young boys. He called upon old friends to visit Charleston and speak. They came in droves, conferring on cadets the benediction of their fame. To boys from small towns dotting the rural South it was a heady introduction to the world. By turns they heard the booming exhortations of big men. General Matthew B. Ridgway lauded their commitment, self-discipline and drive. Barry Goldwater, Curtis E. LeMay, Herbert Hoover, General Maxwell Taylor, Francis Cardinal Spellman, Billy Graham and others saw in those cadets the faces of young patriots and proud Americans devoted to the nation's cause. Indeed, they were. Eisenhower made the point himself, arriving on the campus amid fanfare and reviewing the corps while standing in a moving jeep, flags flapping off the hood. It was a heady and exciting time. Four barracks had been built. And every one of them was nearly full. Here was something grand, those boys believed, something timeless and enduring.

And yet outside those gates, new pressures had begun to build. Deep plates of history were shifting. The French were crushed at Dien Bien Phu. In military circles, the domino theory held sway. In Bond Hall, Clark thundered on about "the threat," and twined it with a new phenomenon at home. Across America, with increasing volume, blacks were calling for an equal place. The Supreme Court ruled in 1954 that separate was not equal. *Brown v. Board of Education* sent a thunderclap across the South. More demands would follow. Clark saw in them a communist plot to weaken his proud land. He opposed integration in the military, and in private letters he described black soldiers as cowardly and inferior. To the editor of the *Charleston Evening Post* he complained about "indiscriminate racial integration." To him, the burgeoning civil rights movement seemed a violation of the natural order of the world, a toxin sent to poison his great nation from within.

Hunkered down beside the Ashley, Clark swore he would resist the era's pull. To a remarkable extent, he succeeded. There, at least, the world retained its shape. Inevitably, his virulent attacks on integrationists seeped into the corps. Confederate flags began to flutter on the campus. In the 1958 *Sphinx,* F Troop (a "duckbutt" company composed of shorter boys and voted "best disciplined" and "best academic" that year) posed for a company portrait standing behind a huge Confederate flag at the top of which was pinned a scrap of paper marked with the letters KKK. "Kleen Kut Kompany," the caption read. Just joking. Everyone was smiling. Their world was good. The Bulldogs excelled on the football field, and in 1958, twenty-two hundred boys were in the barracks, the most in that school's history. Among them, indeed leading them, were the same men who three decades later would return to that holy ground to defend it against a very different enemy—a girl from Powdersville whom one lawyer described as a "toxin" that would weaken the corps and kill it from within. Not long after that, without a trace of irony or wit, Citadel officials suggested that if the judge decreed that she must march she should bunk in the infirmary. ("Mom," joked the subject of all that angst, "they think that I'm a germ.") But it was an old notion and familiar to the men who ran the school. Three decades after they donned their rings, Clark's boys were back and ready for a fight.

Claudius Elmer "Bud" Watts III, the son of Elmer "Tug" Watts Jr., a Citadel graduate from 1932, arrived from Cheraw, South Carolina, in 1954 as a tall, gangly, small-town kid determined to excel. He did, by every standard at the school. By 1958, Bud was a "senior superlative" who headed the honor committee, served as vice president of the Round Table debating society, acted as first sergeant on the Summerall Guards and chaired the senior hop. He was a member of the presidential advisory committee, helped craft the school's new honor code, and was named to *Who's Who Among Students in American Universities & Colleges,* a list of high achievers. He commanded Third Battalion and was voted both "most likely to succeed" and "most in the know" by classmates. A cartoon in the *Sphinx* his senior year showed him with his feet propped on a desk as he tipped backward and blew smoke rings from a fat cigar. A more formal portrait showed him earnest with his chin tucked tight and a white-gloved hand firmly grasping a bright sword. Bud joined the Air Force after graduation. There, among other things, he would fly 276 combat missions over Vietnam, serve as deputy chief of staff for intelligence, then assume the role of comptroller. In 1989, he retired as lieutenant general and, still wearing his uniform, went home to Charleston to run his school as president. "Not bad for a country boy," he said with a stiff smile. At the time he said it, his hometown had three stoplights.

Cadet captain Jimmie Emerson Jones of Greenville joined Watts as a "senior superlative" in 1958. He edited the *Sphinx,* chaired the Miss Citadel contest and served as the commander of I Company. A short-statured "duckbutt," Jones marched with the Summerall Guards and Junior Sword Drill and won the nickname "Outlaw." Affable and eager, he was dubbed "one of the friendliest boys of our class" by the class historian and "biggest politician" by his friends. The same *Sphinx* cartoon that showed Watts with his cigar depicted Jones strutting about wearing a sandwich board that urged his classmates: "VOTE FOR JONES."

They did. In 1995 he chaired the Board of Visitors.

William Lewis Spearman was a slick-haired boy from Columbia with a slowly spreading grin. In 1958, he was a "senior superlative" who commanded the Fourth Battalion and made Who's Who as commander of the Summerall Guards and Bond Volunteers. He had marched in Junior Sword Drill while rooming with Watts and participated in the Round Table with him their senior year. The *Sphinx* dubbed him "best personality" and showed him wearing shorts and a T-shirt, grasping a bottle of liniment oil as he helped prop up a friend ("most unlucky") trussed up with a broken leg and wrist. In 1995, colleagues called him Doctor Spearman, though he never earned the title. It was a suitable name, though. He stilled played that role. In 1995, instead of propping up "most unlucky," he helped his friend Bud Watts, the college president, his former roommate. Preferring a role of wizard back behind the screen, Spearman wrote speeches, helped guide the Faulkner litigation and stoked a campus mood of bitterness.

Other men had drifted back as well. Lawrence Edward McKay Jr., the class president in 1958, served as director of student activities. Walter

Bland Mathis Jr., the regimental executive officer and class historian in 1958, taught English in Capers Hall. James Watson Bradin, member of the Summerall Guards and the Bond Volunteers in 1958, served on the Board of Visitors.

Theirs was a small world of well-known faces and closed doors. When Shannon Faulkner came to march, Mark Clark's boys—the same men who once dominated the barracks—now controlled the school itself. On that ground where tradition was so revered, history would repeat. Just as they had done before, they readied for a fight. But now it was not blacks they vowed to keep away, but women. The arguments they voiced were much the same. The corps would die. Something fine and of long standing would be lost and irretrievable. They spoke with sadness of bad endings in the very same dark courtroom that once resounded with arguments that framed the *Brown v. Board of Education* fight. In that room, they sat on the same chairs and mouthed the same most solemn oaths with the very same intensity. They were old friends, those men, the product of a certain time and place, Mark Clark's boys, each one—proud graduates and proud Americans who thought that they were standing at the center of the world.

As Though God Himself
Walked There

TONY LACKEY was a toddler, playing soldier, while his father fought in World War II. In the cinemas, grainy images in black and white showed soldiers drenched in raging glory, tattered and exhausted, risking all for God and country. Crackling radios were full of howitzers, sparking sniper fire and sudden death on distant shores. Boys longed for that great test. Fueled by such excitement, the war so far away, they imagined blue skies above their peaceful houses filled with bombers surfing death, moving fast in cold formations, swinging silently beneath the clouds. The sounds of heavy machine-gun fire—eh-eh-eh-eh-eh-eh-eh—rattled in their throats. How could a child know what that might mean? In the isolated town of Statesville, North Carolina, where Lackey learned to walk and talk and play with guns, young men marched off to kill the Nazis with long rifles and new skills. Moms and girlfriends said goodbye. They leaned forward with a final kiss and tears of sadness in adoring eyes. . . . *And I will be a soldier, too,* Tony told himself with great solemnity.

In the late afternoon of April 12, 1945, President Franklin Delano Roosevelt suffered a massive cerebral hemorrhage. Two and a half hours later, Harry Truman said the oath of office. "Boys," he told a group of reporters the next day, "if you ever pray, pray for me now. . . . When they told me yesterday what had happened, I felt like the moon, the stars, and all the planets had fallen on me." In the coming days, the full scope of his new powers would come clear. Truman was now commander in chief of a vast military that included more than sixteen million men and women, the largest naval force in history and an Air Force with greater reach and killing power than any military organization in history. That force was then fully engaged. World War II was at its ghastly peak. Almost two hundred thousand Americans lay dead. No end was then in sight.

In his second week in office, Truman received an in-depth briefing from his secretary of war. The $2 billion Manhattan Project was tentatively labeled a success. "Within four months," a formal memo informed the president, "we shall in all probability have completed the most terrible weapon ever known in human history."

Out in small towns and far-off cities, Americans were ignorant of that new power. They knew only that they were winning. News of war arrived in breathless dispatches. Mussolini was killed; Nazi forces foundered; Italian troops surrendered; then Hitler, too, was dead. Lackey waited at the door. One day, now, his father would come home.

Nine days before his sixth birthday, it was done. The end came with "a light not of this world." It flashed twice. Then Japan surrendered. "This is a great day," said Truman, "the day we've been waiting for." In every city, people poured onto the streets. Those distant clouds spelled victory. Soldiers had their absolution. Two enormous bombs had ended years of vicious combat. With them, America became the greatest power in the world. What better nutrient for a young boy?

In flickering images on film and accounts in hometown newspapers, soldiers were pictured grinning, hanging off troop trucks, scattering chocolate bars to hungry children. Some men grabbed total strangers in a steel embrace or happily chugged one last beer before they boarded ships heading for home. Once on familiar shores, they fell and kissed the ground before being swept along in storms of bright confetti. More private homecomings were never shown. They were harder, the homecomings of men who came back crippled, twisted and in pain, the war with them forever. Lackey watched and waited. Now his father would come, too. His dad would stand in uniform—a perfect hero for his son.

Nothing ever was so simple.

Jack Lackey was not the man his son had conjured. An enlisted man, he was an Army sergeant who jumped from airplanes and tromped through muddy fields and came back with a broken spirit and a raging taste for whiskey. "He was a drunk and a slob," Tony said without emotion twenty years after his father's death. "He grew up during Prohibition but was a drunk by the time he turned fifteen. . . . He was an alcoholic as a kid. He got kicked out of high school in the ninth or tenth grade for raising some kind of ruckus. He fought in World War II and then Korea. When he got back, on the weekends he got drunk. Then he went AWOL. He was discharged under less than honorable circumstances."

Jack Lackey was neither a kind man nor an accomplished one. Tony vowed he would be both. A gawky boy with no connections, Jack Lackey's son, John G. Lackey III, dreamed of West Point but fell short. He had neither the grades nor the social entree to forge a path to the nation's service academies. Instead he went south to Charleston and scraped through four years at The Citadel. In 1957, when Bud Watts and his team were seniors, Tony signed up in their midst, under their command. In 1961, he wore the ring. It was "the golden age," he said, a time of peace when all America seemed joined and discipline on campus was tempered by both humor and camaraderie. At The Citadel he found his home, the only place that would abide.

In 1957, ranking officers hovered and corrected. Clothes were expected to be folded in a certain order in the press. Any sloppiness or deviation brought demerits and some trouble. But freshmen quickly learned old tricks and new evasions. Most cadets hid the clothes they wore beneath their bedding and left their drawers immaculate with uniforms they seldom touched. In those days, boys awoke at 4 a.m. to get their rooms spotless for inspections. No perfection was enough. But no failure courted cruel brutalities. "The worst we had," said Lackey, "was a stupid drill inside the guard room when the freshmen took their first leave." He failed on his first try. There was a minor flaw, a detail missed, that sent him back into the quad. In his room he was so angry at himself that he threw his belt against the wall. The scratches on his buckle took an afternoon to fix. It was a long while before he could laugh about that childish outburst. "My own frustration cost me most," he said with typical self-disparagement. "I spent the next few hours in my room." He never did forget it.

In time, the anguish and confusion of the first few weeks diminished. Lackey made new friends and found his way around the campus. By spring, the worst of it was done. On Recognition Day "they shook your hand," he said. "It was incredible." In that instant, he had his name back and was pulled into another world, a world of men and patriots. Here, his father's failures had no place. Lackey could erase them. Others would remember the moment, too, as a time of almost transcendent pride. "On that day, we became part of an elite," said Ed Tivol, a contemporary of Lackey's who knew him only vaguely at The Citadel but better later when their Army careers intersected. "We had made it. We survived. We had done something not everyone could do. I loved it. I must have floated two feet above the ground."

Lackey saw his father for the last time while he was still in school. In 1958, the two men sat together in the cool silence of the college chapel. They made an awkward, though not unprecedented, tableau: a father on his long way down, the son just getting started. After that, the two men spoke infrequently. Nine years later, on the day Jack Lackey died, his son was an Army captain assigned stateside between tours and Jack a cashiered sergeant, twice divorced and foundering, a cautionary tale of alcohol, loneliness and penury. In their last phone call, father and son, two soldiers, drifted from one subject to the next then said a stiff good-bye. Two hours later, Jack Lackey crashed his car into a creek and died. "He was who he was," was all his son would say.

Lackey never talked about his father much. But the wound of him would linger. As a young man, Lackey shaped his life around that wound and strived for something better. At The Citadel, he tried so hard to make a second lieutenant's grade that friends mocked him for the effort, saying he had exhausted his entire life's energies on something trivial. "You'll never earn a higher rank," a roommate taunted. "You've just got nothing left." That assessment badly underestimated Lackey's drive. "I wasn't the smartest kid," he said with a smile. "But I figured that what I lacked in intelligence I could make up for with hard work." He was a soldier's soldier that way; a bulldog once he set his sights, tenacious, single-minded and loyal to a fault. In that, he epitomized the deep philosophy behind his college training. Duty was his driving purpose. He made a life of it and rarely challenged those he served. Instead of picking away at flaws, he stressed successes. Instead of questioning commands, he fulfilled them to the best of his ability. As a soldier he was fearless. As a patriot, unswerving. As a graduate, forever faithful. By habit and by training, Lackey left the big picture to others. He would implement and execute and even risk his life to follow orders. But for the most part, he gave the trust of leadership to men with higher ranks. He was dutiful in that as he was dutiful in all things.

"I really had this strong belief," he said with a vague wave that encompassed a world of values he could barely bring himself to say aloud. "And I was striving."

At school, Lackey balanced barracks life and classroom work. He dated a local girl, made rank, and won a commission in the reserves. It was not the regular Army commission he had hoped for and nowhere near the start that West Point might have offered. But it was enough for a small-town boy to make a good beginning, and to him that was everything. He would have a soldier's life. At The Citadel, with new mentors all around, he had made Mark Clark his hero. Clark's absolutes would leave a deep and lasting imprint. "He left a kind of aura on the campus," Lackey said. "As though God himself walked there."

By most accounts, Clark conspicuously sought such adulation. A Citadel band director composed the "General Clark, Liberator of Rome March," and it was played before parades. More cynical contemporaries called Clark a publicity hound who cared more for heads turned and headlines won than battles fought. That was unfair. He was an able general and widely respected through the ranks. Yet he never lost a chance to make a convert to his views and proved a powerful storyteller and proud connoisseur of his own exploits. To him, an officer's image was almost as important as his field effectiveness. In the art of leading men, Clark emphatically instructed, "a general should *inspire.*" And so he did, consciously painting himself hero, soldier, statesman, patriot. Some colleagues found him arrogant. He didn't mind. Neither did America. When he came home after serving as commander in chief of the United Nations Command in Korea, New York City greeted him with ticker tape.

At The Citadel, Clark enjoyed an even more adoring audience. Strutting about in his uniform, clear in his command, he moved among the students barking orders like a king. In his world there was no room to voice complaint. Like Summerall, Clark loved being the boss. Anyone who crossed him got a sharp comeuppance. Dissent was considered a firing offense, tenure positively un-American. A president's effectiveness, Clark believed, lay in his control, not in his open-mindedness. In Clark's view, the college faculty, staff and students should share the president's values or get out. He kept the staff so nervous that on days when he swept out of his office for "surprise" inspections (moving about the campus in a convoy, his car hood fluttering with four-star flags) a secretary discreetly called ahead to alert employees at each stop.

"He drove around in the biggest black thing that he could get, short of a limo," laughed a staff member from that time. "Men would line up out in front to greet him." By the time the general's entourage pulled up, students were studying, secretaries typing frantically and the ranks were all in order. Everyone in the place stood when the president walked in.

Formal welcomes were exchanged and polite tours quickly arranged. "Very good," the general mused distractedly, after picking away at minor flaws. Once he was out of earshot, someone headed for the phone. "We had a whole rapid alert system," chuckled the staff member. "General Clark didn't go anywhere that we didn't know it first. His world was perfectly controlled."

Cloistered on that closed-off ground and surrounded by admiring boys, Clark hardened his views. He liked the world the way it was. And yet increasingly, his world was being questioned. Issues left hanging after the Civil War were cautiously revisited. Having attained tremendous power, Americans were divided about how to use it and who should share it. A reprise had begun. True, slaves were free and women had the vote. But our dinner tables looked the same. Old lines of authority had mostly held. Our words about equality hung hollow in our midst. They were not true. "I, too, sing America," the black poet Langston Hughes had challenged in 1926. "They send me to eat in the kitchen. . . . But I laugh, And eat well, And grow strong. Tomorrow, I'll be at the table." That challenge still lay hanging. And it grew noisier each year.

In Georgia in the summer of 1946, four blacks (an Army veteran among them) were dragged from a car and slaughtered in a hail of gunfire so intense that the bodies were barely recognizable once those bullets found their mark. Though throngs of people watched, no witnesses came forward. In Batesburg, South Carolina, 130 miles northwest of Charleston, a black sergeant was beaten and blinded in one eye by police after city officials pulled him from a bus. State law enforcement officials said there was nothing they could do. Truman, sickened by those assaults and horrified that black soldiers who risked their lives abroad should come home to risk them once again, moved to use his powers. In an executive order signed on July 26, 1948, he ended segregation in the armed forces. That same year he appealed to Congress to pass new laws ensuring civil rights. It was time, the president said, for the imperatives embodied in the Fourteenth Amendment to be reflected in our daily lives. In his presidential campaign, he stumped in Harlem (the first presidential candidate to do so) and said he wanted an anti-lynching law, the abolition of poll taxes, an end to discrimination in the civil service and the complete desegregation of public transportation.

His were fighting words to many listeners. Strom Thurmond, then the governor of South Carolina, called Truman's proposals "communistic," "un-American," and "anti-Southern." He vowed to run for president himself. In Birmingham, Alabama, that July, southern "Dixiecrats" sought to split the vote and nominated Thurmond as their candidate. But Thurmond was a paper lion. Truman won a second term. In it, a new war would capture our attention. The growing furor of civil rights coincided with new foreign threats. Chinese troops pushed south into Korea. The Soviet Union conducted its first successful nuclear test. The domino theory gained force and favor. Our supremacy was questioned. No longer did we stand alone with the devastating powers we had made.

At that moment, our military was stronger than it had ever been. It was overbuilt and overarmed, a huge industry of many parts and a vast and terrifying potential. "Ours is a world of nuclear giants and ethical infants," cautioned Army General Omar Bradley, the first chairman of the Joint Chiefs of Staff, in a speech to West Point cadets in 1952. "We know more about war than we know about peace, more about killing than we know about living." And yet we had acquired a taste for power, and we would not turn away. The buildup barreled on. The Soviet Union is estimated to have had about 160 nuclear bombs in its entire arsenal in 1957. The United States, seeking absolute supremacy, held roughly 4,200 nuclear devices ready for a launch. No amount of power seemed enough. Yet like the radioactive dust that had drifted over Hiroshima, the weapons that we made left us nervous and afraid. The fear that it unleashed stayed with us, too, and worked its silent havoc. The very vocabulary of war began to change. Instead of speaking of victory, some wise men talked about annihilation. We were afraid. Now we feared even each other.

In 1950, Senator Joseph McCarthy held a piece of paper in the air and said that it contained the names of 205 communists working in the State Department. Nobody took much notice at the time. But soon the phrase "card-carrying communist" had seeped into the culture. We looked for scapegoats in our midst, deflecting new anxieties.

Within two years McCarthy had made an extraordinary reputation for himself. The forty-three-year-old politician (only recently dismissed by Washington correspondents as the worst member of the Senate) was put in charge of a committee investigating the very scare he helped create. He ran it roughly, crudely, hashing reputations by the score. As powerful as we were, we had never felt more vulnerable. What we had created, we could not now control. And so a shift occurred. We held our powers back. In Korea, troops fought with less than their full arsenal for the first time in our history. New realities demanded a more complex approach to war. Some Americans chafed at that new hesitance. "YOU DID IT ONCE BEFORE," an impatient citizen hectored in a telegram delivered to the Truman White House. "DROP ONE OVER THE KREMLIN AND GET IT OVER WITH." Cooler heads prevailed.

In Charleston, Mark Clark believed in flexing muscle. Self-doubt and indecision filled him with disgust. And so he pushed his boys toward absolutes and listened with approval when McCarthy spoke. In 1954, Clark's first year at The Citadel, the famous senator stood before the nation with a map. "Here," McCarthy said in one of the first congressional committee hearings ever to be televised . . . *and here . . . and here . . . and here,* he challenged, brandishing a pointer, were communist enclaves in our midst. As McCarthy railed about a web of spies, Clark not only emphatically nodded in agreement but joined him in the more extravagant assertion that communists had infiltrated the top ranks of the U.S. military. It was an unpopular view and one that taxed his friendship with Eisenhower. Indeed, that speech was a turning point, though not in the way McCarthy intended. To a majority of Americans, the Red-baiting senator came off as a zealot and a demagogue, the very things the country stood against. Senate colleagues shuffled in embarrassment, then turned away. Eleven months later, they censored their one-time ringleader for "conduct unbecoming." Three years later he was dead.

Down beside the Ashley, cocooned among the like-minded and reinforced by the adulation of two thousand boys, Clark hung tenaciously to notions of "the threat" and ordered all incoming freshmen to read J. Edgar Hoover's *Masters of Deceit: The Story of Communism in America and How to Fight It.* In a grand battle between democracy and communism he saw everyone as a potential enemy, himself as a committed hero resisting painful tides. He shared that sentiment with his boys, pledging to create the toughest plebe system in America. On that ground, he swore, they would produce a generation of young men untainted by subversive views. Students grimly pledged to fight the menace of communism both at home and overseas. In college classrooms, faculty members marched to the same tune—or found themselves without a job. New professors were hired only after an interview with the president. In those talks, anyone who proved himself less than an acolyte was immediately ruled out. And lest a professor stray intellectually once hired, Clark held off a tenure system, declining scholars that safety net. Not until 1960, when a state accreditation committee forced the matter, did he finally relent. And even then he saw to it that the change in policy was not well publicized.

Cadets, meanwhile, began to see themselves as soldiers in a holy cause. An air of purpose hung above the campus. Famous men stood before them with their views. Not surprisingly, their views matched those of the college president, who, himself famous, was often away proselytizing around the South. No dissenting voices were welcome. And they were never heard. Instead, from the classroom to the marching field, students marched with single purpose and heard nothing but encouragement. In the midst of that excitement, the institution thrived. From the time that Clark arrived in 1954 to the time that Tony Lackey graduated in 1961, long-neglected buildings were renovated, faded hallways repainted. New buildings—including a library, dozens of units of faculty housing and a well-appointed student activities building—were either on the drawing board or rising out of empty space.

There was a vibrancy to the time that Lackey deeply loved. Like many cadets of that era, he felt a part of something grand. "I think that's really when we got it right," he said years afterward. He was infected with a sense of purpose that would last throughout his life. "We are The Citadel. We have high ideals and high principles that we aren't afraid to talk about. The Citadel has a culture. It operates twenty-four hours a day, seven days a week." In that culture, might was right and all in war was fair. Higher principles were at stake. The nation's future was in jeopardy. In the college newspaper, the *Brigadier,* young editors encouraged censorship, seeing it as a positive and necessary tool for national health.

Outside those gates, Charleston approved. In fact, the city too had a habit of driving off unwelcome critics. Ostracism, shaming and occasional violence preserved the status quo. That was particularly true around the issue of civil rights. No one was exempt; not even the most well-born, well-bred and widely accomplished of her citizens. In 1950, J. Waties Waring, a federal judge and seventh-generation Charlestonian, proved that rule in a long-running scandal that ended only when he left town. First, the judge rubbed his neighbors wrong when he ruled the Democratic Party should fully open up its ranks to blacks. ("Monster!" shouted Mendel Rivers from the floor of Congress.) Later, the judge would give the city fits again, writing in a judgment that would become a frame for the U.S. Supreme Court's decision in *Brown v. Board of Edu-*

cation that segregation should be abolished in South Carolina's public schools. In a 2–1 vote, his argument was a dissent. For the time being, the rules of segregation held.

His were shocking attitudes in a city set on segregation. Though the Warings were a prominent family and an old one on that ground, the clan underwent an ugly split. Judge Waring's nephew Tom, the editor of the *News and Courier,* savaged his uncle in print. Still, the judge pressed on. He invited blacks to dinner at his elegant Charleston home and with his second wife, Elizabeth, swung wide the social gates. Angry Charlestonians reacted crudely. Mrs. Waring was publicly snubbed and called a "whore" and a "bitch" on Charleston's streets. "A stone wall of unpleasantness" met the pair at every turn. Worse troubles followed. Shortly after Judge Waring told a New York City church group that the South's problems with civil rights stemmed not from its "Negro problem" but from a wrong-headed fixation on racial supremacy, a burning cross flickered outside his door. Waring viewed the incident as a warning from the Ku Klux Klan, a group he estimated to have four hundred to five hundred adherents in the town. Charleston police, however, dismissed the cross burning as a "prank." Six months later, shots were fired not far outside the judge's door. Then a fragment of concrete slammed through a downstairs window. In Washington, officials with the U.S. attorney general's office were sufficiently alarmed to assign federal marshals to stand guard. By then it was too late. The judge no longer cared to fight. Instead, he made Manhattan home.

Tom Waring was delighted. In 1954, when the Supreme Court ruled against segregation, he jeered in print that moves to integrate Charleston city schools would take an entire army to enforce. Mark Clark agreed and soon befriended the young man. In Lackey's sophomore year, Tom Waring stood at graduation dressed in scholar's robes as he accepted an honorary doctorate in law. Two years after that, as the civil rights movement gained steam and black students began a series of peaceful protests across the state, Waring would again roar in outrage. Ripping a page from Clark's book, he considered the protesters part of a "worldwide conspiracy" and urged police in print to answer their acts of civil disobedience with "the whip, the rope, the knout, gun or anything else" that they might choose. Still, the tide of change surged in.

The Citadel would remain secure inside a bubble of consensus—and all-white despite the Supreme Court's ruling—until 1965. But if Bud Watts, Jimmie Jones, Lew Spearman and Jim Bradin could easily ignore those growing tensions, Lackey's class could not. When Lackey marched as a senior, city workers moved glumly about the city pulling down Jim Crow signs that ensured segregation at swimming pools, restaurants, drinking fountains and at beaches. The great upheavals of a decade had begun.

A yellowing home movie from Lackey's graduation day shows him crisp and hopeful, splendid in his dress whites, wandering about in the glaring sunlight with a crooked smile and a deep tan. He looks awkward and embarrassed, unused to center stage. His mother stands nearby, beaming and excited. She has come to see him off and claps and smiles amid a sea of silk. Dressed in a simple frock and a cheerful hat that droops in the humidity, she is nervous, staring into the camera lens, tipping her head and waving in her new white gloves. Happily self-conscious, proud enough to nearly burst, she has her son right there beside her, bony and upright, dazzled by the day. In no time he will be married; soon after that, a father. His world would take its shape. In the Army, Lackey's first assignment would be to shuttle secrets up and down the coast at the height of the Cuban missile crisis. That job only underscored his sense that a grand battle was at hand. Soon, he would be posted overseas. Far away, another war was commanding our attention.

The year of Lackey's graduation marked the hundredth anniversary of the start of the Civil War. At The Citadel, it proved an occasion too seductive to ignore. Early that spring, cadets lugged heavy cannons out to Morris Island. There, amid the dunes, under the gaze of the national press, they performed a reenactment. A ship loomed into view. The cannons boomed and smoked. The dunes around them shook. *Life* magazine recorded the moment for all America to share. Nostalgia. America was not the same. The nation had grown in stature and in strength until it towered over the world stage. When Lackey heard those cannons boom, he felt a rush of great emotion. The Citadel had given him a map. He would always follow it. And yet a break point was at hand. Soon, the nation sheared in two. Old issues were revisited with new intensity. *What gives you the right?* a generation asked.

Lackey did not see it then. Instead, he donned his uniform and headed overseas. Army Lieutenant John G. Lackey III arrived in Vietnam early and served four tours. While he inhabited a world of Green Berets, special operations, secret missions and lost friends, a decade came and went. He risked his life and rose in rank. But this was not the war he wanted. It was a gray space of frightful losses and friendly fire, a war that split the nation. He could not be the hero he had conjured from his porch. When he came home, no crowds would cheer nor bright confetti catch in his short hair. In his long absence, a generation had twisted and convulsed. Lackey felt himself a stranger on familiar turf. Only down beside the Ashley, where the seabirds swung down low and the stars and stripes still slowly waved, did his surging sense of pride return. He took his healing there.

Confluence

IN AUGUST 1963, two weeks before the cannons fired for another cycle starting at The Citadel, America's ambassador to Vietnam, Henry Cabot Lodge, unpacked a suitcase in the steamy heat of Saigon in a climate not unlike Charleston's own. While the class of 1967 prepared for school, the new ambassador moved quickly, peppering the White House with memos outlining problems with the American-backed regime of Ngo Dinh Diem. After only seven days in his new post, Lodge proposed that Washington end U.S. support. It was hardly a signal that we were preparing to withdraw. Rather, it was soon followed by a serious escalation of our involvement in Vietnam. We were using our long reach again. Diem had lost his effectiveness, and the Kennedy administration had determined it would back a coup d'etat.

Though U.S. military advisers had been dying on and off in Vietnam since 1959, a new era was suddenly at hand. Washington's commitment to the region now seemed cinched. Ever since the French had fallen in Dien Bien Phu, Washington sent about $400 million a year in assistance to Saigon and kept a network of young soldiers on the ground. But now our investment of both men and money would increase. In 1967, the United States spent $21 billion on the war. Still, the following year, the Tet offensive shook our confidence. From that moment forward soldiers knew that this would be a different fight, a war without front lines in which friends and foes were indistinguishable and sometimes even fellow soldiers could prove deadly.

Hell no, we won't go, said a growing number of young men. It became popular to voice dissent, and soon the din grew louder. In time, a swelling surge of dissidents challenged every structure we had built. From New York to California, protesters merged calls for black power, women's rights and a quick end to our involvement in Vietnam's civil war. The careful order of the dinner table was destroyed. The quiet on our city streets evaporated, too. Police and National Guardsmen met protesters with tear gas and brute force.

In the halls of Congress, Mendel Rivers sped on undeterred. So great was his influence and so deep his generosity back home that admiring voters joked that the ocean at their doorstep was made of "the Cooper, the Ashley and the L. Mendel Rivers." An outspoken conservative who packed a pearl-handled revolver, Rivers had become a master at the helm. During the Korean War he oversaw the expansion of the Charleston Naval Shipyard and pumped millions into Charleston's Air Force Base, a facility that shared its runways with the city's civilian airport—a symbiotic commingling that continues to this day. Momentum only grew from there. The tie between the city and her soldiers deepened. It was written now in steel, in concrete and in blood.

The war in Vietnam would reinforce that old liaison. In 1965, as the first U.S. Marines splashed onto the golden beaches at Da Nang, Rivers rose to assume his chairmanship of the House Armed Services Committee. Like a kite that catches a sharp updraft and suddenly gains altitude with a fierce snap, his new powers coincided with the largest military escalation since World War II. He used the luck of timing well. "Rivers Delivers," the congressman's campaigners always said, and he lived up to that crude slogan. By the war's end, costs had mounted to nearly $120 billion. In Charleston, the congressman opened all the taps. Rivers had the sweetest touch since Midas, observed *Life* magazine. One investment drew another. Du Pont, Lockheed, McDonnell-Douglas and General Electric set root in quick succession, adding to the city's prosperity while extolling its hawkish values. If the country stood divided, well so be it. But Charleston was not. The complexities of Kent State and Detroit were muted in the charming alleyways beneath her Spanish moss.

At The Citadel, 663 boys signed in as freshmen on September 3, 1963. Four years later, more than half the senior class poured into Jenkins Hall to take commissions in the Army, the Navy, the Air Force and Marines. Most of them were wearing uniforms by the time of the Tet offensive. Tony Lackey had already served two tours with the Army's Special Forces by the time the class of 1967 joined him in those fields. Inspired by John F. Kennedy's benedictions over the Green Berets, Lackey had chosen to follow the most dangerous course, participating in what Neil Sheehan would later describe as "the worldwide counterinsurgency mission of the special forces." In 1963, when Army officers asked Lackey what he wanted to do, he answered in three syllables—*Vi-et-nam*—at a time when many Americans could not have found the country on a map.

"I wanted the glory of it all," he remembered. "I was aggrandizing. I didn't understand it. What was important to me were all the trappings." The first death he saw was in Saigon in 1964 during "nap time" when all the American girls went up to the rooftops to sunbathe in their new bikinis. While the city slept a crowd of marchers suddenly appeared in the street below his apartment building. A girl of about ten was caught up in their midst. There was a sudden panic, a whirling mob. "They went crazy," Lackey said. "About 1,800 of them. She got trampled to death. She was frail. It was a frenzy." He watched that madness from his rooftop. He had a daughter of his own by then. That scene stayed with him forever.

In Charleston, the class of 1967 swore their oaths as officers and gave grim-faced salutes. Like Lackey, their training turned them toward that moment. They faced it without fear, their optimism yet untarnished. "We are a proud class and we have the right to be," wrote Steve Dowdney, the class historian. "We are the class most confronted with the realities of a changing world; spawned on the eve of conflict, motivated by change, driven by competition, faced with the horrors of war; we are the class thrust into the flux." He was absolutely right. But the conflicts that he spoke of meant a terrible new urgency inside the corps. Almost imperceptibly, it shifted toward greater harshness.

On the banks beside the Ashley, a dangerous confluence occurred. On July 1, 1965, Mark Clark stepped down as president. The first black cadet, Charles Foster, was coming in the fall. After railing against just such a shift for years, the general had no wish to preside over an integrated corps. He walked away one month before the change took place. Yet boys left straddling his tenure had heard his sour musings. Blacks would make the Army weak, Clark believed; integration would dangerously sap the nation's fighting strength. With Clark gone and a black student now coming, cadets had more to prove than ever. Clark had promised the toughest plebe system in the country? Well, they would deliver it. A second factor influenced them as well. Now a new war was at hand, and cadets took on its ugly imprint. There was no Western Front or beach at Normandy to take. Instead, enemies lay hidden all about. How could they train for that? They learned, but at a cost, then passed that training down.

A new game was invented. As always, it was precisely fitted to the times. On their own, inside their barracks, cadets turned away from coordinated assaults and lessons of massive troop movements to explore instead the maddening maze of a guerrilla war. Rather than playing scout beneath the tabletops or letting fly with cherry bombs over the barrack's parapets, cadets prepared to face the horrors that they witnessed on the nightly news—horrors that, though hardly new to war itself, shocked the viewing public. At The Citadel, boys quickly figured out what they were seeing. The time of an ordered system of hostilities was done. Theirs would be a war of tiger cages, torture and uncertain loyalties. In that environment, no place was safe. Front lines were all erased. So were clear notions of friend and foe. And so they pushed each other to extremes. In training for the Bond Volunteers, a quasi-military group that fed into a precision drill platoon named after General Summerall, cadets submitted to incredible ordeals. Fearful, hopeful, they craved the hardest kind of test. "One hundred thirty B.V.'s rolled out on that fateful day, the greatest turnout since the late fifties," Steve Dowdney reported. "Groveling in the stench of sweat and grimy mud, for three weeks the Bond Volunteers submitted themselves to the severe discipline of the '66 Summerall Guards so that they could be the representatives of our class during our senior year." They took pride in that punishment. They built up new elites.

Junior Sword Drill, a troop of third-year boys who held their swords aloft for seniors at their ring hop, became the holy grail. This was a simple matter of deduction. Bond Volunteers were one hundred or so boys stretching to excel. The Summerall Guards was a group made up of sixty-one, Junior Sword Drill but fourteen. There were elites within elites. In that charged atmosphere, they gained new popularity. "The pleasure devolves upon him," it was said in 1900, "to do unto others as was done unto him." More than half a century later, that proved truer than ever. Each successive class took on a rougher cast. Spurred by taunts and frightened by what they had been taught to hate, young boys reached new heights of strength, endurance and hostility. While soldiers died in lonely anguish far away, the violence on campus grew in its sad shadow. Hardship was a badge of courage, pain their sacred trust. Perhaps they thought—as young people sometimes will—that if they were only strong enough and quick enough, well trained enough and true, they could rise above the odds of fate and come back home a hero.

By the time the class of 1967 stood in its dress whites for graduation,

Clark had established himself in an elegant apartment atop the Francis Marion hotel downtown. From there, perched well above the tree line, that gray-haired general could survey the gracious city he so loved. Down below glimmered a sparkling vision of America. Old mansions south of Broad Street had a timelessness and grace. The cobblestones glowed bright under the sun. The tourists paced and stared. Dolphins swam and shimmered by the Battery. The pace was slow and old formalities endured. Clark himself was lionized and loved. A Charleston newspaper likened him to Robert E. Lee. In Atlanta editors paid homage, too, lavishing his new home with praise as a penthouse perch fit for "The American Eagle." There, amid his memories and memorabilia, the sixty-eight-year-old general held court and entertained, while back inside the barracks his deep influence lived on.

Over the next decade much inside The Citadel would change. After Clark left, two presidents followed in quick succession. Neither kept a firm hand on the corps. Instead, inside the barracks walls, there began a dangerous time of drift. From 1965 to 1975, perhaps more than at any other time in the school's history, the corps ran the corps. Tactical officers cycled in and out more frequently—always needed in the field. With adults paying little attention to barracks life, old ordeals turned newly vicious. Vanished patterns reappeared. Draconian tests of body and of soul were devised and then refined. In that "laboratory" of student life, boys set deep seeds for suffering. Cadets would do unto others as few before had ever done. While the country turned left, moving toward permissiveness, The Citadel marched hard right and took on intricate new layers of discipline and rigor.

When Clark retired, the board had set out to find a worthy successor at a difficult time. The man they found was Hugh Pate Harris, a combat veteran who made the Army his career and rose within the ranks through several wars. In 1964, after commanding the Seventh U.S. Army in Europe, he took over the Continental Army Command wearing the Distinguished Service Medal, the Silver Star, the Legion of Merit with two oak clusters, and a colorful array of other ribbons all pinned neatly side to side. But another war was getting under way just then, and this time, Hugh Harris was ready for a quieter life.

The perfect candidate, the board agreed, a soldier and a patriot with four stars to grace his epaulets. They welcomed him with fanfare.

Born in Anderson, Alabama, in June 1909, Harris was a West Pointer from a class between world wars. After his graduation in 1931, he had charted a fine course. Retired in his prime, in the summer of 1965 he still looked young and quite commanding, blond and blue-eyed, almost Prussian. Archival photographs show him as a slightly puffy figure, vaguely handsome at the age of fifty-six, with a broad nose, a high forehead and a thick mane of hair slicked back out of his face, fastidious in his dress, but rather slack around the jaw. At home, the sherry decanters stood atop mahogany, and everybody posed with perfect postures. News accounts checked off his background and achievements. He seemed perfectly cast. On parade days the new general stretched tall as he surveyed an ordered world. It was a comforting vision even if that history was not his own. Plus, the perquisites were splendid. The general spent long days hunting game in open fields or floating on a back creek, fishing underneath the broiling sun. Charleston nights were full of fine food and ample alcohol in a city with a well-known taste for both. It was a great relief, at first. After a lifetime of stiff regimens, Harris assumed he answered only to himself. He was wrong, of course. Years later, bitter graduates would complain that he retired on the day he arrived.

In his first semester by the Ashley, Harris settled easily into rituals that were long since set. In speeches, he addressed students and staff with lofty rhetoric, sounding the notes of change and growth, of education and military training drawn into a perfect sphere. The Citadel, he said with confidence, would be true to its old standards. But it would also bend. He would fit the school to the future and emphasize the liberal arts. "We are the last of 'the hell-night plebes,'" Steve Dowdney noted optimistically in 1967. "We are the old; yet we are the new." That was Harris's intention. Reality would prove otherwise.

Harris's plans for the college set him early on a disastrous course. Any meddling with old ways was met with automatic disapproval by graduates and board members. They did not want The Citadel to change—especially now. Theirs was a military school. The country was at war. Few among the faithful saw a need for any tinkering. Fewer still embraced Harris's call for an expanded curriculum. Soon, detractors undermined his every move. They called him frivolous and weak. They missed Mark Clark. Harris spent too much time hunting, fishing and drinking, his critics sullenly complained. One story in particular painted him in an offensive light. Many said he played a coward's game, hunting baited fields. One critic went further. "Whenever he went out turkey hunting," said Jim Bradin, "somebody had to go on out there ahead of him and wire turkeys in the trees." What bitterness he stirred.

Students called him Santa Claus. Some admired him. More laughed behind his back. The new president was soft, they mocked. Shocked by the intensity of life inside the corps, he tended to distribute mass pardons to the boys. The sight of whole companies walking back and forth on endless tours inside the quads seemed pointless to the general. He complained about group punishment and curried favor by showing leniency. The boys accepted his kindness but lost all their respect. He was a pushover, they sneered—everything that they were not. Still, Harris pressed on. The Citadel was a college, he huffed, not some tent city in the field.

Caught in those conflicting tides, the school began to list and sink. No longer did the college move in step with the country that it served. Once, across the South, a military education was the norm for men (finishing school and piano lessons the standard rounding off for women). Now, such schools were either closing or setting aside old regimens. The nation's mood had changed. Students across America were burning their draft cards, slipping off to Canada or signing up at graduate school or with the National Guard to skip their turn at war. Colleges meanwhile offered more elective courses and a broader curriculum. Campuses were integrating, and there were new pressures for coeducation, too. In 1969, Princeton and Yale opened their doors to women for the first time. Most other colleges and universities would follow suit. Cadets who chose The Citadel marched purposefully against that tide. But they were in a rapidly dwindling minority. Enrollment numbers dropped. Year by year, the isolation grew.

By the late 1960s, freshmen were welcomed not as volunteers to keep the faith but as flotsam from a world gone mad. The upperclassmen said the new arrivals needed to be trained. Since the society outside was perceived as sick, the old process of breaking a boy down took on a fierce new seriousness. Inside the barracks, hardships increased as older boys purged younger ones of the toxins of their time. Prove yourselves, the older boys challenged. Prove you are not weak, a hippie, a peacenik, some drifting product of permissiveness. They called their harshness love.

In the spring of 1966, Harris expressed his first concerns about the way the system worked. By then, many in the administration also felt a growing sense of discomfort. Major General Reuben H. Tucker, the commandant, advised the president that cadets were losing so much weight that the school laundry was "constantly tailoring the uniforms to fit." Some cadets grew sick from lack of food and sleep. Others simply were too traumatized to do much studying. Boys with shaved heads and dull expressions marched inside a fog of constant reprimand, swallowing their fear, doing as they were told. Visitors to the campus were shocked to see emaciated freshmen sweating through dozens of push-ups in full uniform prior to meals. They were unsettled, too, by the vacant look many freshmen wore, and by older students' general attitude of disrespect. Across the parade field, Harris was terrified of a scandal at the school. In early 1968, spurred by complaints by board members, parents and legislators, he dispatched the commandant to study Marine boot camp techniques. If discipline was taken to extremes and physical tests imposed to excess, Harris reasoned, then *more* discipline and tougher training were the answer. Given the circumstances, it was a twisted bit of logic, as though he saw his house on fire and decided that it needed to be doused with gasoline.

Richard Lovelace, a member of the class of 1968, remembers the time well. Administrators constantly sought scapegoats, hoping to pin the institution's deepening problems on the misbehavior of the few, he said, reflecting on that era during an interview in 1997. In a booming voice, Lovelace mocked the former commandant. "The individual I am seeking is the person we are looking for," Lovelace shouted. "This is the work of the *infinitessimable one percent!*" Most adults downplayed the growing crisis. Hazing, though ubiquitous, was attributed to a few cadets who simply lacked self-discipline—perhaps because they cut their teeth in new, permissive times. Cadets knew better. Hazing was the way the system worked, integral upon that ground. They made T-shirts printed with the slogan "1%" and laughed at the old man, said Lovelace.

Older graduates, meanwhile, peered inside the gates and saw a world unchanged. The cannons boomed. The grass was cut. Gray uniforms looked just the same. Old mannerisms held. It was a seductive scene to many graduates who wanted something constant in a changing world. Cadets picked up that theme—then drove it home. Seeing themselves as the standard-bearers of a culture under attack, they steadily increased their own hardships, vowing to be worthy of their heritage. If America was growing lax and riven with self-doubt, they would be hard and full of firm assurance. If America was weak, they would be strong. Mark Clark's legacy survived. Boys inspired by his promise imposed excruciatingly severe standards of body and of mind.

In Bond Hall, Harris studied declining enrollments and rising attrition rates and looked for somebody to blame. In 1967, before a meeting with new students, he sat at his wide desk to write some notes. "Ninety-five percent of our cadets are not mistreating the fourth classmen," he scribbled, anxious to show support. "But about five percent are, whether they think they are or not. Now that five percent are giving The Citadel a black eye, and they are making me work overtime." He crossed that out. The emphasis of blame would fall to those who quit. True, "immaturity" and "sadistic tendencies" must be stamped out, the president allowed, but the worst problem the school faced was created by weak-willed boys who left and then complained. "The only harm to The Citadel that I know of that is being done is by about five percent who come here, cannot cope and then go home and start rationalizing their weaknesses to mama," he informed the new fourth class. "These people are really hurting us right now—whether or not their complaints are justified." In coming months, that tone would harden. Young men from "families with a permissive environment . . . expect The Citadel to correct in a few months problems that existed at home for years," Harris told all freshmen in his last year. "These are the ones that yell hazing at every stage of correction and development." Loyal cadets, he said, should go home and talk about the school's good points. They had to, he warned, because "anonymous letters, telephone calls, threats of official investigations and irate confrontations with parents" were piling up inside Bond Hall.

As barracks trials went unchecked and class after class of new boys suffered through torrents of verbal abuse and exquisite tests of flesh and stamina, The Citadel's sense of righteous loneliness increased. In 1968, the college yearbook put a sword and shako on its cover in an admiring reference to the fourteen cadets of Junior Sword Drill. A photograph inside showed the muzzle of a cannon looming oversized in front of the main barracks. The warning was quite clear. The battle had been joined. Danger lay outside the gates. Cadets would stand their ground.

"ACHTUNG!" a huge sign written in broken German cautioned outside a sally port in 1969. *"Sie Sind jetzt Fahren Americanish sector."* You are now entering the American sector.

Inside the gates, discipline was godliness. Cadet authority could not be questioned. Honor. Duty. Loyalty. Those were the catchwords that they used, and those values—and the way that they were taught—could not be challenged. The Citadel was sane. America was going wild. But as time went on some cadets were not so sure. Perhaps The Citadel was crazy, and America was sane. Who could tell? Every year grew more confusing. Tucked behind their gates, each boy lived in a kaleidoscope of discipline and pain. Out of those fractured images each took his lessons from that time. Increasingly, they came wrapped in an awful iconography.

In 1967, a casual portrait of the boys from Golf Company published in the *Sphinx* showed one cadet in an infantryman's helmet with his right hand raised in a flat-handed salute. A swastika armband circled his left arm. An iron cross hung from his neck, and several Nazi medals lay across his chest. A nameplate on his shirt paid homage to Hermann Göring. That same year, Alpha Company used the slogan "Rotten to the Corps," and mixed football shirts and sunglasses with chains and Nazi memorabilia.

In 1968, M Company (Mike Reich, as it was widely known) mixed paisley with an enormous swastika flag, while R Company sported long-haired wigs, a five-point star reminiscent of Nazi occupations and a book emblazoned with a swastika. Tango sported a small Confederate flag and a large swastika.

While massive antiwar demonstrations shook all of Washington, K Company showed its students holding a large Nazi flag aloft while cadets smoked cigars and clowned. M Company dressed in prisoners' garb and lounged around a tomb. A huge Nazi flag was draped across a stone memorial. In front of it a cadet dressed as a bishop held up a hand-made sign: "The Corps is SICK," it read.

In the last days of Harris's tenure, freshmen were sometimes herded into stairwells like squealing, frightened pigs. They piled one atop the other in a mass, choking down their fears. Sweat poured from them in waves. Some boys pissed from fright or passed out from fear and sheer exhaustion. Once, cadet initiation was a painful rite of passage that lasted for three months. By the time Harris left, it had expanded into a nine-month torture that ended only in late spring. For their initiation, freshmen were sent to the showers and made to stand naked, pressed in a frightened mass until their skin wrinkled and their heads felt light. They stood against the tile, their bodies touching, nausea rising. There were so many ways to break the new boys down. Some were beaten. Some were ridiculed. Some were taunted the whole year. In the end, they all broke. Then the older boys would build them up again, into a form they recognized. "Welcome," boys with stars and medals coached. "You have made a choice."

In Chicago, smoke rose over demonstrations. Soldiers stood by, nervous with their guns. Citadel graduates were among them, pointing guns at their own countrymen.

In Charleston, still the new boys came. Some were sent by fathers. Some came on their own. They walked through Lesesne Gate as refugees from a chaotic world. They would be heroes. They would be men. They would be soldiers. They would not break.

On January 23, 1968, North Korean gunboats circled a U.S. intelligence ship, the USS *Pueblo,* as it sailed off Korean waters. Communist soldiers captured every man aboard. For the next year, scattered news accounts would show emaciated crew members held captive, shuddering with fright or speaking dully, their faces ashen, their hands listless. From New York, Walter Cronkite appeared on television giving somber explanations of the torture, acute deprivation and psychological abuse of the *Pueblo* crew. "We laughed at those soldiers," said Bubba Kennedy, the director of The Citadel's office of alumni affairs in 1995 and a member of the graduating class of 1970. "They complained that they had sticks put behind their knees and had to squat until they passed out. We heard that and said, 'Oh, hey, just send them here!' For us, life was like that all the time."

A graduate from Bubba's year, a member of the State Law Enforcement Division now, shared some stories from that era one afternoon in 1997 while paying a call on his old friend. The two men laughed as they looked back. "It might as well have been Auschwitz," Bubba's visitor said, running a hand across his knee and studying the floor. He remembered his worst tormentor best. "He could have been an SS guard," he said. "He really had that down."

Auschwitz. The *Pueblo* crew. Malnutrition. Broken bones. Some boys thought it was a game. Others took it all to heart and struggled the whole time. Slowly, a language rife with euphemisms evolved. In the new corps there were "blanket parties," "smokers," "knob showers," "sweat parties" and other ordeals. But for most graduates there almost always was a caveat. It was not the system that had failed the boys, most Citadel men maintained, but a few boys who failed the system. Whatever the analysis, that failure carried with it a vague cost. Some graduates found it hard to reestablish trust after those trials. Others struggled with nightmares and depression. Thirty years after he held his new diploma in his hands, Richard Lovelace said he still woke up in a sweat some nights, convinced that he was back inside it, unable to escape. A comfortable family man and successful professional, he described himself as occasionally given to violent fantasies of revenge. He would enjoy it, he commented casually one day, if he could find his worst abuser and crush both of his legs.

In 1969, the country's chaotic mood spilled onto the streets of Charleston. Nearly four hundred workers, mostly black women, walked off their jobs to strike for equal pay. The strike dragged on one hundred days. South Carolina's governor called in the troops. That spring five thousand members of the National Guard stood in the Holy City. They lined up on rooftops and arrayed themselves along old alleyways, ready with their guns. Finally, the White House acted. The strikers got much of what they wanted. "We gained recognition as human beings," one of the workers said succinctly once that long strike was done.

"You are now entering the American sector." But who was the enemy? It was no longer clear. Was America inside the gates—the thing that they preserved—or was it counterpoint and chaos just outside? Who could claim it? Who deserved it? Who preserved its values best? Was it those who marched for freedom and a voice for the oppressed, or those willing to fight a foreign enemy and hold old standards without question?

In 1970, Hugh Harris resigned. He ended his five-year tenure with a certain eerie calm. He had come full circle. Whether through exhaustion, resignation or epiphany, his tone was now one not of desperation but of pride. When addressing that year's class of freshmen, Harris described an institution built upon the solid rock of tradition and kept strong by the faithful preservation of essential values. If freshmen did as they were told, he promised, they would excel and reap the rewards. Respect the system, he advised. Everything in it was carefully constructed, minutely refined and carefully supervised. "The program is sophisticated, but simple," he said warmly. "If you really try to be a good fourth classman and try to conform and learn—and be a good plebe— you will be rewarded and you will find the system very, very easy." If they resisted, he admonished, they would get "the full treatment."

James W. Duckett, a native of Greenwood, South Carolina, and a 1932 graduate of The Citadel, became the school's thirteenth president. He inherited a legacy of anger and confusion that he was neither prepared for nor equipped to manage. A chemistry professor pulled from the teaching ranks at a time when most military men were still busy in Southeast Asia, Duckett was the first civilian to run The Citadel since the 1920s. To obscure that shift, the college promoted Duckett to the rank of major general in the college's civilian army, a toothless group called the South Carolina Unorganized Militia and better known by the unfortunate acronym SCUM. Five years of drift would come to ten.

"You could say that in the 1960s, General Harris lost touch with the corps," said General James A. Grimsley Jr., a 1942 graduate who would serve as the school's president during the somewhat more halcyon 1980s. "But General Duckett lost interest in it. Cadets took matters into their own hands without any supervision from the president or the commandant's office. He just took the attitude that boys would be boys. He hardly paid attention." By the time Grimsley returned to take his place inside Bond Hall, "you'd wander in the barracks and see these swastikas up. You'd just take them down. It became an educational process. The responsibility that goes with leadership had to be ingrained. It took some years to do that."

Duckett was clearly wrestling with pressing problems of his own while he served as president. Something about the chaotic temper of the 1960s had unhinged him. Hiding in a grim miasma of pure fear, he became skittish and reclusive. While cadets struggled through new trials in the barracks, Duckett kept away from them and battled private demons. Before long, the campus reflected his paranoia. Speed bumps and railings were installed to guard against attack. Terrified that antiwar protesters would physically do battle with cadets, Duckett ordered the maintenance crew to build obstacles to block their path. "He was scared to death of terrorists," said Grimsley. "He was scared of people coming after him. This was his fear. He sequestered himself. He didn't exhibit himself on campus. . . . When I got here, you had to almost walk a maze to go from place to place. The railings were to stop people, to sort of cattleize individuals, have them move just where he wanted."

In 1971, a photograph in the *Sphinx* showed a glistening line of shining swords. Under that broad arc of steel on the magical occasion of ring night, the fourteen cadets of Junior Sword Drill honored seniors heading into the last days of war. Beside them, a girl with silken black hair, a rose clutched in one hand and high heels on her feet, leaned forward with a kiss. How beautiful it sometimes looked. On another page, a crowd of students squeezed together in a cramped space bordered by metal bars. Among them, one boy clenched a dagger hard between his teeth. Another wore a swastika and iron cross pinned to his collar. Not one among them smiled. College days.

Lessons from the Field

L IKE TONY LACKEY, Walt Clark was a poor boy who settled early on the Army. He set his sights on West Point but was told there was no space that year for one more son of Georgia. Instead, he made his bed in Charleston where he soon befriended a student whose very name, Edward Rutledge Ravenel III, was rich with all the splendor and mystery of Charleston's past. Their friendship would be sadly brief. Two years later, Ravenel was killed in combat in Korea. His death created a debt that Clark could not repay. "I call it my Citadel love story," he said long afterward with a slow smile. Within it lay a deeply personal legacy that would pass through generations.

When Ravenel's body was shipped home and his affairs were set in order, Clark found that all his college loans were cleared. A son of wealth and privilege, Ravenel had deftly turned his tragedy into a blessing for a friend. He did it with a single signature, naming Walter Ballard Clark, his former roommate, as the sole beneficiary of his G.I. insurance. Clark thanked the family with a gift, giving them the sword their son had used in college, one that Clark had used himself as a member of the 1950 Junior Sword Drill.

Seven years later, after Clark had fought and nearly died in Korea himself, he and his wife, Ellen, had their first son, Benjamin Ravenel Clark, born July 15, 1957. The birth began another cycle of a twining history. In 1975, while Walt was back at The Citadel as commandant and Ben just signing up as a freshmen, a slender package arrived in the mail. The Ravenel sword had returned. Ben would use it three years later. Stepping smartly in his father's path, he took his place in Junior Sword Drill. But much had changed in the years since his father marched; and Walt's love story worked best if told only in its barest details. The sword became a line dividing father and son. Because what Ben perceived as the apogee of his college achievement was, to his father, part of a misguided elite, almost a cult, that had twisted once simple routines into a sad, sadistic orgy of pain among young men. Forever afterward, Walt would look at Citadel drill teams and nearly spit with his contempt. He called them "Mickey Mouse" and gruffly mocked their every move. Yet he loved his son and admired him. And so the two men never crossed that line. They rarely even spoke of it.

The route away from Charleston and back was one well traveled. Lackey came back on August 20, 1972, as a tac officer to teach ROTC. Walt Clark returned two days later, and those two soldiers became friends. But what they found on that old ground was not what they expected. In the decade between Lackey's graduation from college and his return to it after four tours in Vietnam, the school he so adored had changed. He noticed those changes less than Clark. Assigned as a senior province adviser in the Mekong Delta, Colonel Walt Clark had mostly waged a war for hearts and minds in a region without much fighting. In Lackey's sector, death taunted every step. When he came home to Charleston his heart was still half numb. For him, anything after that experience was destined to seem mild.

Early in the war, Lackey had watched dark bands of B-52s swing low. He loved those massive raids. To him, they brought a glimpse of total war and total victory. An avalanche pounded from the sky. It thrilled him to the core. In his earliest days in Vietnam, he had helped to isolate first targets. Years later, he could still remember every detail. Twenty-eight great planes lumbered close and dropped their payloads. No thunder ever was so loud. When it was done an eerie quiet fell. Then the research started. Helicopters thumped down low, disgorged their men and then pulled back. Lackey landed with a dozen soldiers weighted down with heavy gear. In a rising mist that smelled of sulfur and destruction, they struggled for their bearings. What had been jungle now was waste. They would walk it single file, shooting at phantasms, shooting all the while.

It was not a field of death exactly, but an obliteration of all life. The ground itself was smoking. The air was thick and close with steam. Red soil and black mud had heaved in ragged piles. The earth was dark and cancered. Not a stand of vegetation stood. No tree rose up above them. Smoke and flecks of ash caught in their nostrils, acrid and unpleasant. Their boots caught in root tangles, and their packs weighed down like slabs of stone. Sweat dripped off their faces, down their backs, between their buttocks, under clinging cloth down straining legs. Water oozed inside their socks. In clouds of smoke, they could not catch their breath. In air drifting with the tang of spent explosives, they could hardly find their way. And still, they had to navigate that strange terrain. Step here. Fire. Nothing. Keep the nausea down. Step there. Fire. Nothing. Water sloshed in craters bigger than a city block. Mud and debris clung like fingers. Fire. Volleys of ammunition made a steady din. But there was nothing there to shoot. Nothing moving. Nothing living. Nothing left. Still, the soldiers spilled their ammunition. They shot into the smoke at mud heaps and the figments of their strained imaginations. But only fear walked with those soldiers then. No hostile fire came back.

"I was scared to death," Lackey said. "We walked the box shooting the whole time. You had these huge holes that water had filled up. I had all this equipment. Everything was burning." The only thing he could remember, the only thing that he could see, was several bent and twisted bicycles and a typewriter blasted into junk. He radioed that information home. It was a successful hit. Lackey walked the stretch of it and kept his trigger pulling. He started that long walk with four hundred rounds of ammunition. At the backstretch he had none. "I was terrified," he said. "I was excited. I could hardly breathe." Some craters were probably thirty feet in depth. A man could drown in that red water. A pack, a hand-held radio, an M-16, some heavy boots, a life could vanish with one slip. It did not matter that the enemy was gone. The ground itself was dangerous. The soldiers sprayed their bullets into empty air to every side. It was a relief to feel those pumps of lead explode out of gun barrels.

Before the first B-52 strikes, General William C. Westmoreland and a handful of other generals had made plans. Lackey, an intelligence officer, participated at a distance, gathering reports and helping pinpoint targets. *Here,* said Lackey, guiding them . . . *and here.* Radio signals, fleeting as they were, became the veins and sinew of the enemy. Planes dropped low across that landscape like a net, catching everything beneath them in a whirl of fire and explosives. Lackey followed, breathing hard, making his assessments. After the third strike, fifty helicopters hovered close and landed. They pulled away while fighter jets on combat patrol screamed ribbons overhead. The din of those jet engines drowned out every other sound. "Every now and then," Lackey recalled, "the jets would fly over and hit something just for the hell of dropping ordnance." But that was only pointless fun. The ground by then was clear.

"We didn't find a thing." The enemy had either fled or been reduced to ash.

In a war of intangibles, where death could come from any side, Lackey came to love those bombing runs. If the rest of Vietnam was incremental gain and painful setbacks and lost friends, those air strikes were pure magic. "We weren't seeing a lot of results, but I believed in it. That was the way we ought to do business. This was mean. This was good stuff. This was the way that we should fight the war. This was the Army I had wanted to be a part of." Those strikes showed pure commitment and unquestionable resolve. For a moment, at least, perhaps they drowned the din of protest from back home. Yet such exhilaration was an exception. The rule was lonely jungle treks and swallowed terror, sniper shots and punji sticks and more bad news from home. Even fellow soldiers could be deadly. Lackey watched his back. "Except for a small hard core of people, you didn't trust anybody. There were bad things happening on post." Back at base, cynical young soldiers smoked dope and constantly condemned the things he most believed in. Most waited only to get out. Lackey's world contracted.

In 1972, he watched the enemy gain confidence and strength. He was sick of all of it and ready to get out. A new job awaited him in Charleston. He had made a trade for it, agreeing to serve a final tour in Southeast Asia if at the end of it he could go back home to Charleston to teach cadets and pick up a master's degree in education at his alma mater. He felt more than ready for the change. But up until the end, the fighting was intense, about the hardest he had seen. He watched it coming. North Vietnamese forces were massing along the Ho Chi Minh trail, across the demilitarized zone and over the border in Cambodia. It could mean only one thing. In Lackey's zone, the B-52s were bombing day and night. The sight no longer thrilled him, and the enemy did not seem much affected. January, February and March came and went, and there were small-scale encounters here and there, but the worst lay out there, still. The waiting wore him out.

By 1968, more than half a million American troops had fanned out across Vietnam. There was energy and optimism then. Lackey thought the war was won. But politics and domestic strife reversed the tide. By early 1972, just 140,000 troops remained. The soldiers who were left felt uncomfortably exposed. And now they faced an enemy who seemed larger, more aggressive, more confident and deadlier than ever. After all the napalm and the carpet bombings and the massive weight of the

American war effort, enemy troops still moved on their home ground like a sea of deadly snakes, hidden mostly, but fatal when they struck. In the green, battered land around Pleiku that spring, they came out in the open, taunting. Far away, peace negotiations stumbled on. It was clear that we had lost. Still, Lackey waited for the worst of it.

On March 30, 1972, all the pieces fell together. What Lackey had read for months in maps and deciphered in bursts of radio static now appeared in human form. It was an awesome sight. North Vietnamese troops poured across the demilitarized zone. They moved south and west with little resistance, pushing their way forward with the strength and confidence of an army plunging toward its final victory. Hundreds of tanks cranked over muddy borders into zones Americans once easily controlled. For the first time in the war, the enemy used heavy weapons and TOW missiles made in China. Everyone could feel the heat of it. Lackey watched with an almost fatalistic fascination. In a single day, his troops knocked out eighteen tanks. The scope of it was like nothing he had seen before.

As the offensive wore on, he departed for America. He had one last thing to do at home before his tour was done. In Tennessee that spring, he signed the papers for divorce. His marriage was finished in every detail but that signature. His daughter and his ex-wife were moving to Florida. It had happened slowly, as such collapses sometimes do. First the letters slowed to a trickle. Then, when they did come, they carried no real warmth. He figured he would let it go. He had no heart to struggle. "I'd been through enough fighting. I didn't want emotional battles on top of all that." So he signed his name and in that moment left behind a raft of hope. Then he boarded another plane and went straight back into the war.

In Pleiku, while he was gone, North Vietnamese forces had drawn a circle. Fighting now intensified in every direction. Soldiers compared notes. No cigarettes were getting through. That was a bad sign, the holy shit warning men watched for to see how great their isolation had become. Lackey spent those last few weeks grabbing sleep when he could and eating wherever he could find a meal. It was a tough time, his toughest yet. The fighting came in furious spurts. Lackey felt the pace and surge of it and found his way by instinct. For him, just as it was for most of those last soldiers, the object was not victory. It was simpler. How did one live out the day? What step would find a hidden mine? What tree might hide a soldier? The end was often random and abrupt.

But often it proved tauntingly incomplete, taking a man's legs or arms or sometimes both; or mocking the victim by leaving little visible damage, but a mind so securely fixed in a moment of excruciating terror that nothing in life afterward would ever be the same. For those men, rout or victory, there was no reality beyond the war. It enveloped them completely. Brethren who marched on intact prayed with every footfall that they would not be next. Among the hazards underfoot, Bouncing Bettys were among the worst. Designed to lift into the air before exploding, they might leave nothing but a fine red mist where an unlucky soldier's legs had been or end, forever, a young man's hopes of siring children. For the most part, the enemy remained unseen. A sniper's shot left one neat hole, an ending. A spray of bullets from behind some trees took two men down, their faces startled, frozen at the moment of impact. Sometimes a soldier lay down dead and no one ever heard a shot.

Lackey was tired of it. He was tired, period, and wanted to go home. He distrusted colleagues who came into the Army with the draft, and was disgusted by the excesses of men he once revered. "The officer corps was morally bankrupt. We had been in a war for ten years, and everybody just kept rotating. There was too much drinking and carousing, and the base camps were palatial. The whole thinking was just make everything as good as you can because then you are going to go out there and die. Westmoreland understood that. He knew that our values, all those things I had believed in, had disappeared. The country didn't believe in us as a military." Increasingly, Lackey did not either. He felt no pride in his profession. That half-stoned mob of malcontents was nothing he could boast. To him it was a sacrilege. He needed one thing to believe in. He had found it on the banks of the slow and muddy Ashley River. There, at least, his world had made some sense. He clung to that.

At times, waiting for the end of it, he lost himself in the details. Once, perhaps bored, he counted more than six hundred body parts scattered over a single clearing. Yet massive casualties were rare. "The general who is skilled in defense hides in the most secret recesses of the earth," wrote the famous Chinese strategist Sun Tzu, whom Ho Chi Minh had studied. No ground was safe. The North Vietnamese moved in to strike, then vanished in the green. Until the Easter offensive of 1972, the enemy was mostly a vague and maddening force. Sometimes there was a face in the bushes or a rattle and sparks off in the distance. Mostly, danger creeped around them with no face. For much of Lackey's final tour, his assignments were routine: "Go pick up the bones."

Just before his last home leave, Lackey's radio crackled. *Retrieval of remains.* It was a vulture's hunt conducted under fire. But in that shadow world defined by death, some endings were just accidents. Those only underscored the sense of gross futility. John Paul Vann, the war's civilian architect and to many its most radiant light, died suddenly for no good reason other than that he had beat the odds for far too long. On June 9, 1972, Vann had spent the day in Pleiku. He lingered over dinner, a send-off for a friend. Just after dark, he left for a nearby town, the site of a terrible battle that Vann had earlier described with his customary flair. "Outside Kontum," Vann informed a *Washington Post* reporter before he died, "wherever you dropped bombs, you scattered bodies." On his way back that night his helicopter went down. In the dark, perhaps confused over unfamiliar terrain, his pilot simply wheeled into some trees. Vann died instantly.

Lackey went with a team of men to gather Vann's remains. If Vietnam had a hero, Vann might have been that man. But no one was in the mood for heroes on that night. Instead, to Lackey, Vann was just a corpse like any corpse, and a pain in the ass, too, since he died in an area infested with the enemy. Lackey had known Vann only slightly. He thought of him as an effective but slightly obsessed leader, a man to whom the war had become an utterly amoral landscape. Now, his death was waste for waste's sake, a metaphor if he allowed himself that much. The corpse was zipped up in a body bag and moved along its way. Helicopters crashed. Accidents happened. Death was Lackey's routine. Only this time, the corpse was more important. Vann would soon be buried with great fanfare on green slopes back in Arlington. President Nixon himself would console the family. Lackey had no such grand homecoming in store. Six weeks later, he headed home to the only place he knew that merited the name.

On August 1, 1972, Lackey stood on the tarmac in Pleiku with a handful of other officers and a flight plan that would take him first through Nha Trang, then to Saigon and finally aboard a jet across the Pacific. His part was finished. But he hardly had the time to say good-bye. On the morning of his final day two firefights tied up his troops. He climbed into his jeep and was calling in attack helicopters and troop carriers called "slicks" to move new men into position. Guns and slicks. He sent out twelve that day. Those were men he knew out there. But he had learned to think in terms of hardware.

Shifting from one foot to another in the heat, Lackey crackled orders on the radio, switching from firefight to firefight. Then his replacement came, and at last his war was over. A Red Cross nurse handed him a glass of warm champagne. He downed it and looked around the tarmac once, then gathered his belongings. One minute he was senior operations adviser, Pleiku Province, II Corps Tactical Zone, Republic of Vietnam. The next minute he was "back in the world," as those soldiers came to say, heading off to South Carolina to serve his alma mater. On the plane going back, he decided he would quit. A figure in his imagination saluted once, then handed in his papers. "I was getting out of there," he said. "In my mind, I think I did want to get out." But the Army was the thing he knew and he would end up staying.

Lackey's sense of isolation in the field seemed even worse at home. But signing out just meant a slide from bad to worse. He was no scholar. He had no training that would suit him to civilian life. He could kill and he could command, but he didn't know much else. By 1972, he had transformed his initial reserve officer's position into a credible career. He had moved up through the ranks and won respect. He was right about himself. What he lacked in training and in education he could always make up for in pure drive. And so he did and had succeeded. But none of that translated. In his early thirties now, he had no options that he liked, no home, no wife, no money in the bank, no plan to lead him forward. Just readjusting to America seemed hard enough right then. The figure in his head would slowly fade. He would not quit. He reached a turning point but did not turn. Instead, he let the Army chart his course.

In the short time it took to move from scorched earth to a schoolroom, returning Citadel alumni and Vietnam veterans cycling through as tactical officers and ROTC teachers were called upon to learn a whole new set of trip wires. Even home was hostile now. In airports and in cities and in Army bases all across America, returning soldiers were flatly informed that wearing their uniforms in public was hardly wise. Wearing green fatigues meant only trouble. Why court it? And so they tried to hide among civilians. But their short hair and their rough tans and their sad faces gave them all away. A guy could hardly have a beer without someone coming up to share his views on politics and peace. But what did they know, anyway, if they hadn't been there in the heat? Lackey arrived in Charleston that August. Eleven years after his graduation, Charleston was just as dandy, worn-down elegant as it had ever been. But he was changed. He was traumatized and blank, bitter and half broken. The war had snuffed him out. Anyone could see it.

Walt Clark, a graduate of the class of 1951 who had nearly lost his legs in Korea then went on to serve in Vietnam but in a far more peaceful region to the south, signed back in at The Citadel shortly after Lackey did. Clark liked the younger officer from the moment they first met. He took him home and introduced him all around. Ellen Clark and the couple's children took the tan young soldier straight into their hearts. Clark's son Ben adopted him as mentor. Ellen made him a new friend. She was an Army wife and took pride in that and saw right through the ugly husk that war had left behind. Lackey's health was fine. That was more than some returning soldiers had and more than her own young husband had laid claim to when they walked down the aisle. But something deep inside had cracked. The Clarks would help him find his long way back. Gently, they sat him down to family dinners, bundled him off to football games, reminded him of love. Almost imperceptibly, they smothered him with care. Lackey sparked to life. Gradually, gratefully, he recovered his sense of humor and a taste for family life. Once the Clarks saw that, they winked and fixed him up with a local school-teacher who had recently divorced. Kay was energetic and upbeat, and the chemistry worked fast. Within a year, Lackey was remarried, setting off on a new course. "It was a happy time for me," he said. "It was a healing time."

Lackey came and went. Clark, almost ten years his senior, stayed on. He had come back near the end of his career and soon discovered he was home. He found an old plantation house on James Island (a stone's throw from where the True and Absolute Lords Proprietors of Carolina had dropped anchor three centuries before). It was a short commute to campus. On that hallowed ground the Clarks set about transforming a dowdy and abandoned hulk, a nine-thousand-square-foot "windfall" purchased for just $50,000, and made it their new home. Though Clark was still in his Army uniform and serving on active duty, a life of moving vans and distant posts was at an end. New complexities would soon take over.

After two years back in Charleston, Clark was named the comman-dant. In that role, he faced a major problem. In his long absence from the school, something "parallel to Nazi youth culture," he said, had laid its hand across the corps. He fixed the blame for it on Junior Sword

Drill. Those boys were harder and stronger and more resilient than any-one. They proved it with their sweat, their shaved heads, their bodies rippling with pure muscle. On a campus driven by the rules of power and resilience, bizarre trials proved their dominance. Junior "aspirants" volunteered to stand up to exquisite torment. Exercised to exhaustion, driven until they fainted, they were pushed and then pushed more by seniors who had done the same. In some years, boys pumped hundreds of push-ups while older boys held swords between their legs. Or they were made to hang for hours from aching fingertips, clutching at I-beams and ceiling pipes, their shakos tilting off their sweating foreheads, their clothes drenched, their bodies shaking, a sword held sharp beneath their dangling scrotums while older boys shouted insults and impugned their masculinity. The guys who fell down last were local legends of endurance. "I can't begin to describe the tortures they went through," said Clark. Junior Sword Drill had "great tricks . . . for inflicting pain."

By August 1974, the year Clark took over in Jenkins Hall, a new pres-ident had come to take the place of James Duckett. The school had waited for him for some time. Army Lieutenant General George M. Seignious II, a graduate of The Citadel's illustrious class of 1942, was tied up with the Paris Peace Talks at the end of the Vietnam War, and The Citadel held a place for him until the peace accord was signed. Like Mark Clark, Seignious was a general with a flair. He strutted about the campus in a cape. An air of pure authority surrounded him. Yet he was often preoccupied with matters other than the troubles of cadets. Once on campus, Seignious would be distracted by his involvement in new Strategic Arms Limitation Talks (SALT). Meanwhile, Walt Clark de-manded his attention. Hazing was out of control, he told Seignious. Its root was Junior Sword Drill. "I said, 'General, this is one of the things that they admire. It sets the tone. . . . If we're going to correct hazing and brutality, then we got to start with Sword Drill.'" Clark proposed a series of reforms to limit the number of push-ups and clamp controls on sessions in the closed, overheated fieldhouse during which aspirants were made to run up and down the bleachers until they fainted or col-lapsed. He also demanded that the boys' grueling tests be overseen by an adult. Seignious, a graduate himself, gave the commandant his blessing.

On that ground where tradition, however recently minted, was revered almost by instinct, it was no easy task to kill what years of administrative neglect had allowed to grow. By the time Clark turned his attention to the drill, seniors who had participated one year before (and now were charged with inducting a new team of juniors) were convinced they were untouchable. Self-righteous and indignant over any whisper of adult meddling, they considered themselves above the school itself, the guardians of ancient truths. In their minds, and those of many of their peers, they were the very embodiment of strength and honor, masculinity and southern pride. They answered to no one. Indeed, they had not been required to for years. "So here I am," said Clark, "old fool Army colonel. I called in the regimental commander, the class president and the commander of the Junior Sword Drill. I explained [the changes] to them—and this was like I was talking in a foreign language, especially with the Junior Sword Drill guy." All the students' faces suddenly went blank.

In a yearbook picture from spring of 1974, a handsome, perfectly chiseled blond cadet squats above an emaciated bald figure collapsed in his own sweat. Bare chested, every muscle lean and fit, he bobs lightly on his toes, a riding crop gripped loosely in his hands. Before his squatting form, the second boy, an "aspirant," struggles to get up.

In a photograph from 1973, a boy lies face-down, his legs bent upwards at an angle at the knees, ankles resting on a pipe, head hovering above a pool of either sweat or his own vomit. An older student wearing a Sword Drill T-shirt from the year before squats near, crouched and sullen, cradling a coiled snake.

Jane Barton, a nurse at the school infirmary from 1973 until 1995, came to understand the boys' intensity within the context of the time. During the Vietnam War, she explained, constant news coverage showed Americans soldiers suffering, trapped in tiger cages, tortured, gaunt and desperate or simply piled onto airplanes in plastic body bags. On campus, said the nurse, "they got this idea that they had to take all this to be prepared. [They] just got misguided, as young people sometimes do. They took and incorporated the torture that they saw into their own school system. I think they just got carried away with it." Inside those walls, they re-created rituals of war. To them it was a positive good, something hard to shape men's souls. Soon, a new theme would emerge. It would add another layer of intensity.

In 1972, Title IX legislation passed by Congress banned sex discrimination in any educational institution receiving federal funding. Only military schools were made exempt. And they were under challenge. In 1974, the U.S. Merchant Marine Academy became the first service academy to admit women. One year later, Congress required all the rest to unlock their doors. By the fall of 1976, while Walt Clark served as commandant, women had started wearing plebe uniforms at Annapolis, itchy gray at West Point and Air Force jumpsuits in Colorado. At The Citadel and VMI, however, old patterns would survive. Beside the Ashley, the distinction was a point of pride at first, and then a shared preoccupation. Having the toughest plebe system in the country suddenly came with the afterburn of undiluted masculinity.

Inevitably, the grim ordeals of Junior Sword Drill drifted down throughout the ranks. The nurses saw the worst of it. Sometimes a boy would be brought in on a stretcher in such bad shape that nurse Barton would pray, "Oh, Lord, don't let us lose this one." Many times she gently scolded, "This is not the way. You can't do this. This is sadistic." But the boys did not listen. They believed in those ordeals and patronized those frightened nurses. "You don't understand," they said, as they struggled for their breath. And so the nurses, just like their counterparts in war, became specialized in trauma. They could take a boy who was hyperventilating, his eyes rolled back, his brain all in a jumble, convulsing and half crazed, and bring him back into himself. Hell Night was the worst of it. Barton and other nurses remember looking out the window to see unconscious or hysterical freshmen lugged in on stretchers through the dark. Sometimes they streamed in half the night, like casualties from some great war. In some ways, they were. Al Basso, a paramedic who had served in Vietnam, came back to join the school's small nursing staff. He reached across the sea to find a suitable analogy. "It was just like a MASH ward in here," he said of Hell Nights he recalled. "You could see them out the windows, lined up with their stretchers." Year after year, older students carted in the wounded, the unconscious and the sick.

Nurses did not tell those tales. Nobody did. The rules of secrecy were deeply set. Hugh Harris had made them quite specific, giving the administration's imprimatur to a natural instinct among boys. To keep the system going, he had warned the corps in 1967, silence was the rule. "Anytime a freshmen goes home and starts talking us down because he couldn't take it, it hurts our public relations. We must work to drown out this unfounded criticism." When Barton arrived, she found a campus full of secrets. "I think there are two Citadels," she said. There is "The Citadel the public sees with the uniforms, the parades and the saluting. And then there's the inside Citadel. It's almost a secret society." The dangerous intensity inside those walls was reinforced with each new cycle.

Walt Clark and shy dissidents within the nursing staff were hardly alone with their concerns. In 1973, cadet John R. Chase broke the code of silence. In a guest editorial in the *Brigadier*, he admitted that he was reluctant to air a "hush, hush" problem. No one outside the school, he knew, could imagine those ordeals. "A certain naiveté exists in the minds of all who have not been through The Citadel System," said Chase. "Try to explain to them the physical punishment you received as a knob. I have not a single doubt that the person with whom you are speaking will express complete revulsion and disdain." He believed the hazing served no purpose. "Think for a moment," he urged fellow cadets, "of the worst experiences of your plebe year. Did the pain really stop there?" Quite the contrary, he suggested. "What of the mental scars you harbor . . . have you ever given them any thought? Do. The next time you abuse a knob or, God help you, harm him, try to reason out why you do this thing. Is it not against some sort of Western code of ethics to do so? Of course. Is it not against your religious code to do so? Yes, again." Yet "rarely is the offender caught," he said. "In most cases he is not turned in because his victim has had his head filled with what must be termed propaganda, that it is an honor to take the abuse to truly have 'been through' a plebe year; that to turn in someone for hazing is a cowardly act and, God help us, virtually a dismissal offense."

Hell Night and Recognition Day were bookends to that pain. A year of harassment lay between, different for each boy. For those who made it, one final hurdle awaited them come spring. Before it was all done, knobs gathered one last time and were set upon by gleeful mobs. An orgy of brutality followed. Now, before freshmen were allowed their names and released from nine months of subservience, they had to pass a final test. The time of handshakes and warm acknowledgment was gone. A hand might just as easily be broken. On that day, said R. Gordon Bell Jr., writing in the *Brigadier* in May 1973, "injuries are not only common, but expected, especially broken wrists caused by attempts on the part of the freshmen to deflect the swats of upper classmen." It was true, he said, careful to give the school its due, that some abuses had been curbed. But still the violence persisted. Surely, cadets knew something had gone wrong. To hide that wild melee, they covered up the sally ports with blankets.

In 1973, The Citadel's corps of cadets, designed to accommodate two thousand students, fell to near the sixteen hundred mark. Rumors of the school's troubles were moving across the South. Outside the gates, social pressures were building, too. Military schools were no longer popular. Nor did it make sense any longer to sign up for ROTC with an eye on an officer's uniform and a role as a "Rear Echelon Mother Fucker" (the bitter term made famous by drafted soldiers) who called the shots but often stayed well back from the fighting. That artful dodge no longer served. The war was almost done. The military was contracting. Cadets who signed up for a military career found little advantage in an institution that was bloated with a glut of officers and had no war to fight. Prospects for advancement were poor. The pay was miserable. The inducements were few. Even the proudest veterans sometimes warned their sons away from the world that they had lived in. Dawes Cooke's father was such a man. In Beaufort, South Carolina, as the war drew to a close Cooke heeded the advice of his Marine colonel father and set his sights on a civilian's life. Out of college, Cooke, The Citadel's lead lawyer in 1995, went to law school instead of boot camp. In Charleston, meanwhile, the corps kept right on marching. The boys had made that war their own. Even as it ended, they would not let it go.

On the day that Walt Clark moved to make reforms in Junior Sword Drill, he met a solid wall of defiance and disrespect. The boys listened passively. But they showed no sign of understanding. Clark persisted. Eventually, the class president and the regimental commander grudgingly came over to his view. Sure, they shrugged, reforms were needed. They would help. But the senior who commanded Junior Sword Drill rudely shook his head. Clark would never forget what followed.

"Here was this young buck who was built like a chiseled Greek statue," said Clark, "muscles rippling and *Raaauggghhh!* Kill! Kill! Goddamn it, he was tough. He didn't hear a word I said. I described the problems engendered with the Sword Drill. I let them know that I was in Sword Drill myself, and I told him that this was going to change. I said the following rules are going to be put into effect: *One! Two! Three!* And this guy looked at me, and he said, 'Colonel. You don't understand.' That's what young folks always tell you. 'You just don't understand.' He glared at me and said, 'Sir, *I* command the Junior Sword Drill. . . . Not the president. Nor the commandant. Nor the regimental commander. Nobody tells me what to do. *I* command the Junior Sword Drill.'"

Even after twenty years, that confrontation rankled. "This was the degree to which this had grown on that campus," said Clark. "It was totally out of control. . . . This was the most macho of macho. This was *it*. This was *Junior Sword Drill!* The problem for me was that all the guys looked up to him. Sword Drill had not been kept under control since the 1960s. He looked right at me and said, 'You can't tell me what to do. You have no authority over this.' Well, I kept my temper. He was just some kid to me. It was his motive to intimidate. But I don't intimidate. Not with little boys in particular."

Clark threatened the cadet with expulsion and added that he had the power to disband the drill itself.

"I asked that boy, did he know how to read a compass?"

The cadet responded snidely. "I'm an Army ranger," he said coldly. "I can find my way around."

" 'Well, then, take a reading on Lesesne Gate,' barked the commandant. 'You just do that. And you follow it right out of here, and you don't come back. Out! Go! You just get out. We don't need you people here.' That got his attention. Finally, it began to dawn on this young buck that this old colonel just might be a little bit bigger and meaner than he was. But this was the attitude. That was the attitude of Junior Sword Drill." The boy stayed on to graduate. Clark did not have the heart to throw him out.

Like many soldiers assigned to The Citadel at that time, Clark, for all his careful observations and deeply felt criticism, found it hard to condemn those boys. When he looked outside those gates, he, too, saw things that frightened him. Drug use had increased. Divorce was up as well. Families were splintering, and a new tone of disrespect had crept into the public discourse. Much in America shocked his sensibilities. He considered his own country a nation now at war with itself. At the Pentagon he had been assigned to monitor intelligence information regarding radical groups. And as a soldier on the nation's streets, he had once done the unthinkable, raising arms against his countrymen. In the spring of 1968, during the riots that followed the assassination of Martin Luther King Jr., Clark was based in Illinois, where he commanded an 850-man battalion under the Tenth Infantry. His orders on that day were clear. Chicago was engulfed in rage. Mobs were surging through the streets and lighting fires as they went. Clark moved his men into the Loop, their rifles raised. "Fix your bayonets," he shouted. His troops made rows of Army green, a vision of authority. Protesters spat and flashed them the finger and moved on. Clark was shocked and frightened. "To be going American against American . . ." He let the sentence drift.

At The Citadel as commandant, Walt Clark did what he could to strike a balance. There were values and traditions on that ground that he passionately wanted to preserve. But then there were some things that frightened and disturbed him, too. "I did what I could," he said. "It never was enough." New crises always came.

IN 1976, early on the Sunday morning following Thanksgiving, Officer Carl Olsen of the Montvale, New Jersey, police stopped a car for passing through a stop sign without braking. Olsen flicked on his cruiser lights and tapped his siren briefly. It was 4 a.m. Only the Montvale street lights cast a glow across the scene. The car jerked to a stop. A dark-haired teenager jumped out and started shouting. "They're dead," he yelled, running toward the startled officer. "I found my family dead!"

Home from college for the long Thanksgiving weekend, Harry De La Roche Jr., a gaunt and pale Citadel freshman, gawkish in wire glasses, led Olsen to his home. There, the officer found De La Roche's mother, father and a brother dead in various spots around the house. Another brother was found later. Near dusk on that same day, De La Roche was charged with murdering his family. A signed confession told the story of that sorry night.

De La Roche had started his evening at a discotheque, staying out until well past midnight. When he got home, his family was asleep. Quietly, he pulled off his military jump boots and Army field jacket and removed his pants and socks. He sat alone in his bedroom for several minutes then went down into his parents' room. In the morning, he was due to leave for Charleston. He could not bear to go. Nor could he bear to tell his father he was quitting. "Quitters are failures," his father told him. In his parents' bedroom, De La Roche found a gun. He picked it up. "I was thinking about what I was going to do, thinking I can't go back," he said in his confession.

He stood above his father's sleeping form. "I got real close," he told the police lieutenant on the case. "Must have stood in his room about a half an hour just holding the pistol up. Finally, I said, 'I can't go back,' closed my eyes and pulled the trigger." His father died almost instantly. "That set it off. Shot my mother right then and there. And then I went to my brothers' room."

De La Roche's parents died in bed. His brother Ronald was killed with a single blast to the face. Eric, the youngest, struggled most. Harry shot him repeatedly, then went upstairs to his own room. But the house was not quiet. He could hear Eric breathing. Downstairs, he saw the boy struggling to get up. "I put my hand over his eyes," said Harry. "I was trying to calm him down. But then he got up and started screaming, and I hit him with the pistol butt on the head. Then he went down to the ground. I hit him again."

Two years later, in January 1978, the case went to trial. De La Roche's lawyer, John Taylor, moved to keep the confession out of court and argued that the defendant was innocent by reason of temporary insanity. De La Roche killed only his brother Ronald after coming home to witness a shocking scene, he said. Harry was a victim of dreadful circumstance. It was his *brother* who shot the other three, he argued. Then Harry shot his brother. But the judge ruled that the confession could be used. It was read aloud in court and swayed more than one juror's heart.

On January 24, Taylor called Dr. David J. Gallina, a young, dark-haired psychiatrist, as a witness for the defense. He was hoping to lay the groundwork for a lenient decision. But the psychiatrist's testimony took an unexpected turn. On the stand, Gallina patiently described Harry's state of mind on the night of those four murders. He said the boy's consuming fear of The Citadel coupled with his dread of confronting an overbearing father had sent him into a psychotic state in which he could not tell right from wrong. The psychiatrist portrayed De La Roche as a bright and nonviolent young man trapped in a violent atmosphere at his college. As a freshman at The Citadel, the psychiatrist explained, De La Roche was hazed and ridiculed and pushed to the limits of endurance. Ritualized abuse at the school coupled with the boy's terror of his father's violent rages triggered a complete breakdown of his normal thinking. The murders on that night, he testified, were driven by a savage conflict.

Taylor listened in shock as his entire defense unraveled. Instead of showing his client as a level-headed boy who killed his brother after witnessing an unspeakable tragedy, Gallina's statements portrayed a boy who used a gun to end unendurable anguish. Late that morning, Taylor stood and faced the judge. With all the calm that he could muster, he requested a short recess in the trial. Then he called the psychiatrist to one side. When the men returned, Taylor, in an extraordinary reversal, expanded the boy's defense.

"We are going on an insanity defense to all four counts," he abruptly informed the judge. Harry slayed all four members of his family, Taylor said with urgency. But he did so in an abnormal state of mind. He did so, as the psychiatrist had implied, during an emotional episode so intense that he was not responsible for his actions.

It was a high-wire, last-minute attempt. And it would fail. The pace of the final day in court proved unpleasant for both sides.

Taylor, in a mumbled closing argument that lasted for an hour and a half, said his client had lived inside a "private hell" at the southern military college where he went to school. There, said Taylor "in soft tones that were frequently inaudible," a *New York Times* account reported, De La Roche was forced to live in an environment in which he had been repeatedly kicked by upperclassmen, constantly ridiculed and thrown into a metal locker for punishment. His father, a rigid disciplinarian himself, was a man who did not want to hear of his son's anguish. The murders that occurred, said Taylor, were an act of desperation, the doomed and tragic act of a teenager trying to escape something he could no longer bear. His insanity was written clearly in the actions themselves, the lawyer said. "You cannot tell me that any boy who killed his family is not mentally insane."

It was true that De La Roche was "sick and crazy," prosecutor Richard E. Salkin countered. But that was no defense. He branded De La Roche an "accomplished liar" and urged the jury not to let the truth be his last victim. "You're too intelligent," he pleaded, "too sophisticated, and have too much common sense to fall for eleventh-hour psychosis. You don't turn psychoses on and off like a water faucet."

Two days later, the verdict came down. Taylor read it in the jurors' faces before the foreman ever spoke. "I said: 'Harry, you're screwed,'" he recalled in 1997.

In Charleston in 1976, when news of the murders reached the campus, Ben Clark, then a ranking officer in November Company, called his father, Walt, then commandant. A boy from November had killed his family over Thanksgiving break, Ben said urgently. He shot them while they slept.

It might have been the public relations disaster that Hugh Harris had so feared. But the school escaped deep inquiry. Instead, when reporters called the school, a picture of a troubled boy emerged. De La Roche was described as a liar who told Citadel officials he had to leave the campus early for Thanksgiving because his mother had been diagnosed with cancer. "We did not check on that at all," said D. D. Nicholson, then an administrator in Bond Hall. "We work on an honor system here." An autopsy showed De La Roche's mother with no trace of the disease.

Eventually, in news accounts and a TV documentary on the tragedy, a complex portrait emerged. It showed De La Roche as an awkward and shy youth. In high school, he was mocked and teased by classmates. He seldom dated or went out and found it difficult to make new friends. His was a solitary life that mostly centered on a rare coin collection, his old car and a part-time job teaching target shooting at a nearby rifle range. A girl from his high school would recall him as a frequent subject of abuse. He was, she said, "a weakling . . . a punching bag for other kids." A local Little League coach described the father as verbally abusive.

At The Citadel, De La Roche was brushed off as a notoriously bad cadet. "One of the worst in his class," recalled a fellow student. Contemporaries say he stopped showering altogether and stuffed his clothing underneath his bed instead of laying it neatly in his college bureau (called a press) as was required. He left his shoes unshined and his uniform completely wrinkled. Something in him broke. It never was repaired. Instead, he skipped classes and corps formations. Every misstep made things worse. He never found the tools to navigate. He never found a path to guide him through that strange terrain. Instead, he stumbled and stayed lost. Classmates recall that he had a vacant face and a rank smell. He resisted every order that he could. What price he paid for that only De La Roche and his classmates knew. But he was a terrible cadet in an environment in which even small transgressions sometimes carried a great price.

PART III

Vigilance

Mill Dust

P OWDERSVILLE was a flat town, a no town, a town to drive through
without stopping. It was a crisscross patchwork of lowlands with no
beginning, all middle and no end. In January 1975, when Sandy and Ed
Faulkner brought their newborn daughter home (premature, under-
weight and fighting right from birth, they said), old farms stretched out
under the sky, graceful and constant, at rest before the sapping heat of
summer days. How easy then to think that nothing short of God's own
touch could shape that land. The cycles seemed eternal: the silver teeth
of plows in spring; white thunderclouds come June; cicadas in the still,
hot dusk and the jagged forms of sparrows resting colorless on dark electric lines strung loose against the sun. Yet Shannon and her older
brother, Todd, learned almost nothing of smooth constancies. As they
jousted in the back yard and measured their growth in startling spurts,
the land around those children heaved. Old landmarks fell haphazardly
beneath the blades of growth. Empty acres stood by waiting, pocked
with billboards, thick with lures: *Cash for land. Land for sale. Money for
old farms.* The Sun Belt was declared. New investments multiplied. Old
pine brakes were laid open and adjacent ground transformed.

By the time Shannon entered high school, back roads led to highways
that sucked traffic in all directions in a rush. Farms were sold, divided,
penned and leveled, stripped of drafty dwellings and made neat with
ticktacktoes of modest housing. Old barns with their chipped paint and
wrinkled board lengths fell in sudden heaps under the scraping teeth of
beeping bulldozers. Their shattered frames got trucked to dumps. In
their place, grass and saplings grew on arch-backed acres stretched taut
green with strips of sod. Towering mansions grew from viny underbrush
and left no trace of lifetimes gone. As Greenville stretched, new growth
moved like a combine, taking everything along its path. With a swim-

ming pool here and a new fence line there, a pile of Sheetrock, a load of brick and a tangle of rough tie beams, anything was possible.

Shannon looked around at faux chateaux with chandeliers and doorways that gaped wide between white columns. She "lapped the malls" and dreamed her dreams. From year to year the pace increased. Every road seemed new, and every driver in a hurry. Greenville was the hub of it. Northern money washed in first. Deutschemarks, yen and British pounds soon followed. Developers and bankers cruised those back roads with a vision. Where pastures lay, they conjured cul-de-sacs and small estates, trim enclaves of new homes. Termite-ridden antiquities seemed out of place beside new Taras. Finished off with brick enclosures, walk-in closets, brass faucets and fake marble, old acreage found new purpose. Huge signs promised cheap financing. A sense of tenuousness prevailed.

Sons and daughters of arthritic farmers cashed their checks and said goodbye; to hell with screen doors and no central air. A lot of people were just waiting on some funerals. For them, there was more in a fairy tale without a tree than there ever was in farming. Sentimentality could not pay the bills. To them, tradition meant only poverty. Anyway, if the developers did not get you then the highway department did. North, south, east, and west, asphalt rivers flowed with powerful currents. Even Kmart could hardly keep its footing with a new Wal-Mart opening now. Grandma's home was an interstate. The old interstate was a back road bleached bone white. Between the two lay endless acres of suburban sprawl, a neat terrain devoid of past. The tangling maws of bulldozers reworked whole landscapes in a day. In the span of one lifetime a whole way of life was lost.

In Shannon's family there was no careful homage paid to history. Progress was just fine with them. They had no love for ancestry and made only scant accounting of their forefathers. They kept no fading papers lying crinkled in a safe and laid no claim to aristocracy. Their family tree was simple and utterly without pretense. A childish wood plaque hung in the family's large, untidy kitchen. It showed only four names on a sapling sprouting from an acorn's crown: Ed and Sandy, Todd and Shannon, as though the family's entire substance had surged from seed to leaf in one short span. For them, there was no taproot in a king's grant. From their perch in Powdersville, nestled in a downslope and dwarfed by towering trees, they looked ahead at their best chances, not back at where they had been. The rest was all just stories. Hardly worth remembering.

Sandy Faulkner could tell the family history in ten minutes flat, with all of the embellishments. They were a mix of German, Irish and Scottish folk all running from war and poverty and famines back in Europe. From what she knew, they were humble people on both sides, farmers and handymen and knockabouts who followed the crops and their best chances state to state. Some worked in the quarries. Some worked in the mills. Most of them worked hard, she said, and went to church and made a life.

Sandy's grandmother died as she gave birth to her third child. Her grandfather followed six months later when his car flipped as he sped around a slow horse wagon, showing off. They were doing well back then. But those deaths knocked the family back. Sandy's mother, Evelyn Richey, was packed off to her grandparents' house where she never quite felt welcome. There, she learned hard lessons while still young. "As a family, we've always believed that what you want, you just go after," Richey said smoothly, sipping iced tea on a back porch, her air conditioner humming, her face a web of wrinkles from a life lived full and long.

Evelyn Richey lived by that credo and passed it on. While she was young and about to be married, she approached the foreman in her mill and asked for three days off for herself and her new husband. The foreman grunted and said that she could go ahead and take her honeymoon . . . but her husband had to stay behind. There was a war on then. The foreman needed every man. Richey, insulted, responded with a reckless quip: "Well, then, he quits," she answered, and turned her back and left. The newlyweds went south to Charleston to celebrate their wedding vows. They walked beside the Battery and drank in all that history. On their way back home, Richey gently informed her husband that he no longer had a job. The next morning, when he stood abashed before his boss, the foreman shook his head and sighed, then hired him right back again. Half a century later, Richey still got a laugh from that old victory. What you need, you had to take. She knew that lesson well and taught it firmly, in her way.

Sandy inherited her mother's spunk. When she was just a child and ran away from home one day, packing a bag and stifling a sob that mixed independence with raw fear, her mother helped her pack, then gaily waved goodbye: "Write us when you learn how, honey," Richey called after that small, shuffling figure. Sandy turned around again as soon as she hit pavement. "Mother believed she should give us wings to fly . . .

and then let go," said Sandy. Sandy thought the same. It was a matter of survival.

Ed Faulkner's family was cut of the same cloth. There was a horse thief from Abbeville somewhere generations back and a grandmother killed when a loose apron string got caught up in mill machinery. Everyone else had worked, married, given birth and gotten by in something close to anonymity. Theirs were hard lives, undistinguished and short. Ed's father, Albert Faulkner, the youngest of eleven, started work when he was six, selling newspapers to mill hands for a penny profit here and there. Later, he hawked ice cream from a wagon, then signed up at the mill himself, in 1929, when he was fourteen. He had put the mill work off. His mama had started there when she was eight. She died when he was four. His father worked there, too, and ended life a bitter man, old at fifty-three. Albert never missed him much. He stole his children's earnings and made a rough and frightening drunk.

Albert hated mill work and escaped while he was young. He married a girl from church and opened a diner down the hill from the noisy brick colossus that was the centerpiece of town. That small business became Greenville's church of the profane. Albert built a sign made out of tiles on the outside wall and spelled THE COFFEE POT in huge block letters crisp inside a bright red frame. That place would be his home. He and his wife, Ethel, worked eighteen-hour days there catering to every shift that came and went in the seven mills in town. Soon, they were the central conduit of news. Mill hands came in after work or sat uneasy at the Church of God across the street, swamped with fire and brimstone, then slipped across Tremont Avenue to heave a great sigh of relief. For years, Albert and Ethel saw their business grow and prosper. Then a slow decay set in. After a time, Sandy Faulkner would avoid her in-laws' proud creation, dismissing it as a greasy spoon fit only for bums and derelicts. But Shannon loved to go and twist in circles on The Coffee Pot's old orange stools. She spent long afternoons amid convoluted stories, munching on fat hamburgers and crunching home-cooked fries. The air inside was close and hot with cigarettes and kitchen grease. But the company was good. To many of the men and women who had frequented the place nearly all their lives, it had the certain feel of home. Good times and bad, Albert always took them in. Sundays, Jimmy Swaggart came across the radio, and Albert played along, tapping at a plastic keyboard and turning his establishment into a funky house of worship full of song. The spirit was contagious. It was not unusual for every person there, old and young, fat and thin, solvent or busted down to their last dime to join in Swaggart's hymns while Albert pounded at his electronic omnichord and raised his voice in harmony.

By then, The Coffee Pot served not only as a restaurant but as a pawnshop, general store, rumor mill and local bank. It was packed with ancient bicycles, dusty Kodak film, household goods, greasy tools, plastic Barbies and countless other children's toys. (Albert's favorite was a snoring bear he kept beside him on the counter.) People slammed in through the swinging door and asked for anything that they might need. From diapers to door locks, Albert kept it all somewhere. Great haphazard heaps of junk grew tall along the floor. Huge piles crawled up the walls, on teetering shelves and down beneath a long glass counter. The kitchen, the dining room and the pool hall back behind them acquired the look of a basement packed with castaways. One old shoe? Why throw it out, thought Albert, someone just might need it. That stuff grew like kudzu. "Hey Albert!" old friends shouted with one foot barely through his door. You got . . . an old chain saw? A box of birthday candles? A set of lug nuts?

In its heyday, The Coffee Pot had been considerably more mundane. A jukebox played, and tidy booths were full of customers and tips. A billiard room was added. Glinting mirrors lined the walls and home-cooked food was served by waitresses in crisply ironed uniforms. Albert and Ethel served a constant stream of customers. Ed helped out as soon as he could walk and proved adept behind the stove. "Two meats and a vegetable" was the trademark meal. Fresh pie was served up à la mode. Coffee and iced tea were poured in endless refills. Ethel bought some chandeliers and tried for elegance and style. But one by one the mills closed down. Then traffic on the roadways stopped, pulled off by a new interstate. What had been a surging river of commerce became a stagnant backwater. Progress passed them by.

Ed's parents were too old to start again. Instead, they watched as unemployment soared and a drug culture set root. Albert ran long, penciled tabs without the slightest hope of payment. Ethel complained sourly but did not interfere. Outside, frustrated teenagers played target practice, pitching rocks at Albert's pride and joy, a sign made like a coffeepot and finished off with neon. Albert shooed them off. But more and more, the lights stayed out and the damage never got repaired. Now, a marquee offered HOME COOKED EALS UMBOS LLA. Tiles fell off the outside wall. A sense of endings had begun.

A drifter came and stayed awhile but then turned mean and left. He told Albert he would burn the place. In 1988 Albert and Ethel went out one night and came back home to flames. The next morning, Albert stood shuffling and half dazed in the smoking ruin of his life. "It was charcoal," he said bitterly. But folks came in that day and sniffed and poked and sighed, then placed their orders anyway. Albert eyed them warily, then gave his stove a try. It started, and he set to work. For months, he juggled buzzsaws and frying pans, too proud to ask his son for help, rebuilding while he cooked. In time, the damage got repaired. Still, something died for good that night. The Coffee Pot's old shine was permanently extinguished now. The Christmas lights stayed up all year. Bugs scuttered down the countertops. A film of greasy neglect lay heavy as a fishing net.

On days when Shannon slammed through that screen door, Albert winked and brightened. "My hero," he said, beaming. In her he saw the future.

Sandy had begun her life with certain aspirations. When she met Ed she was fourteen and easily impressed. He walked onto the high school baseball lot wearing a brown corduroy suit with a wide-ribbed vest and a slim tie. To her, a country girl, he was the picture of a city sophisticate and a better prospect than gap-toothed kids from pig farms and tobacco fields. She sidled up and caught his eye and hid her age from him at first. They fell together easily and married young and made a start. In time, Ed moved away from his father's enterprise and made a business for himself. It was not the life that Sandy had envisioned. But dreams of glamour soon gave way. Her husband was a working man who spent his days in blue jeans digging postholes in the sun. His callused hands paid all the bills. While that family was still young, the Faulkners moved from a cramped starter house in Greenville to a larger home down back roads where the kids had room to roam. A swimming pool glistened turquoise in the yard. Ed's business slowly grew. Life was not so bad.

As soon as Shannon learned to talk her mother went right back to school. Women in her family always worked. But now, buoyed by the thinking of the time, Sandy set her sights high. Before long she had a teaching job at the local public school and a college diploma on the wall. She was proud of those accomplishments. Beside the diploma hung a needlepoint that soberly advised: "The tassel is worth the hassle." Shannon took that rule to heart. Friends from high school wore small engagement rings that cast bright sparkles on the walls. Shannon held out for a different fate. Sandy watched her with great bursts of pride. Her own life was well set by then, and it was fine by her. She had gained some weight and let her hair go white and settled into middle age. At Christmas, she played Mrs. Claus to pay for extras for the kids. After anguish and some therapy she made her peace with who she was. It showed in her soft features. In her floppy hat and bright red suit, old glasses slipping down her nose, she looked the part of Santa's wife. But Shannon wanted more than that. In her rash, unbridled hope, Sandy saw herself when she was young. And why shouldn't Shannon have her dreams? That girl of theirs had talent and competitive drive to spare. There was nothing that she could not do.

In court, the family's history was pared to bare essentials.

"Your parents, are they South Carolina residents?" a lawyer for The Citadel asked Shannon early on.

"Yes, sir," she answered warily. She was a southerner was what she meant, a South Carolina girl and proud of it, not some crazy radical come down there to make trouble.

"And has your family always lived in Powdersville?"

Shannon shifted in her chair and looked at Bobby Hood, one of the school's attorneys. "Well, they lived in Greenville for a little while. And then Powdersville, yes, sir."

"What does your father do?"

"He owns his own fence company."

"F-e-n-c-e, fence?"

"Fence, f-e-n-c-e."

"What kind of fences does he . . ."

"Chain-link, brick, wood . . ."

"All kind of fences?"

". . . iron."

It hardly took her long to draw her background for the experts. Her father finished high school, then started up a business. Her mother taught psychology and social studies at Wren High School. Todd was in the Navy, aboard the USS *Ashland.* She saw him change in that sharp uniform and craved the same self-discipline.

The lawyers prodded. And what about her grandparents?

"My mother's parents are both retired," Shannon said without inflection.

"What did they do?" asked Hood.

Shannon shrugged and looked impatient. "I have no earthly idea."

What was he getting at? You worked; you paid your bills. What did all that have to do with her? After a pause she frowned and then complied. "I believe my grandfather worked for J. P. Stevens."

On the margin of that interview a lawyer made a note: "Greenville mill family."

She was an unlikely rebel, poured from the same mold as many of the male cadets. But she was unwelcome even so. For a quarter of a century, The Citadel had braced for such a challenge. In 1966, Hugh Harris promised alumni and cadets that there would be no girls, no hippies, and no peaceniks. It was a joke then, preposterous. A decade later, when Shannon celebrated her first birthday and the service academies prepared to open up their ranks to women, the matter took on greater urgency. Still, The Citadel resisted calls for change. The school defined itself in that. Mark Clark's pledge was now effectively a sacred trust. The Citadel had—and would maintain—the toughest plebe system in America. Among the aging board members (themselves so far from barracks life), the issue was a point of pride. Graduates considered it a central piece of their identity. The school's personality was tuned and fixed. It left no room for females. By 1979, when Shannon started the first grade, the question of women in the barracks had become an explosive litmus test for any prospective president. From there, deep passions only grew.

In the wake of the Denmark Vesey–inspired slave revolt of 1822, the city fathers of Charleston approved new instruments of torture and measures of control. Among them was a treadmill much like this one built to punish workers in Jamaica. The Charleston device helped turn a wheel used in grinding corn. In that same era, city fathers also called for a citadel to protect white citizens from harm. Soon one was being built on Marion Square.

Inside the Charleston workhouse (above), unruly slaves were whipped, denied food and subjected to grueling sessions on the treadmill. Not far away, Citadel cadets—whose first task was described as keeping Charleston's black population "compleatly subordinate"—occupied a building with a strikingly similar design. The Citadel was transformed into a school in 1842. On its new campus, opened in 1922, anachronistic turrets and gothic crenelations repeated the workhouse's most distinctive features. That design is faithfully copied even in new barracks built today.

Citadel cadets fired upon the *Star of the West* as it steamed toward Fort Sumter with fresh supplie for federal troops in January 1861. With no orders to fight, the ship's captain retreated, putting of the start of the Civil War. Three months later the war began in earnest when Confederate troop launched a massive and successful attack on the Union-held fort.

Charleston's famous harbor, her quiet streets and many elegant mansions would be charred ruins b war's end. But in late 1861 the city remained both proud and confident as rebel soldiers moved dow Broad Street.

Once peace was won, new political realities emerged. In Washington in 1866, women and blacks gathered outside the galleries of the House of Representatives to cheer the passage of the Fourteenth Amendment, which ensured civil rights and voting privileges for freed slaves. Some of those rights would long exist on paper but not in practice.

In Charleston in 1866, the sudden inversion of power led to riots in the streets. One particularly fierce melee erupted outside The Citadel's gates and surged throughout the city, leaving windows broken and many businesses badly damaged.

Poor white boys gained entry into a new world at The Citadel by willingly subjecting themselves to the paddlings and "ass whippings" of upperclassmen—sometimes with an audience in attendance. The Citadel had become an institution bent on changing undisciplined young boys into self-sacrificing, hard-willed men, and such rough rituals were an open secret in the ranks.

By the start of the new century, The Citadel was known for the many humiliations heaped upon incoming cadets. Here, three freshmen (known then as "rats") are shown with their heads completely shorn, an event the 1906 yearbook described as "the biggest joke of all." By the late 1960s—when hair was a combustive social issue—freshmen were no longer "rats" but "knobs," so named because their exposed craniums resembled doorknobs.

Almost a century would pass before The Citadel accepted its first woman into the corps, but early yearbooks included a variety of sketches showing what such a change might look like. In some sketches, cadet women wore pants and shakos, as at left. In others they wore skirts down to their ankles and elaborate hairstyles.

During his tenure as president, from 1931 to 1954, General Charles P. Summerall instituted tough fiscal policies and kept a firm hand on the corps, which helped the school survive. It emerged intact from hard Depression years and began to grow in size and gain respect across the South. Once dismissed as nothing but a "dude factory," The Citadel at last began to earn attention for its academics as well as its attitude.

Mark Clark was a four-star general and commander of the U.S. Fifth Army in Italy during World War II before succeeding Summerall as The Citadel's eleventh president. A staunch opponent of integration and an outspoken warrior in the Cold War, Clark invited dozens of prominent speakers to the Charleston campus, among them President Dwight Eisenhower, to whom he granted an honorary doctorate. Clark's tenure came at a time when the Cold War was young and cadets were full of patriotic zeal. But by the time he retired in 1965, times were changing. The Vietnam War had begun, and The Citadel's first black cadet started marching just weeks after Clark's departure.

Claudius (Bud) Watts III became president of The Citadel in 1989 and led the school's opposition to allowing women in the corps. Thirty years earlier, as a top-ranking cadet (above) under Mark Clark, Watts was praised as "Most Likely to Succeed" in the 1958 college yearbook.

A new era began with the start of the Vietnam War. In 1965, Hugh Pate Harris inherited a thriving institution, but during his five years as president, enrollment declined as military schools lost favor across the South. Inside the barracks, meanwhile, hazing intensified as boys pushed each other to new extremes in the name of wartime training. Harris spoke out against barracks abuses but could not stop them.

"THE CORPS IS SICK," advised a sign in The Citadel's M Company in 1970.

In the 1960s, gaining membership in the Junior Sword Drill, a fourteen-member drill team that was once a relatively banal part of college life, became a grueling test of strength, commitment and endurance. Some rituals, such as hanging for long periods of time from pipes and then running endlessly up and down gymnasium stairs, unconsciously mirrored ordeals once imposed on restive slaves forced to run the work-house treadmill. But cadets who wanted to be part of the Sword Drill's small elite volunteered for that treatment.

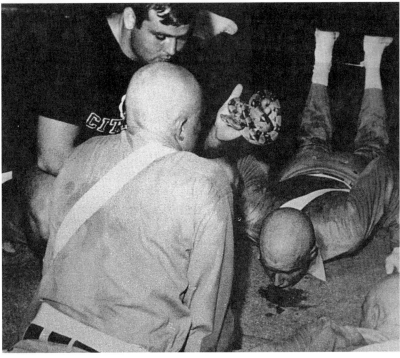

As seniors, Junior Sword Drill members from the previous year were charged with training junior aspirants. Some used unusual means to heighten the tryouts' tension.

Armed troops with the National Guard fanned out across Charleston in the summer of 1969 during a strike by black hospital workers seeking better pay and treatment. That high drama on Charleston's usually quiet streets underscored some Citadel cadets' growing sense that the world outside their gates had gone berserk—not them.

As commandant of cadets in the early 1970s, Walter Clark was shocked by Junior Sword Drill's practices and distrusted the group's elevated status. But any move to bring women into the school, Clark said, would threaten his alma mater with the same "softening down" he believed was occurring in the nation's coed military academies.

During Thanksgiving break in 1974, Citadel freshman Harry De La Roche Jr. was arrested and charged with murdering his parents and two brothers. At his trial two years later (here he is escorted into the New Jersey courthouse), a psychiatrist testified that the student had suffered a "psychotic break" when forced to choose between returning to a culture of ritualized abuse inside the barracks and telling a rigid, disciplinarian father that he did not want to go back.

In 1991, Tony Lackey retired from the Army. Soon afterward he headed south to his alma mater.

Shannon Faulkner at the age of five outside Peggy's School of Dance in Powdersville, South Carolina.

Shannon's grandparents on her father's side, Albert and Ethel Faulkner, cheered Shannon's challenge to The Citadel. Having worked eighteen-hour days, seven days a week, throughout their lives, they knew that it took guts and determination to succeed in life. "She's my hero," Albert said.

Before the Faulkner case began, Pat Johnson and two other Navy women tried to get into a Citadel program tailored for male veterans. The women sued when they were rejected on the basis of their sex. Citadel officials sidestepped that attack by shutting the entire veterans program down. In January 1994, Johnson wore her uniform as a sign of protest on the day Shannon signed in as a day student, barred from barracks life. Both women were represented by Valorie Vojdik (far left) of the powerful New York firm of Shearman & Sterling, and Sara L. Mandelbaum (shown behind Faulkner and Johnson) of the ACLU.

For a year and a half, Shannon was allowed to attend classes with cadets but was barred from all other aspects of student life until her lawsuit was resolved. Some students taunted and teased. Most simply ignored her. Off campus, meanwhile, there were death threats and acts of sabotage.

In the mid-1970s, Dawes Cooke's father, a much-decorated Marine colonel, advised his son against joining the military. With the Vietnam War finished, officers' ranks were bloated, morale was poor, and there were few prospects for promotion. Dawes opted for a law degree instead and as a lawyer for The Citadel spent most of his time in the early 1990s defending the school against proposals to introduce women to the all-male corps.

The night before Shannon took her first steps as a full cadet, her core supporters gathered to celebrate. From left: Her mother, Sandy, Valorie Vojdik, Shannon, Melinda Black, her husband, Bob Black (a Charleston lawyer who prided himself on being the only "true Southerner" arguing on Shannon's behalf in court) and Shannon's father, Ed, dressed provocatively in the T-shirt of a rival school.

Another of Shannon's lawyers, Henry Weisburg, flashed the V sign on the day Shannon started marching with the corps. With little fanfare, a 153-year tradition ended as a woman joined a student body comprising about 1,800 men.

On her first day as a full-fledged cadet, Shannon moved into spartan quarters that she would occupy alone. In class as in the barracks, she had no female companions.

As military training got under way, a member of Shannon's training cadre urged her to "think!"

Even with federal marshals standing near and charged with protecting her, Shannon quickly showed the strain.

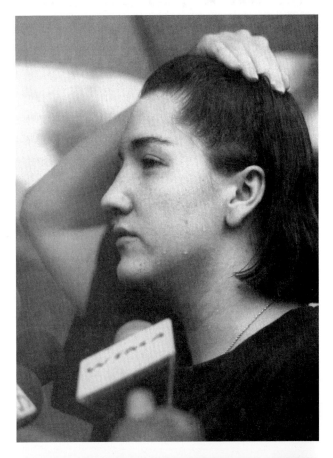

In a pouring rain, a tearful Shannon Faulkner announced she was leaving the school after just one week.

Cadets, hearing of Shannon's withdrawal, celebrated in a noisy, joyous outburst.

Bruised by the long and vicious battle over admitting women, Bud Watts resigned his post as president in the spring of 1996. His successor, John S. Grinalds (above), installed a small military field desk in the president's office and pledged a broad range of reforms. By then, a small band of alumni were publicly condemning barracks abuses, saying that they traumatized men as well as women.

In 1999, Shannon (shown here with her father) graduated from Anderson College in South Carolina and embarked on a career as a teacher in the South Carolina public school system.

Rip Tide

IN THE SPRING OF 1979, Vice Admiral James Bond Stockdale, a former prisoner of war best known for once having bludgeoned his own face with a prison stool rather than give his Vietnamese captors a filmed confession to be used for propaganda, received an unexpected letter postmarked Charleston, South Carolina. Written with warm deference, the letter was an invitation to apply to be the institution's fifteenth president. Stockdale was delighted. He had a vaguely positive sense of that old school. But more important was the fact that the letter came just as he was thinking of a change. In that, he saw his destiny.

To The Citadel's board, Stockdale was a natural choice. Shot down in the Gulf of Tonkin in 1965, he had survived eight years of captivity and emerged a national hero. The U.S. Naval Academy awarded the James Bond Stockdale Trophy for Inspirational Leadership. His glinting Congressional Medal of Honor confirmed his status as a man of grit. And he had some powerful friends. His Annapolis classmate Jimmy Carter sat in the White House that year. Later, Stockdale would aspire to such ranks himself when Ross Perot put him in the national spotlight as his selection for vice president.

When The Citadel came calling, Stockdale was serving as president of the Naval War College in Newport, Rhode Island, but was ready to retire. In the southern school, he saw a perfect opportunity. There he hoped to merge his military experience with his growing interest in scholarship and the training of young men. But when he stepped on The Citadel's clipped turf he experienced a strange sensation. Instead of capturing the calm repose of an institution of higher learning, The Citadel's archaic design recalled his prison camp in Vietnam. The turrets and the gateways seemed familiar, he later wrote, those "high, whitewashed exterior walls identical." Memory swept him suddenly. As his hosts laughed and bantered, the former prisoner was pulled into the past. "I was looking out into the cell blocks off Heartbreak Hotel courtyard, Hoa Lo prison, in Hanoi. I could hear the guard's heel clicks echoing," he wrote in his memoir. A sense of total vigilance consumed him. "This was the first time since I had returned that I had ever had such clear visions and sound recollections of prison. I quickly doused them with positive thoughts."

It was pointless. All his senses were alert. He became aware of small details and invested them with great significance. The license plate on his host's car was printed: "CITADEL 1." A perquisite for the board president, it was a signal of the institution's power. Stockdale did not like it. To him it called to mind the North Vietnamese and all their casual tyrannies. He flinched, too, when he learned the tightly controlled makeup of the board. Only Citadel men could serve, and each man had to make his home in that underpopulated state. The insularity disturbed him. He struggled against a rising sensation of entrapment.

Later that same day, in a cozy private club in Charleston, Stockdale settled into a formal interview with board members. He had a vision for the school, he said. He planned to focus most on academics. To his surprise, several men chuckled. Then the topic turned. Board members expressed concern that the admission of women at the military academies had led to a "softening down" that would rob the nation of its military edge. What did Stockdale think of that? Did he see the full significance of The Citadel's status as one of the nation's last all-male training grounds?

Stockdale nodded casually and answered that the hazing he experienced at the Naval Academy had probably been key to his survival during his long imprisonment. There was a quiet shuffle in the room. Heads bobbed and several men shifted in their chairs, visibly pleased. But they were not quite done. When Stockdale's wife, Sybil, joined the group, the same question was repeated. Women played their hand behind the scenes. Board members wanted unity. Did she agree that single-sex education had its place? Indeed she did. She had studied at an all-girls' school herself.

That spring, Stockdale was named president. The family's moving van arrived in Charleston in August 1979. Gracious introductions followed. The president's household staff was deferential and well trained.

Employees seemed genuinely awed to have a hero in their midst. They gave the couple every courtesy. But Stockdale felt uneasy from the start. In his desk drawer in Bond Hall, he found a letter from a father who complained that a short stint at the college had transformed his son from a "level-headed, optimistic, aggressive individual" into a "fatigued, irrational, confused and bitter" one. Stockdale wondered why.

Most of his colleagues did not. Instead, they viewed student anguish as a normal part of a time-honored process that prepared young men to face life's bigger tests. Outside The Citadel's gates, shifting currents in the social debate now seemed to reinforce that view. Conservative social critics fretted that the country had grown weak after years of self-indulgence. America's confidence was waning. The nation's military supremacy was being questioned, too. Not only were leftist movements proliferating near our border in Nicaragua, El Salvador and Guatemala, but an armed mob stormed the U.S. embassy in Teheran on November 4, 1979, and took fifty-three American citizens hostage. For more than a year, Jimmy Carter tried to win their freedom. But a series of embarrassing mishaps corroded public faith. Helicopters crashed in the desert. Rescues were botched. Back at home, gas lines stretched for city blocks. The inflation rate rose to its highest point in thirty-three years, and the national debt was bloating so rapidly that by 1985 it would be the largest in the world. Not since 1914 had the nation owed more money than it was due. It seemed an almost unthinkable reversal of our fortunes, a sure sign of ill health. Accustomed to being held as the mightiest nation in the world, we worried we had lost our edge.

In that atmosphere, a new mood of nostalgia formed. Tom Wolfe's *The Right Stuff*, celebrating an unapologetically macho military culture, rose high on the best-seller lists. In movie theaters, meanwhile, *Kramer vs. Kramer* showed a mother walking out on her young son to find fulfillment, a notion that would have been unthinkable one generation back. In some quarters now, a rapacious "me generation" that valued personal gratification over social responsibility was blamed for a wide range of ills. Conservatives rang the bells of vindication. That winter, Carter moved out of the White House. The man who pardoned draft evaders and made human rights a formal component of American foreign policy had lasted just one term. America looked instead for heroes and the simpler template of our past. In 1981, Ronald Reagan would provide both as he traded in Carter's famous cardigans for a pair of cowboy boots. His politics matched his attire. When air traffic controllers struck over wages, Reagan simply fired them. "The law is the law," he announced without apology. Permissiveness had lost its chic.

At The Citadel, where boys had marched in the opposite direction for the better part of two decades, a very different set of problems preoccupied the new president. There, freshmen found themselves lost inside an exquisite maze, faced with layer on layer on layer of rules. In that environment, obedience was valued above logic and even common sense. To older cadets intoxicated with notions of power and control, the substance of a command meant less than the simple fact that a boy with stripes upon his shoulder could bark it out and see it followed.

Yet with Mark Clark gone and blacks marching on that ground, something novel was needed to organize the younger boys and reinforce their sense of mission. Since black cadets might now impose their will upon white freshmen, the game of slave and master faltered. It hardly made much sense. In its place, a new dialectic of contempt was needed. Soon a new vocabulary evolved as metaphors of supremacy shifted from race to gender. For the first time, a transparent hostility toward women showed. Soon, it would be knit into the complex patterns of the corps.

Once, mothers and girlfriends were sponsors and dates, ladies in hats and gloves, adoring admirers with endless patience, or seductive Miss Citadels with buxom bodies and sweet smiles. None of those roles challenged expectations. But now women were calling loudly for an equal place. Old assumptions of their proper role were fast disintegrating. Cadets responded crudely with reminders of their dominance. In the *Sphinx* of 1971 a photograph showed twenty-five young men in shorts and bathing suits standing in a huddle on a beach, an American flag fluttering handsomely behind them. Leaning forward as a group—one boy circling his fingers into small binoculars—they ogled two bikini-clad girls who lounged nearby in the sand. The caption read: "Who's First!"

In Charleston, a vast seduction guided new recruits. Theirs would be the toughest and most *manly* of the nation's schools. In 1973, an editorial in the *Brigadier* entitled "The Straw That Will Break America's Back" identified the Equal Rights Amendment as that straw. Quoting an unnamed expert from Yale, the writer, Sidney L. Wise Jr. of the class of 1974, suggested that the amendment would weaken the social order by increasing the incidence of divorce, alcoholism, suicide and homosexuality. Anarchy would be the sure result, concluded Wise, bringing "joy to the hearts of our enemies, who would like nothing more than to have the United States fall apart socially, especially if the downfall were the result of a move initiated within the country." The argument was familiar; Mark Clark had made it once himself. Only the focal point had changed.

On campus, new rituals showed a heightened preoccupation with strength and masculinity. If "hippies" with their unkempt clothes and wild hair had been the signals of a society twisting itself into a strange new shape, a nearly shaved head indicated a stern repudiation of those same social experiments. Now a stubbly scalping was a rite of passage for all new boys. The footprint of that shift lay with Junior Sword Drill. From the 1960s on, Sword Drill "aspirants" were easily identified by their bald heads. Those scalpings were their brand as true believers. Later, in the gray doldrums of February, scores of other boys with less cachet sported a similar style. ("Bald Heads and Lots of Guts," trumpeted one *Brigadier* headline describing the Bond Volunteers.) Soon enough, freshmen found those razors aimed at them. Walt Clark was shocked to see the change. "When I was a cadet in the 1940s," he recalled, "we didn't get knob haircuts. Noooo! Hair was not a social issue." When Stockdale arrived, it was. Freshmen were shaved nearly to the skull. And they were not rats as they had been once, nor plebes. Now, with a nod of approval from board members who chose not to have the school confused with "softened down" service academies, they were part of a dialogue of mastery that centered on sex. From that time forward they would be *knobs* (a term signifying the tip of a man's penis in British slang), shaved as smooth as doorknobs and immediately recognizable for a look that virtually branded them as male.

For many boys, that radical first shaving marked a point of no return. Shorn of their most obvious allegiance to the culture they came out of, freshmen were made to look so odd in those "baldy" haircuts that they could not easily leave campus without an attack of acute embarrassment. To self-conscious eighteen-year-olds it was hard business going back. Even in Charleston, those haircuts hinted at a growing distance. There, residents at least knew the drill. Everywhere else, recruits who quit were freaks until their hair grew back. Among the knobs, a quick defensiveness arose. They became part of something new with that first shaving. A deep camaraderie evolved. Only other cadets could understand what they went through. Only other cadets realized what their sacrifice might mean. Only other cadets could see what their commitment signified.

In the barracks, Stockdale would survey a world shaped by its harshest antecedents. Like Walt Clark, the new president recoiled, then moved to make some changes. To his dismay, he soon discovered that for every reform devised by adults, students found a coy evasion. Push-ups were a prime example. Once, upperclassmen had assigned them by the hundreds, driving freshmen to exhaustion. Now, they were expressly limited in number, yet not in execution. As a result, a remarkable innovation allowed for equal pain by other means. Though upperclassmen could assign only a few push-ups at a time, a new process involved ordering knobs to "rest" with their elbows bent and their bodies suspended halfway between the floor and a full stretch. In that way, just a few push-ups could become a long experiment that ended only when a student collapsed in sweat and pain. Technically, no rule was broken.

Early in the school year, Stockdale ordered freshmen to his office one by one. The admiral found himself repulsed by their demeanor. They would not relax. And they would not speak freely. Instead, most of them stared straight ahead, dazed and unresponsive. Almost every one had lost all sense of his own agency. Stockdale watched them in a rising fury. "I would have been less alarmed if they had been brought in on stretchers with black eyes and leg splints, rather than as walking spooks," he noted sadly. At least that way he would have known that they fought back.

That fall, moving quickly, the new president launched a campaign to curb abuse. He also assigned a prominent Citadel alumnus, lawyer Francis P. Mood of Columbia, South Carolina, to begin a broad investigation. Hazing would be abolished at the school, the admiral vowed. He made his outrage public. A storm of letters followed. Some were angry and insulting. Others conveyed expressions of relieved support.

"Oh, how I pray you don't resign!" wrote the mother of a knob.

"Sleeping was often on the floor so as not to be punished if there was a crease in the bed," one grandmother advised.

A 1968 graduate said he was surprised no one had yet died.

Another graduate wrote to say he did not defecate for a week. He simply was too terrified to walk down his long hallway.

"Only the lunatic fringe of graduates would fail to recognize the urgency for change," another said.

One parent took a humble tone as she described her stepson's fate. "We do not want to sound like 'sour grapes,'" she said, "but we have a family tragedy. . . . Our son is in the South Carolina State hospital."

Though a standout while in high school, twenty years later, when Shannon filed her lawsuit, he was a sad and frightened loner, only recently deinstitutionalized, who bagged groceries for small tips and did not wear The Citadel ring.

Many graduates resented Stockdale's moves. They called him a publicity hound for speaking out and denied that there was anything wrong inside those walls. Sweat parties were just jokes, they said. Naked boys with shaved heads and shaking bodies were packed into the showers, flesh to flesh. The faucets went full blast. Just kidding. The imagery was grim, but the taps held only water. Boys always played their games. If you couldn't take it, then you left. If you left, you invented some sad story.

"The fight goes on here," Stockdale scribbled in the margins of a dozen letters. In fact it would intensify and soon become entwined with the vague and as yet unfounded fear that women would be marching next.

Colonel James W. Bradin, one of Mark Clark's boys and later a member of the board, stood at the mouth of that volcano. He sat in Jenkins Hall that year and served as a professor of military science. In that role, he found himself caught between two masters. The U.S. Army and the college president wanted different things of him. Stockdale demanded more control inside the barracks. The Army wanted Bradin to focus instead on expanding the size and quality of local ROTC programs. That spring, those issues merged with fateful impact.

On March 26, 1980 (just several days before Frank Mood's critical analysis of campus hazing was released), Bradin wrote a letter to his Army commander at Fort Bragg saying that he had approached the College of Charleston to see if it had any interest in accepting an Army ROTC program on its campus. A side note added that the College of Charleston administrator believed "most support will come from female students." Faculty at the College of Charleston quickly rejected the idea. Still mindful of the havoc of the Vietnam years, they did not welcome having uniformed officers on campus. At The Citadel, however, a time bomb had been set, and it was ticking out of sight. Inside Jenkins Hall, someone had misread the letter, taking it to mean that women would be marching sharp not at the College of Charleston at all but among men beside the Ashley. Soon, pirated copies of the letter (mimeographed in secret and shared in tandem with that basic misconception) became a central part of a coordinated campaign to drive Stockdale out of town.

Bradin, it was said, was using a back door to sneak girls into the corps of cadets. If that happened, The Citadel would be no different from the academies. Stockdale was allowing it, the rumors went, or else he was so out of touch that he did not know enough to stop it.

Bradin made an unlikely Antichrist upon that ground. As an air cavalry officer in Vietnam, he thrived in a unit known for its mad exploits and made famous in the film *Apocalypse Now.* Cavalry soldiers swooped down in shrieking helicopters, the wildest of wild men. Bradin did not let that image go. Instead, he nurtured it, strutting about campus in knee-high tanker boots that closed with straps instead of laces and gave him something of a look of a stern Luftwaffe general. For a swagger stick, he waved an ax handle. Of course, there was a story behind that. Bradin always told it with a smile.

In the spring and early summer of 1964 while he was a young Army captain serving in Georgia in an exercise named Air Assault Two, Bradin was put in charge of distributing supplies to bases scattered across the midlands of South Carolina. It was a tiring round-the-clock operation slowed by bad morale. Nothing seemed to get those soldiers to look sharp. "By day three or four, I was ready to start marching these guys into turning aircraft props, [one] platoon at a time," he said, laughing. A better solution presented itself. One morning, a young sergeant eyed him sympathetically and leaned forward with an ax handle. "Here," the soldier said, tossing his heavy club of hickory at the seething captain. "You need this worse than this ax does."

Bradin looked at him irritably. "What in the hell am I supposed to do with this?"

"Just carry it and bang it on things," the sergeant said with a wide grin. "They'll come around pretty quick."

Later that day, Bradin had that ax handle in hand when he saw a sergeant bumping merrily across an open field inside his forklift. Like everybody else, fumed Bradin, that black soldier was just wasting precious time. Bradin moved in front of him and ordered him to stop. Furious, he slammed the ax handle across that forklift's hood then walked away abruptly, telling the startled soldier to sit tight until Bradin told him he could move. Hours later, Bradin was roused by a junior officer. Sorry to wake you, sir, the man began apologetically. But some fool sergeant was sitting in the field, frozen in his forklift. Bradin had to come. That soldier wouldn't listen to anybody else.

Bradin dressed hastily and dashed outside. In the constant press of duty he had forgotten all about that man. With a warm pat and a sincere apology, he sent the soldier on his way. He was embarrassed by his lapse and felt badly for the sergeant. Yet something in the exchange had thrilled him, too. From that day forward, he always kept that ax handle close by.

Whether the young officer knew it or not, a lawn ornament then popular across the South paid homage to a similar story of obedience. When George Washington prepared to cross the Delaware, he asked his personal slave to hold a lamp to guide his soldiers back to camp. It was a long crossing on a bitter day and as legend had it, when the troops at last returned, that slave was dead and frozen stiff; his lamp still held aloft. Washington commissioned a statue in his honor, and soon copies of it appeared across the South as a reminder to black workers to behave and a boast to whites that local slaves were docile and subservient. Not until the civil rights movement reached its peak did those black jockeys disappear.

With his swagger stick in hand and his boots kept black and polished, Bradin hardly seemed the sort of man to let The Citadel go soft. But fears of such a shift were great. Social pressures had been building. Staff members whispered of a dire conspiracy. The academies had given in. Perhaps their campus would be next. From Jenkins Hall, an old associate of Walt Clark's raised an alarm. Clark listened, outraged, then stormed out of retirement. He faced Bradin down inside his office and shouted that he was reckless and a fool, out to kill their alma mater.

"Having come by this information . . . that they expressed interest . . . which I got clandestinely, I went to Bradin," Clark recalled in a voice roughened by decades of alcohol and smoke. "And I said, 'Bradin! You are negotiating with the College of Charleston to have ROTC students—*some of whom will be female*—come to The Citadel. And in my opinion you are driving a nail in the coffin in the future of The Citadel. And I'll see you in hell before I let you see females in here to water down this program. . . .' We parted enemies. He was hot and I was hot."

Soon, the fighting ricocheted. Men like Clark who had been appalled by campus violence were now *more* outraged at the idea that the school's all-male history might end. Clark, encouraged by friends, set off on reconnaissance, then set the seeds of malcontent. He talked to cadets, faculty and others and concluded that the problem lay not with Bradin but with Stockdale and all of his reforms. Stockdale was not a Citadel man, Clark snorted. He did not understand the school's traditions. "I was after Stockdale," Clark said bluntly. "One of my classmates was a member of the Board of Visitors. I called him and I said, 'Are you people on the Board of Visitors aware that from within The Citadel there are negotiations to permit women on the campus to take ROTC?'

"He said, 'Noooo!'

"I said, 'Well, I'm prepared to tell you what I know about it.'"

A small group of men met shortly after that. Clark was well prepared. He showed them the Bradin letter and told them Stockdale "should be lynched" if he knew of any plan to sneak women into the corps. If he did not, then he should be removed on grounds of gross incompetence. The board members, also misreading that letter, agreed. Years later, Clark would look back warmly on that moment. "I had Army handouts for the students and maps and charts and whatnot. I said, 'This just shows you that this man Stockdale is detrimental to The Citadel, and I give you this as ammunition.' I gave them a whole variety of reasons." *One. Two. Three.* Clark laughed. "As it turned out, Stockdale was not aware at *all* that his subordinate Bradin was trying to get the College of Charleston into the ROTC program." Clark tapped his pipe out in an ashtray with a shrug. The larger point was made. The school would stay all-male. New battle lines were drawn.

It was an ugly struggle over a nonissue. But it sealed Stockdale's fate. All spring, the crisis escalated.

In Jenkins Hall in those next months, Bradin reeled between conflicting commands. The Mood Report suggested that active-duty tac officers be posted inside the barracks. The change would have meant a measure of oversight and adult control, but Bradin worried that he did not have the manpower for such a shift. He told superior officers at Fort Bragg that their own priorities regarding the Army's "expand the base" program would suffer if the Mood Report were put in place. Tac officers inside the barracks would mean a "drastic" change, Bradin warned.

"Stay out of Citadel politics," Bradin's commanding officer snapped back. And so he did. The recommendations of the Mood Report (informally renamed "the Stockdale Plan" by suspicious detractors) would mostly languish on a shelf.

Clark, meanwhile, continued to push for Stockdale's ouster. At an alumni meeting late that spring, Clark approached Stockdale and laid out his complaints. "For the first time in my life," said Clark, "I went to an alumni association meeting. And when the floor was open I said to Admiral Stockdale, eyeball to eyeball, about a five-minute pitch." As

Clark attacked, the famous former prisoner withdrew. "He had sort of an *I'm not here* stare. The combat one-thousand-yard stare," remembered Clark. Alumni at that meeting quickly took Clark's side. "I got a standing ovation," he said. "Everyone stood up and cheered, which wasn't what I wanted."

Two weeks later, still wired and engaged, Clark held to his attack. Hunkered down in his cluttered basement office, sitting in a haze of smoke, he wrote several urgent memos outlining his fears. In them, he described himself as an "arch conservative" who believed that his college had survived the upheavals of the time "with values and principles more intact than did the institutions of church, family, Armed Services, government, education, etc., etc." To his thinking, the new mood in Bond Hall marked a turn toward moral drift. If Stockdale remained in place, Clark feared, The Citadel would join the very revolution it had so resolutely fought.

He was careful to seek balance. Like his adversary, Clark objected to the "demeaning and violent" tactics so prevalent among the upperclassmen. "I am personally *not* upset by Administration efforts to curb abuses in the Fourth Class system," he wrote. "I am disturbed by the overall thrust of an administration that projects that all things Citadel are guilty & suspect until proven innocent." He found Stockdale's tone imperious. He detected a certain Navy elitism and suspected that all Stockdale wanted was to make his old school more like the academies. That wounded Walt Clark's pride. True, he conceded, some tinkering was needed. But why let the tumult of a generation destroy what more than a century of history had built?

That summer, a whirl of bitter politics swept the campus like a fire. Stockdale confronted the Board of Visitors and said that he would leave the college unless they gave him more authority. It was a dizzying time, he recalled in his memoir, one in which he was caught in "the crosscurrents of factionalism, backstabbing, rumor and hate." In the end, the fire consumed him. Five days before his first full year was up, Stockdale resigned. He described a vague "back channel" that seemed to undermine his efforts. He said his relationship with the board had soured that March, then disintegrated further. "The forces of the status quo were marshaled," he told a Charleston reporter. "And they won."

Buddy Prioleau, the board president, described Stockdale as a "great American," then moved rapidly to seat another president. This time the board's choice was a Citadel man, an Army general who had almost won out against Stockdale in a secret ballot the year before. Prioleau introduced General James A. Grimsley to alumni and supportive Charlestonians as "one of our own." Though in the days of Charles Summerall and Mark Clark that issue had not mattered, by 1980 it was a crucial distinction. The Citadel was marching to its own tune now, one crafted from traditions that predated the Civil War. On James Island, Walt Clark heaved an enormous sigh of relief. Old lines would hold. Familiar faces were in place. His school would keep its shape. Yet when he thought back, it was not the issue of women that first sprang to mind. Instead, a single memory stung most. At one time during his tenure, Stockdale was quoted comparing The Citadel to his jail in Vietnam. Walt Clark recoiled in disgust. To him, danger lay outside those gates, not there among his own.

An Astringent for the Soul

IN AN EASIER DAY at a simpler time, the first of a series of elegant yachts cruised the waters just beyond the Battery's low sea wall. Sometimes men in uniform paced back and forth on board, cradling drinks and canapés. Floating out beyond the last line of palmettos in the dying light, those boats stood in dark silhouette against great sweeps of azure sky and made a splendid backdrop for that city and her steeples. Seeming to emerge from an antique world of orderly elegance, they cruised slowly past the crumbling rubble of Fort Sumter and then diminished into dots at sea. Back on shore, tourists leaned in toward the railing at the Battery's edge and watched that drifting pageantry with sighs of envy and delight. But the photographs they snapped could never capture what they had seen. For like the last light from a star already gone to black, The Citadel's elegant seagoing vessels were a glimmer from a world already gone. Indeed, to some, they were the ghost of Never Was.

It was an odd preening in any case. For all its watery boundaries, the Military College of South Carolina, as Jim Stockdale's tenure perhaps showed, never was at ease at sea. The Navy fought at a remove and focused most on strategy. The Citadel, dominated by the Army and deeply wedded to more earthy trials, rumbled in the mud. There, generations were instructed that adversity was an astringent for the soul, a natural good. Even in changing times, few doubted that philosophy's essential merit.

The same theory had long held in the military academies where a vicious hazing was often part of an important rite of passage. Yet, over time, that pattern had begun to shift. The spur, in part, was war itself, and a growing national awareness that violence and terror in all its forms carried a cost in mental scars as well as physical damage.

Combat veterans had always understood that truth. But to a wider populace the spiritual toll of trauma was made powerfully clear in World War I. Britain's Royal Army Medical Corps treated more than eighty thousand troops for shell shock and related ills. Hundreds of thousands suffered later, more privately, at home. Though physically unharmed, they clearly paid an awful price. It lingered after guns fell still. Shell shock, hysteria and "disordered action of the heart" were the terms used then. They were not terms of honor. In the ancient code of Western nations, war was glorious, soldiers brave. There was no place for terror. Those who felt it were despised.

Indeed, young men suffering from what they had endured made for a frightening sight. There was nothing of glory and patriotism to early film stock that documented young soldiers shaking convulsively, their eyes rolled back, their minds caught in a frightful tangle. In military hospitals, many medical professionals used shame and humiliation to knock those soldiers to their senses. Electric shock, a routine psychiatric treatment of the time, was commonly administered as well. That double punch was justified with doctrine. "It could be assumed that soldiers developed symptoms of hysteria because they were weak, mentally and morally," wrote Allan Young in his history of psychiatric thinking about trauma. Military doctors had their orders. Their goal was not a cure, but victory. They wanted those men marching.

Top officers, though usually positioned at the rear of the worst fighting, often experienced similarly debilitating symptoms. Yet it proved awkward, even unpatriotic, perhaps, to blame members of the highest echelons of the military command as weak. Ranking officers therefore required a semantic dodge. Doctors generously supplied it. According to Young, yellowing military records show that men with senior rank, rather than being stigmatized with diagnoses of hysteria and shell shock, were more apt to be diagnosed with the less despised condition of "neurasthenia," or better yet, simple exhaustion, the remedy for which was likely to be a combination of rest, hot food and plenty of encouragement—in short, a reconnection to the world.

The fact was, most doctors had no idea what to do. Confronted with incredible evidence of private human torment, doctors found themselves both overwhelmed and underqualified. Suffering veterans, meanwhile, found that aggressive "cures" sometimes only magnified their pain. As a result, those who could do so cauterized their emotions or blurred their difficulties in a fog of drugs or alcohol or beneath the hard integument of careful manners. "Once you fall, human nature is on you," said Septimus Warren Smith, a troubled war veteran sketched in Virginia Woolf's 1925 novel, *Mrs. Dalloway.* "The rack and the thumb-screw are applied. Human nature is remorseless." Septimus killed himself rather than go to a psychiatric ward. "Coward," screamed his psychiatrist as the haunted veteran leapt through an open window.

Only a few pioneering psychiatrists took a more empathic view. They believed the debilitating mental fallout of war should be considered a natural reaction to unnatural stress. True, the bravest officer could crack. To them that fact made sense. The wounds of war were not only those etched in flesh and blood. They seared the spirit, too. In time, that view gained favor. Vietnam veterans in particular had a powerful new incentive to come to grips with their psychological disintegration. Where soldiers of past wars were welcomed back into society as men of valor and self-sacrifice (or warehoused out of sight in veterans homes with sweeping lawns and careful plantings), veterans pouring back from Southeast Asia were often shunned as grunts and baby killers or dismissed with hardly a thought as hateful figures of contempt. Denied their self-respect and any recognition of their sacrifice, some veterans demanded that doctors and psychiatrists give more weight and understanding to their pain. By 1980, their private agonies had a new name and a more sympathetic diagnosis. In its large compendium of mental illness published that year, the American Psychiatric Association included post-traumatic stress disorder among its many ailments. In time, that diagnosis would extend to victims of rape, domestic abuse and other trauma in the civilian sphere.

Inside the Veterans Administration, a shift in policy occurred. Cowardice no longer sufficed to describe a soldier's struggles. The days of shell shock and hysteria were done. Now, soldiers suffering from mental trauma could share their sadness without shame. It was a profound change, and it came in tandem with another major shift inside the ranks. By 1978, the Army had its first female two-star general. In everything but combat, women worked shoulder to shoulder alongside men. There would be no turning back. An agonizing reorientation had begun. Nothing about it would be easy. Even if new maps were incomplete, old maps no longer served.

At The Citadel, meanwhile, ancient shibboleths held firm. School officials did not spin the mirror back or question what they built. A wall of purposeful oblivion was raised. Cadets still marched with pride in bright reflections of their past. Ancient lines of order held. A series of old absolutes would guide them: Soldiers were not victims. Women were not soldiers. Suffering forged a sacred bond. Those who could not take it quit. They were reviled as weak. Those who stayed on won great praise. Bathed in the support of classmates and old graduates, cadets saw themselves not as survivors of some vast anachronistic test but as courageous victors in a fundamental human drama. The world was tough. They were in training for its hardships. Down beside the Ashley River, Citadel men proudly claimed the high ground. The Pentagon had caved to social pressure, Citadel boosters chided. That deepest of allegiances began to fray.

Privately, some who wore the ring suspected something had gone wrong. Faced with disturbing proof of barracks terrors, they moved to implement reforms. Loyal to the school, yet shocked by what they witnessed, critics struggled to find a balance that would fit. Always, their reforms fell short. It was hard to break tradition where tradition was so highly valued. And it was hard to admit failure while condemning others in the outside world as failed. And yet, time and again, efforts were made.

In 1968, when hazing at The Citadel was arguably at its worst, Hugh Harris ordered a comprehensive study of The Citadel's fourth class system. He assigned James M. Whitmire Jr., a graduate of the class of 1938, to the task. The resulting report acknowledged the presence of "significant and extensive abuses" but stopped short of providing specifics on the grounds that such details would only sensationalize an already difficult problem. In place of examples that might shock, the Whitmire Report generated vague conclusions that showed a college deep in crisis. "Instead of one well-defined, understood and organized system," the authors explained, "there are presently some seventeen major and about fourteen hundred minor plebe systems at The Citadel tied strictly to individual personalities, attitudes and interpretations." Fourteen hundred equaled roughly the number of cadets, excluding freshmen. Seventeen referred to the number of cadet companies. The result, the authors said, was an anarchic environment in which cadets had such deep contempt for college rules that specific prohibitions outlined in the Blue Book merely "served to suggest ideas for abuses."

The Whitmire committee recommended a broad overhaul. "There needs to be reorientation," the study warned in 1968, "away from the idea of having the toughest plebe system in the country to one of pride in having the most meaningful." That reorientation did not occur.

Twelve years later, the Mood committee would reach a resoundingly similar conclusion. In an environment dedicated to training young men in the qualities of "integrity, honesty, compassion," its authors said, the purposeful interference with study, sleep or meals was entirely counter-productive. A more "positive approach" was suggested, one that would underscore "the essential worth and dignity of the individual." That, in sum, was the Stockdale Plan. Designed to rid the institution of "instant traditions" and a barracks atmosphere of "almost pure ritualism," it was roughly in line with changes then occurring in the service academies. But that was precisely its problem. The Citadel's board, convinced that the coed academies had lost their way, wanted no part of a new philosophy. Students paid the price for that intransigence.

Though the extensive details of the Mood Report were not publicly released, by the early 1980s the world outside of Lesesne Gate was becoming sadly aware of the college's failings. Violence among young men was the unspoken secret. But more important to prospective employers were the institution's academic lapses. Once, Citadel graduates were virtually guaranteed jobs if they but flashed their rings. That was no longer true. All across the South, the economy was growing more complex. Networking, nearly the sole criterion for landing employment in a relatively simple economy, no longer was enough for most graduates to thrive. Instead, they needed skills and training to succeed. Citadel professors—themselves more highly educated than at any other time in the school's history—knew that, yet found themselves frustrated. Day by day, they stood in front of boys more concerned with survival outside class than a good performance in it. The tests and fascinations of barracks life overwhelmed all but the few.

Squeezed between the extreme demands imposed by the corps and the increasing expectations of the world outside of it, many students struggled harder than ever before. David Epps, a 1980 graduate who by his own account came to Charleston with a "lack of motivation, lack of focus, minor troubles," defended The Citadel's environment as precisely his best medicine. He loved the school for having taught him discipline. Yet he felt that the rewards for his long sacrifice were hardly clear and certainly not understood outside those gates. As a cadet, he was picked on by city boys. As a white male, he said, he no longer felt respected.

When he graduated, married, and later fought for custody of his children in a difficult divorce, he sat in a courtroom surrounded by posters showing deadbeat dads. At the Navy base where Epps worked as a civilian, he clashed constantly with female colleagues and came away believing that they wanted to be heard, but not to listen. His own arguments, he felt, were sneered at.

At home, he found relief working on a novel late into the night. In it, he continually relived his college days, teasing out an 800-page opus about Junior Sword Drill. In those pages, Epps marched with the fourteen and, in the novel's closing moments, executed a perfect drill. When it was done, he wrote, "I was where I dreamed of being, yet it was too good to be true. My life was forever changed, and my first thing to do was to break my most solemn vow. I didn't move, but just stood at perfect 'full arc' as the crowd continued its storm, and I could feel a tear start to roll down my face. I just couldn't help it. From hoodlum to hero, my dream was now a reality. I was Sword Drill."

The glory of Junior Sword Drill and thus of The Citadel, to him, was that it was neither bland nor compromised, "not for the weak of heart, nor the unfit." It was a place of rules and limits, clearly set. "Knighthood becomes really the point of it," Epps explained. In a clear system of authority in which everybody found his place, a man who passed extraordinary tests could expect extraordinary reward. The king's daughter took his hand. His future was secured. He stood above all other men. It was a lovely story. But its ending was no longer happy. On his beloved campus, old routines replayed. Knobs who crumpled or complained were heaped with burning shame. Those who made it wore the ring. But only on ground matted by the steps of generations did those grim trials matter. There the swords flashed bright and flags fluttered undisturbed. Turrets rose into a brilliant sky. Theirs was the heroic imagery of time long gone. But nobody was watching now. Cadets were marching for themselves, narcissistically transfixed. Outside, in a new age molding itself to subtle and difficult new realities, knights were no longer recognized. Instead, they walked like mortals on the street, their sacrifice ignored.

Hurricane

THEIRS WAS A WORLD encased in glass. A crack was bound to show. But it was a long time forming. In 1981, with Jim Stockdale come and gone, one writer called the school "more popular, more arrogant, more self-possessed, and seemingly stronger than ever." Enrollment was up. A nagging sense of crisis passed. The tough encasement held. Though conditions in the barracks remained demanding, cannon muzzles no longer bristled with implicit warning from the *Sphinx*. A more temperate period had begun. It would be brief. The Citadel was badly out of step with the culture that it served. Soon, new fault lines would appear.

On October 23, 1986, five white cadets dressed in white robes and hoods burst into the room of Kevin Nesmith, a black freshman, carrying a small burnt cross. Nesmith's Filipino roommate, Michael Mendoza, rose out of his bed and drove them off. A fissure grew within the ranks. At the college's next football game, white cadets rose and sang "Dixie," just as they had always done. In protest, several dozen black cadets stayed seated. Tensions on the campus soared.

That November, the governor assigned a four-member team with the South Carolina Human Affairs Commission to issue a report on race relations at The Citadel. The study's authors described an institution that tolerated integration but was not at all transformed by it. Twenty years after the first black cadet marched, the door of race was unlocked but still not quite ajar. Only 6 percent of the cadets were black, and a string of statistics showed the college lagging far behind other South Carolina schools in terms of racially integrating the college staff. Bond Hall was run by four white men. The faculty consisted of 164 white men, nine white women and one black man. The Supreme Court had just upheld affirmative action laws. But the nation—and The Citadel— still boiled with debate. In a review of all such programs in four-year colleges around South Carolina, the committee observed, The Citadel ranked last.

Theirs was a telling checklist. But there were other, more symbolic, signals of persistent racial attitudes as well. Twenty years after the campus was integrated, not one black man or woman had ever appeared on campus to give a "Greater Issues" speech. The Confederate flag was proudly waved at sporting events, and "Dixie" was the school's fight song. Only six among 188 Citadel Scholar awards granted over a dozen years had gone to black cadets. And every single member of the committee assigning those coveted scholarships was white. To press that point, the NAACP unearthed a college yearbook photograph from 1977 that showed cadets from Tango Company in Ku Klux Klan garb surrounding a black cadet with a noose around his neck and a gun pointed at his head. "We were just having a good time," a former cadet informed the *News and Courier* as the controversy swelled.

Jim Bradin was in Germany then, serving under the command of General Colin Powell. But news of his alma mater's sudden notoriety traveled across the sea. In an integrated Army unit run by a black general, news accounts of the Nesmith incident and those Tango Company boys in their white hoods left a deeply unpleasant aftertaste. Powell called Bradin to his office. What in the world was going on down there? the general asked. Bradin felt his color rise. It was an ugly thing. Bradin could only imagine that discipline had lapsed. But the conversation lingered after it was done. Bradin admired his commanding officer and, for perhaps the first time in his life, felt ashamed of his old school.

In early September 1989, Hurricane Hugo hit Charleston straight on. To Bud Watts, who had returned that summer to run his alma mater, it was an awful christening for an ugly time. New problems would soon follow. Racial tensions were not resolved. Years of history lay behind them. Issues involving women would be next. In the spring of 1990, Justice Department lawyers filed suit against the Virginia Military Institute, charging that the school's exclusionary practices (though expressly allowed through an exemption written into Title IX laws) violated women's rights and did not satisfy the Equal Protection Clause of the Fourteenth Amendment. Two weeks later, Justice Department lawyers would be knocking on The Citadel's door. Soon after that, a female legislator introduced a bill to force the Military College of South Carolina to admit women into the corps. The measure was tabled in committee meetings. But the shift in mood was clear. The glass was finally cracking.

With the prospect of female cadets once again pushed to the fore, the threat of impending weakness reappeared. Boys responded in familiar ways, underscoring an old vow. They had and would maintain the toughest system in the country. To ensure that that tradition held, they beat and harassed younger boys. In 1991, Jane Barton was shocked by much of what she saw. Students were sometimes brought to the infirmary at polar extremes of catatonia and hysteria. If older boys hung near, she knew there had been trouble. They made a ring around their victim, keeping information close, echoing bland explanations. Knobs showed the new intensity with an array of symptoms. "Sometimes they would sleep twenty-four and thirty-six hours without even waking," Barton explained. Or they would lie down, "fists clenched, almost bracing, completely stiff in the bed. They just could not relax." To her, the year took on a "cultlike" feeling. "It just suddenly hit me. . . . They don't eat enough. They have sleep deprivation. Then it's just easier to gain control of somebody's mind."

In early 1991, students writing in the *Brigadier* laughed off freshman terrors, using an ugly campus event to take a poke at nervous knobs. Early that spring, a female raccoon had wandered through the boggy marshes and up onto the campus grounds. Some time after midnight, it was captured by several high-ranking cadets and slowly tortured to death. The animal's terrified shrieks awakened many on the campus. The faculty was shaken. But students used the incident as an opening for dark comedy. "A knob death resulted on Thursday when certain sword-bearing exterminators had mistaken him for a raccoon," tweaked the April Fool's edition of the *Brigadier*. "When the culprits were asked for the reason behind the slaying, they replied, 'The beady eyes! The squeaky noises that he made! It was easy to mistake a knob for a raccoon.'"

In fact, student violence would soon be in the news. Early the next fall, four freshman athletes dropped out of the school, charging that they were beaten and abused by upperclassmen. An article about the case in *Sports Illustrated* triggered yet another study of secret campus rituals. The Lane Commission, after an investigation stretching over several months, would reach the same conclusions as every one of its predecessors. Food, sleep and study remained problems for all freshmen. Hazing was widespread. Reforms were recommended.

At the *Brigadier*, the stories of those four athletes became fodder for a season's thinking. But now, instead of embracing censorship as a positive good (as editors had done in Mark Clark's time), student reporters had the audacity to expose administration doublespeak and mock a state hazing law which, though prompted by the Nesmith incident, specifically excluded The Citadel from its purview. That aggressive new journalistic approach did not sit well with Mark Clark's boys. Subsequent issues of the *Brigadier* were firmly back on track, full of articles extolling cadet virtues and emphasizing the school's more positive aspects. One front-page item hinted why: "Newspaper Censored by Administration," announced a huge headline concerning a conflict at *another* school.

Over in Bond Hall, spitballs from the *Brigadier* were perhaps the least of General Watts's concerns. As The Citadel's seventeenth president sat at his enormous wood desk, a swirl of difficult events required his attention. By the spring of 1992, the chronically short-tempered president faced a deepening crisis in enrollment and a surge of racial tension on the campus that focused on the continued playing of "Dixie" and the ubiquitous presence of the Confederate flag. Meanwhile, a Justice Department investigation loomed, and the president had normal administrative duties to attend to. A $50 million construction project was planned to upgrade the college's infrastructure and replace its aging barracks. Cautiously, Watts started to make changes.

In the fall of 1991, Watts had ordered a college Race Relations Advisory Committee reconvened. That committee's findings were filed on March 4, 1992. The report was relatively mild; its authors simply noted that five years after the Nesmith incident, black employees still worked almost exclusively in the kitchen, for the grounds crew and in the janitorial ranks. The black student population had not grown, and few among them held leadership positions. Yet the committee believed that the school was on the right track. "As a preamble to our detailed report," the authors wrote, "it should be noted that race relations in general on The Citadel campus since the Nesmith incident in 1986 are not at the same level of negativism as has been reported at many campuses in the United States." Positive steps were being taken by the Watts administration; they should continue, the writers urged. Meanwhile, two symbolic matters needed fixing. The committee recommended that Confederate flags be banned at Citadel-sponsored events. And the playing of "Dixie" finally had to go. Instead of serving as the school's fight song, it should be reserved for special occasions.

The Confederate flag fell first. For decades, a house-sized version of the flag had adorned the college's enormous water tank. Now the school painted it over with The Citadel's trademark baby blue. Other steps would follow. None of them were popular. It was a moody, brooding time on campus.

On March 12, one week after the report on race relations was issued, a short pop sounded beside the Ashley. A startled black cadet staggered forward several feet, then fell. A bullet had entered his chest about an inch above his heart. It tore beneath his clavicle and exited through his humerus bone, piercing one lung and shattering his upper arm. He crumpled in a heap behind the Padgett-Thomas Barracks. One inch lower, and that bullet would have ripped right through his heart.

On that bright Thursday afternoon, Colonel Ben Legare, a fifth-generation Citadel man, was working in the Bond Hall annex. He remembered the moment vividly. For him, it brought back a rush of memories from Vietnam. "There was blood all over the place. It was right before the evening mess. He had staggered down from where he was shot to go and try to find someone to help him. He was out by the bookstore when he fell. They were loading him onto an ambulance when I got there. I hadn't smelled blood since 1965."

Watts summoned the Charleston police, the South Carolina Law Enforcement Division and the Federal Bureau of Investigation. But he did not order a general lockdown of the barracks. Nor did he demand a search from room to room. Instead, he let the Charleston police take charge. They pushed out onto the river in small boats and combed the grassy marshland by the bank, searching for evidence. In the ensuing days, cadets submitted to short interviews. Nobody reported having seen or heard a thing that afternoon. No weapon was recovered. No powder-dusted shell casing was dropped into a plastic bag. The shot seemed to have come from nowhere.

Berra Lee Byrd Jr., his plans for an Army career suddenly dashed, spent five months at home recovering, then returned to The Citadel to graduate. Meanwhile, a sense of mystery prevailed. School officials insinuated that Byrd knew his assailant all along. He doubtless brought it on himself, they said, and chose to keep the matter secret. Perhaps there was a love triangle? Or a fight among some local blacks? He must have been involved in something. Or else it could have been a random shot, fired by a reckless hunter somewhere off across the river.

Jimmie Jones, ever defensive of his alma mater, wrote it off as a "personal episode" and drew no broader significance. "I have a gut feeling," the board chairman explained, "right here in the pit of my gut, that this was probably a couple guys who had a spat over a girl." Or a random shot. It could have been that, too, he added.

Jones's wife described the shooting as the "strangest thing that ever happened on that campus." To her, it was a symptom of the times. America had become a dangerous place. Crime was rampant. The society's fabric was badly torn. Our moral structure was decayed. There were drive-by shootings in inner cities and random crimes from coast to coast. "A drive-by shooting," said Nancy Jones. "That's what I thought." Soon enough the whole event just drifted from her mind.

In Bond Hall that spring, there was little time to fret about the implications of that shooting. Five days after Byrd went down, a new distraction loomed. Patricia Johnson, a Navy reserve officer, applied to attend The Citadel's all-male day program for veterans seeking an advanced degree in engineering. She owned a house in the area and had a job she liked. She did not want to move. Yet her best option for further schooling was choked off. Barred from The Citadel's program because of her sex, Johnson had to cobble classes together at other schools to earn a degree which—unlike that offered by The Citadel—would not carry the imprimatur of accreditation. "There's something wrong with that," Johnson told a friend. It gnawed at her.

In January 1992, Johnson was lying on a couch at home near the North Charleston Naval Base, watching a television movie about the *Roe v. Wade* case, when, "Wham!" she said, grinning, "it was like a lightbulb went on. The next day I started going through the phone book calling lawyers." At first, she called only women. One among them led her to Bob Black. Black answered the call himself. Yes, he agreed, the situation was not fair. Black had taught at the college himself not so long before, and carried a certain bitterness about the school. Johnson liked him from the start. Though the middle-aged lawyer changed careers midstream and had barely started his law practice, she found him "extremely intelligent and worldly." When Black spoke, she said, "his speech was perfect. It was eloquent. Well above my own language."

Johnson was a tomboy from Florida. Though born in New England, from the age of eight she lived in Deerfield Beach: dead end on a sea coast, last stop to the blue. She spent her childhood out of doors and never looked ahead. When she dreamed, she dreamed of her father, a Navy man who walked away from the family's home when she was two. Johnson kept a picture of him in her head. In her mind, he was young and handsome and always crisp in his white uniform. Her mother was a waitress. No romance there. After high school, Johnson drifted aimlessly from job to job. Then, at twenty-two, she walked into a Navy recruitment office and asked what they might have for her. "I thought to myself that whatever I picked now, this is what I will do and be proficient at for the rest of my life." The Navy sent her to Orlando. She went to boot camp there and then started technical training. For years, the Navy would define her life. "Hell, I even liked boot camp!" she recalled.

In 1981, when Shannon Faulkner was just starting first grade, Johnson was posted to the USS *Canopus*, where she was one of fifty women working with twelve hundred men. Johnson did not think about it much. The Navy was a job. Standing at the vanguard was nothing she had planned. "I worked with all men, and they weren't very happy about it," she remembered with a shrug. For the most part, she ignored the tension or managed to break it with a joke. Hassle was part of the job. But one day a sailor of lower rank called her a "fucking WAVE," and Johnson reported him for insubordination. Shortly after that, her work reports declined. Errors showed up everywhere. She grew more cautious, but her problems did not end. Eventually, a superior officer approached with a solution. "He didn't say it outright, he more or less insinuated that if I just pulled the chit [complaint] back my life would be much easier." She finally acquiesced. The complaint was withdrawn. The blemishes on her record disappeared. "Everything just went away," she said.

Johnson reenlisted once, then took an extension to expand her technical expertise. Her salary rose, and her benefits accrued. She rose to her father's rank, petty officer first class, and gained seniority as a specialist in precision measurements. Then new troubles started. Eager to purge its ranks of homosexuals, a Navy investigation put a handful of women sailors on the spot. Johnson had everything at stake by then. Asked to respond to an allegation that she and a female friend had had sex, she denied it. The investigating officer threw his hand out in an arc. "This is classic," he responded with contempt. The investigation widened. Many of Johnson's friends were driven from the service. She was not. She figured her proficiency in an arcane field saved her. But her taste for Navy life had soured, and in early 1990 she left that life behind. Ten days later, missing it, she signed up with the reserves. But she was angry now, and trained for attack. She wanted something to take on.

Johnson was thirty-two by then and found life outside the Navy strange. "I was used to protocol. . . . You wear a uniform every day of your life. You are at their beck and call. I went for years and years with them mandating what I did, where I went, who I answered to. It was all taken away, or not taken away, it was all gone. I wasn't used to feeling free." She hated it at first.

Civilian life meant a drop in pay, no health insurance and all the same commitments. Everything felt odd. "I was going to work, and I didn't stand in a formation in the morning at quarters for muster and instruction and inspection. Now, I wasn't around huge groups of people anymore. I worked in a little, tiny laboratory with just one or two other people. And it was just real laid back, and I wasn't used to that. It's almost like there's reverse culture shock. I felt bizarre. I felt as though I didn't really know how to act. A major portion of my adult life was in a structured, what I would consider repressed, repressive, environment. But now I would wake up in the morning and couldn't believe that I was actually putting on regular clothes. That, to me, was amazing. I did not like it." She even had trouble figuring out what she should wear.

In the reserves, during a conversation with a fellow female veteran, Johnson found an outlet for her rage. It would burn upon The Citadel. And so in the spring of 1992, while the school was reeling from the shooting of Berra Byrd, she and two other female veterans, Elizabeth A. Lacey and Angela C. Chapman, submitted applications for The Citadel's veterans program in engineering. Their desire was not to march in the corps of cadets or participate in any way with barracks life ("Who would want to?" Johnson wondered) but to sit in class in the only accredited engineering program in the South Carolina low country.

When the women were rejected, they filed suit, describing them- selves in depositions as "outraged," "frustrated," and "deprived" by the school's policies and demanding their full rights under the Constitution. Their language was stilted, but their point was clear. Other veterans, men who in some cases had served their country far less time than they, were receiving important benefits that they were denied.

When word of that lawsuit reached New York, lawyers with the American Civil Liberties Union were immediately attracted to the case. It fit perfectly their politics and their interpretation of the law. In that conflict they saw a clear violation of the Equal Protection Clause of the Fourteenth Amendment to the Constitution. But more money and more clout were clearly required. Soon, an informal search began. At Shearman & Sterling, an ambitious young attorney named Val Vojdik got a call from Isabelle Pinzler of the ACLU. There was this interesting case down in South Carolina, Pinzler explained, launching into the basics. "I'll take it," Vojdik snapped after hardly a moment's thought. "To me it was the quintessential case on gender discrimination." The instant she hung up, she rushed down the quiet hallway to Henry Weis- burg's office, where she began to wheedle and convince. It was an impor- tant case, Vojdik told her colleague passionately. It might be a landmark case. The firm should say yes, or someone else would pick it up. "I knew we had to move fast," she said. "It was just one of those things."

In that moment, the axis of power shifted. Instead of being located in Bob Black's dusty, one-man, one-room, walk-up office near Charleston's famous "four corners of the law" at the intersection of Broad and Meet- ing Streets, all energy was suddenly swept seven hundred miles north, to the immaculate corporate headquarters of Shearman & Sterling, a hum- ming, arrogant behemoth suspended in Manhattan's skyline.

"So it's a female network that's operating," Vojdik said proudly of that start. In no time at all, Pat Johnson was dealing with some of the sharpest young lawyers in New York, lawyers who were inclined to see the case in the broadest possible terms. For years, the Supreme Court had applied something called "intermediate scrutiny" to cases involving women. The terminology meant that women need not tolerate overt discrimination but lacked the stronger protections or "strict scrutiny" provided in matters involving race. In layman's terms, because of physi- cal differences and distinctions such as pregnancies, gender differences could have a mitigating effect in some legal issues while race could not. Lawyers like Vojdik wanted that standard changed. They wanted gender- blind equality. Only the Supreme Court had the power to grant it. From the start, Vojdik and her colleagues set their sights on Washington.

Bob Black, hearing their arguments, sadly shook his head. They missed the point, he thought to himself. The Citadel was nothing but an antiquated world that needed busting up. "It's an old-boy thing," he said. "It's a whole system." He thought it should be closed. He bucked that system the moment he took on Johnson's case. In Charleston, that stance would cost him dearly.

The Citadel, meanwhile, reacted with a surgical strike. Instead of fighting the veterans' case in court, college officials moved to make it moot. They abruptly terminated the program, throwing seventy-eight male veterans out of class. Theirs was a neat bit of logic. Since The Citadel no longer offered a daytime program for the education of any military veterans, there were no grounds for a lawsuit brought by female veterans.

"Their whole thing was like this," Johnson said. "If we can get rid of the guys, we can get rid of the girls. That's equal discrimination. So that's equality. The whole thing was just dead."

The veterans' case drew only scant notice off the campus grounds. But many members of The Citadel's faculty were disturbed by the administration's attitude. On September 10, 1992, The Citadel's Faculty Council held a special meeting to draft a resolution expressing their objections. Several professors argued that the administration's move to close the program altogether was an appalling affront to veterans across the country and thus an inappropriate stance for a military school to take. Saul J. Adelman, a physics professor, pushed for a harsh condemnation of the board. The closure of the veterans program, he said, was "unethical and without honor." In the end, softer language was adopted. It captured the faculty's dismay in the careful verbiage of scholars.

"Be it resolved," they agreed, "that the Faculty Council requests that The Citadel's Board of Visitors honor the moral contract a college assumes when it admits a student and allow current veteran students in good academic standing to continue in the day program until they complete their bachelor's degrees.

"Be it resolved," they added, "that the Faculty Council notes with concern the failure of the administration (1) to consult with the faculty prior to eliminating the veteran student day program, (2) to notify the faculty prior to announcing the elimination of the veteran student day program, and (3) to provide, as of the present time, the faculty with any formal notice with respect to the elimination of the veteran student day program."

Their real ire and sense of insult were held back, however, until the third and final resolution. "Be it resolved," they concluded with the hollow thunder of men and women finding themselves without a voice on their own campus, "that Faculty Council deplores and opposes the elimination of the veteran student day program and strongly urges the immediate restoration of the program."

No such thing happened. Not only were Pat Johnson, Liz Lacey and Angela Chapman out of luck. So were all the male veterans who had chosen to pursue their studies at The Citadel.

Caught up in a tide of righteous mutiny, the faculty soon took the matter further. This time, they challenged sacred sanctions against women. It was a bold move but taken shyly, under the cloak of anonymity. On October 22, 1992, the Faculty Council met again. Aware of the lawsuit being pressed by the Justice Department against VMI, The Citadel's teaching staff took up the matter of admitting women not only to the now-defunct veterans program but to the corps itself. And they took it on with an unusual, even subversive, zeal that stunned administrators ensconced in Bond Hall. Using a list obtained from the vice president's office, the Faculty Council distributed a secret ballot to 149 tenured and tenure-track professors. The ballot contained four questions regarding the possible integration of women into the corps of cadets. Question number three addressed the issue dead-on: "Do you favor the admission of women to the now all-male The Citadel Corps of Cadets?"

Their answers ran directly counter to the board's actions and the school's much professed bias for single-gender education. Of the faculty who responded, 82, or 64 percent, answered that the corps should welcome women in its ranks. Thirty-three said it should not. Looking over their shoulders at possible court action like that facing VMI, the survey writers next presented a narrower set of options predicated on the notion that the Justice Department just might win its point. That question allowed professors to either dodge the matter by supporting a move to make the college private; skirt it by establishing a separate corps for women; or embrace it by welcoming coeducation. In that case, the faculty proved even more emphatic. Seventeen suggested that the school go private. Eight said a separate corps for women held appeal. But 99 professors—77 percent of those responding—said women should march, too. In their minds, the time for change had come.

The survey caused a storm of protest in Bond Hall. Intentionally ignoring the wording of question three—*Do you favor the admission of women to the now all-male The Citadel Corps of Cadets?*—the school's public relations officer, Rick Mill (a 1978 Citadel graduate who served in the Marines), challenged the survey as "unscientific," not "valid," and filled with results of "no obvious merit." In a press release issued to startled reporters, Mill introduced the survey, then argued that it had no bearing on school policy or practice and should be utterly discounted. Moving fast to catch reporters off guard before the faculty reached out themselves, Mill included some of the survey's findings—but not all—while at the same time dismissing the survey's merit and impact. He closed with a point that could not have been more true. Results of the questionnaire, he assured, "should not be misconstrued as a precursor to future policy of The Citadel." Nothing was about to change.

Bud Watts, quoted in that same press release, was a bit more circumspect. He allowed that the school stood behind its faculty but added that their survey had contained a deeply misleading oversight. The faculty's "support and belief in single-gender education was not offered as an option," he chided, totally ignoring the thrust of question three. And yet, he argued, those teachers clearly spoke out every day. They voted with their feet. Citadel professors were "free to teach anywhere they so choose," he said. "Their presence here indicates their belief."

Outraged faculty members shot back. But theirs was a feeble retort from a popgun heard only inside their own walls. In a December meeting, Peter Mailloux, then serving as faculty chair, glumly reported that a private letter had been sent to the press office to protest "the bias and inaccuracy of the press release." It accomplished nothing. No correction was made. And no further action was taken by the faculty. Few professors had missed the president's soft warning shot. And though they had the benefits of tenure, they knew full well that their careers rested in large measure on the backing and support of administrators in Bond Hall. With the flood of students provided by the baby boom having petered out and the job market contracting, few of those scholars could hope for teaching jobs elsewhere. It would be five years before they spoke up again. The administration had outmaneuvered them by simply pulling rank.

Board members were hardly fazed by a minor insurrection of the SCUM. Instead, speaking in an early deposition taken on November 24, 1992, Jimmie Jones ("most political") described the board's decision to terminate the veterans day program as something made in an almost offhand way. The purpose of that maneuver, the board chairman explained, was purely preventative. By closing down the veterans program, board members hoped to thwart any future challenge to the all-male corps.

Did Jones remember whether there had been previous discussion about closing the veterans program down?

He shook his head and frowned. No. Not that he could recall. "We didn't realize that was a problem until that happened," he said vaguely.

"Until what happened?"

"Until we had the applications from three—two or three female veterans."

"Understood," the lawyer said. But the question, rather, was when the board first considered closing the program altogether.

"After the young ladies made application," Jones responded tartly. There was immediate concern that the women's appearance in the day program would open the door to letting women march in the corps. And no one on the board approved of that. The issue was as old as stone. They hardly needed to discuss it. "We felt that there was an effect there," Jones said calmly. And so they closed the program down. That's all there really was to it.

"That was the puff of smoke that indicated we were going to be in trench warfare," said Henry Weisburg. After that, agreed Vojdik, "we argued over every grain of sand."

Four hours by car to the north at about that same time, a magazine article concerning the hazing of four athletes at The Citadel was being passed around a classroom at Wren High School. Shannon Faulkner scanned it and found herself intrigued. It was not the hazing charges that caught her eye. It was that she wondered why a public school in her home state did not admit women. She did not think it fair.

By that time, in the state capital, some public officials agreed and found themselves less inclined than ever to indulge the whims of that old school. Fred R. Sheheen, the South Carolina commissioner of education, would publicly recommend that The Citadel finally change its ways. He felt the time had come for the institution to admit women and would later testify to that effect in court. Meanwhile, a publication issued by the state's Commission on Higher Education captured a new philosophy that embodied the thinking of an era that had begun in earnest in the 1960s. On the front page of a thick study titled "Choosing South Carolina's Future: A Plan for Higher Education in the 1990's," a call to action appeared beneath the state's elegant seal: "In the end," it said, "it is important to remember that we cannot become what we need to be by remaining what we are."

Nowhere were those words less welcome than in the gleaming, polished corridors then occupied by Mark Clark's boys.

The Engineer

VALORIE KAY VOJDIK was born on Christmas Eve, 1959, in a hospital outside Detroit. Hawaii and Alaska had earlier that year become our last two states. The building of a nation now was finished. But Vojdik would grow up in a culture deeply reconsidering some of its basic tenets. We peered into the looking glass and questioned what we had built. Among the catalysts was war. On July 8, 1959, six months before Vojdik was bundled up against a winter wind and taken home to Grand Blanc, Michigan, an affluent suburb of the industrial city of Flint, Major Dale R. Buis and Master Sergeant Chester N. Ovnard stood up to stretch during a movie break after evening mess in Bien-hoa, Vietnam. While a projectionist changed reels in that normally quiet provincial capital, the room was sprayed with automatic weapons fire. In the aftermath of that attack, two South Vietnamese guards, an eight-year-old Vietnamese boy, and Buis and Ovnard lay dead. Years later, those two American advisers would appear first and second among nearly 58,000 names listed on a slab of polished granite in Washington, D.C.

Vojdik was four when the Tonkin Gulf resolution was signed, the same year that Stanley Kubrick's *Dr. Strangelove* mocked a military mind-set gone berserk. She was five when Alice Herz, an eighty-two-year-old refugee from Nazi Germany, set herself on fire in Detroit to protest the war that followed. Let her death, Herz told stunned citizens in a note she left behind, serve as a signal of respect to Buddhists half a world away. Let her sacrifice, she wrote, serve "to protest against a great country trying to wipe out a small country for no reason." Vojdik had barely celebrated her eighth birthday (with a cake shaped like a Christmas tree and covered with green sprinkles) when the Tet offensive sent the nation into shock. She was eleven when the *New York Times* published the Pentagon Papers; twelve when Richard M. Nixon announced the intensification of bombing in North Vietnam; thirteen when the Watergate crisis peaked; fourteen when the House Judiciary Committee recommended that the president be impeached; and fifteen when the last Americans left Saigon in a chaotic evacuation captured on TV.

Against that backdrop of war and political turmoil, Vojdik learned early that nothing was quite fixed. In her world, wars could be won *or* lost, presidents honored *or* ousted and laws radically changed to suit the changing times. Those notions were as deeply knit in her as Tony Lackey's more absolute assumptions about honor, duty and patriotism were set in him. And like him, she would use those childhood lessons to shape her aspirations. The restless daughter of a lawyer (an Army veteran who had hated everything about his military service and came home badly wounded after the Battle of the Bulge), Vojdik set her sights on a legal career before entering her teens. By then, new laws and new enthusiasms were redefining America. The civil rights movement had peaked. With it came new calls for women's rights. For the most part, victories came after years of careful struggle and agonizing sacrifice. But some came about almost by chance. Indeed, one of the most potent weapons women's rights activists would lay claim to was created only as a joke, by men.

At the height of the civil rights movement, when feminism had yet to find its roar, a "Dixiecrat" from Virginia, Howard W. Smith, attempted a ruse that became law and made an awkward match of race and sex. In essence, it was a political potshot that exploded in Smith's face. In an effort to quash the Civil Rights Act then being considered on the House floor, Smith introduced what he considered the preposterous idea of gender to a subclause, Title VII, which was intended to ban racial discrimination in employment. The Virginia Democrat's thinking was that if the confounding matter of sex were to be included in the bill it would generate such wild furor in the House that the entire effort would fail. In a parody delivered to his colleagues on the floor, Smith postulated a world in which Title VII could "protect our spinster friends" by ensuring them what all American girls dreamed of: "their right to a nice husband and family." He drew appreciative titters from several of his peers. But the fact was, he miscalculated. Amusing as the matter may have been to Smith and his conservative colleagues, several liberals soon found themselves smiling for quite another reason. They saw in his amendment a wedge with which to push for new powers of their own.

Among the most enthusiastic backers of the Smith proposal was a representative from Vojdik's home state, Martha Griffiths, a Michigan Democrat. Griffiths and several other representatives pushed for Smith's new language. It was approved by a vote of 168 to 133. When the act itself came to a vote, the sides reversed. Most of Smith's cronies, as always intended, voted no. But supporters, including Griffiths, carried the day. Instead of crashing to defeat as Smith had predicted, the Civil Rights Act—complete with its new tagline about sex—went straight to the Senate. There, despite a seventy-five-day filibuster led by southern senators, the new legislation was gaveled into being and signed into law by President Lyndon Johnson. From that moment forward, matters of race and sex, so inherently different and yet so naturally aligned, were merged in law as well as history.

Two years later, in 1966, Griffiths would push Smith's little joke into the foreground once again. "What is this sickness," she demanded of fellow representatives when the Equal Employment and Opportunity Commission failed to enforce the sex-discrimination clause, "that causes an official to ridicule the law he swore to uphold and enforce? . . . What kind of mentality is it that can ignore the fact that women's wages are much less than men's, and that Negro women's wages are least of all?" From that frustration sprang new energy. The National Organization for Women was invented over lunch soon afterward when Betty Friedan, the author of one of Vojdik's favorite books, the 1963 treatise *The Feminine Mystique,* scribbled across a napkin that a new group was needed to "bring women into full participation in the mainstream of American society *NOW.*"

Within just several years, the notion of sex discrimination had worked its way so deeply into the thinking of the time that in 1967 Lyndon Johnson signed Executive Order 11375 declaring that no federal contractor or subcontractor could practice discrimination based on gender. In a breathtakingly short time old assumptions were reversed. Once again women's rights lagged behind those granted blacks. But here was an astounding leap. In the span of less than twenty years we had moved from President Truman's offhand (yet surely representative) remarks about "a lot of hooey" over equal rights to something extraordinarily close to the establishment of those new rights. To many women already in the workplace that shift brought needed remedy. By the 1970s, nearly half of all married women (and 90 percent of all women with college degrees) held jobs outside the home. Yet for most of those women, toiling in relative obscurity and breaking ancient barriers with every step, equal work did not mean either equal pay or equal opportunity. Even with new laws in place, they had to fight for what they got.

By the time Walt Clark and Tony Lackey returned to their alma mater, calls for women's rights and the slow easing of an established order based on sex had supplanted conversation about race. In 1978, more women than men would show up at America's colleges as freshmen for the first time. Higher education was changing, too. In that decade, the number of women receiving law degrees jumped from 5.4 percent to 28.5 percent. The number of women holding Ph.D.'s doubled; and medical doctorates nearly tripled from 8 percent to 23 percent. At The Citadel, hostility to such changes was extreme and attacks on the leaders of the movement deeply personal. Above the *Brigadier's* 1973 editorial against the ERA was a cartoon showing a heavyset woman in pants and a tight-fitting T-shirt, her eyes obscured by aviator sunglasses, a cigarette dangling from her thick-lipped mouth, smoke curling in her dark, kinky hair as she held a sign demanding: "We Want Freedom N.O.W." (An impish figure in the corner quipped: "And they call *us* pigs?")

Some women meanwhile made women's rights the centerpiece not of political activism on the streets but of impressive new careers. Among them was Ruth Bader Ginsburg. By that time, the small, bespectacled attorney—born in Brooklyn in 1933 and a member of the Harvard Law School class of 1958 (she earned her J.D. at Columbia Law School in 1959)—a determined scrapper with jet black hair and equally unambiguous opinions, was on her way to fame and influence. Hers was an elegant rise within the ranks of the establishment. In time, through a combination of luck, pluck, acute political instincts and intelligence, she would be catapulted to the highest court in America, propelled, at least in part, by the very shifts she helped create.

In 1971, Professor Ginsburg, then a member of the staff at Rutgers University School of Law, appeared before the Supreme Court to argue against a law that gave automatic preference to males over females in disputes involving the administration of estates. She won. The Idaho law was overturned. In 1973, she was back before the Supreme Court again, this time arguing that Air Force Lieutenant Sharron Frontiero should be allowed the same family benefits as those afforded men of her same rank, whether or not her spouse was financially dependent. Again, the court ruled in her favor. By then, matters of sex discrimination were Ginsburg's specialty. In addition to teaching and other work, she coauthored a book on sex-based discrimination and founded the Women's Rights

Project, a specialized legal arm of the ACLU that would later bring Isabelle Katz Pinzler and Sara L. Mandelbaum to Shannon Faulkner's defense.

Val Vojdik, in her childhood, was mostly ignorant of those great waves of change, and certainly of their potential to shape her own life and career. Instead, she grew up thinking that the law had always granted women equal rights. To her, that was an absolute. She never found the need to question it. And surely at the age of twelve she had more compelling preoccupations. Let the nuances of history find her later; in 1972, she set herself to learning basics. With a book from the public library she taught herself to type by pounding her fingers endlessly against a mock-up keyboard made of paper. In Catholic schools, she learned the rudimentaries of debate. At her father's knee, she learned ambition. When she daydreamed of life ahead and mused aloud that she might like to be a nurse, her father barked back: "Doctor." His advice was short and simple. Aim high, he told Val and her younger sister, Catherine. "Don't waste time." Val did not, even as a child.

By the age of twelve, supported by her mother, pushed by her father, Vojdik often pounded out legal briefs on a clunky office typewriter and handled basic correspondence at her father's firm. Happily ensconced in the mysterious world of adults, there she answered telephone calls, consumed legal arcana, ran errands and learned the give and take of case law. She wove the law into her language and then that language deep into her life. She would be a consummate lawyer in time, thrilled by conflict, flushed in victory, unremorseful toward her foes. But she had another passion, too. *Ms.* magazine appeared on newsstands in 1972. A voracious reader, Vojdik found herself entranced with the notion that a woman might mold a whole identity based only on her brain. For her, the allure held a particularly personal appeal. Diagnosed with scoliosis at the age of eight, she spent much of her childhood locked inside a metal brace. The device, necessary to counteract the debilitating effects of a disease better known for its crippling, slow "curvature of the spine," kept her separate from the rush and tumble of her friends. She felt stigmatized and ugly. Her brain was her best hope, and she explored its potential with both energy and pleasure. In the tenth grade she proudly embroidered "MS" in green across a peach-colored T-shirt. A geeky teenager then, "just, oh so typically '70s," she tromped around in nerdy glasses, tight jeans and a thin smile. Later she would cringe when she looked at those old yearbooks. But for the moment it was bliss. "There was this whole popular culture thing," she said in Charleston after court one day. "There was that Helen Reddy thing, 'I am woman. . . . Hear me roar!' God, I loved it."

The women's movement crested as Vojdik entered adolescence. In 1972, the Equal Rights Amendment passed the Senate by a vote of eighty-four to eight. Almost immediately it was caught up in emotional debates about subjecting women to the draft. Slowly, it would die a tick-tock death. In 1982, the ERA's window for approval closed while the bill still lacked sufficient state backing to become law. Battles in the interim had showed a devastating fault line that transcended gender and obscured even the alarm over potential military requirements. Though it was always easy for facile critics to dismiss the ERA as some vast battle of the sexes, the fact was that many women balked—not at the thought of military duty, really, but at the more basic notion of blurring sex distinctions and tipping a balance of power many women had already quite comfortably built their lives around.

Arguments in the Vojdik household followed familiar lines. Val argued hotly with her mother and dubbed her "pre-evolved." Even in that liberal Catholic family the gap of generations took some time to bridge. But Val and Mary Ann Vojdik were hardly alone in that long struggle. By 1982, it was all too clear that some of the most bitter and effective critics of the ERA included older women who defined themselves through their relationships to men and children and had no wish to change that old equation. Accustomed to finding both status and fulfillment as "loyal wives" and "good mothers," many women were insulted to think they might now have to doubt either the basic value of their contributions and commitments or come up with a new set of goals and aspirations altogether. As Val described it, her mother gravitated to new imperatives "gradually," under Val's careful and persistent prodding. "It was clear to see why," Vojdik said almost apologetically. "She grew up in the 1950s. I mean, my mother was like queen of the sock hop. She was the homecoming queen. She was really smart, but . . ." Vojdik waved a hand for lack of words, then shook her head with fresh dismay. "Then again, *her* mother was in that generation of women that simply got screwed."

Detractors of the Equal Rights Amendment capitalized on such discomfort and raised the specter of an end to social cohesion and family primacy, two things few women were willing to easily let go. Debate soon centered not on distribution of power or such fundamental issues as equal pay and job opportunity, but on a woman's "proper" role in the social hierarchy, suggesting that Mom and apple pie would be forever torn asunder. The National Committee to Stop the ERA, headed by Phyllis Schlafly, flatly encouraged women to resist this latest drift of social tinkering. It was folly and dangerous, Schlafly warned, to destroy respect for "the American woman as a wife and mother . . . [and] the family as the basic unit of society." Not above a bit of coy campaigning, members of the Schlafly group were sent back to the kitchen and told to set up "jam brigades." Members of the group sent jars of homemade jelly to state legislators along with notes that sweetly pleaded: "Preserve us from a congressional jam. Vote against the ERA sham." Of course then, as now, it was primarily men who served on state legislatures and opened all those jam jars. Many of them needed no further prodding to vote no.

In many military families, the rise of the women's rights movement came with an uncomfortable history and fell with a particularly unpleasant force. The two were longtime enemies. Accustomed to strict hierarchies at work, and often quite comfortable duplicating them at home (sometimes with an almost eerie fidelity to military forms and ranking), many soldiers not only considered their unassailable primacy as head of household suddenly under attack, but felt that their professional purpose was derided, too. Historically, the women's movement had always hit them where they worked. In 1915, in the last stretch of their own long fight for women's suffrage, three thousand women met in Washington to form the Women's Peace Party. In 1924, the Women's Peace Union launched a campaign to end all war. During a parade in sleepy Washington, D.C., that year, Peace Union members wearing long skirts and flowing dresses carried stenciled banners urging America to: "Make War Illegal. Abolish the Army and Navy." Irritating as that protest may have been, a lot of military officers found that sentiment almost quaint. Those women posed no real threat. Given the right to vote just four years before, they had neither influence nor clout in halls of power. Indeed, some military men argued then that it was all quite natural for women to speak out for peace; since women were biologically designed for procreation, they naturally carried a strain of pacifism that men could ill afford.

Such arguments were considerably more complex by the time Vojdik passed her bar exam. Women were soldiers, too, by then, and moving ever upward in the ranks. Vojdik understood the impulse. She chafed at anything that blocked her way and used that instinct as her guide. When the veterans' case fell on her desk, she felt the same disgust that had driven Pat Johnson to take action. Soon, the case consumed her. If Shearman & Sterling would be the engine, she would be the engineer. "As a female litigator in one of the largest law firms in the world . . . the notion that women couldn't perform under stress, it was really laughable . . . it definitely made me want to take the case." With that passion fueling her, she dominated Shannon's team from the start. And the more she learned about The Citadel and the more she fought with its lawyers in court, the more she matched the school's outrage and vigilance with equal measures of her own. "I think the best thing that could happen to those men is that they admit women," she sputtered angrily one day. "To keep women out, at that age, where it plays up to this hyper-masculine image is inherently degrading to women. They are defined as the *other*. . . . The bottom line is that . . . it's not as good, what we're doing. The whole definition is that [women are] the *other* and therefore different, and therefore worse. That's the whole problem." Charleston was part of the problem too, she supposed. She came to think of it as a charming but peculiar backwater.

Vojdik came from a different place. Leaving in a rush, squeezing into taxis and fighting the traffic to La Guardia Airport, she clambered onto roaring jets. Time and again she left New York, cutting it close, jamming responsibilities together in a too-tight schedule full of deadlines. In a moment, the dark valleys of Manhattan fell away. She rose into the skies and watched the blue Atlantic pass below. It was a short flight. She usually worked through most of it. Then there was a bump. She clicked open her seat buckle and stepped into the slam of heat that lay between the cockpit and the cooled-down grayness of Charleston's new airport. It was a madcap commute that thrust her into a different world. The voyage jarred her every time. She might as well have gotten out her passport; the transition was that sharp.

From the first step outside, everything was green. Vojdik loved that. There were palmettos in the parking lot and always the moist tang of sea. She gathered her belongings and set out, a portable telephone tucked inside her briefcase, a mass of files in her arms. Spinning down white highways under the arch of towering trees, she approached Charleston's pastel harmonies, the famous shoreline and grand steeples, thinking only of the case. Even so, the city administered a slight shock every time. It stopped her heart. She came to love it. But she never felt at home. Too deep patterns of behavior made her queasy. And antiquated courtesies nearly stopped her in her tracks. One afternoon an older man turned and tipped his hat. Vojdik laughed about it later. No man had ever tipped his hat to her before. She was flustered and amused and responded with a casual greeting. But he just hurried off. "He looked so distressed," Val said, and then pitched back and laughed. "Wow! Was I supposed to smile sweetly and say nothing? I don't know. I think it was a bowler hat. I guess I broke some rule." She sighed and scratched her knee. She found it quaint and charming. But as she strode to her hotel, one question kept repeating: "Did I say the right thing back?" The appeal and the oppressiveness could mingle in a second. It set her nerves on edge.

Masculine All the Way Through . . .

As the veterans' case took shape, Shannon Faulkner was busy starting her senior year at Wren High School. She had yet to look ahead. Restless on the cusp of life, a tomboy wedged between childhood and a future that led her no place certain, she whirled from one thing to another, yet let her college applications slide. Her mother fretted constantly. "I nagged and nagged," said Sandy. Football season started. Then basketball began. In Powdersville, the leaves turned gold, then fell. Winter settled down like smoke. Sandy watched the weeks slip by. Her daughter would not budge. The world could wait. Shannon was confident that way, or too proud to reveal her insecurities. From time to time, she stopped in at The Coffee Pot and loudly called hello. Albert perked up every time. She wandered in the local mall and played touch football with her friends, oscillating between womanhood and all the wildness of youth. Meanwhile, stacks of papers sat at home. "I just went crazy," said Sandy. Shannon had ambition, but no plan.

On November 9, 1992, two days after she took her SATs and shortly after reading a *Sports Illustrated* article about the Military College of South Carolina, Shannon took a pen and scribbled out a simple application for The Citadel. She did nothing with it for two months. Then one day she burst into her mother's classroom with a pile of papers and a mischievous expression. Sandy turned from her students with an apology, then gave her younger child the sternest look that she could summon. Shannon stared back with a defiant grin and held out four completed applications. While Sandy rifled around for her checkbook, her daughter stood aside with her arms folded, waiting for her mother to spin her future forward.

Sandy had four checks to write. The last one stopped her with a thump. She peered into her daughter's face. But Shannon stood before her full of impish challenge. Sandy could almost hear her heart. That is one willful girl, Sandy thought to herself with a deep sigh. And smart. Her class was getting restless, and Sandy was boxed in. This was no place for her to make a scene. As a parent, she almost had to laugh. What a smooth maneuver, she conceded with grudging admiration: "classic Shannon." Sandy tried to look displeased as she signed that final check. But Shannon merely smiled. With all four checks in hand, she chirped, "Thanks, Mom," and practically ran out of that room.

Martha Dolge, Shannon's guidance counselor, sat down to work on Shannon's transcripts on January 11, 1993. At Shannon's request, she used a bottle of Wite-Out to remove all references to gender that appeared on Shannon's transcripts. Then she finished her own appraisal on The Citadel's student description form, noting that Shannon Richey Faulkner, born the twentieth day of January, 1975, in Greenville, South Carolina, now a resident of Anderson County, South Carolina, a United Methodist by religion and white by race, ranked fortieth in a senior class of 234 with a grade point average of 3.35. Eight questions followed. Dolge gave Shannon high marks on every one. The student "always accepts fully" personal responsibility, she noted. Other checkmarks confirmed that the applicant was "always involved, often initiated" class discussions; had "considerable" aptitude for independent study; possessed a critical and questioning attitude and was "always considerate of others." She ranked "very high" in involvement in all classroom activities, Dolge added, and was "exceptionally consistent" in her school performance. A personal note was scrawled across the bottom in lieu of a longer letter of recommendation.

"Shannon has been a valuable part of our student body during all four years of high school," her guidance counselor wrote, carefully avoiding any pronouns. "I recommend Shannon to you." She signed the form, dated the papers and sent them on their way. But before she finished, she looked right into Shannon's eyes. Then she asked the same question that had first crossed Sandy's mind.

"Honey, are you sure you want to do this?"

Shannon nodded. She was sure.

Dolge shrugged and signed her name. "It was clear to me," she said later with a defensiveness born of troubled times, "that she had the right to submit the application without gender. Because of Title IX. Because of the Constitution."

Privately, Dolge was just a little proud of Shannon's bold initiative. Most students at Wren High School never gave a thought to politics. The Miss Wrenicycle contest got more attention every year. Scores of girls competed. They practiced makeup styles and graceful walks and had their hair sprayed stiff to hold elaborate swirls. Onstage, they swished about in evening gowns and smiled coy seductions. Miss South Carolina was a Wren High School girl herself around that time. "That sort of thing is important," Dolge had to say. Politics was harder. School board policies forbade teachers from discussing religion, birth control or abortion in class. State laws barred discussion of homosexuality. More implicit constraints kept other issues out of reach as well. Controversy was unwelcome, and to Dolge's mind, more or less unknown. "I'm not sure that in the South at this particular time [students] have strong political views about anything," she sighed. Everybody tried to hold their tongue. But the guidance counselor found herself put off by all that silence. The product of a small mill town herself, Dolge came of age in the 1960s and tore through Winthrop College in three years. She loved the sense of freedom she felt then and the cauldron of ideas. Thirty years later, she missed it, and Shannon's whisper of revolt caught her sharply in the heart. She was right, Dolge thought to herself, painting over Shannon's transcript. Didn't the Constitution allow for equal rights?

Later, Wren's principal made sure that no one else would soon repeat that Wite-Out ruse. With the issue in the headlines and the school's behavior under question, colleagues gently turned away. The principal issued a press release to say that the counselor was disciplined. In fact, said Dolge, all he did was say she should have asked him first. Yet she could feel the shift. Some colleagues cooled when she came by. "There were times when I thought, Oh my God! What have I done? I had worked in education twenty years or more and considered myself a professional and to suddenly have the people I worked with say I had been disciplined. I lost sleep over it. All those men at The Citadel said we had altered a transcript and whatnot, and they went on and on and on . . . and suddenly it sounded like I was a criminal! I just don't think I was prepared for how strong the feelings were."

Nor did she have any idea that a loophole lay hidden deep in the language used in Title IX. Under the law, The Citadel was perfectly within its rights to turn down Shannon simply on the grounds of sex. But it did not. Instead, The Citadel sent a letter of acceptance. Someone in the admissions office simply mistook her for a boy.

Not ten days after the application arrived in Charleston, Wallace I. West Jr., The Citadel's director of admissions, dictated an acceptance letter to Mr. Shannon Richey Faulkner. It was mailed on January 22, 1993, two days after Shannon turned eighteen and not two weeks after Martha Dolge had dried her Wite-Out with a gentle blow of air. Shannon had four applications pending. She was nervous and impatient and checked the mailbox every day. Though all four schools would accept her in due time, The Citadel's approval came through first. Early one afternoon, once the postman's Jeep had driven by, Shannon skipped up the driveway and flipped through all the mail. In it, there was a letter from Charleston. She tore it open, breathing hard. Then she let out a resounding whoop. Sandy looked up the driveway and saw her daughter running. But Shannon's mother had an awful premonition on that day.

"She came flying down the driveway, running, jumping, kind of leaping in the air," Sandy said later, thinking back. "She kept shouting, 'I'm in! I'm in!' I went and hugged her and asked, 'Which one?'" Shannon said, "The Citadel," and Sandy just went quiet. She believed her daughter had a right to go. Ed and Sandy paid their taxes. It was a public school. Like Shannon, they thought it only fair. Still, Sandy felt her stomach clutch. "Right then, I knew that if she went, she was going to get hurt."

While Shannon read the letter through, her mother made an effort to seem pleased. "Dear Mr. Faulkner," Shannon said, half laughing. "It is my pleasure to inform you that the Fourth Class Admissions Advisory Committee of The Citadel has given you provisional acceptance for admission." Sandy struggled to produce a smile. "To gain full acceptance and be permitted to matriculate as a freshman in August of 1993, you must accomplish the following. . . ." Shannon was jumping from foot to foot. She didn't necessarily intend to go to The Citadel. She just wanted to make a point. She wanted to prove to herself and everybody else that—boy *or* girl—she was good enough to march. The letter proved it. And it was the first to confirm that she qualified for college life. Several bureaucratic requirements were carefully spelled out. But the most important was so ancient that it was never ever mentioned. To join the corps of cadets, as that letter invited her to do, Shannon had to be a boy. Congress itself said so.

News of Shannon's ploy drifted south over the telephone. According to Jimmie Jones, the board chairman, it was Jamie Clark, a junior at The Citadel, who first sounded an alarm. Jamie was the son of Shannon's assistant principal at Wren. He heard from his father, Larry Clark Sr., that a mix-up had occurred. It didn't sit too well with him so he called Jim Boyd, a Citadel friend whose father then served on the board. They had a problem, Jamie announced. There was another call. This Shannon Faulkner is a girl, Jim Boyd informed his dad. David Boyd took the news glumly. Soon he called Jones and Jones called West to let the director of admissions know that he made a mistake. Then West wrote a second letter, and they all thought they were done with it. From time to time a kid would play a prank like that. "I thought it was a dare," Jones recalled. If he remembered right, there even was a Shannon Faulkner on the football team one year. "It sounded masculine all the way through."

On Wednesday, February 10, West wrote to Ms. Faulkner to tell her she was out. Shannon scanned it quickly: "The Citadel day program is a single-gender college program for males under the provisions of Title IX and the Federal Education Act of 1972," West wrote, carefully citing the legal protections of the school. He refunded her application fee, voided her acceptance letter, rejected her application and withdrew the school's invitation to visit the campus as a provisionally accepted member of the corps. Enclosed with that letter was a second one, addressed to Mrs. Faulkner, notifying Sandy that her daughter was no longer welcome.

Yet more than landscapes had been changing in that state. For some, the mood had changed as well. And the more that Shannon thought about it, the angrier she grew. Like Val Vojdik, she was of a generation that could hardly imagine a time when women were not equal. Nor could she conceive of any reason why they should not be. To her way of thinking, The Citadel was not a brave protector of tradition at all, but something profoundly *un*-American. It opposed one of the nation's most essential precepts, Shannon thought, the basic rule of equal rights that guided true democracy. And so she set a countervailing force in motion.

Suzanne Coe never read the newspapers much. Her life was wholly consumed by work. Little outside it penetrated. She knew nothing of Pat Johnson or of the veterans program and very little about The Citadel. While a student at Converse College, a private, all-female college in Spartanburg, South Carolina, she had considered The Citadel as a "brother school," but hardly stopped to think about it more. Nevertheless, when Shannon laid out her complaints, the twice-divorced, twenty-eight-year-old lawyer was instantly intrigued. Awkward causes were her specialty. She thrived in their chaotic atmosphere. "Well, you better come on in," she said, "and bring your letters with you." Shannon showed up wearing sweatpants and snapping at a piece of gum. Coe liked her instantly and found herself pulled in. As she read through the correspondence, she nodded to herself. "Once I saw that they accepted her, I was like: 'Wow! Somebody's job is going to roll!'" She knew they had a case.

That afternoon, when it came time to sign a contract establishing that Coe's small Greenville firm would act on Shannon's behalf, the long-haired lawyer pushed the paperwork toward Shannon's mother. But Shannon stopped her with a question.

"How old do you have to be to sign a contract in this state?" the high school senior asked.

"Eighteen," came the reply.

"Well, I'm eighteen," Shannon said. She signed the papers herself. It was her case from the start, and she would run it.

For Coe, that kind of litigation was a joy. Straight out of law school she had started piling up high-profile cases. "I kind of went on a rampage and put a lot of people in jail and pretty much tried to clean up the protester scene in Greenville, which was a hotbed of antiabortion activity," she said with mischievous pride. Coe made powerful enemies that way. She also stirred the ire of many Bible-toting Baptists. "You get these threats—usually illegible—by some crazed person, and they mention God about sixteen times," she said irritably. "But if Jesus was here I don't think he'd buy that at all."

Liberation theology, with its celebration of the human spirit and rejection of oppression in all forms, best captured the young lawyer's thinking. She had studied it at Converse College and called the class the most important of her student years. In fact, it spoke to her at a profoundly personal level. For two years, from the age of sixteen to eighteen, while other students were in high school, Coe was locked inside a Florida drug rehabilitation program that she likened to a Korean prison camp. Bored at school, she had turned to marijuana for recreation. The program was intended to stop a cycle of dependence. Parents saw in it a way to help their children. Judges agreed, and gave some troubled youths a choice between participating in the program or going to jail. In Coe's case, her parents signed her in. Once there, she signed her own agreement, one that she described as elicited under pressure. After that, she said, she was deprived of basic freedoms and monitored both day and night. "Think of a smart kid locked up in a place like that," she said. "They scream at you all day long and say you aren't worth shit. . . . I was, like, where's my rights? Read me my rights. I've got a right to a trial. I've got a right to a hearing. Where's my lawyer? But, you're in lockup. You're completely in lockup. . . . You can't see your parents. You aren't allowed a phone call. You are not allowed to go to school. . . . I was, like, do they not know that there are [all these] kids here? And if they don't, then why in the hell did they let Nancy Reagan come here crying crocodile tears about brave children?" Later, struggling against charges of human rights abuses, the institution closed its doors. "People stood up," said Coe. "That was all it took."

From that time forward, Coe set her sights on a career in law. Two years inside the drug rehab program had utterly transformed her. By the age of eighteen she had changed from a reckless high school student with no compass into a determined advocate for the oppressed. Friends in Greenville knew nothing of those years. She kept them hidden. Yet they guided her completely. "I think it's one reason why I'm so paranoid, so antsy now. I always was hyper in the first place; but that put me more on edge. I think of it as kind of like the ACLU motto that vigilance is your eternal duty. That's ingrained in me. Everyone has a right to one life. You don't know if you get to come back, and you really don't know if there's a heaven. And there's a lot of things that can go wrong in this life that people can do to you." Coe found strength in that fierce battle of wills. She also found direction. "I'm almost the only liberal lawyer in this town," she said in a staccato rush. "I take on the stuff nobody else will touch. I represent abortion clinics. I represent bikers. I represent strip clubs." She paused, then shrugged. "I represent Shannon. I am out there on the fringe. I have a lot of conservative friends; but they say, 'Oh, well, that's just Suzanne.' . . . To me, it's a question of who's going to dare defy the powerful. . . . All of a sudden I realize, it's like life's war. Unless you are willing to stand up to these people, they will walk all over you."

With Shannon now in tow, she called the first press conference. Jimmie Jones learned about it with disgust. He had never liked that long-haired lawyer much. Though she had hardly been in practice more than a year, she managed always to find some issue that caught him in the craw. He knew just who his adversary was. Jones, an affluent Greenville real estate developer, had seen her staring into the camera lens, speaking out on this or that. He watched her with contempt. As far as The Citadel's board chairman was concerned, that young lawyer had no morals. "If a truck full of pigs was in an accident," Jones reflected bitterly, "then Suzanne would represent the pigs."

At first, Shannon loved the ruckus. "My parents pay their taxes," she said, cool and articulate every time the cameras rolled. "The law just isn't right."

Coe stood beside her, smiling with approval. "One gender should not have to fund its own exclusion," she agreed. "And that, in South Carolina, is exactly what we do."

When the two women first talked, it almost sounded easy. But Shannon's parents and grandparents expressed some reservations. Evelyn Richey considered herself a lady and did not think it seemly for her granddaughter to take The Citadel on. Sandy and Ed worried what forces that school would unleash. It had a reputation. Almost no one dared to cross it. Shannon's older brother, Todd, had reservations, too. If Shannon filed suit, he knew the school would fight. Again and again, Shannon made her case. In the end, even Evelyn could not disagree. "If you want something, go for it. In a nutshell, that's how it's always been with us." And so the family drew together. If Shannon chose to push, they would close in right behind her, adding whatever weight they could.

Soon, more lawyers came tumbling through the door. One week after Wally West wrote to Shannon saying that she could never march, Steven J. Bates, the executive director of the American Civil Liberties Union Foundation of South Carolina, wrote urging her to use the ACLU's resources. Shannon's public challenge was a "heroic endeavor," he cheered enthusiastically. "Your courage in taking on such a large and entrenched institution has my highest respect and admiration." Yet he was "curious," he had to admit, as to why Shannon had not sought out his organization for help. The ACLU's involvement in the veterans' case and its participation in the legal challenge against VMI were matters of public record. Because of those two lawsuits, the ACLU had a vast amount of research material at hand and broad expertise in matters of that kind. He offered all of it to Shannon, free of charge.

Before long, Suzanne Coe was on her way to Charleston to introduce herself around. There, she found Bob Black in his cramped office: "One room. Sort of cluttered. On Broad Street. . . . Bunch of files." Val Vojdik was there to introduce herself as well. But when they settled down to business, Coe was stunned to grasp the scope of it. "All of a sudden, I realized how much money had already been spent and how many people were involved. . . . It was huge. Val knew all the experts. She had been in it more than a year . . . and here she was a member of a firm with, like, seven hundred lawyers." By then, a complex machine was working at full power. At first, Coe was naive enough to think that it would work for her. "I'm stupid about things," she laughed. "I walk right into them. . . . I'm spouting off ideas because I just got this case. . . . At first I actually thought I'd be lead counsel. I was a young attorney. Not even two years at it. And I was under the impression that we could resolve it fairly quickly. Of course, that wasn't true." Once she realized that, she took her ego out of it and merely did what she could do. Yet even in a minor role, she found the case took all her time.

From the start, Vojdik was anxious to move Shannon front and center. She knew the girl would be their hook. With the veterans' case in limbo, she felt uncharacteristically insecure. She wanted headlines and swashbuckling and something clean and clear. But the veterans' case was dissolving in an unappealing tangle of arcana. Even if they won it, the corps would stay all-male. Vojdik craved someone young and passionate to stand up to that Goliath. She wanted Judge Houck to weigh not an abstract issue but the individual fate of one girl who claimed that she was unfairly disadvantaged in her own home state. Like it or not, human emotions had a central place in court. And Shannon made a perfect plaintiff. Direct yet polite, feminine but tough, she was the answer to Vojdik's prayers. Instead of lashing out obliquely, the crowd of lawyers could strike directly at the institution's heart. Shannon would be their battering ram. Almost overnight, Vojdik's interest in the veterans ebbed. (Pat Johnson felt it instantly.) It was the corps Val wanted to transform, and all it represented. Back in her Catholic high school, deeply engrossed in liberation theology herself, she hardly could have imagined a case better suited to her temperament.

Once Shannon was drawn in, the energy exploded. Vojdik would lead. Shannon would display her strengths. Stubbornness was one of them. Shannon did not easily give ground but instead stood resiliently in place and quoted from the Constitution. "Shannon was great," Suzanne Coe said warmly. "She was full of ambition and energy and vigor. At the time she was sort of lean and mean and ready to go." In Charleston, emotions quickly overflowed. Shannon's lawyers loved it. You can make history, they cheered. They left no room for easy exits. And they paid all the bills.

On March 2, 1993, civil action number 29304882 was filed in the United States District Court's Charleston division. In that complaint, Shannon Richey Faulkner sued Wally West, Bud Watts, Jimmie Jones, Jim Bradin and the rest of the Board of Visitors. The complaint argued that Shannon was wrongfully excluded from a public school. She wanted to march, those lawyers said. The names of eight attorneys appeared on that complaint on her behalf. Suzanne Coe and Stephen Henry were listed as Shannon's Greenville representatives. Bob Black provided a Charleston link. Shearman & Sterling, from its six hundred lawyers, added Vojdik, Henry Weisburg and Jonathan Greenblatt (along with teams of ambitious assistants out of sight). Isabelle Katz Pinzler and Sara L. Mandelbaum identified themselves only by their address in New York: 132 West Forty-third Street. What they did not spell out was that the building, a small and slightly scruffy midtown low-rise near the theater district, served as the headquarters of the Women's Rights Project at the ACLU, Ruth Ginsburg's onetime home. For now, that detail was intentionally obscured. In South Carolina, some things were better left unsaid. A lot of folks in Greenville thought that group was made up of communists; and even Shannon was not completely comfortable about that link.

Pat Johnson watched with pleasure as her revolution grew. She adored taking The Citadel on. "I was like a dog biting into the jugular, and I wouldn't stop biting until I was told I killed it, it's dead, and I had to be told that," she said. "But all along it occurred to me that I was using my own money to fight myself—my tax dollars were being used against me." Almost as painful was the fact that neither her passion nor her fierce persistence proved enough to keep her in that mix. Dozens of lawyers came and went—always saying Shannon's name. In huddles and in pairs, they moved like harried commuters through the complex alleys of the case. A strict hierarchy held. Though Mandelbaum from the ACLU and Sandy Beber of the Justice Department would track the litigation through its every move, Vojdik always seemed the one on point. Coe kept her hand in but tried to juggle other work. "I have to make money," she apologized. "I can't sit there and fool with this all the time." Bob Black was less pragmatic. Instead of disengaging—or even trying to—he followed every twist and turn like a man hurtling downward on a luge.

His passions were too complex and his distaste for The Citadel too deep to allow him room for much other work. The case won him local fame, but not a long list of new clients. Outspent and outgunned from day one, he never served as a major strategist and was forever overshadowed by New York.

Geography was part of it. For Black, it served as both a liability and an asset. His office in Charleston kept him in the litigation from start to finish, but it also meant that he was worlds away from its busy New York nerve center. The real work of *Faulkner v. Jones et al.* was tucked down a back hallway somewhere high above East Fifty-third Street, seven hundred miles to the north. There, in a cramped and windowless storage space on the thirty-first floor of a high-rise on Lexington Avenue, a team of overworked lawyers drove the case flat out on all its cylinders. Inside their nondescript back room, an ever-shifting crew made up of lawyers, assistants, paralegals, secretaries and interns worked incessantly, swilling coffee and writing briefs in an airless enclosure dominated by a towering bookshelf so laden with files that it occasionally tipped forward to spill its contents out into the room. The only decoration was a Lichtenstein print of yellow lemons that hung crooked and ignored upon one wall. Otherwise, the lights were harsh, the rug stained, the table plain and the chairs mostly purloined from nearby offices. In that odd encampment, morning, noon and often far into the night, a high-wattage band made up of mostly women pored earnestly over endless paperwork, filling trash cans through the day with crumpled yellow legal paper, scattered notes, pink message slips, soiled paper plates and teetering cups of coffee thrown aside when they turned cold.

Visitors to Shearman & Sterling got no glimpse of that strange war room. While Vojdik and her team struggled with heavy books and twisting legal theory under their fluorescent lights, clients and Lycra-clad messenger boys spilled out into the main foyer. After soaring skyward on a hushed express elevator, those visitors moved shyly, adjusting to a quiet world of expensive fabrics, muted lighting, towering flower arrangements, polished marble and bright brass. The firm's name was etched in stone along one wall. That ancient rock seemed out of place in those surroundings, swamped by modern sheets of steel and glass, but eye-catching, as though communicating the subliminal message that the firm's founding in 1873 was only the beginning of an enterprise that would itself endure. To the left and right, soft carpeting connected hall-ways to office spaces and conference rooms decorated in ways intended to both soothe and subtly impress. All day long the elevators glided, then settled to a cushioned stop. When their gleaming doors slid open, some passengers hurried off and disappeared down silent hallways. Others looked about, dazed and groping for their bearings. For all of them, a certain bland solemnity prevailed. Normally rowdy bike boys with neon helmets and long dreadlocks instinctively lowered their voices in that hall, as though the messages they carried might be felt around the world. Sometimes, indeed, they were.

Inside Shearman & Sterling's maze of offices, soft conversations bubbled here and there. Top-ranking lawyers like Henry Weisburg commanded rooftop views. When the lawyers took their seats around their polished, room-length conference table, they settled high above a world played out in miniature. Far below, jostling pedestrians, harried tourists, honking taxicabs and idling limousines made up a silent show. In their own cool and quiet world, Shearman & Sterling's lawyers could ignore it if they chose. Most did. They were far more focused on each other, vying for laughter and for points while sharing their thoughts beneath the portraits of such modern giants as Pablo Casals, Henry Moore, Winston Churchill, Muhammad Ali, Albert Einstein, Georgia O'Keeffe and Pablo Picasso. Humility was not their style.

To most of the firm's partners, the Faulkner case was just a footnote in a much vaster practice that more often dealt with foreign nations, international negotiations and billion-dollar deals. Yet even relegated to its storage space and fueled with the passions and talents of junior lawyers and their young assistants, the Faulkner litigation made headlines regularly and brought Shearman & Sterling's name into the public eye. Partners and accountants loosely estimated that what the firm invested in Charleston was easily reclaimed through free publicity. And in time, there was a chance that all that effort would be paid off in cash as well. If Shannon won her case, the state of South Carolina would be billed not only for much of The Citadel's fight but for all of Shannon's legal services as well. The tally was considerable. It would rise to more than $6 million before the fight was done. Then that would be contested, too.

Toiling far to the south, holed up in his one-room office, Bob Black was like a pilot fish separated from his whale. But more than distance undercut his role. He lacked the clout, the money and the staff to do the job. He was one man, alone. "My war is with my country, with my people," he said darkly. That was how it started. Judge Houck called him the spark that lit the flame. Black was proud of that. For a long time, he kept a pink memo from Pat Johnson's first phone call folded neatly in his wallet. Until the end, he attended every court session and did what work he could. But one thing bothered him throughout. He was the only real southerner on Shannon's side. Suzanne Coe, though she grew up in Florida, came from solid Massachusetts stock. Vojdik grew up in Michigan. Weisburg came from Brooklyn. So did Sara Mandelbaum. Everyone else was from some other place. Black resented the imbalance. To him, the realities of the South, and of The Citadel especially, were something you had to carry in your bones to comprehend.

Black Magic

T WO MONTHS AFTER Shannon's complaint was filed, she sat down to her first deposition. Suzanne Coe, Bob Black and Val Vojdik flanked her, facing Dawes Cooke across the table. To Shannon, Cooke seemed kind, if rather condescending. "He talked down to me," she said years later, "treating me like the naive little girl they all thought I was . . . [not] the stubborn, bullheaded teenager I happened to be." In his neat suit and cheerful tie, The Citadel's primary lawyer had the boyish look of a comfortable man. His clothes were well tailored but hung slightly wrinkled on his midsized frame. He smiled easily and laughed without self-consciousness. He kept his thick brown hair groomed close. It showed no early trace of gray. His hands were warm, and his manner gracious. At thirty-eight, he exuded a distracted sense of welcome to the world. Cooke's Charleston office, impossibly cluttered but full of life, reflected the same interior ease. Tennis and soccer trophies vied for space with duck paperweights of polished brass. His walls were crowded with diplomas (an honorary doctorate from The Citadel soon to rest among them), and his bookshelves overflowed with a jumble of mementos from a life lived busily in midcareer. Snapshots of his family stood amid a cyclone on his desk. Files poured across the floor.

Other than the mess inside his office, Cooke led an orderly existence. The son of a Marine colonel, he was a traditionalist at heart and a man whose own life conformed to rigid social expectations. His indulgences were modest. He did not drink and never had. His passions did not show. His wife, Helen, was a homemaker. Two sons attended private school. A daughter would be born before the trial was resolved. Their life was solidly constructed and enviably safe. The couple never bothered to lock their attractive Victorian house in the tidy township of Mount Pleasant. Cooke wasn't even sure if he could find his key. Indeed, if anything bothered him at all, it was that life had presented him with so few obstacles. His father proved himself in World War II and again in wars that followed. But Dawes had lived a smoother life, without great notes of conflict. There lay his only obvious insecurity. Sometimes, he would admit, he actually envied those cadets their harshest trials.

The hushed offices of Barnwell, Whaley, Patterson & Helms on Meeting Street were meticulously maintained and well appointed. Although unable to match the size and vast complexity of Shearman & Sterling's operations (the Charleston firm had but twelve lawyers), Cooke's law office was well established in the state and not without its influence. Only in recent years had the firm expanded from a small group of well-connected partners to a more complicated enterprise more defined by billing hours and profit sheets. Cooke straddled that transition. He had an older partner's sense of decorum and pace but a younger man's taste for competition. While not considered quite as ruthless as some colleagues of his age, he was admired and valued as a smart attorney with a deeply rooted sense of decency. Clients and adversaries tended to think of him as both likable and fair. He was "nice," was what so many people said. He had a calming manner and a good grip on the law. The only time his staff ever saw him truly lose his temper was once when he thought that someone had swiped a brownie from his desk. Assistants suspected he had eaten it himself and just forgot. He was a little scatterbrained that way.

Cooke had quite consciously selected the low country as home. A son of both the North and the South, that link came from his mother's side. She called two generations of Beaufort County sheriffs kin. "The high sheriff of the low country," as Cooke's grandfather liked to call himself, in fact had several claims to fame. Not only did he preserve a family tradition of low-country law enforcement but in his spare time he held a second job as a witch doctor. His training for that role fell at the foot of slavery. In 1912, recalled James Edwin McTeer in a book of reminiscences, "When my family purchased our farm of four hundred acres, we gained, in the bargain, Aunt Emmeline and Uncle Tony Legare. Their parents had been slaves on the farm, and when reconstruction came and they were free, both of them chose to stay on the land they knew. . . . Little did I know that it would be these two ancient Africans who would introduce me to African black magic and witch craft, and who would enlarge my vocabulary with such words as 'Ju Ju,' 'put mouth on you,' 'root,' 'hex,' and 'spirits of the night.'"

Sheriff McTeer's chosen turf was a complex landscape ruled by fear. In that world, the anxieties of both races worked in perpetual interplay. Terror, as William Tecumseh Sherman observed fiercely when he burned his way to victory, "was a power. And I intended to utilize it." Many before him used it first. Throughout slavery, whites employed the threat of rape, castration, amputation and hanging to keep restive blacks in check. Sometimes those threats were carried out. Whites had the whip in hand and the rule of law to back them up. Yet power lay not only in established limits of authority. It also existed more vaguely in a nether-world of spells and sorcery. To believers, explained Cooke's grandfather in his book *Fifty Years as a Low Country Witch Doctor,* "the night is more than dark. It is accentuated by an extra darkness. It is a blackness that was carried to this new land by their forefathers, a darkness sensed rather than seen . . . the darkness of voodoo, Satanism, the black art known here as 'Root.'" Many whites came to fear and respect such powers. Cooke's great-grandmother was among them. Convinced that the supernatural held secrets beyond knowing, she studied the occult her-self. The allure to a young woman living on an isolated plantation was obvious. Observed Dawes's grandfather: "No overseer or owner of a rice plantation could make a slave refuse his witch doctor's command." It was the single force that exceeded that exerted by white men.

Two generations of McTeer's forbears worked with Ouija boards and studied European notions of the supernatural. But Dawes's grandfather would look to Africa to find his inspiration. From the age of nine, he made himself apprentice, learning the Gullah dialect and studying the words and spells of doctors known as Snake and Crow, Hawk, Bug and Buzzard. As a white witch doctor, however, he did not cast spells but pulled them off, presiding over exorcisms and making wretched symp-toms go away. What delicious stories he could tell. And how that humid coastline came alive as his grandchildren gathered at his knees. Towering at six feet two, his pockets jammed with candy, and his office thick with bones and magic cures, African masks and sorcerers' tools, Sheriff McTeer could not help but entertain. Dawes was transfixed and adoring. And though later he would look upon witchcraft with a lawyer's cool remove, he could still in 1993 produce small amulets from his desk drawer. Those soft packets made of felt were gentle fragments of his past. On hot, cicada nights on Coffin Point when he was young, Dawes's mother and grandmother sewed magic down a long dirt road, their faces toward the sea.

By the time Dawes entered college, his grandfather had formally dedicated himself to doing only good. After a confrontation with Doctor Buzzard, "Fate was with me," the sheriff explained in his memoir. "Shortly after we put our respective 'spells' to work, Dr. Buzzard's son ran his car off a causeway during a rain storm, and drowned. One afternoon shortly afterward, I drove up in my back yard. Dr. Buzzard was sitting in his car, waiting for me. 'I've brought you two fine chickens,' he said. 'Let's you and me be friends. I've got power and so have you, I can tell.'" That balance was rare. But the sheriff responded by saying that he was giving up black witchcraft altogether. "All I want to do from now on," he told his visitor, "is help afflicted people."

As Sheriff McTeer well knew, profound, unquenchable terror lay at the heart of voodoo practice. Sometimes, it was strong enough to kill. Jim McTeer knew of several such cases. Like most literature concerning voodoo they detailed otherwise inexplicable fatalities and mental scars that occasionally lasted for a lifetime though no physical harm was ever done. Modern studies of mental trauma in fact begin not with the shock of war at all but with the study of black magic. According to one early student of the phenomenon of voodoo deaths, a victim's condition can be expected to worsen through three predictable stages. First, explained Walter B. Cannon, there must be a public laying on of a curse ("Die Shannon," said the sign). Next comes the isolation of the subject ("Faulkner: Alone in Victory," observed the *Post and Courier*). Finally, the group gathers together ("1,952 Bulldogs and 1 Bitch," taunted a popular T-shirt), leaving the victim overcome with a sense of "powerless misery." Allan Young, in his more modern examination of theories of post-traumatic stress disorder, quoted Cannon's work in noting that the trauma of fear can almost equal, perhaps even exceed, that of actual physical injury. "Intense fear—characteristically, fear plus the element of surprise—is an assault equivalent or analogous to physical violence," he explained. Deprived of the ability to either fight or flee, victims become "bathed in fear and anger," sometimes to the point of death.

Sheriff McTeer, writing less clinically, reached the same conclusion. "No one can account for some of the things which have happened to the unfortunate victims of the hex doll," he reflected. Yet the results were undeniable. "I have saved literally hundreds from insanity, murder, suicide, and have also saved many marriages," Dawes's grandfather would boast.

The northern half of Dawes's family was considerably less colorful.

But just like the McTeers, it also laid claim to long tradition. Three generations of Dawes's forbears attended the St. Paul's School in New Hampshire, then went on to study at Princeton. Cooke arrived at St. Paul's when he was thirteen. When he graduated in 1972, Dawes was a staunch conservative and chairman of the school's committee to reelect Richard Nixon. Deeming Princeton too liberal for his taste, he turned away from his forbears' school and went to the University of Virginia. In that, he was not only being faithful to his politics but beginning a long journey back to the only place he knew as home. Though his father's side boasted an important Yankee general and generations of wealthy and well-connected northerners, Cooke's own alliances were set in the Deep South, where the McTeers traced a direct link to Thomas Heyward Jr., a prominent South Carolinian who signed the Declaration of Independence. For law school he chose the University of South Carolina. For a home, he made his bed in Charleston.

To some degree, in making those choices he was rejecting the world that Val Vojdik, five years his junior, was then so happily embracing. His prep school class was the first to graduate girls among its ranks. Yet while St. Paul's changed, the Cooke family did not. It never occurred to Morris D. Cooke Sr. that his daughter Betsy might follow her brother, father and several ancestors into that famous boarding school. "There was no tradition for it," both Dawes and his father explained. It was Cooke *sons* who tacked those sheepskins on their walls. Betsy stayed at home.

Unlike Dawes, Betsy had no great expectations to fulfill and no long line of tradition to guide her in the world. At home, the pecking order was quite clear. During high school, "the sore point," said Betsy, "was that there was special treatment for the boy who'd been away at school." She resented it. When Colonel Cooke was off in Vietnam working in military intelligence and Dawes settled in his place in front of the television set, Betsy invariably was called upon to serve him. "It was just like, 'Get his tray. Carry his tray to him.' That kind of thing. Then, when we'd be finished, it was, 'Could you take his tray into the kitchen?'" Betsy boiled at those orders and struggled with depression. In college, she fended off thoughts of suicide. Afterward, she slowly found her peace. "I'm the helper and the caregiver in the family, and he's the lawyer in the family," Betsy explained from the remove of many years. Once, she told herself she never would go home. But time had softened those hard feelings. Now, when she looked ahead, she looked south toward

Beaufort, where she expected she would someday soon be caring for her parents.

By her late thirties, Betsy could laugh about her childhood anguish and Dawes's propensity for taunting and for teasing her. That was just his way, she said. He knocked her down when they went skating. He slipped her guppies into his piranha tank. He flew a shark kite on the beach. He had that kind of humor. His parents found him boyishly reckless. They never made too much of it. Once, they said, Dawes destroyed a car by never bothering to change the oil or take it in for maintenance. Another time, in his glove compartment, Mrs. Cooke unearthed a yellowing wad of unpaid traffic tickets. But that was long ago.

Betsy herself rarely looked back. She had her own life now. It was a simple life made up of home and work and hobbies. Though the sole expectation of her childhood was that she would marry and have children, she lived alone instead inside a world of pets and angels. In her large garden in the small inland town of Bamberg, South Carolina, she grew miniature forests of bonsai, making majestic oaks and gnarly pines in careful replica. The past was past, she said while standing in that garden in the sun. The time was gone when she had thought of jumping out of windows or standing up in front of speeding trucks.

"You're not supposed to get depressed," she shrugged. "It's a weakness. It's a character weakness. It's a flaw." So deep was that rule in her family that when Betsy joined the Peace Corps and moved to Africa, she asked her mother if she wanted "the good news, the bad news or the truth?" Her mother did not hesitate. "The good news," Mrs. Cooke responded. It was the "southern way," explained her daughter, "not rocking the boat."

For all of that, there were some things that still chafed. Though Betsy had grown quite close to her brother and loved and respected his wife, Helen, too, she recoiled on occasions when she watched old patterns in replay. Once, while visiting Dawes's family in Mount Pleasant, Betsy overheard someone saying that his daughter, Celia, was playing doctor. No, quipped Dawes, "she's playing nurse." Betsy shook her head with some distaste. "He's a male chauvinist," she said with fatigue. "It's part of Dawes. It just is."

Dawes remembered that day, too. It was a joke, he corrected. At work, he used the same humor in another guise. "He is always talking about this paralegal named Bob," said Tish Solomon, a paralegal assigned to the Faulkner case. "He's always saying that *Bob* could do the work better. Dawes teases me. He'll say: 'Maybe he'd be better at this because he's a *male* paralegal. Maybe I should get *Bob* to do this.'" Tish gave a sour smile. Then she gently rolled her eyes. "But I love Dawes," she added with almost stern emphasis.

Helen admitted that her husband could sometimes appear insensitive. But she viewed his humor through a special lens. As the daughter of a Marine colonel who had once commanded the Basic School at Quantico where he taught Oliver North, Helen inherited the same world as her sister-in-law. Yet she had an advantage. Unlike Betsy, she had sisters she could cling to in a world heavily oriented toward males. "We would commiserate and make jokes about how important the boys are and we are, you know . . . just little pigs living in our sty. That's what we would say." Helen said those comments held no anger. They merely helped those girls survive. Betsy, deprived of a similar outlet, "internalized it," Helen said sympathetically. "There was no one to bounce it off of. There was no one to show her that she wasn't just being singled out."

By the time the Faulkner case came around with all its stabbing at convention, the Cooke family was perhaps more conscious of tradition than ever, and more keenly aware of its slow passing. Dawes's father described a world dying by degrees. One ending haunted him particularly. To the north of Philadelphia while Shannon Faulkner marched, a garish "For Sale" appeared outside "Dawesfield," an old Ambler mansion that had housed nine generations of the colonel's forbears. To Colonel Cooke, that 1727 estate represented a vanishing way of life. When he lived there, nearly a dozen servants worked to keep that property in shape. A calming sense of order held. After cocktails every night, a butler gently called the family in to dine. That image lived in amber. Yet from the age of ten, when his mother died and his father moved the kids away, Dawes's father could look upon those days only with longing from a distance. Someone else took on that house. Now it was leaving the family altogether. Younger generations scattered. None among them wanted a nine-bedroom mansion in a city that had itself seen better days. And so the ground that held the colonel's fondest memories sat empty and unclaimed, its sloping lawns neglected, its azaleas run wild.

For military brats like Dawes and Betsy, home was not a grand residence with a respectful staff. Instead, it was almost any place they unpacked. And so, to them, the constancy of Coffin Point held an appeal. Dawes loved the place and went back every time he could. During one holiday, while he was teaching sailing, he met Helen. Helen had no interest in him at the start. She considered Dawes too "straight" for her and went on dating other boys. But after college something shifted. The very qualities she first objected to began to draw her in. "It was just immediate," she said of that transition. Suddenly his values, his conservatism, his self-confidence and goals seemed not stuffy, but attractive. "I had never been that much in love," Helen said shaking her head. "Probably I had matured and saw what Dawes was [compared to] the people I was dating and saw the differences. He was just, I don't know. . . . He was nice. He had an open mind. He was just very secure with himself. And we had a lot of fun together. We got along real well."

During Shannon's first deposition, Dawes was persistent and skillful and flawlessly polite. Carefully, he moved her through some basic questions, probing gently for a motivation. He could not understand it. Why, he asked, would a woman want to march?

Shannon walked him through the start of it. She said she was in a class when the topic first came up. She wondered right away why women weren't allowed to go. Cooke pursued it.

Why did she think that she would like it there?

Shannon told him graduates talked mysteriously about a "brotherhood" that lasted all their lives. She liked the sense of that and saw in it a cushion for one's future.

And could *she* be part of that brotherhood? he pressed.

Shannon stared straight at him. "I don't think it would be a brotherhood anymore," she corrected coolly. "It would be a family."

Far outside the courtroom then, deep animosities already showed. In ensuing months, they would only grow. The Faulkners' house was spattered with eggs. After Thanksgiving, Ed and Sandy were roused by a neighbor in the night and told that someone had vandalized the exterior of their house. When Shannon's parents went outside they found graffiti scrawled in huge red streaks across white clapboard: "Dyke," "Bitch," "Whore," "Get Out!" In the dark before dawn, Ed used white paint to make those letters disappear. But the trace of fear they left behind increased. Warnings and malicious tamperings occurred in quick succession. On three different occasions, unseen hands bashed in the Faulkners' street-side mailbox. A car screeched down the block, bumped off the curb and drove across the Faulkners' lawn, cutting ugly circles in Sandy's favorite flower bed. Once, Ed discovered that the house's water heater—accessible through a crawl space from outside—had been tampered with in a way that might have caused a fire. Ed felt lucky to have caught it. But a chilling terror set its hook. Threatening phone calls came both day and night. Twice, the family's Southern Bell voice-mail message was erased. In its place, someone substituted a rap song about a "bitch" with a "big butt." Worse were callers who threatened and harangued. One in particular sent Sandy through the roof. "I was so hysterical, I could hardly drive. But I don't think it was that one phone call," she amended. "I think it's the buildup. My emotions are just shot."

Slowly, Sandy gained weight. She ate when she was nervous. That meant she ate a lot. Before long, she carried the results in soft pouches on her cheeks, around her thighs and on her stomach. White-haired and bespectacled, she laughed and shrugged it off. Despite some lingering vanity, Sandy did not really care. Nor did she care when people called them ugly names. If Shannon was the "divine bovine from Powdersville," Sandy merely shrugged. "That was no big thing," she said with a slight frown. "We are a country place out here." Sandy herself thought of Powdersville as "that wide space in the road." She had no great pretensions. No, she said, she could tolerate even the "1,952 Bulldogs and 1 Bitch" T-shirt that showed her daughter as a dog in high heels and red lipstick standing out in front of a pack of snarling bulldogs trussed up in cadet uniforms. "See who's out in front?" joked Shannon. "I'm leading the parade." Sometimes Shannon wore that T-shirt herself and autographed it, too—as if to say: Just watch, I'll beat you in the end.

For Sandy, the harder part was fielding phone calls and opening the mail. The thought of rape and murder wore heavily on her nerves. She was disgusted by suggestions that Shannon belonged in "O" Company and terrified her daughter would be harmed inside those walls. Some callers were explicit. So were the many messages that appeared on billboards, on T-shirts and in anonymous letters to the house. One shirt Sandy never will forget showed Shannon standing in front of a mob of cadets outside a barracks gate, each leveling a gun: "Over My Dead Body!" the writing on the T-shirt warned. By contrast, supporters called from here and there to offer any help they could. "Pray for us," urged Sandy. It was the only thing that she could think to say. And so they had a prayer circle that stretched from California to New York.

Still, Shannon persisted. The lawyers prepared her and approved. She was calm under pressure and articulate, if abrasive. What she started she would finish. She had no intention now of leaving. Nor could she have found an easy exit. Millions were being spent on both sides of the case. She stood there at the center. Meanwhile, the more she learned about the school, the more she came to see in it a path toward almost guaranteed success. If you survived that first hard year you had it made, she thought. Someone would be there to always help you on your way. Shannon wanted that challenge. And she wanted that reward. That's what she told Dawes Cooke on May 3, 1993. He asked her to elaborate. Shannon struggled to explain it.

"It is a link between anyone who graduates from The Citadel and wears that ring," she said. "It is a high honor to wear the ring. You can almost get anything you want by wearing that ring, by knowing someone. It's just—you're linked together. You might not know each other but . . . you are together in a way." It was "common knowledge around South Carolina," Shannon told Dawes Cooke. No other school could match it. That ring was like a key. It opened many doors.

Down in Charleston, in an office crowded with college paraphernalia and a dozen pint-sized bulldogs, Bubba Kennedy, the short, hawk-nosed director of alumni affairs whose real first name was Henry, began to feel the strain. On his bookshelf he kept an odd array of soothing New Age music. There, Yanni stood beside "Oceans," "Sounds of the Forest," "Whispering Winds," "Gentle Surf," "Stormy Night," and Vivaldi's "Four Seasons." He played them in varied sequences throughout the day. But even that could not still his burning moods or quiet his upset stomach. Because just as he began to feel relaxed the phone would ring and some alumnus would vent a torrent of emotion. "Bubba!" near strangers shouted out, having met him at some barbecue. "What are you guys down there going to do about this girl?" Some men made their cases carefully. Others raved and shouted. Bubba tried to sound polite and jocular with every one. He could honestly assure them that the college was doing all it could. A special fund had been established to fight the case in court. Money was now pouring in. Sure, they could contribute. Meanwhile, they ought to know, Bud Watts would fight this to the end. Some callers hung up quite appeased. Others spewed out venom and hung up while still sputtering. Bubba heard it all. Some callers made him laugh so hard he almost lost his breath. He tacked to the back of his office door a poem from a Citadel chat group on the Internet. It almost always made him smile.

REAL MEN DON'T WEAR HEELS

Shave her head and call her mister
She don't know a boy ain't a sister
She says she is, We says she ain't
She says she can, We says she can't
There must be a difference or so it seems to me
We don't ripe like apples and drop off trees
The world's gone crazy, over run by fools
There must be standards, there must be rules
What's wrong with tradition or honoring the past
Or shooting those cannons in a star spangled blast
She can call her lawyer friends and fuss when she can
She can wear pants and ties but she still ain't a man
I got me a good education, learned some about the world
I'm proud I was a cadet and my momma was a girl
So shave her head and call her mister
Who in their right mind would want a brother for a sister?

In court, arguments over coeducation were framed in far more sober terms. But the gist was the same. Even if Shannon did sign in, Citadel representatives patiently explained, she would never be accepted in the network that she so desperately sought to join. More likely, she would destroy it.

That first fall after her lawsuit was filed, Shannon enrolled at the University of South Carolina. But while she studied and attended parties and made friends, her lawyers argued that she was being seriously deprived of an education that had no match elsewhere in the state. Judge Houck agreed, and ruled that as of January 1994, Shannon could take classes with cadets, but could have no access to the barracks until the broader case was resolved. He also ruled that the veterans' case was moot. "Right after the veterans decision, on a Friday," Jimmie Jones remembered, Sara Lister, the assistant secretary of the Army for manpower and reserve affairs, called The Citadel to inform the school that its commandant, a 1969 Citadel graduate named Joseph William Trez, could no longer work on active duty. "We realized that we were in trouble," said the board chairman. "She just told us that active-duty officers were not going to be involved as commandant of cadets. Watts called Trez in and relieved him of duty that afternoon." Shortly after that, Trez would retire from the Army and take back his job as commandant. By then, officially as well as unofficially, all energy had shifted to Shannon.

That Christmas, she packed her bags. On January 20, her nineteenth birthday, she signed in at The Citadel in a category of one. Johnson stood on campus that same morning. Looking out across a small sea of cadets, the crop-haired Navy veteran tried to hide her disappointment.

The three women veterans who first challenged The Citadel were forgotten, she said bitterly. "But during Shannon's registration, I showed up in my dress blues. . . . I made a huge statement by showing up in that old uniform." It was a fleeting final moment. Johnson and the other veterans were out of the case entirely. And though Johnson tried to stay in touch and sent Val Vojdik cards and asked after her cats, Muffler and Buster, the correspondence never flourished. The veterans were history. It was left to Shannon now to fight what Johnson considered "the invisible octopus effect," a pervasive and consuming network of power that seemed to reach out everywhere with The Citadel always at its head.

In some ways, Johnson might have liked to let it go. But she could not. The case followed her everywhere. Newspapers were full of it. Radio commentators chuckled. It was the talk of Charleston. "SAVE THE MALES" bumper stickers started appearing throughout town. As Shannon gained some weight and the fight centered on whether or not she should get a knob haircut, they changed to "SHAVE THE WHALE." At Trident Technical College, where Johnson was still tacking courses together for her degree, it was impossible to ignore the vitriol behind the case. Once in a Spanish class, a female student wrote *"Va, Shannon, Va!"* on the blackboard. "This guy erased the last *va*," said Johnson, "and he was trying to write 'go to hell' in Spanish but the teacher was just saying, 'Go, get out of here.' It was at the end of class." On another occasion, a male student sneered that he would like to see Shannon "with a bullet in her head." There was a meanness to it Johnson just could not believe.

For the next year, Shannon took day classes and lived with Bob Black's family in their modest house on James Island. She baby-sat for the Blacks' kids and did her homework and got by. It was not a happy time. She sometimes fought with Bob and always felt the pressure rising. Mail came almost every day. Up in Powdersville, Sandy opened it warily, then weeded out the worst.

On campus, Shannon's welcome was mixed. Several cadets were warm and made their support quite widely known. Others signaled secretly that they wished she would succeed. Many more kept their opinions to themselves or met her with open hostility. In the *Brigadier*, the anonymous Scarlet Pimpernel speculated repeatedly about her sex life, taking scattershots that linked her romantically with a black cadet or insinuated that her sexual preference was for women. Shannon, ever the pragmatist, brushed off taunts suggesting she was homosexual. "If I was a lesbian," she asked brusquely, winding up for a good laugh, "why would I want to go to a school with only men?" Meanwhile, Shannon struggled to align herself with those inside the gates. Knobs had it worse, she said protectively. She watched them at a distance, wishing to belong. Every Friday, during parade, she stood at the edge of Summerall Field, a thumb in every eye.

In that first year, Sandy often caught herself thinking back to Shannon's birth. "She's a survivor," Sandy reminded herself firmly, hoping to find peace. Born prematurely, Shannon hovered between life and death in her first weeks. Sandy liked to think that fight was deeply etched inside her soul. "She was this tiny, fragile little kid," Sandy said distractedly late one afternoon. "We didn't know if she was going to live or die." Yet once her health stabilized, a profound determination showed. It never did let up. Shannon was a fighter. She was one from the start. When Shannon learned to walk, recalled her mother, she did not bother with tentative forays from chair to chair. Instead, "at sixteen months, she just got up and walked around the room. There were no toddler steps." When Shannon started swimming lessons at the age of three, she cried at first, then looked into her mother's eyes: "You're going to make me do this, ain't you?" she said, tears streaming down her face. Sandy answered that she was. "You don't have to do it ever again," she soothed. "But we paid for these lessons." Shannon thought about it for a while. "Then she said, 'Okay,' and jumped into the pool and started paddling." Sandy loved her for it. She had a bit of that gumption herself. In 1982, when she became the first person in her family to finish college, she set a pillow proudly on the living room couch. "The greatest oak," that small needlepoint reminded, "was once a little nut that held its ground."

At The Citadel, Shannon built upon that spirit. "The only thing that can stop me now is the Supreme Court," she said gamely early on. "I'm hated by some. I'm honored by others. Some people say that I'm a pawn. All I can say to that is: *Checkmate.*"

With her lawyers, though, Shannon sometimes fell into awkward silences. She hated to repeat some of the names she had been called and eventually found ways to guide Vojdik and Mandelbaum to the correct obscenities. "It's another word for cat." "It's part of a woman's person." Slowly, a crude vocabulary came clear. Knobs were "douching the galleries" when they swept down open hallways with their mops and buckets. Cadets in slim cloth hats were wearing "cunt caps." Boys who cried or whimpered were "pussies," "cunts" and "whores."

Outside those gates, increasingly, Shannon was embraced as a feminist. She rejected the label. "I'm not a feminist," she corrected briskly. "I am an individualist." She stated her philosophy simply, subconsciously quoting her own grandmother. "If you think you have the ability to do something and you have the quality to do it, then you should do it." A young girl from Virginia put it best, Shannon thought. Shannon memorized that note. "Wake up and smell the Nineties!" the girl had written. "We're about to go into the Twenty-first Century here, and we're *still* fighting discrimination?" Shannon tipped her head back and laughed appreciatively. "God, I loved that note."

While not taking depositions, Shannon's lawyers gradually became immersed in the language and rituals of barracks life. Some proved boyish and immature. Others were plainly shocking. Company marching ditties tended toward the obscene. They often mixed sex and violence. In some, women were dismembered and blinded, killed in any number of ways. One in particular made Vojdik nearly sick. Sung to the tune of "The Candy Man," its lyrics were an ugly rage. "Who can take two jumper cables / Clip 'em to her tit / Turn on the battery / And watch the bitch twitch."

"She has a right to be safe," Vojdik argued in court that spring. "She is the only woman in that environment."

In the midst of all that ugliness Evelyn Richey started to nearly rise out of her chair whenever Shannon's name came up. She did not understand the temper of the corps. She could not fathom its crude hostility or the fact that few boys on that old campus ever offered any help. "I'm sorry," Shannon's grandmother said unapologetically. "You see a dog get run over out here, and you're going to try to get it out of traffic. You're not going to just let it go. This is really hard for me to understand. . . . I mean, when is all this gentlemanly attitude supposed to take effect? When they walk out of the gate? Just when does it kick in?" By then, Sandy's mother had no lingering ambivalence. Her mind was set, and her heart was firmly with her granddaughter. "Tradition," she sniffed angrily. "Well, slavery was tradition, too. And it wasn't right." Down at The Coffee Pot, Albert had never wavered. He showered perfect strangers with tales of Shannon's exploits. "That girl, she's my hero," he repeated proudly, waving pages torn from *Time* and *Newsweek*. "That girl, she's the best."

In Charleston, Shannon said she would not be a coward. She vowed she would not quit. Nobody would get to her. She grew tearful as she said it. Though she bore no disrespect for those who left, the guys whom she revered the most were those who stayed and kept themselves intact. To face so hard a test and to excel . . . well, that was what she wanted. She admired those who made it through. She set her sights on that. It was the same challenge generations of boys had sought. She would walk across those burning coals and not be burned.

From the Ashes

O N AUGUST 1, 1991, Tony Lackey stiffened with a last salute and retired from the Army. He had made four tries for a general's star and was dealt four disappointments. His wife, Kay, stood close and took a photograph of her proud colonel with his medals. But as the last few minutes of his long career wound down, Lackey did not smile. Instead, he stood with a crook in his posture and a sad grimace in his eyes. "There is a primary zone," he would explain. "And then you get too old." The only life he had ever known was lost.

He tried to take the impact gracefully. But there were petty insults on the way, and those were harder to forgive. One year the general officers list came out just a day before he was due to relinquish a command. Everyone thought he had a star that time. So did he. The signs were there. "All the generals called to say that they were coming to visit with me and Kay," Lackey said with a dry smile. "Then all the generals canceled." When the new promotions list was posted, he still wore a colonel's rank. "Hey, you were just right there," a friend consoled. But Lackey took no comfort from near misses. Bullets and promotions were the same. You hit the target or you missed. "That was the closest that I ever got," he concluded with a dismissive wave. "The generals . . . well, of course, now that's a club."

Lackey was fifty-one when he retired, three weeks short a birthday. As he shook General Wayne Downing's hand and said goodbye to a man whom he revered and an institution that he deeply loved in the place he called "the center of the universe," Fort Bragg, he had no clear plans for his future and no house that he called home. He lingered on the Army's sidelines for a while, working under the secretary of defense as the special assistant for human intelligence and special operations. Then, early in the summer of 1993, he moved Kay and their daughter Laura to

Charleston and took a job teaching high school students how to march. Junior ROTC instruction made for an enormous change after working at the highest reaches of the military. He lasted only a year. Then he did what many Citadel men had done before him. On June 1, 1994, he drove through Lesesne Gate and settled back inside an old, familiar world.

It was a long circle that had finally brought him home. Now, as assistant commandant of cadets in Jenkins Hall, he had an office all his own and a small brass nameplate on his desk. His walls were lined with photographs, fond caricatures, Army memorabilia and the idiosyncratic maps of a career. For thirty years he had served his country faithfully. In retirement, he kept the signs of that commitment close. In one image, he was immortalized running in the night, his face covered with greasepaint, an M-16 raised in one hand, his intentions deadly. In another he was depicted in pastels with a too-big head while two black soldiers argued with a female colleague on a nearby couch. On bases far away, men gathered on a tarmac, frozen with their fond goodbyes. A more recent picture showed his oldest friends, "the grumpy old colonels," their figures softened, their faces lined. A heavy saber glinted on a long wood plaque. A slender Citadel sword hung near it. Lackey was young there, too, straight-backed and almost handsome as he took General Mark Clark's hand.

In a long Army career, he had played his many roles. Each was framed by an early twist in his career. As a young soldier, he longed to join the infantry but was shuttled off instead into what he described as a "super-duper CIA course." His would be a sensitive specialty, fraught with danger and filled with controversy. Tasked to do what superior officers ordered but did not always publicly admit, he was drawn into a world outside the world, one in which civilian rules did not apply and the only imperative was mission orders. Back home, those soldiers could not boast of their successes; they could not even tell their wives. But Lackey was Mark Clark's man, well made and perfectly suited to such work. His loyalty was unswerving, and his patriotism absolute. The nation that he served would never prove so trusting.

In Lackey's first few years of soldiering, while he was assigned to the First Special Forces in Okinawa and then at the U.S. Army Intelligence School at Fort Holabird in Maryland, his fledgling career in military intelligence several times intersected with a secret training operation known as Project X. Lackey denied having had any knowledge of the program as a young soldier. But by 1998 he and everyone else in the armed services knew of its controversial history. It was widely in the news, and in a most unflattering light. Begun in the mid-1960s under the auspices of the first Joint Foreign Intelligence Assistance Program, Project X was devised for the guerrilla war in Southeast Asia and perhaps used as a model for the Phoenix program, then later exported to friendly governments fighting communist-inspired uprisings elsewhere. But what began in the 1960s as a natural outgrowth of an ugly war was considered thirty years later one of the darkest chapters of Pentagon history. By 1991, liberal opponents of Project X saw not a glorious and effective means by which to undergird American strength outside our borders but suspected instead that it trained death squads and promoted dirty wars outside the public view. To them, it exemplified the awful hazard of power wielded with impunity.

Project X was dropped by the Pentagon as part of its training repertoire in 1991. In a changing political climate the Defense Intelligence Agency raised ethical and legal challenges to a program based on manuals that taught blackmail, torture, kidnappings, threats to family members, "abduction, exile, physical beatings and executions," as described by the assistant deputy director for counterintelligence that year. Shortly afterward, almost all manuals used in that program were destroyed. The official explanation for the mass shredding was that such methods should never again be used or taught by U.S. military personnel at home or overseas. A more plausible explanation was that by the early 1990s that bit of Army history had become quite an embarrassment. In a time of relative peace, civilians feared that a secret segment of the military had become lost in the back alleyways of intrigue and hidden violence.

Lackey had a soldier's view. He was a killer when he had to be. To him, war was deadly business and required deadly practices to win. His own specialty was infiltration and the training of foreign agents. That preparation, he said, led him to write the special forces plan for the Phoenix program. He volunteered to serve in that program during his last tour but was rebuffed in a classic military snafu once he arrived in Vietnam. "When I got there," he said, laughing, "because I had never gone to the Phoenix course, the *Phung Hoang* course in Fort Bragg, they decided I wasn't qualified." He found it ironic. "Actually I was part of the original . . . ," he scribbled a circle on a pad of paper, lost in thought. "I helped write the original plan."

From a distance of many years, Lackey explained the Phoenix program in its simplest details and made no effort to obscure the abuses that had brought it public shame. "In each hamlet, each village, each city, there was a Viet Cong infrastructure, a people's government," he said. Intelligence officers in the CIA determined "to ferret this thing out, choke off the infrastructure, choke off the support." Lackey's job was to help infiltrate those shadow governments to allow special forces units to provide cities and military bases with early warnings of attack. To do that, the special forces needed spies and double agents. They found them among the Montagnards, Cambodians, Chinese and others who worked on U.S. payrolls. Lackey stopped in the middle of his narrative and smiled, spreading his arms. "So it's the Phoenix plan. Big bird. Big white bird. Greek mythology. That was their symbol and thus *Phung Hoang.*" The driving idea was to match guerrilla tactics with guerrilla tactics and pull a victory from the ashes.

Yet such intelligence networks did not always function as intended. After province and district intelligence units shared their information, "you would take these groups out and you would visit them and determine whether they would be VC or not," he explained, "and you can see how that would get out of hand? If you went to ah, Mrs. Nu Win down there, and beat her up, then all kinds of bad things could happen. Then you had provincial reconnaissance units. PRUs. And the PRUs were kind of like raid parties. They would go out and attack the infrastructure. They might be really in the structure, or they might be just bad guys, or they might really be vigilante groups that went out and got money for themselves and—you see how all that might get out of hand? If you had legitimate government, it worked. If you had renegade government . . . it didn't work. So you had all these abuses, mini My Lais, you know, by the Vietnamese themselves. So that was the Phoenix program." It was a sound concept, he believed, but sometimes badly mangled in the chaos of a civil war.

After the Vietnam War, the Phoenix program retained some passionate supporters who believed that in it lay a key to victory had we only acted sooner or stayed longer in that land. Because of such support, its imprint and that of Project X lived on. In a new world defined by small-scale encounters between clashing ideologies, some military theorists believed that techniques learned in Vietnam should be transposed onto simmering "low-intensity conflicts" fought between leftist peasant groups inspired by liberation theology and right-wing governments in such countries as Nicaragua, El Salvador and the Philippines. Lessons from Vietnam were handily transferred. At the School of the Americas at

Fort Benning, Project X training manuals virtually unchanged from those written at Fort Holabird in 1968 were used throughout the 1980s to teach new generations of soldiers techniques that embodied the ugliest aspects of guerrilla warfare. In time, like the Vietnam War itself, those manuals fell under the grinding teeth of politics.

In his critical Congressional Report on the School of the Americas, Congressman Joseph P. Kennedy II of Massachusetts documented that trail and found in it a blueprint for abuse and criminality. "Somehow in the vast and powerful military bureaucracy the message was delivered repeatedly from the upper echelons of power that the rules don't matter," the Kennedy report concluded. "The most graphic part of the Interrogation Manual is the section discussing 'coercive techniques,'" those pages advised. "The manual . . . [recommends] psychological techniques to break an individual's will to resist. The techniques include: prolonged constraint; prolonged exertion; extremes of heat, cold, or moisture; deprivation of food or sleep; disrupting routines; solitary confinement; threats of pain; deprivation of sensory stimuli; hypnosis; and use of drugs or placebos." Actual injury was not always necessary. In fact, beatings and physical torture could prove counterproductive, those manuals advised, only more firmly setting a victim's mind against his captors. Instead, the *fear* of pain was recommended. And more effective, still, the sense that the victim was hurting himself or somehow responsible for threats made to his loved ones.

"The torture situation is an external conflict, a contest between the subject and his tormentor," explained the Project X Human Resource Exploitation Manual (1983). "The pain which is being inflicted upon him from outside himself may actually intensify his will to resist. On the other hand, pain which he feels he is inflicting upon himself is more likely to sap his resistance." Blame was shifted to the victim. It was *his* fault that he was being hurt. If he only would cooperate, all his troubles would evaporate.

The history of the School of the Americas (the "School of Assassins," to its critics) "begins with Project X," Kennedy said. "There are countless victims," the Kennedy report stated. "Archbishop Oscar Romero was gunned down in cold blood by SOA graduates because he stood up for the powerless against the powerful. Four Ursuline nuns were ravaged and mutilated and thrown into a ditch for the crime of teaching children to read. . . ." The list went on and on.

By the late 1980s, with the threat of communism suddenly withering,

Americans were in no mood to hear such tales. Just as Lackey reached his "primary zone" for advancement to a general's rank, a Democratic Congress turned against the Reagan White House, accusing the president of supporting military operations that operated behind a cloak of secrecy with disdain for the law. Lackey's career was at a lofty height just as the Iran-Contra scandal broke. While Congress cast a skeptical eye on the military's secret operations, Lackey commanded United States Army Intelligence Support Activity, a sensitive special mission unit. His had been a steady climb. It ended rather suddenly. At the very moment that Project X was under scrutiny by the secretary of defense, he snapped a last salute. In that environment, "you're not politically correct," he shrugged. "Intelligence and special operations, everything they do is controversial. And everything comes with the risk of failure." Awkward questions were inevitable. He kept his colonel's stripes. It was a profound disappointment after an illustrious career. But the atmosphere had changed.

Former commanders praised Lackey as a "great patriot" but acknowledged that his best work was relegated to secret files and top secret accountings, condemned to stay forever out of sight. One former commander described him as a "great combat soldier," then paused to think of Lackey's equals. "Most of them are dead," he said at last. "And they did not die peacefully." To Lackey's face, Pentagon officials denied it was an issue. The mix just wasn't right, those generals said. There were gaps in expertise to fill. Lackey's specialties were not required. His friend Ed Tivol, a retired colonel working in Virginia as a military subcontractor with Electronic Warfare Associates, Inc., put Lackey's fate in simpler terms. "The green machine never likes to promote the guys who do the dirty work," he said. "They send you out there, let you risk your life . . ." He shrugged.

At The Citadel, Lackey's life took on a softer shape. A guitar leaned against the wall behind his office door. Handsome portraits of his wife and daughters graced the windowsill beside an old computer. A change of clothing hung behind his door, and a duffel bag on most days held the crumpled laundry from his daily run. Even so, he still marched to a soldier's clock. He rose before sunup and drove himself all day. The life of soldiering would never leave him. He had cleaved to it completely. On days when colleagues dressed their best and pinned their medals high, he shimmered with the heavy legacy of service under fire. Among his honors were the Distinguished Service Medal, four Legion of Merit awards, two Bronze Stars, three awards for Meritorious Service, four Air Medals, five Army Commendation Medals, the Cross of Gallantry, the Combat Infantryman Badge, the Master Parachutist Badge, the Vietnam Service Medal with nine stars, the Southwest Asia Service Medal and the Purple Heart. There was no pin to say what each had cost.

In Mount Pleasant, several tree-lined blocks from where Dawes and Helen Cooke were raising their young family, Lackey's neatly tended bungalow was painted a pale Citadel blue. He kept an enormous boxer named Rocky for a pet and made the Ashley his horizon. If a cartoon map could capture his perspective late in life, it would have shown his alma mater in the foreground like a holy fire. Charleston would glimmer behind it, washed in light. Behind those giant houses and lush gardens, the Ashley and the Cooper would forever vie for space with the Atlantic. In the distance, Southeast Asia, El Salvador, Germany, Grenada and Panama would sparkle like small glints of glass under a burning sky. Above it all, of course, Fort Bragg would shine—the brightest star. He never questioned that.

"The Citadel is an ideal," he remarked early one morning after a predawn run. "It is an ideal of values more than anything." In that school's toughness, he saw valor. In its challenge, he saw pride. In the boys, he saw himself and perhaps the son he never sired. With women coming, he feared much of that would change. He liked the hardships that he saw. He thought those hardships built good men. "Maybe I'm a dinosaur," he said, wondering aloud. "I guess I just believe in manly men."

Asked to intervene in violent cadet conflicts he found himself dutiful but often quite ambivalent. Talking at length about a corps-wide football free-for-all known as the Turkey Bowl, he laughed as he explained it. "It's just a brawl," he said. "But I've got to stop it. Because it's dangerous. Last year we had probably fifteen that ended up in Roper [Hospital] . . . dislocated shoulders, broken ankles and smashed teeth. The freshmen try to get back at the upperclassmen, and the upperclassmen kill them. It's good for them. . . . It just is. That's part of the bonding. . . . In my little heart of hearts, I don't blame them. They're in college. They are growing. That's part of it. . . . I'll walk out there . . . because it's my duty. But inside I'm saying, *Hit 'em harder. Hit 'em harder!* Because you remember those things when you grow up." He made no apology for that. On that ground he never had to.

Colonel Joe Trez was in Tacoma, Washington, as 1994 began. A commanding buzz-cut figure who stood stiff and straight at six feet three and always spoke in a precise and almost oddly simple way, he was conforming to his duties as the chief of staff for the Army's Seventh Infantry Division when he got a call to come back home. His alma mater needed him, Bud Watts explained. Between the Faulkner case, a nearly fatal injury in Junior Sword Drill, persistent campus tensions over race and the constant howling of the press, it was time for a deep revamp of the corps. Against a bitter tide of alumni protest, The Citadel was cautiously initiating change. Watts needed a new team. Lackey would be part of it. So would Roger Popham of the class of 1963. Watts wanted Trez to serve as commandant. He appealed to Trez's patriotism, his loyalties, his sense of purpose and his pride. He hit every weak spot Trez had ever had.

Trez agreed to take the job. He knew the school should change. Several recent experiences had told him that his alma mater needed a revamping. "I was worried," he said plainly. In the service, among young soldiers wearing Citadel rings, he said, "I didn't like what I was seeing." One encounter rankled particularly. After confronting a Citadel graduate over "an almost total breakdown in command and a failure to adhere to standards," he asked the soldier why he did not get his men under control. "We have to instill fear!" the man responded. "We have to prepare them for combat. We must replicate war!" Trez stared at him in disbelief. "That was the *wrong* stuff," he said glumly. "I relieved him of his command."

Trez, a graduate of the class of 1969, was an outspoken opponent of hazing. He thought it served no purpose and based that judgment on his own experience. "The thing about that process," he said, "and this is key to the develpment of Trez as a cadet leader and Trez today, is that the thing it taught me is—*number one*—how to hate." When Watts came calling, Trez wanted to be part of it. He was an optimist that way.

PART IV

Lone Wolf

Smile, Because Tomorrow
Will Be Worse

F OR A YEAR the balance held. Shannon sat through day classes. The corps remained all-male. But theirs was a stalemate that could not last. Late in the damp, cloying summer of 1995, it broke. The signs were clear before the term began. On campus, expecting defeat and instructed by the judge to make room for a woman in the barracks, Citadel officials prepared spartan quarters for the student they had spent three years and many millions of dollars struggling to repel. Still, in the last few days before the term began, a false sense of timelessness hung over that old campus. To those who knew and loved the school that time was a sad requiem.

In the final weeks before the new school year, The Citadel was quiet. Summer school was ending, and cadets who had lingered to earn final credits seemed hesitant to leave. A tall, sandy-haired senior named Bryon Frost was heading off to medical school. He looked as though he could not bear to go. Lingering on the open quad, he fumbled for his words. With Shannon Faulkner coming now, he said, everything would change. "It would be like a world without gardens," he observed dejectedly, struggling for a metaphor. "If women were cadets, then who would make things beautiful?" He stared out across the concrete checkerboard that had been his home for those four years. "What do those lawyers know?" he said. "Women should not be trained like men."

In tandem, as if to prove his point, two young women suddenly appeared out by the sally port, bobbing in that open entryway, their figures framed by iron gates. They peered in past the line beyond which no females could then pass. Waving and laughing, they leaned forward as though straining over a low, imaginary wall. Bryon watched them for a moment as they jittered up and down in skirts and sandals, their arms waving, broad smiles beckoning. Then he stepped forward with a shy smile and stood stiffly in their warmth. "We just baked these," the women said, bouncing restlessly from foot to foot and leaning into one another until their shoulders touched. "They're still hot." And they were. Bryon took two cookies from the plastic container that they offered and gave his visitors a smile. Then he turned away again, back into his own world. "They bring brownies and things," he said, chewing. "It's real nice." Out in the shimmering heat rising from the wide square quadrangle of Zoo barracks, two bare-chested black men in bleached white tradesmen pants were repainting antique squares in careful alternations of red and white. Every barracks looked the same. It was a Citadel trademark, a game board at the center of every cadet's life. Each summer, just before the new boys came, the quads were carefully repainted. The men worked slowly but methodically, red square to red square, stepping white to white, a straw hat mashed on one man's head, a baseball cap slung low across his colleague's forehead. While cadets moved casually around the periphery, walking from room to room and shouting out goodbyes, the workers dipped their rollers down. A hard sun baked the colors dry in minutes. It was the same each summer, a red carpet for the new boys. Every corner of the school was made pristine. The campus gleamed with paint and polish. Bryon struggled to explain why even that had meaning. Everything at The Citadel, he said, was done for a good reason. Early August had its patterns. Traditions were what made the place so great.

That August, before the knobs, the training cadre and the school officials all arrived, the campus lay stock-still, hard-baked and stark beneath a sun that blanched the sky from end to end. Hurricane Hugo had done away with most of The Citadel's old trees six years before. In the absence of their green and arching lines, the school was even more barren now than usual. Few low-slung branches provided shade and respite. No arboretums or quaint lakes and fountains offered room to muse. Seen from the air, The Citadel's campus was just a thin rectangle of white stretched taut around the parade ground's wide central expanse, its border made of tools of war, an idled jet, an armored tank, a missile and an enormous cannon that shot blanks at big parades. Inside those strict geometries, the lives and hopes of generations of young men were concentrated in a space not much bigger than a football field. It was tough training in tight quarters, one whole world on those few acres.

Everything about the campus communicated a certain clean rigidity. Where Charleston was all curved lines and shady gardens, The Citadel was severity and burning sunlight. Here, the old lore went, thousands of young boys had found one truth, one set of rules, one shared experience. The rest of the world could heave and change, but The Citadel would not. It was destined, each new generation thought, always to be a special place, the city's complement, the center axle in a secret wheel of power. Like the cobbled streets of Charleston, or the coffee cups and silver spoons and dark portraits of inheritance, some things always had their place and purpose. New boys arrived believing that. Inside those gates the world was fixed. Duty, honor, discipline and truth. They had read the school's brochures. They signed up full of hope and expectation. They knew it would be hard. But they wanted what it offered. And they wanted to belong.

To new boys, The Citadel's tidy campus was an essay on control. It offered no distractions. Bleach white and blood red inside its gates, theirs would be a home of concrete, asphalt, iron and shaved grass. That barren landscape made no reference to the chintz and lace next door. Southern indulgence was abandoned at the gates. That was how it was meant to be. Once, the legend went, when plantation boys wore frilly lace and grew up spoiled by mothers and attentive slaves, that training stripped a child of his soft dependencies. "Reared from infancy to man-hood with servants at his command to bring his water, brush his shoes, saddle his horse and, in fine, to minister to his personal wants, the aver-age Southern boy grew up in some points of character dependent, and lazy and inefficient," wrote John Peyre Thomas in his history of the school. The image, painted in 1893, was but a nostalgic dream, never true but for the slenderest minority of cadets. In fact, rich boys almost always studied elsewhere. But one century later, that promise, unexam-ined, lay unbroken. New classes of young boys were always viewed as soft. The Citadel would be their touchstone, one fashioned from a set of perceptions which never could be moved. That was the point and, to supporters, its dark poetry.

"The success of Citadel men is no mystery," Bud Watts informed all incoming cadets. "It results from the benefits of a well-rounded educa-tion which develops cadets academically, morally, spiritually and physi-cally; all within a framework of a demanding, strict, disciplined military environment. This experience builds character and self-confidence, instills integrity and honor." Citadel men liked that notion. They framed their lives around its promise. So did many of their mothers, their girlfriends and their wives. It told them who they were. And it said that they were special. Even the architecture carried out the theme. Walls rose in white, four-story cliffs. A master fantasist had been at work. Theirs was a prison and a palace joined, a place which, once embraced, would never lose its hold.

Some cadets called it "Disneyland," and scowled at the tour buses that slid across the campus at a crawl. Unpopulated, it did have that strange cast. In the summer, before the start of things, The Citadel stood empty and unreal. Across the marsh, the Ashley rolled in muddy streaks. A breeze silked by while all the rest of Charleston was steaming. Crows called. Workers puttered here and there. The sun bore down. The days slipped by. In the lull before the corps arrived the campus was a strange oasis of pure quiet. It seemed innocuous, if odd. But cadets had left their mark behind. Grim warnings greeted every new boy at the gate.

From floor to floor in all four barracks, small, perfectly worked paintings pictured death and violence. One sign showed a former platoon leader as a monster with a bleached white skull, bloody teeth and fires burning hollows deep in holes that once were eyes. A Kilo Company athletics board showed a bulldog with its fangs bared. It growled in a rabid, drooling rage above a leather collar full of spikes. Another sign recording regimental standings showed the black-cloaked angel of death standing smug beside a skeleton cradling an M-16. In the Thundering Third Herd, as cadets called Third Battalion, someone had pressed a bottle cap into a stairwell wall. It was painted with a sunny yellow smiley face that bore a bullet hole between the eyes.

"SMILE," that message warned in careful stenciling. "Because tomorrow will be worse."

Shannon arrived in front of a handful of reporters late on a Friday afternoon. She had stayed home for the last few court hearings, finally bored by all the endless back and forth. By then, even the judge seemed tired of the legal bickering. "Mr. Cooke, you know you can't answer interrogatories with broad objections," Judge Houck said wearily on one occasion that July. "There's not a district judge in this state that would permit that." The judge took a long breath as Cooke squirmed under his hard scrutiny. "I mean, it doesn't do anything except give you the ability to totally control what you furnish." All that summer, Shannon's lawyers had peppered The Citadel with requests for information, statistics and odd facts. But The Citadel persistently kept its records from the court while parrying with last-ditch efforts of its own. That August, in a last-minute, closed-door appeal before the judge, Cooke and other lawyers argued that the female candidate did not meet the school's height and weight requirements. Records from that meeting were sealed. But within days, Shannon's precise weight was well known and widely distributed. With school about to start, Judge Houck's patience was near its end. In the midst of that last ugliness, he left no room for Cooke to move.

Cooke stood rocking back and forth under the judge's gentle blasts. Houck's displeasure was not new. Three years into it, the judge seemed to carry a distinct distaste for this long battle. Cooke had felt his heat often in the past. Yet Watts and his old roommate, Lew Spearman, always pushed their point man further, wanting more, urging him to fight it out. For Cooke it was an awkward squeeze. The judge sat before him, clear in his displeasure, while behind Dawes's back, stony-faced Citadel officials whom he served and answered to whispered that their sweet-faced Charleston lawyer lacked the stomach for attack.

In truth, Citadel officials reserved their harshest criticism not for Cooke but for the judge. They had come to hate his mocking attitude and distrust his motivations. The judge was biased, they complained. He had set his mind against them. Out of court and safely beyond earshot, they spread dark insinuations about the judge's private life, suggesting to reporters that they dig into his first marriage and examine what they called "Houck's new housing arrangement." With Rick Mill gone, Terry Leedom lustily took up the cause. "Check him out," he coached. "That would tell you a lot." He let a spate of implications hang, hinting that the judge's opinions were not fashioned by the law, but by his passion for his blond assistant, a woman whom Leedom called "a rabid feminist."

"Do your homework," Leedom nudged. "You'll see who pulls his strings."

Everyone who knew the case could feel the pressure rising. Indeed, courtroom tensions had percolated back behind the scenes for years. But as Shannon readied herself to march, Judge Houck played a stronger hand than usual. Though his decisions had often been second-guessed by the court of appeals in Richmond, Virginia, now even that judicial panel seemed disinclined to stand in Shannon's way. Hardly seventy-two hours before Shannon was due back in Charleston, the Fourth U.S. Circuit Court of Appeals had refused to stay Houck's ruling that Shannon should join the corps that fall. The decision abruptly ended an expensive chapter in the fight. Inspired by VMI, which had created a "separate but equal" program for women at Mary Baldwin College, a women's school in Virginia, Citadel officials, late in the case, had persuaded Converse College in Spartanburg to launch the South Carolina Institute for Leadership (SCIL), a cadet program for women, on its own meticulously landscaped grounds.

Late that summer, after an emergency mailing of thousands of letters to high school seniors and prospective students, twenty-two girls joined the newly minted, still unfinished SCIL program. Converse's cooperation was secured shortly after Sandra Thomas, a forceful Texan, took the reins. Though the school had earlier resisted overtures from its "brother school" in the low country 190 miles to the south, serious financial woes made for compelling motivation. When Thomas took the job it was with a mandate to revive the college's ailing financial health. As her predecessor put it, the administration's top priorities at the time were an alliterative trio consisting of: "conscientious cost-cutting"; "fantastic fund-raising"; and "rigorous recruitment and retention." The SCIL program promised the private school relief on all three fronts. Without spending a nickel of its own, the struggling liberal arts college received a nonrefundable $5 million startup check from The Citadel, and was promised an additional $3.4 million from the state. Those first SCIL cadets were showered with scholarships worth up to 100 percent of their college costs. It was a hard deal not to like. And Sandra Thomas loved it.

Val Vojdik compared the programs with a bitter laugh. "Summer camp," she sputtered after spending months preparing to argue the matter before the Charleston judge. "They're not comparable at all. It's just a joke. It really pisses me off." Outside the courtroom, she dubbed it a "glorified Girl Scout program." In front of Judge Houck she said the financial inducements "read like a blue light special." She made no effort to hide her disgust. That August, the SCIL's first days did have much the feel of a girls camp. Before the academics started, all twenty-two students began their regimen with an Outward Bound adventure in the mountains of North Carolina. Thomas sent them off into the hills bathed in warm encouragement. The girls quickly repaid her. Before they trudged away, they broke out in a boisterous chant: "Dr. Thomas, she's our friend. She says SCIL will never end. . . . We're the first and we're the best; set the mark for all the rest!" Despite that optimism, the Richmond court, by a 2–1 vote, decided not to block Judge Houck's ruling to place Shannon in the barracks with Citadel cadets. Though VMI dodged a bullet by setting up its parallel program, the SCIL program would never be approved by Judge Houck as an alternative.

With that door closed, Citadel officials thrashed about for some other last-minute reprieve. While Shannon packed up for the fall, Citadel lawyers launched a final, desperate overture in Washington. Just hours after the Richmond judges ruled, The Citadel delivered a 161-page plea to the Supreme Court beseeching Chief Justice William Rehnquist to do what no court beneath him would do. "If there is any room at all under the Constitution for public single-sex education," the lawyers argued, pushing for an emergency stay, "then surely The Citadel's Corps of Cadets qualifies." Theirs was the slenderest thread of hope. But they wound boundless strands of optimism around it. "It's not over yet," Leedom told reporters. "We're all waiting on Washington. We know we've got a chance." Vojdik, meanwhile, felt the surge of certain victory. "One down, one to go," she said. "They haven't got a chance."

The subject of all that controversy was grinning broadly on that Friday evening as she stepped up in front of reporters for what she thought was her last press conference. After that, she explained, she would be a cadet like everybody else and no longer available. But on that night, she took a final turn at center stage. Walking down a mossy passageway toward the small Charleston garden her lawyers had reserved for the occasion, Shannon distributed hugs and handshakes to those who had stood beside her in those years. Only Sara Mandelbaum was absent. She had stayed in New York, banished along with the ACLU after an angry disagreement. The rupture occurred over something minor, a bumper sticker promoting coeducation that obviously alluded to the case but did not even mention Shannon's name. For Shannon, though, three years of taunts and mockery in her home state had been enough. Never comfortable with that link in the first place, Shannon finally severed it in a confrontation that left the ACLU lawyer in tears. The group was capitalizing on her painful quest, Shannon argued heatedly. She never really wanted their involvement. With vicious words, she cut it off. "And I don't need a lawyer who cries when there is a conflict," Shannon finished with an ugly stab. It was a bruising clash in a long and bruising battle. After three years, everybody's nerves were worn. Now, the core group included just Vojdik and Henry Weisburg, Suzanne Coe and Bob Black.

Vojdik looked at Shannon and grinned. "You're in," she whispered, flinging her arms around her client. Then Vojdik moved on to Sandy and hugged her so hard that Sandy's glasses tilted. The last countdown had begun. The time of arguments was done. Shannon moved out front and produced her broadest smile. "Well," she said, "here we go."

Dressed in a long T-shirt, a short white skirt and tennis shoes, Shannon laced her hands together and began. "If traditions didn't end," she said, speaking calmly into a cluster of microphones, "you'd have to think where we'd be now."

A veteran of major news shows, winner of national awards, she had developed considerable poise under the lights, facing questioners straight on and answering their queries with both humor and assurance. Friends and supporters whispered that she should try a life in politics. But Shannon demurred and kept her plans snapped shut and out of sight. "People say I should run for governor," she had joked once, "but first I guess I need to finish college." She was charming when she cared to be and tough when she felt threatened. That night, she spoke with confidence tinged only slightly with a case of nerves.

"Are you ready?" came the question.

Shannon pursed her lips and nodded. "Well, I guess I'm ready. I sure ought to be."

Vojdik, nervous and jiggling, standing to one side, had dressed for the cameras in a dark blue dress, fuchsia jacket and her trademark strand of pearls. Framed by towering palmettos, a papaya tree, azaleas and boxwood, she stood back and to one side like a proud parent, grinning while Shannon talked and nervously shredding a tissue into snow between her fingers. On the verge of the biggest legal victory of her career, Vojdik's adrenaline was rushing hard. It all came down to this.

"We're so pleased to be here," she said happily when her turn came. It was one of the great understatements of her life.

As reporters drifted off toward evening deadlines, Shannon's victory party retired into the air-conditioned safety of a tiny two-story house that Shearman & Sterling had rented for the visit. While Shannon stood with her parents and accepted congratulations, four bottles of Napa Valley champagne were brought from a back kitchen. Forty plastic tumblers leaned in stacks along a table. Vojdik and Melinda Black, Bob's wife, fussed playfully and laughed as they laid out that simple celebration. Both women were nervous. Tomorrow it would start. Shannon popped the first cork. Glasses moved from hand to hand amid soft sprays of rising bubbles. But as Vojdik prepared to make a toast, her underage client raised her empty hands in protest. "Oh my God!" laughed Val. "Shannon doesn't have a glass!" She dumped some water out of an ice bucket and offered it to her. Shannon grinned and licked her lips. "All this," she said, pausing dramatically, "and I can't drink a glass of my own champagne."

"To Cadet Faulkner!" Vojdik shouted, raising the first toast. Everybody cheered. Then a telephone rang, and the last good news came in. Antonin Scalia, the most conservative justice on the Supreme Court, had just dashed The Citadel's last hopes. "Scalia denied the stay!" someone shouted. The sally ports yawned open. The room exploded in a noisy cheer.

"Well," said Ed Faulkner, gazing warmly at his wife, "we won."

A dozen cameras clicked. Frozen in that moment, Sandy, Ed and Shannon, Melinda and Bob Black and Val Vojdik pulled close, smiles creasing every face.

With that small celebration finished, the group dispersed, and Shannon went off to a local mall with Melinda to find a bathing suit for the next term. She selected a red, white and blue Speedo fashioned after the nation's flag. "It just seemed appropriate," she quipped later with a smile.

The following morning, when the Faulkners' family van drove onto campus there was a brand-new bumper sticker on the vehicle's rear fender: "WE ARE A CITADEL FAMILY," it proudly announced. Nearby, a parent pointed and stared, then nudged his wife and mumbled, "Well, let's see." In a day of drop-offs and tearful goodbyes other cars had other sentiments to share. "SHAVE SHANNON'S HEAD," some urged. "SHAVE THE WHALE," said others.

James T. Hammond, a reporter with the *Greenville News* who had covered the case from start to finish, shook his head and made a note. "I swear," he said sourly, "if they shaved her head, there'd be folks selling clumps of it on every street corner in Charleston."

Hell Week started two days late that year. Although school tradition dictated that the shock of change should occur in those first moments, in 1995 administrators decided to take two days to remind everyone involved that theirs was as much a college as a military school. Academic orientation kicked off the fall semester. Not until Monday would cadre take command. That slight and yet important shift left many sophomores jumpy. They watched with distaste as parents deposited their sons in spare, un-air-conditioned rooms and then, instead of being banished from the campus, stayed on to see the boys again. Always in the past, first drop-off was final. In one searing moment, those boys left childhood behind. The wheel of power turned. It cycled on to the sophomores. The practice of leave-taking, Citadel lawyers had once argued in court, was crucial, "part of the pedagogy of the institution." Every aspect of a Citadel cadet's career, those lawyers stressed, every ritual, every rule and every order was the result of sophisticated knowledge about how best to build young men. Cadets believed that absolutely. But now, old rituals were changing.

While Shannon and her parents moved about the campus, parents watched their gangly sons and drifted around aimlessly hoping they did not look as lost and out of place as their disoriented offspring did. Returning upperclassmen stood aside, commenting. When they were freshmen, as soon as they stepped into the barracks the cadre was in charge. From that moment until Recognition Day, knobs were upperclassmen's property, expected to snap to at every order. Now, all they got was sweet talk and pointless blather for two days. The boys blamed Shannon for the change. That weekend was their proof. "The softening down" had started. "When I came," complained a scowling upperclassman, "the military stuff, it started right away. I mean, *right* away." There was no time for fond goodbyes. There was not meant to be.

"It hasn't really started," a disgruntled sophomore advised impatiently. "Come Monday," he declared, "*then* it will begin. That's when the fourth class system starts." A friend came close and slapped him hard across his tightly muscled upper arm. "Monday, man. . . . It's our turn. I can't wait." Then he threw his head back and howled so loud that several parents turned to stare.

Administrators grappled with that change of schedule, too. While parents drifted back and forth waiting for reunions, first impressions, one last hug, men in uniform hung back, directing from afar. In Jenkins Hall, on Lackey's desk, an enormous document detailed every move that each company should make—and when. But out in the barracks, where the students were in charge, there was scant coordination. Schedules and directives did not always match. Old patterns were disrupted. No one knew quite what to do. Though students in crisp uniforms moved with purposeful intensity, many orders were contradictory and utter chaos ruled. "Monday," repeated a cadre member. "Monday it will start. This is all just bull."

David Abrams, a new graduate who had spent his summer as an aide to Bud Watts, wandered around breathing in the awed compliments of underclassmen. He looked sharp, the younger boys observed. Trim haircut. Blue blazer. Nice pants. Good shine on those shoes. Starch on that crisp collar. He looked fine. Several underclassmen asked to see his ring. He held it up. They peered closely. A palmetto tree. A star for the first shots fired in the Civil War. Cannonballs. A rifle. A saber and a wreath. Class of 1995. "Never thought you'd get that," said a lanky senior with a crew cut and deep scarring left behind by teenage acne. "On your way to a career in politics, no doubt." Abrams denied it. But he had the smoothness of class president as he waved the notion off.

A cadet stopped and saluted. Abrams smiled loosely and told him he looked tired. "Just getting back," the cadet reported. He and several friends had stayed up late the night before immolating cockroaches with a can of hair spray and a lighter. "We played a little 'fried palmetto bug,'" he grinned. Abrams gave him a soldierly pat, then turned away to weave around a huge construction truck.

Abrams had The Citadel glide, moving sort of loose. Every move he made, he said, was designed to get him one step closer to some goal. "Moving with a purpose" was a cornerstone of the school's entire philosophy, he explained. "You should always be going somewhere. That's the whole point of this place. Everything we do—even if it doesn't seem like it—everything we do has a reason behind it. Everything is leadership training. There is a purpose and a meaning to it. Sometimes you just don't see it right away."

As he moved around the campus, he pointed to one building and the next. Almost everything was scheduled for upgrading, even the pipes below the ground. Old barracks wore fresh paint. But inside them the wiring was old, the plumbing was outmoded, and the doors did not hang true. Millions would be spent on new construction just that year. Watts Barracks—with air-conditioning—was being built off to the east. Major renovations were under way elsewhere. Even the roads on campus were torn up. Orange tape fluttered above deep trenches that soon would carry new drainage pipe laid neatly end to end. A film of white clay dust lay over everything in sight. "We're growing," Abrams said, striding from place to place. "We're doing all this for the new guys."

Outside the front gates, the scene was equally chaotic early on that Saturday. One alumnus had sworn he would come and burn his old diploma publicly as he renounced the school for letting Shannon in. After that, he planned to throw his class ring in the Ashley. Clustered beneath a "Save the Males" banner, a small crowd waited for him to arrive. While they waited out on Moultrie Street, they waved joyously at every car that passed. "You are more of a show dog than a bulldog," said one sign waving high up in the air. "You're in it for the show and the money."

Pat Johnson, who stood by that day to watch history being made by someone else, regarded those protesters with hatred. She had long since coined a term for women who came out in support of The Citadel. In her mind, they were not courageous women standing by their men, but vicious traitors to their gender. "I call them the L.A.W.," she said dourly, "standing for 'Ladies Against Women.'"

Sally Baldwin, a small but indefatigable supporter of The Citadel's long fight, arrived with a wide smile and a black armband tied tight around one sleeve. "It's a black day in The Citadel's history," she said flatly. "We're determined that other women won't be coming here." Another protester said she thought the whole affair was "a step for mankind in the wrong direction," like some kind of a reverse moon landing.

Across the street, not thirty feet away, a small array of Shannon's supporters countered with slogans of their own. "The Males Are Saved!" their sign decreed. That group, formed hastily to go against the more well-organized Women in Support of The Citadel, dubbed itself COED, Citizens Organizing to End Discrimination. On that important day, they huddled close in the bright heat, leaning toward the street with words of welcome for the school's first female cadet. "Hang In There Shannon," urged a cheerful cardboard square. "WE SUPPORT YOU!"

The Women in Support of The Citadel, a loose-knit group of the like-minded, had bonded together early in the fight under the leadership of Connie Haynie, the wife of a recent graduate. Haynie came up with the Save the Males slogan while watching a program about endangered whales. Soon, the success of her first bumper sticker expanded into a growing business in her home. She called that enterprise The Reveille Company, because "America needs one big wake-up call." By that year, third- and fourth-generation slogans existed. The most popular bumper stickers that week took pokes at Shannon's weight. A more old-fashioned sign was tacked up out near Hagood Stadium. During the night, someone clambered up a telephone pole to nail up a cardboard square that simply urged: "Go Home."

Shannon arrived early in a traffic jam of nervous families. Immediately, a television cameraman, sweating and intense, lunged at the family's van. He raised his camera to his shoulder but was pulled back roughly by a Citadel employee. "You're out of order!" the official shouted. "Not here! Not now!" The cameraman twisted away from him with a threatening look. "You are out of order!" came the barked rebuke again. The cameraman gestured in disgust and then took off in Shannon's wake. Behind him, the college employee grabbed a walkie-talkie and sputtered into empty air. "I need help here!" he cried into the mouthpiece. "We've got a situation. I need some help out here!" The receiver crackled, then fell silent. Nobody was listening.

On a long, sloping lawn out by the music building where Shannon had started her day with a tryout for the band, Vojdik and Weisburg stood shifting foot to foot. Vojdik had come all prim and proper in a dress that fell below her knees. Weisburg looked more at ease, like a Brooklyn kid just home from camp. His long, graying hair fuzzed out beneath the tight rim of a baseball cap. His pants were wrinkled at the knees, and his blue chambray shirt had eased its way out of the clasp of an expensive belt. "It's good. It's good," he repeated to himself. Both lawyers had the look of victory. Vojdik bobbed up and down, spurting off excess energies. Weisburg grinned and shuffled, too. All of The Citadel's last gambles had failed. Shannon's lawyers looked across the campus with obvious satisfaction. Nothing could stop them now. All they had to do was celebrate.

Tar Baby

Early that first Saturday, while Shannon sat inside the cool, clean refuge of the music building moving through her tryout for the band, a black cadet was packing up to leave. Though he had arrived a week before to take part in fall sports training, now he wanted only to get out. Dressed in his cadet uniform and carefully weighing every move he made, he filled his bags hastily and then walked downstairs into the quad. At the desk beneath the entrance gate he reported to a student guard. The guard glanced up and roughly tapped a sheet of paper. "Sign here," he commanded.

"Punching out," a sophomore jeered. As the boy went through his final paces, several cadets provided hostile commentary just loud enough so everyone could hear. "He's getting out. His knobby cap's not on. He doesn't have a shirt tuck. Must be an athlete. They got here last week. Yeah, that one's gone. Lost cause. Goodbye."

Another cadet squinted in the boy's direction. "Look at that sorry-assed knob. He hasn't shined those shoes. Look at that belt. His shirt's not tucked. He's out," the upperclassman said with satisfaction. "One down. Six hundred little knobby boys to go."

At the sidewalk, the cadet's uncle took the suitcase and threw it into the back of a black Pathfinder. The boy had called that morning. He sounded desperate. His uncle hoisted a bag up in the back seat with a grunt. "He said if no one got down here by 11 o'clock, he'd be on the bus," the uncle said, heaving another bag inside the car. "Yeah, there's a story to it. But I don't know if he will ever tell it." The car doors slammed. The winnowing process had begun.

Outside the third barracks, the traffic started thickening before the sun was up above the barracks wall. A Lumina van from Texas pulled up behind an Oldsmobile from Indiana. An Infinity sedan from Virginia

208

was followed by a red rental car from Hertz. A lot of the boys were unloading from towns so small that they would say the name, then shyly add, "It has a stoplight." Or, "It has two stop signs." Or, "It's Mayberry."

They wanted something different. That was why they came.

Middle-aged women dressed in tightly cut pastels and bright cotton sweaters hugged their awkward boys goodbye. Fathers in khakis and sports shirts walked solemnly toward the sally ports and then gave handshakes or a stiff embrace. Everyone stood shifting about, not quite sure of what to say. Fathers choked back unfamiliar emotion while boys stood by looking frightened but quite stern, trying hard to keep their faces fixed. They would not cry. They would not smile. They came today as boys. But they wanted to be men. Almost instinctively, they pulled their shoulders back and set their mouths in a grim line.

One woman, an attractive investment banker from the Midwest, kissed her resisting son goodbye and then hopped nervously a few steps back. She got a bad feeling from those older boys, she whispered. The way they looked made her uneasy. She wasn't sure why. She laughed nervously. They were polite. It wasn't that. She shrugged. "We are liberals," she said apologetically. "At least I think we're fairly liberal. But he just always liked the military. Guns and tanks and all that stuff. This was what he wanted." She pointed without comment at a cadet wearing a T-shirt painted with a cartoon tease: "It's not over till the fat lady wears the ring." Another boy wore a shirt with "Absolut Male" printed neatly underneath the college seal. The woman took a breath, then made a line straight for her car.

Hundreds of other parents, caught up in first-day nerves, strutted back and forth without a word. Some waited with their boys, standing unsure next to mounds of boxes while sharing stories no one heard. Some couples moved in lockstep, clinging nervously. Others made short, awkward forays back and forth like scientists on expedition. Some held hands as they watched their sons go into that new life. But many merely hung back, peering past invisible barriers that would keep them at a distance from then on.

At the south side of Law Barracks, a crowd drifted and turned behind a line kept tight by a cadet. Fathers were quietly informed that they could cross the line this once to help their sons move in. But mothers had to drop behind. The fathers nodded nervously, then went to tell their wives. The arrangement left a dozen or so mothers, sisters, aunts and girlfriends huddled in small strips of shade. All morning long, middle-aged men climbed those stairs and set their sons' belongings down in cramped dorm rooms equipped with metal bunks and desks and chairs. Clothing was hastily folded and slipped into metal bureaus. Computers were unpacked but not plugged in. Everything felt rushed. Standard-issue shorts and tops were slipped on in place of old blue jeans. The leveling process had begun. Most boys emerged from their new rooms in college-issued clothing, bony-kneed studies in dark blue, anxious to excel; overweight in matching shorts and shirts, nervous and already sweating. Fathers, stepping awkwardly in that ancient ballet, stood tall and let their sons go on. Then they shrank back with heavy sighs that left them feeling old.

The Faulkners arrived in the midst of it, buoyed by good news. Shannon's flute tryout had gone so well that Herb Day, the band director, would have told her on the spot that she could have won a place in Band Company. But college officials had advised Day to keep his appraisals to himself that year. Even so, Shannon knew she had played well. She could feel it in each note. Her confidence was flowing.

For the moment, room 3344 in Law Barracks had Shannon Faulkner's name on it. A private bathroom—the barracks' first for women—was just down the hall. School officials griped that those renovations had cost $25,000. It was a leaf in the forest of a multimillion-dollar lawsuit. But few inside The Citadel juxtaposed the two. Instead, they focused on every minor change required in a landscape they had memorized in every detail. In Shannon's room, venetian blinds afforded a small veil of privacy. Two video cameras positioned just outside her door, a panic button and a whistle granted thin layers of protection. A sign nearby warned that the area around her room was monitored. Cadets observed those changes with disgust.

Sandy found the precautions both comforting and sad. Federal marshals asked Shannon for a password to use in case of an emergency. She shared one from infancy: "It was like she was reaching home to us, to childhood," said Sandy. By then, every provision for her daughter's safety stabbed her heart. "Here we have a young woman surrounded by federal marshals," she said, holding back her tears. "We went to Kmart to pick up a few things, and we had one agent on point and two on flank. Her room has been secured. She has a beeper around her neck. All these things are saying, *You are in danger! You are in danger! You are in danger!*" Sandy closed her eyes and let out a long breath. Back home, as she packed to leave, Shannon had broken down and sobbed once her boyfriend said goodbye. In the last few months before the new school year she sometimes crept into her parents' bed or slept in her brother's vacant room, anything for comfort, anything to keep them near. For the first time in her life, she locked her car when she went out, terrified that someone might plant drugs or something worse inside.

For Sandy, Shannon's growing fear proved almost impossible to watch. "It hurts my heart," she said. "All that hatred focused on my baby. . . . Anything bad that happens to her and they're happy, incredibly happy." Once, while the family relaxed in a restaurant nestled by the Cooper River, Ed Faulkner got up for something and overheard three cadets talking about his daughter. They laughed as one suggested that they should toss her in the river. Ed moved close and said they'd have to get past him first. Startled, one of the cadets turned and asked Ed why. "Because I'm her daddy," he said, then walked away.

By an arrangement with the judge, federal marshals would stay on campus, watching out for Shannon's safety. The court-ordered precaution was taken as a crude insult by cadets and men in the administration. Both tended to repeat a refrain most pithily expressed by Terry Leedom. "What do you think her real agenda is?" the school's spokesman wondered aloud. "She'll be here for a while, and then she'll cry 'sexual harassment' and get out and make her movie. Those cameras won't protect her. They'll protect us *from* her. That's how it will work."

Cadets favored a more colorful version. "We're the ones that will need proof," a senior remarked bitterly as a stream of freshmen lugged their boxes up the stairs. "We'll need the film to prove that all her accusations are just lies."

From the bench, however, Judge Houck advised the school to take those cameras seriously. Mindful of the threats of violence that had swirled around the case, he warned administrators and students alike not to let a few rogue cadets tarnish South Carolina's reputation. Someone, the judge said, would always be there watching.

When Shannon appeared after her band tryout, all conversation stopped abruptly. A woman nudged her husband and then pointed. He shook his head and frowned. "We'll see how long she lasts," he said. "This is no place for a girl."

To one side, a junior named Alex Pettett watched the scene and worried. "There are a lot of bridges coming up," he said. "We'll just cross them when we get there."

While Ed and Sandy Faulkner hoisted Shannon's boxes out onto the sidewalk, a senior went over every rule. No mothers in the barracks. No small children. No women. And no girlfriends. The barracks were for men. Shannon slipped inside and changed her clothes and reemerged in white shorts and a pink T-shirt. Soon enough, she hoped, she would be lost in that new class, a knob dressed in blue like all the rest. "I was nervous this morning," she conceded stiffly. "I'm okay now, though. I'm okay."

In the mess hall, an American flag stood limp in every window. The mood that day was quite relaxed. Outside the door, a crowd watched Shannon getting measured for her physical-training clothes. Then, after lunch, all the knobs were herded together and sent marching off to Mark Clark Hall.

"Okay guys, listen up!" shouted a cadet once they had gathered in the auditorium upstairs. "Move up to the front and fill all the empty chairs. I don't want any empty chairs. Do it now!" Most freshmen were talking, sharing hometowns and fragmentary bits of who they were. Shannon sat among them, reading. At 2 o'clock exactly a sharp call sounded. "All rise!" Almost six hundred men and one woman struggled hurriedly to their feet. Then Cliff Poole, the school's vice president in charge of academic affairs, took over, his rounded glasses twinkling in the light.

"Fortunately," he cracked, as thermometers outside hovered near 100 degrees, "it's not a hot day in Charleston."

Not a sound met that pronouncement.

The reserve officer looked down and shook his head. "That was supposed to be humor," he informed them.

Scattered laughter floated from the boys.

"You all need to loosen up a little. Now. Why are you here?"

Silence.

"It's a chance to change your life in terms of your lifestyle. Get out of the house. Start something new. Basically, why you're here is to get an education." That was first. But it came in a unique environment, the general said. Staring out across a sea of acne and anxiety, the man in charge of academic affairs said he wanted to share with each new student that he understood what they all faced. He knew the glory and the agony of leaving childhood behind. He had been there. He had marched in their shoes, too. He wore a ring from 1959. He held it in the air. "By making this decision," he told a sea of fidgeting recruits, "you have changed your lives forever. It's like a tar baby. Once you get the tar baby, you're stuck with it. You are marked for life with this decision. And I hope you carry it proudly."

In the warm recess of the auditorium in Mark Clark Hall there was nervous squirming by a ghostly pale freshman on the right. A member of the training cadre slammed a fist into his open palm as an admonition to behave. But military training had not started yet. The cadre member scowled and gave the boy a look of pure disgust but let it go. Elsewhere, other boys jiggled their feet and rocked as older boys looked on with ugly sneers.

"You have zero options about attending class," Poole announced from the front stage. Classwork, he announced, would be their primary concern. Academics was the key to any knob's success. "You miss a class, and Colonel Trez will come and visit you. And you don't need that." He quoted Robert Frost and then wished them well. "You are creating a brotherhood like your mind cannot imagine and a bond that you cannot fathom," he said with a warm smile. "You have miles to go and promises to keep. But I swear to you, the journey is well worth it."

A student officer took the lectern with a crisp salute. Then he gazed coldly out across a sea of frightened faces. "Now we go to the egress plan," he said.

Not a single new recruit reacted. "Well, hey!" the student laughed, leaning out over the lectern. "This is college. That's just a fancy word for: How the hell do we get out of here?"

For two days, the knobs rambled around campus while their parents heard again and again that they had their own job to do. Every mother and father, stepmother and fond uncle would be vital to this grand experiment.

"Welcome," Lieutenant General Claudius E. Watts III boomed after a sea of parents surged into McAlister Field House late on that first Saturday. "You all know why we are here."

Heads bobbed and nodded. There was a general murmur of agreement and a round of loud applause. Most parents were nervous and intense. They wanted to impress. They wanted to fit in and follow all the rules. They wore their hopes out front, trying to exude the careful hesitance of solid families of fine stock. They were upbeat and polite and full of expectations. This was, they had been told time and time again, a holy transformation. Some recalled words printed at the front of that year's *Guidon*, a small handbook of general knowledge. *We live in an age disturbed, confused, bewildered, afraid of its own forces, in search not merely of its road but even its direction. . . . It is our duty to find ourselves.*

The quote was from Woodrow Wilson and dated back to 1907. But Watts found it appropriate still, and many parents agreed. There, at The Citadel, generations found their way out of that confusion. By taking on that challenge, Watts assured, students would find "the voices of vision."

On that stifling Saturday afternoon, Watts enlisted every parent's help. Standing alone on the gleaming basketball court, the retired Air Force officer stood tall and trim and ghostly white inside his crisp, star-studded uniform. Confident, commanding and serene, he let the silence wash around him as the parents' expectations intensified in their long wait for him to speak. Then the general held his hand out, palm first, in what seemed a benediction. Finally, he spoke.

"This is the seventh time Jane Watts and I have had the opportunity to welcome parents," he announced with a stiff smile. And yet this year was a special challenge. He nodded, as though entirely to himself. This year they met in crisis.

In the bleachers, parents nodded.

"The courts have ruled," Watts declared, his voice swelling in the emptiness, "that we will take a female into this class. I want to talk about that subject first." He waved his hand in awkward reassurance. No. He did not like it. But he was a trained professional, a soldier and a man of honor. The courts had ruled. His college would abide by that court's ruling.

"I stand before you as the leader of the Citadel family," he said gravely. "And without equivocation, without hesitation, without any qualification, I tell you that this institution will comply." There was a respectful hush across the bleachers. He would lead his flock through all its troubles. "As a military person, I salute, and I move forward," he said firmly. "But let me make an analogy. We are today in a hurricane. And you can put your name on that hurricane." He cleared his throat. "The Citadel finds itself in the eye of the storm. Here, it's calm. It's serene. It is tranquil, and the course is set to take us into the twenty-first century. Only when you get out of the calm do you encounter that hurricane. And then you get beat up."

The Faulkners, seated in the bleachers, stayed stiff and silent in that crowd. That hurricane bore Shannon's name. And every parent knew it.

Watts waved his hand again and rocked back on his heels. There was something else he had to say that afternoon. He turned his gaze to meet the eyes of parents in the stands. *"Each of you!"* he declared with his voice rising, each man and woman who had given The Citadel their sons, would have to trust the institution. True, he said, those boys might call and say all sorts of horrid things were happening. "You should ignore that." The boys would cry and say that they were lonely. That was just a part of growing up. They would cry and ask to come on home. "You should refuse them." They would make up stories. "It is your job to see right through that." Yes, parents could be supportive. Of course they should be. But the best support that they could offer their boys now would be to let those young men grow.

"It's total immersion from the time you leave this weekend to the time you pick him up in four years," the general explained. Parents had their orders, too. Their duty, the president announced, was much like that asked of their sons. Parents must believe that a Citadel education was something worth the sacrifice. They had to trust that the institution was fine-tuned to assure their sons' success. They had to know that everything that happened, happened for a reason. They had to understand it would be tough. "It *will* be tough," he stressed. But every parent was crucial to a son's success, as central to a boy's achievement as any teacher would be. The parents nodded and believed.

Watts had built a team to manage this transition. He swept his arm across a row of bleachers pointing to a line of men. These were the president's men. Cadet commanders. They were the best among the best. "They are handpicked," the general smoothly reassured. "They have my total confidence to meet the challenges that we will face in weeks to come."

These men, Watts explained, would help their sons past every hurdle in the coming days. They would assist those new fourth classmen as they moved from a world of comfort and indulgence into a life defined by challenge and by stress. That was the calm inside the hurricane. They knew what they were doing. Tradition shaped their every move. Trust them. Trust The Citadel. The system worked. "Our system is designed for success."

Watts beamed and turned away. Cadet commanders raised their hands in flashy white-gloved salutes. Every son was on his way.

Flushed and committed, mothers and fathers streamed down onto the basketball court in one common exhalation of relief. They had been welcomed into the clan, pulled into the center of an eternally turning circle. Everyone belonged. Smiling and shy, they tumbled out of their chairs and into the welcoming arms of teachers, ROTC officers, school administrators and friendly volunteers from the ranks of other parents. An immense blue curtain that had been strung across the court was suddenly pulled back to reveal a score of welcome booths. Parents filled with vigor and resolve spilled out across the floor. Citadel parents and alumni met them with everything from bumper stickers to advice. Everyone seemed to have a story of a son's struggle and great triumph. Everyone had shared the same initial doubts. They were all in this together. The Citadel family, it was called. Here was something they could share. Home telephone numbers were scribbled hastily on envelopes, grocery receipts, scraps of paper and the backs of hands. A new class was launched. The family would grow. The cycle would repeat.

Most parents took Watts's admonitions to their hearts. Though their instincts might rebel, they heard his words again when their sons called up in pain. That year as in other years, parents would ignore those plaintive cries. For one mother the worst would come at a time when she believed most of the strains and challenges of initiation were well behind her adored child. Just as Watts had said, one day he called in tears. When she took the telephone he was sobbing uncontrollably and almost incoherent. She soothed and listened. He called her "Mommy," which he had not done since he was four. He begged for her to bring him home.

She sat down on her bed. Watts had warned of this. She heard his voice again. "They will call you." He had known. Her son whimpered and choked. But Watts's words were coming back. She would heed them. She would behave as every parent had been taught. She calmed her son and soothed him and told him he was strong. She said that he could make it. She sent him her respect and love but said she would not help him. Her son whimpered and struggled for his breath. He said an upperclassman had taken him into his barracks room and broken him completely. His mother had no notion what he meant. He stuttered out the words without details. His mother soothed. But she had been warned. And she would do as she was told. One year later she would speak of the school with only praise.

Slowly, the boy regained his composure. But his voice shook as he pleaded with her to send applications to other schools. She very gently told him she would not. She told him how she loved him. She told him he was brave. But he was a big boy now. They were so proud of him. She would be down for the holiday. She would buy him a big dinner. He had to hold on until then. Everything would be all right. When she set down the receiver, she lay across her bed and wept.

Almost six hundred men and one young woman had arrived to join the group that August. At least two boys left almost immediately. More would leave during the year until the school found itself fighting just to keep the barracks filled. Year by year, the corps was dwindling. It was failing, now, quietly struggling for its life. To most Americans, The Citadel had come to seem anachronistic and quite strange. It was not the absence of women that made the college so distinct. It was the whole odd theater of the place, its regimentation and its rules, its uniforms and starchy parades and its reputation as a holdover from an era long since dead.

Some cadets signed in because they thought they might not make it elsewhere. They worried they would lose their way or fall into slothful habits and deadly addictions. Some came because they had something to prove to fathers, teachers, coaches or themselves. Some wanted definitions, limits and set goals. Some were pushed by anxious parents. Some came with academic honors and ROTC scholarships. Others arrived with Ritalin prescriptions they could endlessly refill. Some came with hope. Some came with fear. Some, incredibly, came not even knowing that The Citadel was a military school, a place built on the bedrock of old assumptions and fixed ways. They were tall and short and hefty and thin and shaggy-haired and crew-cut. What they all wanted was not to fail. It was the same reason Shannon had once given to the court. At another school, she told Judge Houck, she might just drift. We had become a society of strange seductions. There were drugs and alcohol on every campus. It was easy just to lose one's way.

At The Citadel, Shannon believed, "I would have to work twice as hard on the studies, whereas in another college I might loaf off and just kind of throw them to the side." She wanted discipline, she told the court. She wanted the honor of a ring.

As ebullient crowds surfed across the basketball court making hearty introductions, Ed and Sandy Faulkner clung together watching proud alumni and their spouses. By then, Shannon's view had darkened. She told her parents not to trust a single word they heard. She said the people there would be perfectly polite, but then, she warned, they would turn and drive a blade into their backs. In fact there *were* signals of distress. In the college chapel an older woman hissed at Shannon when she entered. Another woman called her "bitch" just loud enough for rows around to hear. Strained smiles and looks of cautious welcome came, too. But Sandy was uncomfortable. After Watts's speech she wanted only to get out of there. "Oh, it's fine so far," she said to Ed half hopefully. "I think everything is going fine. Some people have actually been quite nice." Ed gave her a look. Sandy paused, then let her ample shoulders fall. "All I really want," she said with a huge sigh, "is to go back to my hotel and put my mouthpiece in before I bite a hole right through my mouth."

Ed was surveying the receiving line. Whatever thoughts he had he kept completely to himself. He was used to keeping quiet. Making fences six and sometimes seven days a week, he had developed deep habits of silence. From dawn to dusk as long as the dry weather held he worked under the sky marking undulating borders for those with something to protect. He dug postholes in old farmland squeezed in by pinching suburbs. He ran picket fences around new homes all of which were built to look alike. He built steel-webbed boundaries for parking lots and freight yards, small businesses and schools. He knew everything a man could know about limits. He spent his life defining them, outlining who had what and what went where.

That life had left Ed so taciturn that some people thought him slow. Sandy knew better. Ed just had his ways. They had married young and then stayed with it. They had a rhythm now and they communicated, sometimes, without a word exchanged. After a while, Ed turned to her and pulled a squeak of air in through his teeth. Sandy gently took his arm and gave a pat that soothed them both. "Well," she said with a false smile. "Let's go act like Mom and Dad." And so they did.

In Jenkins Hall late that afternoon, Tony Lackey sat behind his desk. Cadets came in all day, he said, telling him that Shannon already had "the I-26 eyes," the vacant and dazed expression drivers got after spending too long on the road. A lot of knobs got I-26 eyes after a while. It was a standing joke on campus. But Lackey seemed surprised that Shannon would already show some strain. None of the more difficult aspects of that regimen had started yet. His thoughts that afternoon echoed Terry Leedom's. "What do you think her agenda is?" Lackey wondered. "Stay awhile, cry foul, then leave and write a book? That's what everybody says."

Headlines in the Sunday papers caught the spirit of the day. "Faulkner: Alone in victory," reported the *Post and Courier*. "Faulkner faces isolation at Citadel," echoed a full-page headline in the *Atlanta Constitution*. The most powerful photograph from that first immersion showed Shannon standing alone off to one side while a cluster of boys from her company huddled together feet away. In Charleston that evening, the weather prediction was for temperatures in the high 90s. All week, the mercury would only rise.

Old Maps for a New World

AFTER ALL THE GOODBYES, the kisses on the cheek and the sharp, fatherly slaps on young men's shoulders, after church services and parents' breakfasts, countless handshakes and innumerable introductions, mothers, fathers, stepparents and siblings headed off to other points and home. In Charleston, as that influx dispersed, the campus quickly settled back into itself. With the niceties done and the hotel bills paid, power, pure if undefinable, shifted to the boys. Monday, they would start to use it. There was an immediate heightening of the mood.

In the darkness before dawn on the first morning of military training, the campus lay dead still under a hazy trace of moonlight. Gnats settled weightlessly on slopes of skin, then bit down hard. It was hot that morning. Even the ground was warm. A thin blue light shone weakly from a guardhouse near the campus gates. Somewhere a radio crackled unintelligibly. A flagpole stood in empty silhouette. Not a soul was stirring.

Well before the sun came up a barked command in the Zoo signaled the first life. Soon the sound of marching drifted up and down the campus. Inside Fourth Barracks' freshly painted quad, the boys from November Company moved up and out. Dressed in dark shorts and dark T-shirts, they stomped about in tight formation, traversing the checkerboard concrete while chanting loudly in the dark. *"November!"* They cried it out in unison, making an eerie racket that ricocheted against the walls. *"Oooh aah . . ."* Soon, lights flicked on around them.

At the corner of Law Barracks, in a squad room busy with the movements of half a dozen uniformed cadets, the members of training cadre were talking and relaxing. A small group ran past them chanting, but nobody looked up. Then, in one sweeping commotion, the sleepy barracks sprang to life. Uniformed cadre members started running from room to room, yelling and shouting, slamming doors and beating wooden poles on metal grating. Over in the Zoo, the boys from Tango Company lined up behind a light blue guidon marked with their company letter. "The boys are back!" they chanted. Over and over they repeated it while new boys in their physical training outfits, called PTs, with polished shoes and black socks pulled up high to near their knees, stood idle in gawkish clusters.

On the third floor of Law Barracks, where Shannon spent the night without a roommate, shadows moved from floor to floor. Outside the barracks guardroom, a car idled in the dark. Two federal marshals sat up front.

As the first hint of light traced across the sky, nervous knobs in loose formations stood outside the barracks' gates. Waiting awkwardly in their limp clothes with plastic bags strung loose around their necks, they weaved and flinched with every order. When they marched, they stumbled. When they ran they bumped each other clumsily. Outside all four barracks, the scene was just the same. By 6:10 a.m. cadre and the new boys whom they were assigned to teach had gathered in the cavernous but nearly empty mess hall for a hearty breakfast to prepare them for a long, demanding day. At 6:45 uniformed cadets ordered all new students to their feet then marched them off toward their next stop. There, Joe Trez prepared to send them toward nine months of constant challenge.

"Today," announced the towering commandant, "you will begin to learn standards." After his short speech, cadets would move back to the barracks, where training cadre would take charge completely. "Today marks the formal transition," Trez announced. It would prove a major shift. But thousands had gone before them. Like Cliff Poole, Trez had walked where they were walking now, he reassured. "When I arrived here thirty years ago," he said, carefully enunciating every word, "I was a seventeen-year-old young punk from the state of New Jersey." Now, he held himself as an example. "I returned on one June of last year to assume the duties of a professor of military science and commandant," he said. He had superior training for that role. In the Army, he had commanded platoons, companies, battalions and finally a full brigade. But now, he told his anxious, silent listeners, he was sacrificing all of that—for them.

"On one August," he continued gravely, "I retired from the U.S. Army to become your commandant of cadets." He expected them to understand just what that meant. But what he did not add was that he made the change with bitterness. He had expected to be on active duty while serving them in Jenkins Hall. But with the school pinned under a harsh and unforgiving spotlight, Pentagon officials imposed a sudden change in policy. Trez, crushed by that sharp order, was forced to leave a life of soldiering behind. He laid that sacrifice before the new recruits, then straightened, cleared his throat and sent those students on their way with warnings and advice.

"College is a noun. Military is an adjective," he advised. He expected every boy to pay attention to his studies. Stress outside the class as well as in it was to be expected. "That stress that you are feeling right now is the fourth class system," Trez announced. That stress served an important purpose. Everything those boys did conformed to a grand plan. They should not fear. The system would protect them. "The greatest fear of all is fear of the unknown," he said. Knobs were yawning and stretching in their seats. Some listened attentively, but others brought the looser habits of the outside world into that hall. Cadre members paced off to the side, waiting. "Each of you should be able to conquer that fear that's inside of you," Trez went on. In that challenge, he assured, each cadet would find himself. A boy with cropped brown hair dropped his head and slept. Trez raised his voice. "For the last two days," he boomed, "you have stayed in dorm rooms on a college campus." Now military training would begin. Freshmen must relinquish their old lives, bond together as a group and devote themselves to one another. "Individuals will not make it here," the stone-faced colonel warned. "If you are an individual and you want to stay an individual, every day will be a very tough day."

Trez drew himself up until his posture made a rigid arrow of his back. "You had breakfast this morning, right?" Several knobs looked up and nodded. "Well, the eggs came from a chicken. But the bacon, the bacon comes from a pig. The chicken contributed to that breakfast. But the pig was committed to it. Here, you have to be pigs." They could expect no middle ground. "Your greatness will be made possible by the extremes of your personalities," he continued. "In commitment, you will subordinate yourselves to your classmates. You must first learn to follow before you can lead. While I'm being your cheerleader, I will also be your roughest taskmaster." He spoke admiringly of Attila the Hun and told them that a cadet's desire to meet the challenge that they faced must be all consuming. Finally, he waved his hand and broke into a smile.

"Gentlemen—and lady," he added, belatedly acknowledging Shannon's presence in that room, "I am proud to have you as members of the class of 1999."

With a stiff salute, he turned the lectern over to Matthew William Pantsari, a handsome, smooth-skinned senior who had risen through the ranks and now commanded a cadet staff of twenty-two. As the corps' regimental commander and top-ranking cadet officer, Pantsari was to send the new class on its way. "Sit up straight in your chairs," he said gently. "And keep your hands away from your face." He sprinkled his commands with encouragement. "My worst day as a cadet," he told the pale and silent teenagers, "is better than my best day at any other college. I am going to teach those of you who are studs to succeed and to excel. But there are going to be those of you who are the duds. You will fall by the wayside."

Over to one side, Trez observed Pantsari's first comments with approval. "I have jumped out of a plane sixty-one times," Trez remarked as he watched the new class start that journey. "Every time you feel the fear. I was here until two in the morning talking kids into staying." His mind took him back to Army days. "It's the first time in 153 years that the commandant had to leave active duty," Trez added distractedly. "The first time. My turn." In the Army, he thought he had a chance at making general. Now that chance was gone. These kids had better make it worth it.

Nearby, Sergeant Louis A. Venable Sr., the commandant's head of cadet operations known universally as "Gunny," commented that the new class arrived with "the shortest hair I've seen in many a year." He was encouraged by the change. Perhaps the gap outside the gates was narrowing. "Some years," he added, raising both eyebrows in an arc, "we've had kids come in with purple hair. Now that's something."

With a sudden explosion, the freshmen stood to leave. Gathered together by company, they marched in caricatures of soldierliness across the smooth parade field and then disappeared inside respective barracks. Sophomores were there, waiting. Amid a welter of commands, the new boys formed in shaky lines by company, making a dark outline around the perimeter of every barracks' quadrangle. In jerky and uncertain steps, one by one the knobs moved forward. Each company had set up a table on a barracks checkerboard. Seated and already sweating, cadre members moved the knobs through initial steps. Signing in was the first hurdle. New boys waited silently in turn, then ran up fast and screeched to a halt in front of older boys. Invariably, everything they did was wrong. The point of the exercise was to ratchet up the tension and to show who held command. With their faces twisted with exertion and resolve, the new boys stopped short in front of staring eyes, screaming out their names until their voices broke. Most barely made it to a full stop and had no chance to sign their names before corrections started.

"I can't *hear* you!"

From side to side, male voices shouted "Sir, yes sir" in a strange chorus, as a new class turned and bent to a world of new demands. It was a simple sentence—the most important of that year—that would set a groove deep in their souls. Obedience was critical. If they did not master that, then they would have to leave.

By 8 a.m. every table was busy with an antique drama.

"Again!"

A knob raced back to his line, turned sharply on one heel and then ran back again to start the process over. For twenty steps his legs pumped. Then he broke to a hard stop several feet back from a wood table. "Sir!" he shouted, off balance from that sprint, "Cadet recruit . . ."

"I can't hear you."

"*Sir!*"

From one table to the next, the new boys tried again. And then again. And then again until they were informed that they could go. In every barracks, for every company, the scene was much the same. When the knobs screamed, the older boys screamed louder. When the knobs showed fear, the training cadre pushed them harder. Disgust curled like vapor through the stagnant air inside those buildings. No new boy got it right. That was the whole point.

"Sir!" The shout rang off the barracks walls and burst from aching lungs. One after another, shaking new recruits made awkward, gawkish salutes. They tried their best, then ran away to start again.

"Sir!" they screamed, their faces flushed and bulging.

Over to one side, David Abrams provided running commentary. "Here, you have serious responsibilities," he observed approvingly. "It is not a game. This whole process puts us way out in front of the power curve in the real world."

Step by step, knob by knob, Shannon moved forward. At last she stood in front. When her turn came, she took off toward the India Company table at a run. But before she could stop she was ordered back. Up and back. Up and back while an India Company first sergeant fumed and sputtered in a rage. "Sound off!" he shouted angrily. She tried and tried again.

At a table to the right, a knob with Lima Company fumbled with a ballpoint pen, then watched in agony as it dropped to the ground. The sophomore at the desk began to swell and rage. Rising from his chair, he pointed at the recruit's feet and bellowed. The boy looked down, ashamed. "Look up!" the black sergeant screamed. "You look at me when I talk to you." The boy looked up. At that moment, the boy in front of him pointed again toward the pen lying useless by his shoes. The new boy bent to reach for it.

"Did I tell you to move?"

He straightened up. Again the company leader pointed, now trembling with anger. Up and down the knob's eyes traveled. Up and down he bobbed. Nothing he could do was right. Finally, he snatched the pen. An upperclassman standing near just shook his head and laughed.

Shannon did not see them. She had problems of her own. Arriving at India Company's sign-in table for a third time, she jolted to a stop. By the sally ports, cameras focused and then flashed. But fifteen cadets circled the school's first female recruit to block the line of sight. *"Cadet Shannon Faulkner reporting for duty, sir!"* Shannon shouted time and time again. *"Sir!"* She was too close. *"Sir!"* She was too far. *"Sir!"* She was too quiet. *"Sir!"* She was all wrong.

"Move back!"

"Move up!"

The cadet in charge of India Company's sign-in sheet reddened and jumped to his feet. With a sudden burst, he pounded his fist down on the wood table. *"Pop off!"* he screamed.

"Sir!"

She was too near.

She tried again. The sergeant looked at her with pure disgust.

"Sound off!"

She shouted louder.

He pounded both fists on the table.

"Sir!" She let the air burst from her body with all the force she had. But the sergeant raised the table off the ground with both his knees, then slammed it down with the full force of both his arms.

"Sound *off!*" he said hysterically.

"Sir!"

"Sound *off!*" The sergeant's feet pounded the concrete—in slaps, in syncopation. His face darkened, and a river of sweat left a growing stain across his shirt. He pulled off his hat then slapped it back again.

"Sir! Cadet recruit . . ."

The sergeant was hyperventilating. Nothing was enough. He rose to his feet and leaned in close and shouted directly into Shannon's face.

Shannon looked right through him. "Sir!"

He sat again and rocked his knees together back and forth then punched his fist into the air. While Shannon looked straight, he crashed both fists down on the table then jumped to his feet before slamming back into his chair. Still standing, Shannon kept her mouth gripped tight and her eyes immobile. The sergeant flailed his hat against the table, screamed at her and then inhaled.

"Pop off!" he shrieked.

Shannon stood still and started that routine again. Breathing hard now, the sergeant rose to his feet and lifted the table with him then smashed it down with so much force it nearly splintered. Shannon did not move. The sergeant stood again and ran a soiled glove across his dripping forehead.

"Sir!"

After that long drama, Shannon signed her name, and it was done. As she turned and ran back to rejoin her group, the sergeant crashed his head onto the table with a bang and lay quiet for a spell as if in shame. The Citadel's first woman had signed in as a cadet. After a long, theatrical pause, the sergeant lifted his head and tensed his body: "Next!"

Near the east gate a woman adjusted her tennis visor and stared across the quad looking for her son. Four companies were inside signing up new boys. At each table, boys with one stripe on their shoulder screamed and shouted in the din. The woman jumped and clasped her hands. Oh, there he was! She bobbed up on the balls of her feet and waved her arm in wild, cheerful arcs. That was her son, she told a stranger. He was starting, too. Crazy and violent as it all looked, she longed to have her boy claim a part of that tradition.

All that morning, knobs were run from one place to another, stopping for water, stopping for air, but always hearing the same deep, welling anger from commanders who treated each of them with hatred and disgust. Some cadets moved in close and shouted directly into new boys' ears. Others stood back a bit and watched in cold disdain. The knobs, now drenched in sweat and pockmarked with their fears, were herded here and there, running single file. In the barbershop that day knobs moved in and out of chairs, two minutes at a time. Six barbers buzzed their skulls to a close shave, leaving virtually no hair on the sides and only patches on the top.

While waiting for that shearing, new boys stared intently at their *Guidons*, poring over words that would guide them all year long. "The life of a cadet is far removed from your former way of living," they read as they waited to be shaved. In the *Guidon*'s instructions governing "conduct and well-being," the new recruits found all the basics. "A 'lone wolf,'" the palm-sized book explained, "will find it impossible to survive within the Corps. Your classmates are your only companions, since fraternization with upperclassmen is prohibited. Start off right by getting acquainted with your classmates. However, never be afraid to ask an upperclassman a question; request permission first and you will find him ready and willing to assist you at any time. When you are allowed to leave campus, it is best to go in a group so that no one will feel left out. These classmates are your sole source of support and aid at this time. They will be your friends for life."

"We're so close to reality, they don't realize it," David Abrams said smoothly, sliding easily into his role as a spokesman for the school. "They see us yelling and they think we're trying to be mean. But we are just training them. This is training for life. It is the best training you can get." He loved the school. It gave him everything he wanted.

In the hall, a knob stood stiff and yellow, his eyes locked forward, his chin quivering. "Where are you from, knob?" an older boy inquired in a sneering tone.

"Sir! November Company. The company of *pride,* sir!"

A woman walked into the hallway with a camera. She said her son was in that group, and she wanted to get a photograph of him in his first knob haircut. An upperclassman blocked her way. Outraged, he burst into the barbershop and stood at attention in front of Abrams. "I need clearance," he said urgently. "She has a camera. We don't know what they might do with it. She might be after Faulkner."

Abrams observed him coolly. All civilians, he calmly informed the nervous cadre member, were to be kept as far from Shannon as possible. The boy rushed off. Then Abrams shrugged. "If I were a reporter," he said, "I'd come in here looking like a priest. That's what I'd do. I'd dress up like a priest. It's called infiltrating. I'm mission oriented. The point is, get what you need."

In the hallway, a knob stood frozen with his *Guidon* poised hardly two inches from his face. Like others around him, his arm was locked at a stiff angle. Only his eyes moved. "The purpose of the cadet system at The Citadel is to develop and graduate the 'whole man,'" the book advised. "The Citadel System is the completeness [*sic*] with which it matures, refines, trains and schools the totality of a young man's character. This finely balanced process is called the 'whole man' concept. During four years, cadets will be developed academically, physically, militarily, and spiritually."

"Feel better, now?" a cadet inquired of a newly shorn recruit who seemed near tears.

"Sir! Yes sir!" the knob responded.

"Louder."

"*Sir!*" the knob replied, his voice breaking. "Yes sir!"

"Well, you *look* a lot better."

"You are no longer a civilian," the *Guidon* informed those still waiting. "Certain answers such as 'yeah' and 'okay' will no longer be part of your vocabulary. The three 'knob answers' are: 'Sir, yes sir. Sir, no sir. and Sir, no excuse sir.' In all communication, you must refer to an upperclassman as 'Mister.'"

"These boys are going to be under a lot of stress tonight," Abrams said jovially. "I'd call it a 'very intimidating evening,'" he added with a laugh.

In the barbershop, cadre members motioned to those waiting to sit down. Even that was hardly easy.

"Sit up straight," a sophomore ordered.

A gangly boy looked up, startled and afraid.

"Don't look at me, boy. I said sit up. You sit up and look straight ahead. Move, man. Move! Knob, don't you look at me. Move up. Sit your butt up at the end of that chair. This isn't some rock concert. You don't settle in." The boy slid forward until he barely had a perch. His legs were shaking at sharp angles. His hands were gathered into fists.

To the left, another sophomore gave the same instructions with a gentler tone. "No, not like that," he told a knob quite calmly. "Just move up. You can't sit back." The second knob shifted in his metal chair. Then another. And another until thirteen boys sat in a row, their postures in alignment. Cadets around them joked and laughed while the new boys sat like stones.

"What looks like hate is just a form of stress, really," Abrams continued. "We all are master stressors. Stress is good. Stress is what you get in
life. The ones who succeed are the ones who can handle it."

Shannon arrived with India Company and left again with a full head
of hair. A tremendous amount of court time had been spent on discussions about her locks. First, Judge Houck allowed that in the interest of
full equality the college could have her head shaved like those of all the
other knobs. Attorney General Janet Reno objected and asked the judge
to reconsider. In reply, the judged stressed that he merely left it to the
college to decide; soon after that Citadel officials (aware that they were
being mocked as petty and mean-spirited) announced that Shannon
could keep her hair long after all. But in the barbershop that morning,
no one near her spoke. The boys of India Company were now deep
inside a cyclone of their own. Razors buzzed and whirred. Shannon
waited. Then the group walked out. Abrams kept on talking. The
school, he said, gave students an advantage later on in life. "You know
the way they have their hands on each other's shoulders? That's symbolic
of their whole first year. They get locked on in the process. They have to
bond together."

Out in the hallway, a knob moved alone in front of tight clusters of
his fellow students. A sophomore stopped him with a bark. "Where are
you supposed to be, boy?"

"Sir. I'm going . . ."

"Is that a knob answer?"

"Sir. No sir."

"Then get your ugly face out of my face."

While the boy shuffled off, upperclassmen hugged and grinned and
asked about each other's summers. Occasionally one or another among
them turned a spotlight on a new recruit.

"What company are you freaks in?"

"Sir! C Company, sir."

The upperclassman moved his hips and raised his voice an octave.
"Sir," he hissed in mockery, making the sentence long and sibilant, "C
Company, sir." He smiled at a friend, then pushed in close to one knob's
face. "Are you grinning at me, freak? Shut your face down, knob. Shut it
down! I'm not here to soothe your mood."

Down the hall, Shannon and several other knobs squeezed together
in a line with their backs pressed hard against the wall. Every one of
them stood with their shoulders high, chests pumped out and one arm

at an angle that put their *Guidons* up in front. Some words would soon be seared into every new recruit's memory. "A cadet holds the highest esteem for the uniform he wears. For many years it has commanded recognition and respect. Never injure that respect by acting in a manner that will reflect discredit upon you or The Citadel. Such actions would constitute a serious infraction of regulations, and would dishonor the traditions of The Citadel."

When Shannon's group walked back into the heat, Abrams clicked on a walkie-talkie at his side. "Elvis has left the building," he said playfully. "Next," he advised, returning the walkie-talkie to his belt, "we go to the haze maze." There, in The Citadel shop situated next to the laundry and the tailor shop, every knob would get a uniform and other standard-issue supplies. Though designed as merely a pickup point for items every student would need, the "haze maze" lived up to its name by providing new levels of hardship and insult. Inside the shop on that bright morning, a tall young man stood swaying under the hard gaze of a cadet.

"What would make a big city boy like you want to come to The Citadel?" the older boy inquired snidely.

"Sir. I wanted to attend a military school, sir."

"Is that one of the three knob answers?" the cadre member hissed, pulling in close. Every question held a trap.

"Sir! No sir."

A black recruit stepped up to be measured for a hat.

"Do you like it here, knob?"

"Sir! No sir," the boy shouted.

"You don't?"

The knob stayed stiff and quiet.

A fat boy from Mobile, Alabama, approached next. Drenched in sweat and shaking, he had the look of someone near collapse. An upperclassman touched him gently on the arm. "Calm down. Now you calm down, and you stay focused," he said in a soft voice.

The boy blinked hard, his eyes glistening. "Sir. Yes sir," he quaked.

"You'll make it. You'll be all right."

"Sir! Yes sir."

Shyly, he looked for reassurance in those eyes. There was none. Instead, the other student snapped and drew away: "Don't you look at me, knob! You look straight ahead. Get out of my face, freak! You hear me? You got ears?" The boy's whole body jolted.

Knobs shuffled forward from one aisle to the next, filling up huge bags with gear.

"Hey, spic," someone shouted. "Where are you from?"

"Sir!" the boy choked.

"Get up here, boy. Get up here."

"I don't think their hearts are really in it," Abrams remarked distractedly. "This is the quietest I've ever seen it in here."

White cloth sacks slowly filled with hats and shoes and other items, gaining weight and bulk with every stop. Knobs wrestled silently with their growing cargo. Still, the sophomores pushed at every turn.

"Hold that bag out straight, freak," an upperclassman yelled. "Hold it out in front of you. That's it. Straight out. Arms straight. Bag out. Don't bend those elbows. Now you keep it out. This isn't Montessori school."

Jeremy Wilson yanked a knob's white bag, pulling it far in front of the boy's chest. "Now, if you're going to be so strong, then you just hold your bag out there," he said acidly. The boy grimaced but stayed silent, then squeezed his eyes in pain. When he opened them, a sophomore was busy throwing punches near his face.

A rail-thin teenager with red stubble on his head and freckles all across his face broke into loud, stuttering sobs. Matt Pantsari and Wilson pulled him aside, then dropped their voices near a whisper. Wilson drew him close, wrapping his steel band of an arm around the knob's quaking shoulder and staring straight into that contorted face.

"I can't do it," the boy sobbed, his chest heaving. "I can't. I can't do it. I can't." Wilson rocked him back and forth.

"Look," Pantsari softly consoled, "you are doing something most people can't do. You are going to make it. You'll be fine. You're a strong guy. You'll do it."

Wilson was with him in an echo. "You'll be all right," he soothed. "You'll be okay. Don't try so hard. Everybody messes up." Tears rolled down the boy's splotched face and fell in quiet spatters on the floor.

"I can't. I can't . . ." he stammered, breathing hard.

Pantsari rested a calming hand on his thin shoulder. "You hang in there. Just catch your breath and then go back out there. You can do this. I know you can. You'll be tough. You're just learning, that's all. We've all been through it."

Nearby, another cadet's throat convulsed. His eyes drifted, but he did not move or flinch. An upperclassman strolled by and nodded in approval. Then the boy exhaled.

Down the line, one by one, the new boys filled their bags, then left. Some looked numb. Some stumbled. Some cried. Some already moved like robots, firm and blank.

Shannon missed the haze maze. She was next door in the tailor shop being measured for new uniforms. Other aspects of her training were different as well. Only five people were allowed to speak with her. Any command that she was given had to come from her squad sergeant, platoon leader, the company commander, battalion commander or Pantsari, the regimental commander, himself. No other boys could tell her what to do. All weekend, cadets said that they resented it. That rule alone meant special treatment. Most cadets did not find it fair, and they did not think it would work—not for her and not for their old school. The point of all that training was treating everybody just the same. "Well, we all know how it is," said an upperclassman that morning. "She's the only one in here with a bunch of lawyers and a room full of federal marshals to protect her. What a joke."

From the cadet store, new students were moved along toward lunch. The mess hall was less than one hundred yards away. But Shannon would later say that it was there that her will faltered. As India Company knobs were herded up a dusty asphalt road, Shannon said she heard a voice. It came from over by a tree outside the tailor shop where several people stood. The words were simple: "The heat in Charleston makes some folks crazy," someone said. "It can play tricks on people's minds." There was nothing more than that. But Shannon felt a shock. She thought she recognized that voice. Turning, she saw a huddle of men beneath the tree. Several smiled and waved. Shannon felt her stomach go.

It would be months before Shannon told her parents of that voice. When she did, she connected it to another she had heard four days before. On the Thursday before she left Powdersville, she said, she went to a local grocery store to pick up several items she would need for the school year. There, a man approached her from behind. "He put his hand over my mouth," Shannon said. "He held me back and talked real low, right in my ear. I'll never forget what he said. He said: 'I can't touch you while you're on that campus. But I can get to your parents. I know a place where I can watch them burn.'" The man was gone as quickly as he came. She said she never saw his face.

Shannon told no one of that encounter. Death threats had come before. She did not want to scare her parents. She put no faith in the police. She had no proof. It was just a voice in her ear, her word against a ghost. But on that Monday morning, three years of fear came into focus.

At lunch, working her way through a plate of beef and pasta, Shannon felt her stomach wrench. She made it halfway through the meal. Then a violent bout of nausea gripped her. She turned stiffly to the cadet seated next to her. "Sir," she told him weakly. "I think I'm going to be sick." He motioned her off to a bathroom. She did not make it to the stall.

During that meal, up in front beneath the lectern, cadet commanders dined with men from the administration. They were utterly relaxed amid the uproar, and focused mainly on the food. One upperclassman kept grumbling about the lunch. The Citadel always served hamburgers on the knobs' first day, but that year there were no hamburgers. He was incensed by that. "It's always been hamburgers," he complained over and over.

Several tables away, a cadet stood and started slamming silver and china on the table. Terrified freshmen tried to follow orders. But every time they moved, more china hit the table. Pantsari coolly told them all to quiet down.

"As a knob," a member of the training cadre explained, like a coach explaining football maneuvers, "you've got to master the one-thousand-yard stare. You can't look at your plate. You can't look left or right. You look over at the forehead of the knob across the table. And you only move if you are told to, which is all the time. I lost twenty-three pounds in my first year."

Plastic mugs slopped full of Italian dressing, mayonnaise, peanut butter, jelly and hot sauce were passing back and forth. Platters of spaghetti were passed down every table's length. In Lima Company, a cadre member was busy screaming at his new boys. "Eat!" he commanded. "Eat!" At the far end of his table another cadet yelled out: "Chew!"

Pantsari rose and stood before them like a father hopelessly annoyed with a car full of screaming kids. "Everyone shut up for ten minutes," he ordered. "I don't want to hear a peep."

A member of his regimental command looked at The Citadel's ranking cadet with friendly affection and respect. "Matt Pantsari is like the CEO, and we are like his staff," he said with a broad grin. "The great thing about The Citadel is that it's just like a corporation. First you learn to take orders. Then you learn to lead. This is the best training you could ever get to face the outside world."

Outside, in the bright sunlight after lunch, Shannon, looking pale and drained, belatedly rejoined her group.

"What's the purpose of marking time?" shouted an India Company leader.

"Cover and alignment," came an answer offered up in unison.

"Cover," the leader yelled, "means standing right below. Alignment means next to. When you march you need to keep in line." They were the building blocks for perfect order in formation. But on that first day loose-limbed recruits drifted and wandered with each step, their every movement out of order.

Cadre members circled and corrected here and there. Most wore their black hats low. Dark visors hid their eyes. Knobs could not see their faces. Instead, they stared straight and moved inside a torrent of commands.

"Get up!" They stood.

"Sit down." They sat.

"Get up!" They stood.

After five rounds of it Shannon broke away with a cadet escort. She was getting sick again.

Over in the band's quiet practice room, Herb Day introduced himself to the new band members. He tried to put those boys at ease. "Relax," he said. "This is a different environment here. Stand at ease, please. Things are different here. It's like a classroom. Take a breath."

But the boys could not relax. Instead, they stood staring straight and ignored his kind entreaties.

Day moved back and forth across the room with infinite patience. "Okay, go ahead and sit down."

They slammed into their chairs like children playing odd man out. Then every single one of them sat frozen in their silence. Day shook his head with something like sadness.

"Sir," croaked a trombonist. "May I clean my glasses, sir?"

Day smiled. "Yes, yes," he said. "You guys relax. You let your shoulders down now. You all clean your faces and take a breath. You have to relax."

Later, in his office, Day said the whole Faulkner thing had simply worn him out. Alumni cast a shadow on his integrity, suggesting that he had changed the rules for Shannon or asking him to fix things so as to keep her from the band. He was insulted and outraged. The judge had seemed suspicious, too. That had hurt him more than anything. If it were his decision, he said cautiously, he would have let girls in. He had a daughter who was as tough as anyone he knew. He beamed and told a story about how she had given someone the "vertical bird" once for suggesting that she was incompetent just because she was a girl. "I just loved her for that," he said, nodding affectionately. "Just flashed that guy the bird."

Shannon checked into the Mary Bennett Murray Memorial Infirmary and was diagnosed with heat exhaustion. The nurses were attentive and quite gentle with their patient. But tensions coursed through that hall, too. Moments after Shannon first checked in, Abrams went to see how she was doing. In the cool front hall, he ran into the chief nurse, Beth Summerford, who made her own attitude quite clear.

"We had six cadets in here before," the dark-haired nurse, the wife of a Citadel graduate, told Abrams conspiratorially. Suddenly she grinned and moved her fist like a sports fan, pump, pump, pump. "Now, Shannon makes it *seven.*"

When Abrams turned away, Summerford had something else to say. "If it were me," she added snappishly in a quick aside between two women, "I'd be out there bringing honor to my general right now. I'd be marching. I would have trained ahead of time. I would have made my gender proud."

Outside, Terry Leedom flicked on his walkie-talkie and called his assistant, Judith Fluck. "This is Papa Bear," he said, "calling Mama Bear." The device crackled. "Well," he said with a half-smile, turning to address himself to a television cameraman. "The cadet, from what I hear, may have come down with a little stomach distress. We are trying to get exact information now. As you see," he continued cheerfully, "we have a heat situation here. The heat index, a complicated measurement combining temperature, humidity and rate of absorption, reads 92.3 degrees."

Across the parade field, a black flag, the signal for danger, was flying over Mark Clark Hall. Back on Leedom's desk, huge piles of messages were growing at odd angles, some marked "friendly," some marked "hostile."

Knobs marched through their paces holding bottles of Evian water. Nervous officials moved about, warning cadre members to be vigilant.

"Plenty of rest. Ample fluids," they ordered one cadre member and the next. "Yes sir," the upperclassmen replied with a salute.

David Atwood, a sophomore from Greenwich, Connecticut, shook his head with some disgust. "This year is just totally different," he said. "In the first four minutes of my first mess last year the corporal broke two glasses and a plate. The corporals ran everything. Now," he looked around at sweaty boys chugging bottled water, "well, these guys, they are just being a little inconvenienced."

He was depressed by all the changes. Last year's sophomore class, he said, had stood around during Hell Week "talking about how cruel and tough they could be." This year's cadre had to sign in early and take classes on correct behavior. He grimaced. To him, it was the end of something admirable. "You know, I went to West Point for a game last year," he said finally. There, uniformed women walked everywhere around the campus. "I thought it was a joke."

Shannon was treated in the infirmary and released. She rejoined her company briefly but found she could not stay. Soon she was back again and lying in the room Citadel officials had earlier proposed as her living quarters. Shannon saw no humor in it now. When nurses peeked in, she was lying balled up in her bed, her stomach twisting.

In Jenkins Hall on that hot Monday, Colonel Roger Popham, Lackey's colleague as assistant commandant, leaned through an open doorway and set his lips into a frown. "Well," he said, sighing heavily, biding his time until Lackey got around to looking up, "she lasted an hour and a half out of the infirmary. Now she's back."

Down on the parade field late that afternoon, Val Vojdik was busy shooting home movies of lawyers standing on the grass. One by one, they approached and waved and gave the thumbs up sign for victory. Henry Weisburg grinned and smiled. None among them knew yet that Shannon was not marching.

Once Bob Black heard of Shannon's condition, he spewed venom at the school. "'You're a bitch,'" he mimicked them. "'You're a woman. You're a whore. You look sick. Let's take you off to bed.'"

Black said he understood the way all those men thought. "It's time to tear the whole thing down," he had sputtered in a rage one day outside the courtroom. "I'd like to hose the whole thing down, the whole old-boy thing that runs the South. That's what I'd like to do."

A cannon shot caused half the crowd to jump. White smoke drifted

west across the field. The crowd swelled. Mothers were there with children. Men brought wives and friends. Some graduates arrived in Army
camouflage. Others came in business suits, or in shorts and old tank
tops. The first parade was always something special. The crowd mixed
straw hats and sundresses, T-shirts and priest's collars. A breeze stirred,
and the sun lay spent and white above the trees. A flag flapped to life and
coasted up and down against the wind, oversized and brilliant against
the blue. For a moment, that whole campus was at peace. Then the band
played the national anthem, and several people started crying.

Gunny Venable, whose primary job consisted of telling everyone just
where to stand during parades, gave a broad, comic wink. He had just
heard that Shannon had checked into the infirmary. "We're not missing
a cadet," he whispered, wagging one finger in the air. "We are missing a
nominee. There's a big difference. They don't become cadets until they
take the oath."

That night, relaxing after a hard day in the whirlwind of reporters,
Terry Leedom sat back in his office chair and took a long, deep breath.
"What a day," he laughed. For him, it ended badly. "My last interview,"
he said plaintively, was with "a real oinker from Washington, the ugliest
reporter that I ever saw." Leedom yawned and stretched. "All the scotch
in Charleston," he laughed, "and still you couldn't drink her pretty."

Leedom would go home soon to get some needed sleep. But for the
knobs and for their cadre, the day was not yet done. The new recruits
were put to bed at 9 o'clock. But they were roused one hour later by the
sound of screams and yells.

The Rocks

THE GATES CLOSED. The world contracted. Shannon lay exhausted and dehydrated in the infirmary, her stomach empty, one arm sore from several nurses' attempts to find a vein for intravenous fluids. Yet as much as her arrival had traumatized the school, Shannon's absence was hardly noticed in the barracks that first evening. There, divested of watches, private talismans and all reminders of the world they'd left behind, the new boys were swept into a new world. There was no longer such a thing as time. Time was only light and dark. The hours themselves were forced and framed by training cadre. There was no privacy. From their feet, shod in Citadel shoes, to their hair, shaved nearly bald in pinprick Citadel stubble, every aspect of their lives had changed on that first day. From that night forward, every move they made would be observed, controlled, corrected. There was no outside world, no respite, no voice of soft encouragement, no mother, father, girlfriend or beloved sibling. There was the corps, and the corps was everything. The new recruits were nothing. They did not even keep their names. That first year they would be knobs and freaks and worse. They touched the tar baby that night. It was "hell with a purpose," Terry Leedom had explained. And it lasted for nine months.

For the next few weeks, it was the hour to awaken when the cadre said so. It was time to sleep when cadre allowed it. It was time to eat and drink and shower and urinate on cadre schedules according to cadre plans. Permission granted. Permission refused. "Sir, can I scratch my nose, sir?" Take a drink? Take a pee? Eat a bite? Recruits could scratch when cadre said so. "Sir, yes sir." They took their rest when cadre gave it. But the cadre did not give them rest. "What is it, freak, you tired?" "Sir, no sir." That was the tradition.

At one time, knobs were assigned to seniors as their slaves. Vestiges of that system still remained. Sophomores assigned to training cadre held total power those first weeks. Then all upperclassmen had their day. Delta, Echo, Bravo, Band, each company functioned like an old plantation, each with a distinct personality and reputation, benevolent or brutal, combining law, judge and jury all in one. Charlie. F-Troop. The Mike Reich. In their midst, the administrators moved. They were proud of their old school. It was a human laboratory, they said, a constant in a changing world, a place that they could count on and a place where they felt safe. They leaned on it and found it strong. And so they smiled and gave their tacit blessings. How could they fault those boys? That system made them who they were. The grass was clipped. Salutes were crisp. A sense of order held. Yet all the while the corps lived in a different world, a world of chaos and intimidation, a world that was renewed on that hot night.

"Knobs are like chattel," a senior carefully explained. "If a knob has been told to do something or not to do something by a superior officer and someone from another company interferes with those orders, then that person—the superior officer—not the knob, is held to account." It was a matter of honor. It was a question of property. And it was older than any of them.

Every class that went through that old system passed it on, then added something of its own. Knobmores, as most sophomores were disparagingly called by upperclassmen, could treat those new recruits just as they pleased. Only on Recognition Day, during one final harrowing ordeal, would those freshmen find a place among their peers. Later, proudly, they turned their swallowed rage toward younger brothers like a flame. That year, without Shannon in their midst, the stark ordeal would be what it had always been, a severe induction into a culture of raw power run by men. Love and honor, truth and courage, the new boys knew the bywords. Patriots and poor boys, young men with high hopes, lost souls with no direction, they wanted light and dark inside a world of absolutes. The Citadel promised them that much. And the promise was repeated those first days. There would be hardship, yes. But hardship led to glory, they were assured, and every boy who ever came had wanted some of that.

Not an hour after the knobs were put to bed on that first Monday there was a whoop in second barracks and yelling to the east and west. From room to room the cadre moved, banging screen doors, slamming terror into every new boy's heart. In Law Barracks, sophomores flicked on lights and moved with purpose back and forth from floor to floor emitting screams and hollering their orders. Wood splintered against metal. Metal banged across concrete. Flesh slapped flesh, and flashbulbs popped. One cadet inside Law Barracks rode a bicycle in circles screaming incoherently into the sultry night.

Knobs were ordered up and out. Shuffling and still struggling with their clothes, they moved in frightened steps to stand inside their quads. "Close your eyes," a voice commanded. The knobs complied, and then the lights went out. For ten minutes there was total silence while mosquitoes buzzed and struck. Some knobs shook their arms and legs and squirmed. But most stood rigid in the dark and struggled just to breathe.

In a corner of Law Barracks, inside a well-lighted squad room, cadre members wearing black hats moved quietly about. Ten minutes passed, then twenty as the knobs swayed in their fear. Then there was a thundering of feet. A dozen cadets goose-stepped center stage. The marching stopped. Quiet. It was a weird ballet. The cadre moved from boy to boy, teaching each one how to brace. Chin down. Shoulders back. From company to company, the boys responded with stern looks of pure obedience. Every posture changed. Chins were driven into necks, and shoulders snapped to full attention. One by one those bodies locked. Rigid forms were broken at the waist. Arms were tucked into the sides then locked at right angles at the hip. Every hand became a fist.

The regimental commander's gentle voice drifted calmly through the loudspeakers. "Gentlemen of the class of 1999," he said, addressing those terrified recruits with both mildness and constraint. "The founding fathers of The Citadel based their educational style on self-discipline and self-sacrifice. Those concepts are contained in The Citadel's fourth class system. . . . The fourth class system is not meant to demean or degrade you in any way."

The sound of bagpipes floated from the Zoo. Brass belt buckles and smudged eyeglasses glowed and sparkled in the dark. Here and there a lightning bug popped into sight with a sharp glow, then faded in the darkness. At the sally port an upperclassman pulled his girlfriend closer to the gate.

There was a roar when Pantsari sent those new boys on their way. Cadets floated like boxers through the quads, ducking and weaving and delivering false blows. They barked commands and screamed and smiled as the new boys gulped and ran, more frenzied with each order.

The cadre swept the knobs from floor to floor. Soon, knobs were shivering in bathrobes waiting for knob showers, short hot latherings that left no time for a quick rinse. They kept their chins down now, their eyes locked, their elbows bent and their hands crushed into balls. They drove their nails down into flesh. They kept their heads locked straight, their necks throbbing with pain. The cadre ran among them here and there. Shadows in the galleries moved in and out of rooms, appearing on the balconies and vanishing behind closed doors.

"Sir. Yes sir!" those knobs exploded louder with each order.

Outside, a comely young woman from Charleston complained that this was nothing. "My ex-boyfriend said they worked him until he passed out," she said primly. "They make this whole thing so much softer every year."

Two of her friends began to whisper. Peering in through the locked gates, they drifted deep into a conversation.

"Those are some pigheaded men," one of them, a junior at the College of Charleston, commented.

Her friend squinted at the scene and nodded in agreement. "They are supposed to have this honor code, this sacred honor code. But they are like the biggest liars."

A campus police officer pulled his car up to the gate. Two headlights laid a streak of yellow in the quad. "The president gave me a call," he said slowly, scratching at a tooth with a short fingernail. "He doesn't want civilians observing this." And so the women left, and all those boys were left there on their own.

Early on the morning after Hell Night, Bud Watts stood tall and commanding before the class of 1999. He peered down at the trembling figures and the ashen faces, blank stares and earnest expressions of resolve they wore and offered them the courage to go on. "Here at The Citadel," he said in a flat monotone, "we are going to inculcate you in higher beliefs and higher standards."

The knobs stared straight ahead, impassive.

"We have already talked about The Citadel as an institution of higher learning, right?"

"*Sir! Yes sir.*" It was an explosion.

He would tell them about honor and earned pride. "I want you to be gentlemen as you go through this experience," he said calmly. "Understand the importance of knowing the feelings of your fellow cadets. Know the minds of your fellow cadets," he urged. "Remember that when you give a man your word, that is your bond, without equivocation." Every time he paused, the knobs shouted their consent.

"You all should know that five hundred ninety-two of you began on our orientation."

"Sir! Yes sir."

"There are five hundred eighty-five of you here right now. We understand what you are doing and what you are aspiring to do and the price that you are willing to pay." The general talked rousingly of spirit, mind and body. Then he wound back down. "I'm not long on questions," he said uninvitingly. "But I will answer any that you have."

No one raised a hand.

Watts nodded with obvious satisfaction. Then he asked, "Is everybody happy?"

"Sir! Yes sir."

"How many think you can do it?" It was a challenge and a dare.

About a hundred hands shot in the air.

"Uh-huh." The general smiled. "And how many of you were homesick last night?"

A dozen hands were meekly raised.

"Well, let me tell you a story. When I got down here, I was alone. The first night I went to bed, I don't think I knew anybody. I had a feeling in the pit of my stomach. I sort of curled up and rammed my fist into my stomach to make the feeling go away. It's always darkest just before you see the light."

Dismissed.

The class of 1999 stood and marched back into the open air in bumping, uneven steps. Sophomores started shouting at them before they made it out the door. All that day, knobs ran from one place to another responding to the endless cascades from commanders who found them always falling short. Tired and disoriented, drenched in sweat and half crazy with their fears, the knobs were herded here and there like skittish sheep.

"Baaaaa," mocked an upperclassman. "Baaaaa."

In the background, several seniors reminisced about a mouse. One year, they said jovially, they adopted a company mascot and named him "Airborne Willie." Airborne Willie parachuted from the upper floors. He was a "noble mouse," they said, a veteran of scores of dangerous missions. But one night his parachute malfunctioned and Airborne Willie splattered on the quad. There was some talk of sabotage. But that was never proved. A knob cleaned up the mess.

On Monday, the temperature had soared above 100 degrees by late afternoon. "Whew, 102!" read the headline in the *Post and Courier*. A reporter put the heat index as high as 115. Records were shattered for a second day. Below the weather story ran another headline: "Faulkner falls ill, misses the oath." A photograph showed Shannon drinking a cup of water near the haze maze. Tuesday would be just as hot. Shannon stayed inside the cool infirmary and slept.

Initiated with a howl of rage, Hell Week rushed on in heat and hardship day by day. Boys wrestled with themselves. Should they stay or should they go? That year they left in droves, telling company commanders, cadre members and anyone in authority that they wanted out, then finding themselves segregated from the rest as though they carried a contagion. One day they were marching. The next they were gone, erased, the duds, the didn't-make-its, the soft boys going back to Mama. All that outflow kept the commandant's office busy. Getting in was easy. But getting out was something else altogether, a two-day ordeal of priests and colonels pressing with a biting air. Boys who indicated their desire to leave were taken off to Thompson Hall and kept under cadet guard until their parents came. The imperative was clear. Don't let the washouts infect the rest. Don't let the numbers drop. There was a plan for that. There was a plan for everything.

Once a new boy made up his mind to go, almost no amount of cajoling or encouragement or sheer humiliation won him back. Yet more knobs stayed than left, and those who left looked back and sometimes wondered. Was there a higher purpose to that pain? Those who stayed believed it. The Citadel was tough, and they wanted to be tough. The school was challenging, and they wanted challenge. They hoped, more than anything, to find their true temper in blends of strength and stoic resilience, pride and focus. What they wanted drove them on. They wanted to be men. And they knew that they were boys. Suffer. It was a word, alien to much of America, that they learned fast and lived with for four years. But at graduation they could stand and win respect, at least, and adulation—hopefully. They would have their sashes neat and sabers sparkling and hold the envy of a thousand eyes beneath a blue spring sky. Suffer, and they would find success. Suffer, whatever sacrifice it took, and they would find their self-respect. Suffer, and the world would come together, not fall apart as they had feared. That's what they were told. Most of them believed it.

A lot of those boys were already spooked by life when they arrived. They had scared themselves in high school or starting out at other colleges with fewer rules. Some could feel a kind of reckless self-destruction growing in their souls. Too many beers on Friday nights. Too much sex in high school. Too many classes skipped. Drugs and boredom, fear of failure, and a father watching all that adolescent tumult with contempt. Or no father at all. They had a lot to prove. Some wanted West Point but fell short. Some wanted something more than community colleges and back-seat sex on Friday nights. Some wanted to be heroes. Some wanted to be rich. Some merely wanted to survive, test their mettle, then get out. Anyone who knew the school respected that survival. So one by one they went to Charleston. They went to find their way, as though old maps could help them navigate in a new world.

The black flag flew above Mark Clark Hall for most of that first week. The temperature rose and rose. The air was still. Even the grass looked tired. Shannon stayed sequestered, sick and out of it. Terry Leedom gave daily reports, barely hiding his own glee. "Noon today is the earliest," he said early one hot morning. Noon came and went. Shannon's release was announced, updated and then revised. She was fine, Leedom said, then grinned. Just a little tired. Just a little sick. The heat was a little bit too much for her, he said with unctuous shows of his concern. "She'll be all right." When reporters asked him about Hell Week, Leedom snapped and told them there was no such thing. "You guys are the ones who made that up," he accused. "You made it up to hype your stories, to sell a couple newspapers. That is your invention. This is *indoctrination* week," he said sharply. "It has always been indoctrination week." He rushed away. In his cool office in Bond Hall, the desks were piling high with message slips as harried staffers fielded questions from every point around the globe. From hour to hour and day to day, the answer stayed the same. Shannon Faulkner was fine. Yes, she'd had a little trouble with the heat. Yes, nurses in the infirmary were giving her good care.

Out on the parade field, in the barracks and the mess hall, the knobs paid no attention. They were treading water in a whirlpool, foundering and frightened.

On August 16, while the board of visitors was preparing for a two-day retreat to review the school's vast public relations problems, the knobs gathered on the dry parade ground with their *Guidon*s stiff and close. Standing in a nervous cluster they read words of inspiration: "*What does it mean to be a gentleman?* It is to be honest, to be gentle, to be generous, to be brave, to be wise; and possessing all these qualities, to exercise them in the most graceful outward manner." Pale and sweaty, they stood frozen in the heat, their world one endless contradiction. While cadre members dressed in gray shouted and condemned, the new boys learned new absolutes: "*What is honor?* Sir, honor is the most cherished principle of the cadet's life. *What is duty?* Sir, duty is the sublimest word in the English language." Every answer was provided and only one answer would do. Those words could stir the soul. And so the new boys, wanting to believe, read their *Guidon*s every time they slammed to a full stop, over and over, until the pages turned to silk and repetition became memory.

With a rough bark, Charlie Company jolted suddenly to life. Heyuuup! With that sharp and unintelligible command, they stumbled forward. Theirs was an awkward birth. Some boys bumped the boys ahead of them. Some boys lagged behind. One by one, they raised their hands to rest upon the shoulder of the next in line. Some knobs jerked with impatience at the touch, flinching with complaint. But when the chain broke an upperclassman shouted, and soon everyone was shuffling hard to keep the line. As they jerked forward, sophomores moved among them, picking and cajoling. "You're embarrassing yourselves," a flush-faced corporal told a group of frantic knobs as he found fault with every step. His color deepened as he raised his voice. "You are only doing this to yourselves. Heeeyup. Move up. Move up! Let's get some order here. You look like a bunch of freaks."

They looked foolish. They looked boyish. They looked young. A bark drove them up the stairs and into Mark Clark Hall. Another bark dropped them down into their seats. Stragglers shuffled and jumped while older boys looked on in dark disgust. Roger Popham was up front that day. White-haired and chinless, he was trying to shout and be a tough guy for their benefit. But he was not like that. His voice was better tuned to a soft, reassuring roll than an angry outburst of authority. He was a faithful Army man, a man accustomed to its ways who had retired and then tried to live as a civilian only to find himself adrift and out of step. After his Army life ended he put on a suit and tie and tried a new life as a businessman. But he never felt at ease with it. He was at his best when he could memorize set hierarchies and well-established rules, when a shoulder bar or collar pin announced just who was who. That gave his world some order. Popham lasted a year as a civilian. Then he moved to Charleston to settle back into familiar ways. Like many of his peers, he wore his class ring sliding heavily above his wedding band. That was the proper fit for him. After all, he stood at that altar first as a member of the class of 1963. Now his ring was worn to a smooth sheen, the numbers so soft that they were barely legible.

Addressing the new class, he tried to share the profundity of that attachment with another generation. Shouting in his reedy voice, he adjusted his glasses, cleared his throat and tried not to seem avuncular. "I am Colonel Popham," he told a sea of sleepy faces. "I am assistant commandant in charge of leadership and discipline." He dropped into a more colloquial tone. "There's twelve guys already that started with you that ain't here anymore. And there are eleven more right now that have indicated that they don't want to be here anymore."

It was a hemorrhage. Popham tried to be the man to stop it. "Look around you," he yelled in his thin voice. "You guys are the rocks!"

There was a booming response.

"You've made it this far, and you've got what it takes!"

"Sir! Yes sir!"

"You can come out of your trance now. You have to keep looking ahead. Saturday night. That's the next milestone, all right?"

"Sir! Yes sir!"

"That's when you get some time off. You just tell yourselves: 'If I can just make it through this week's racking session, I've got it made!'"

"Sir! Yes sir!"

Popham leaned into it. "I mean," he shouted, letting his thin voice break, "'If I can just make it through this next day, *I've got it made!*'"

This was the time for inspiration. He introduced the upperclasses' superachievers in sports and academics. Honor roll cadets stood up and won a round of praise. Then he turned his gaze to the new boys. "Maybe you haven't got the feel yet," he said. "That feel . . ." he drew the word out. He pumped his pelvis and pushed his arm into the air. "You need that *feel* of excellence."

Sophomore corporals moved down long rows of metal chairs and poked at sleeping boys. The knobs woke up with a start and, exposed, stifled sheepish looks of failure. After only several days, many had adopted the combat soldier's empty stare. Shannon had it earlier. By then, everyone knew the term: "1-26 eyes." Knobs who were not dozing or locked upright in their seats stared forward dully and rubbed their stubbly heads. Popham got it right. They were deep inside a trance. Fingers ran along a dozen well-cropped craniums. They had left the world behind.

"A tour," Popham shouted with what was left of his weak voice, "is fifty minutes of walking back and forth across the quad with your rifle. You don't want tours." A sleeping knob was awakened and led away to stand alone, nervous and duncelike at one side, a sulking public example of indiscipline.

"A tour is something that you do not want. A demerit is something that you do not want. You do not want us down on you. You do not want us in your face. You do not want us at your door. So you stick to unquestioning obedience and mental and physical toughness. Because I don't want to see any of you in my office because you have given up. You are going to stand there. And you are going to brace your little heart out while we tell you all the dumb things you've done. You are going to listen. And you are not going to get peed off. I'll tell you right here that swearing, shouting and the use of profane language is not a part of our system."

Several knobs laughed, but hostile stares and an occasional rough poke transformed the laughter into coughing fits and then the room fell silent.

"Your cadre members are not allowed to hit you or punch you or knock things out of your hand. That's negative leadership. That's not supposed to be going on. You have heard of behavior modification?"

"Sir! Yes sir!"

"Well, we are here to modify your behavior. And this is day five. Day five. You guys are the rocks, the ones who are left. Those guys who are gone are gone. But these guys right here, every one of you, you are the rocks. One of you guys is going to be regimental commander some day. I don't know who yet. But you're going to be leaders. You've got what it takes. You guys are great. I love every one of you, and you're all going to make it."

He cleared his throat. He leaned forward and stiffly drew things to a close. "I appreciate your time."

A new voice barked, "All rise!" One thousand feet responded. "Carry on," Popham said politely, then he walked down the aisle, drinking in their youth and their obedience, walking proudly out the door. Before he left, he turned to flash a trim salute, then disappeared off toward his office. More boys were checking out. He had some holes to plug.

Once Popham drifted out of earshot, the boys stiffened as the hammer fell. "The next time a colonel comes in here and takes his time," Spencer Bodison of Green Pond, South Carolina, screamed, "you better show him some respect. This is not Camp Crazyland."

Band Company had arrived late. They were the first to leave. They had that reputation, the "Q-boys," always slightly out of step. Every company had a reputation in the corps. Band was soft. Tango was wild. Echo was violent. The legends tended to repeat.

Band members were given first-floor rooms and a powerful advocate in the retired Marine who led them through their paces. Herb Day was their tough shepherd, giving them time out for band practice and heaps of his support. Envious classmates called the band boys privileged. "Shit," a corporal hissed that day. "Q Company. Queer boys. You faggots. Always the same thing." Day bristled at the name. He had tried without success to stamp it out. "You ignore that," he instructed new boys that first week. "You let that just roll over you." The band boys were his chosen and his charges, and he balanced out their pain with special care and unapologetic love. "Now, I would never tell these boys I love them," he confided with a smile. "Never. Never. Never." But in a thousand different ways, he did. His boys knew it, and they loved him back.

Downstairs in Mark Clark Hall, as small groups of boys rushed to the bathroom or stiffly waited for new orders, a half-dozen knobs from Alpha Company lingered under the stairs as the boy in charge of them singled out several for reprimands. Moving like a prison guard in stiff steps with a scowl, the corporal paced back and forth and found his targets. He stopped in front of one trembling knob, leaned close and shouted in his face. "Knob!" he screamed, letting his spittle drift down the new boy's face. "Were you laughing in mess today?"

The knob stared into space. 1-26 eyes. He learned fast. Stay vacant. Show nothing. No smiling. Eyes empty. Heart closed. "Sir. No excuse, sir."

The older boy stayed on him. "Knob. You don't laugh. You don't smile. We aren't here to entertain you, boy. We aren't here to make you beauty queen. Go look up 'malingering' in your blue book, freak. You get locked on. You don't get sick. And if you're not sick, you don't go to the infirmary and take up the nice lady's time. You hear me, knob?"

Ten sets of eyes stared forward into nothing. Ten faces did not move. Then a knob spoke up unexpectedly.

"Sir, cadet recruit York requests permission to make a move, sir."

"Make a move."

The boy scratched his nose.

Down the line another boy dropped a bottle of water in a fit of nerves.

"What was that?"

He locked back into place. "Sir . . ."

"Pick it up, fuckhead."

In time, they all marched off.

For anyone not marching in the corps for those first days, the campus had an odd air that seemed to balance intense activity with summer list-lessness. The days stayed hot and muggy. The insects scratched their way through screen doors, loose clothing and closed windows. Employees working in Bond Hall appeared relaxed and jovial, slipping down the quiet hallway past the president's thick wood door, trading stories and feeling the tempo gradually increase. Hell Week was a demanding and difficult time for new students. But it was familiar to the staff, and they walked through it with a peaceful air. The shouts on the parade field and the sight of scratchy gray meant the wheel had turned again and everything was in its place.

From a distance, small clusters of cadets looked orderly and even calm. Salutes were exchanged, marching steps were quickly mastered. From a haphazard band of adolescents the new class soon took the shape and look of generations that had walked that grass. History would repeat. There was a certain comfort to it. In the air-conditioned quiet of Bond Hall, military order prevailed and old customs stayed on course. Women in sundresses sat primly behind desks. Men in uniforms moved purposefully here and there. Students, polite and shy on that foreign turf, made tentative requests peppered with "sir" and "ma'am" as they sorted out the final details of matriculation. Everything began with "Please" and ended with "Thank you." The magic held. It was easy to ignore the angry shouts that sometimes drifted in through open doors and wafted over Muzak and muffled conversation. Everybody had a task. And everybody did it with a certain pride and purpose.

In that first week, upperclassmen who did not have a role in cadre training drifted back to Charleston and stayed with friends or lounged around the beaches until classes started. Professors readied their lessons and brushed up on time-worn lectures. The construction equipment beeped, and the new boys marched their jagged march. Summer would cool down to fall. The corps would swell in size when all the older boys returned, then shrink throughout the year as more and more within the ranks dropped out. In the past several years, an increasing number of seniors left at Christmas never to return. Cadets were picking up their final credits elsewhere and drifting off into the world before their time was up. It drove the numbers men wild. Those students received their rings and earned degrees but did not stay through that last year. No one asked those weary upperclassmen why. Yet the upperclass attrition rate affected income for the school and led to confused and angry exchanges about changing values and diminishing commitment. Men who had worn their rings for thirty years or more assumed the problem was to be found in the shifting culture out there past the gates. Kids these days, they complained among themselves, did not have the keen commitment that had driven them when they were young. Instead, this generation worked the angles and found shortcuts and had no pride in their accomplishment. In the meantime, every departure risked much-needed revenue.

Citadel lobbyists had a hard time explaining the drop to legislators who held the purse strings in Columbia. The school was shrinking year by year. A lot of Citadel alumni blamed the Faulkner litigation for the falling numbers. But in fact the drain had started well before the lawyers got involved. As early as February 20, 1992, Professor Linda Elksnin, an education specialist, had informed her colleagues that standards must be dropped to get all those beds filled. Still, the admissions office had already long been scouring the country for its applicants.

"Only thirty percent of the class is from South Carolina at this point," Elksnin said. The significance of her words was clear. South Carolina had always paid its share. Yet with fewer state students now and overall enrollment dropping, old assumptions might no longer hold. There were formulas to meet and, for the politicians, constituents to serve. The South Carolina legislature paid proudly when The Citadel was fat and full. But by the time Shannon Faulkner challenged it, there were quiet questions about old warhorses and lost dreams. A lot of people wanted change. The Board of Visitors did not. It was a tension that the Citadel's well-paid lobbyists knew all too well.

Cadets could feel that pressure rising. As the corps dwindled to numbers not seen since the 1960s, cadets grew more defensive and increasingly isolated. But first shots had been fired. And school officials vowed to fight. The armies were arrayed. To lose would bring dishonor. But to quit was not an option. By the end of the long Faulkner war, many millions would be spent to keep the school all-male. Every penny was well worth it, the hard-liners said. They had names for quitters at The Citadel. They were blunt and often quite obscene.

"South Carolina has had a lot of little Alamos," board member Jim Bradin said of that long fight. "For us, a lot of times when we say, 'No,' it's not just 'No.' It's '*Hell, no!*'" When Shannon filed her lawsuit, his colleagues on the board prepared for all-out war. "We were consumed by it," said Bradin. "It was an overriding cloud that covered everything." He sat in the boardroom then, so frustrated by the arguments at times that he chipped the finish off the table where he sat, tapping his Citadel ring nervously while those board members raged.

Outprocessing

TALL AND THIN, with muscles like a swimmer's, Craig had joined the Reserve Officers' Training Corps in high school and filled his room at home with Citadel memorabilia. He wanted nothing else than to march in tight formation behind Lesesne Gate. He wanted South Carolina's pride to be his own and dreamed of wearing a cadet uniform and grand black shako with its towering plumed flourish. He craved the status a gold ring conveyed and all the lifelong connections it assumed. Rank and privilege were his future. He would bend his will to those two goals. Craig's parents were skeptical. But he insisted and they let him go. And so that August as Shannon unpacked, Craig had signed in, too.

All throughout his senior year, Craig had entertained no doubts. He dreamed of marching, smooth and disciplined, then serving as a proud alumnus with a house filled up with baby blue. He wanted all of it, he said, the college pillows scattered in the living room, the football blankets, the armchair with its emblem and one day, perhaps, even a Citadel baby in a Citadel nightshirt, chewing on a Citadel rattle. Some people in his town had that. He had sat among their memorabilia and listened to their stories. To him, there was something mystical about the place. It consumed his imagination and set him on a stable course. He trained all summer for its rigors and arrived with his body tuned to near perfection, a seamless arrow of male strength. But at the end of his first week, he wavered. Though his heart was set and his muscles trained, he struggled with his choice. The shouting wore him down, he said quietly. He lost himself amid the din. Everything that he revered in the abstract now brought him disillusionment. In a rare break, while waiting for an appointment with his academic adviser, he squatted on a hallway floor and fixed his eyes on a blank wall.

"You lose all sense of time," he said dully. "It's night: It's dark. It's day:

It's light. That's all you ever know." He was disoriented and confused. The heat was nothing, he said. The exercise was fine. He flexed his muscles and made a fist that caused his forearm to jump in rivers down beneath the skin. He said that he would make it through. But he seemed listless and unsure. "This school"—he gathered up his words with care—"this school was all I wanted."

Yet here he was, day five, and he was wondering why he had come. He cried at night. He felt alone. His neck ached from constant bracing. Even when he got things right, someone shouted just for shouting's sake. "I'm an athlete," he said in tentative self-defense, sharing his real name but asking that it not be used. He talked about his high school grades. He had excelled. He had ambition. But that day he had learned how low the freshman grade point average was. In his company, he said bitterly, "It's two point something. I mean, it's so low I don't think half those guys could sign their names. Why didn't they ever tell us that?"

Craig's adviser, a gentle, dark-haired woman with a maternal air, called him in for his appointment. Before she closed the door, she wagged her head and said that many boys broke down in that first week—and later, too. "It's a tough place," she said with resignation. "We do what we can to make it better, to give these kids a place that's safe." The door closed with a click.

A second boy was waiting. Short and muscular, he had captained several high school teams. In basketball, other players towered over him. "Even though I'm short and I don't have much upper-body strength, the guys respected me," he said firmly. He was probably five feet five. "I scrambled harder. That won their respect. When I said something, I didn't have to shout, because everybody knew that anything I asked I would give out even harder. That was how I led them. That was why they made me captain." He stared down at the floor. He was having his doubts, too.

Gesturing at the closed door, he dropped his voice a bit and said that he liked Craig well enough but that Craig was a complainer. "I don't complain. I just do it," he said glumly. He planned to make it through. It was a pledge he made in private. No matter what they threw at him, he vowed, he would take it. But suddenly he slumped against the wall. "The problem is," he said hesitantly, "Craig is right about some things." He looked up, earnest, gauging his reception. "Most of this stuff is just kid stuff. I don't care. It's like a game. It doesn't bother me a bit. But you know, in high school we heard about The Citadel. There was always all this talk about honor and dignity, how we would all learn discipline. It's bull. I can take the shouting. I tune it out. That's okay. I just tell myself: *Turn off. Zone out. Stare straight. Do right. Don't complain. Don't show anything. Never give your heart to anyone.*" Yet the cadre corrected him no matter what he did. "It's just dumb stuff. 'Shut up, dumb knob. Freak. Chin down, country boy.'" He rattled off the litany. He could even tolerate the swearing, though no one in his family swore. He looked down the hallway. A figure appeared and then moved on, taking a flight of stairs two at a time.

"On Hell Night," he continued, almost whispering now, "my company was all together in the dark down on the quad. One of the cadre guys came up to me and stood behind me in the dark. I couldn't see him. Then, right by my ear, so no one else could hear it, he whispered in this real weird voice, 'I'm your daddy. I'm your daddy, and I'm going to fuck you all year long. I'm going to fuck you in the ass.'" The boy stretched his chin out as though relieving a sharp crick. "Excuse me for my language. But that's what he said. 'I'm going to fuck you in the ass.'"

He stared down at the carpeting, pulling strands of it between his thumb and forefinger. "The problem for me is, now I can't get it off my mind."

When the lights came up, he could not tell one face from the next. The cadre in their uniforms moved around him in a shifting mass. He thought the sophomore who addressed him was taller than he was. But that was all he could remember, and he was not even sure of that. With their hair shaved tight and their visors slung down low, they all looked the same. "I wanted to see who this guy was. I looked left and right. But then someone came up close to me. 'What are you looking at, freak?' I just locked my eyes ahead and braced."

For the rest of it he marched and followed orders. But the whisper kept replaying. "I'm not afraid," he said. "It's not that. It's just, I can't seem to let it go."

At night, his roommate cried himself to sleep. He listened and tossed in his own bed, and heard the voice again. "I'm your father . . ." The fear inside him grew.

The academic counselor released Craig with a warm pat. Then she called the other boy. He stiffened and walked in with a solid gait. During a short interview, the counselor asked him about his course load and his first few days at the school. She seemed kind, he said later, but he answered monosyllabically, divulging nothing of what he felt. "Yes, ma'am. No, ma'am. That's all I really said." He remained polite and far away. When they were done he put his body back into a brace and almost ran down the long hall.

Craig lingered, eager to talk. He was due back with his company, he said. But he was sweaty with anxiety. The day before, he had left his cap with everyone else's in a downstairs room while all the knobs went jogging in formation. When he returned, his cap was gone. Now he had a bunch of problems. If he had no cap, he would get punished. If he said that it was stolen, that would challenge the effectiveness of the school's much-valued honor code.

"I know how it will go," he said, playing the scene out.

"'Where's your cap, freak?'"

"Sir, my cap was stolen, sir."

"'We don't lie here, knob. And we don't steal. We have an honor code. So where's your cap?'"

"Sir, my cap was stolen, sir."

"'*Knob!*'"

He weighed his options in a sweat. If he stopped at the cadet store for a new cap, he would arrive late for his next duty and would need an explanation. But if he had no cap, it would mean more trouble still. The line of least resistance was to buy a new cap and perhaps lie about how much time the counseling session took. That way he wouldn't have to accuse anyone or question the effectiveness of the honor code. He would not run the risk of being charged with carelessness or, worse yet, filing a false accusation. He tried it out. He simply had to bend the truth. He would purchase a new cap and show up late and take the heat. Day five. Survive. Minimize the pain. Bend reality until it fits the explanation that's required. Lie, if you have to. Brace for anything. Brace for everything. That was how he saw it.

Craig headed for the cadet store, talking shyly about his high school accomplishments and his family and his frustration with the cap. He spoke about a girlfriend out of state and the friends he left back home. At the shop, he charged a new cap to his account and then headed back into his barracks. Nearing the corner of the building, he quickly turned away, struggling not to cry. With a sudden jolt, he took the corner sharply, tucked his chin and moved along. At the sally port, he turned once more with a snap, took several steps and then jerked to a full stop as a member of the cadre moved to block his path. The sophomore started shouting. Craig kept his face rigid and his shoulders back, hands thrust out in fists. The corporal shouted again. Craig inhaled, then shouted back. They seesawed back and forth. Question. Retort. Question. Retort. At last, the sophomore moved and Craig rushed through the gate, his long legs pumping.

Suffer and make do. Suffer and move on. Suffer and then pass the suffering down. In that first week, most cadets learned to walk around the campus in the synch of it, noting to themselves that this boy or that one seemed important to avoid. Some were cruel and took pleasure in inflicting pain. Others seemed more halfhearted. Some screamed and then sat back, watching fear rise in their charges like foam adrift on a wave. Others did not sit back at all but moved in closer and got louder. The urgent knobs ran through those blades never once complaining. But in the quiet of their rooms at night, they cried themselves to sleep.

Across the campus that first week, pools of activity formed and then evaporated. Some rooms were alive with noise. Two cadets talking. A sophomore member of cadre screaming. Doors slammed. Young men shrieked. Sometimes a radio would play or an office telephone would ring, strange noises from another world. Rhythmic poundings sounded along the quads at dawn as companies gathered and then jogged together, their feet marching step for step. Inside the barracks knobs stuttered up and down the stairs following conflicting orders and fighting back strange tides of strong emotion. A transom rod crashed down against a metal rail. "We are not hurting children," said the quote in Matt Pantsari's room.

By midweek, it was quite clear who might get singled out. Groups of cadre members, hoarse from days of shouting, clustered around hapless knobs and did their job as they saw fit. Isolated, frantic and confused, the new boys stood frail and trembling while the sophomores drank their panic like a drug. Extremes of any kind were instant death. Knobs who showed their fear too much or not at all were in for more.

In court, the philosophy sounded grand and well devised: "Males tend to need an atmosphere of adversativeness or ritual combat," the school's lawyers wrote in a brief submitted to the federal judge early in Shannon's case. Cadets in The Citadel's unique environment took benefit from an "adversarial environment," Dawes Cooke and his colleagues argued, "by becoming free to express themselves artistically and creatively without fear of embarrassment." In front of girls, their inhibitions would show.

Meanwhile, many upperclassmen growled that the system had gone soft. Four years ago, a senior explained, transom poles were used to whack the new boys into shape. Now, he said nostalgically, those "knobby wands" were out of bounds. Hitting with broom handles was prohibited, too, as was physical contact of any sort. "Of course, sometimes someone gets drunk," he shrugged, leaving the matter open to interpretation. "But that's not the leadership that we are taught. We are not allowed physical violence."

The talk on campus tended to drift back to the old days. The Citadel had been through one reform after another over the years. Grand plans were made and endorsed and then left moldy on the shelf. The worst abuses were reshaped. But new anguish always found a form. The system moved like mercury. Compressed and confined in one area, it blew out somewhere else. Squeezed here, it compensated there, and fell back into seamless forms as though no exterior force had ever broken it.

In that first week, cadets gathered to compare racking sessions from years past. Almost compulsively, they examined the particulars of how the system worked. Many of the older boys wanted push-ups reinstated as a means of punishment. They were straightforward, at least, they said. Once those push-ups were done, muscles healed and boys recovered. Mental anguish was much worse.

"Now, they get into your head," said one cadet. "And then you're really gone. Your muscles can take anything. But when they get inside your brain it's worse. And the brain work leaves no bruises."

A senior pointed out the only real way to survive. "The dud brains tend to stay," he said. "But that's good." Their vacant stares meant they were "locked on" and in step. "Those dud brains don't even know where they are," he laughed. "They don't feel any pain. No brain. No pain." He made a face, then said it louder. "No brain? No pain! Welcome to Camp Crazyland."

The ones who had a harder time could almost always be picked out. A knob was going off the deep end if he braced for hours without stopping or trembled uncontrollably or wept until his shoulders shook and he could hardly breathe. Everybody had a breaking point. Some broke and then recovered. Some broke and never were the same. Some lasted for a while, then called their parents and went home.

It was common, even expected, for knobs to sob all night. The ones having a harder time showed up at morning mess appearing gray and dead-eyed and confused. On the fourth day, a knob in Echo Company stumbled in after his peers. He was stopped abruptly at the door. A cadre

member, sharp and neatly pressed, his face a granite wall of pure contempt, greeted him by moving close. The boy stood at attention with his
eyes fixed in a stare. "Bad night, boy?" inquired the upperclassman.

"Sir! No sir!"

"You miss your mama?"

"Sir! No sir!"

"You miss your old, warm, cozy bed?" He taunted and drew close.
The ashen boy blinked hard. "You want to curl up in your mama's bed?"

The knob pulled a gulp of air into his chest and then exploded. *"Sir!
No sir!"*

Some boys simply lost it. They smashed their rooms to pieces in the
night, then left the campus quietly without much fuss. They retreated
far within themselves and kept a vacant look out to the world. There
were signs when someone neared the edge. Those were culled and
weeded and urgently pushed out. There were second chances and third
chances. But it was usually clear who would leave. Best, the new boys
whispered, sharing instant secrets, to be a "ghost knob," always present,
yet seldom seen or singled out.

One boy who sobbed violently on Monday had recovered by midweek. "Everything's all right," he said aggressively in response to a casual
question. Any flicker of familiarity was gone. "I'm fine," he snapped.
"It's supposed to be tough. I'm fine. I'll do just fine here."

There were countless legends of the ones who failed. It was whispered
from class to class that one boy locked into a brace so hard he had to be
hospitalized and heavily sedated before his muscles would relax. Another
boy shouted his knob answers relentlessly but could not handle classwork of any kind. Others swallowed Ritalin and alcohol and ampheta-
mines, living with odd cocktails always on their breath. One boy, a
teetotaling Baptist forced to drink himself to stupefaction, never was the
same again, an upperclassman from his company explained. Thrown
into a cold shower to sober up, he made it through that night. But he
was blue, "cyanotic," the other boy said. The older boy was forced to
drink as a knob himself, he said, but "only until I threw up."

Upperclassmen sometimes had their troubles, too. One cadet came
into his barracks drunk one night and broke a transom rod and flailed
against his roommate. Students wrestled him to the ground until he lay
beneath them, roaring with blind rage.

A mother from Annapolis said her son had barely missed that
drunken spearing. Now, she brought a second son into the school. She

sighed and wagged her head. The younger boy was sensitive, she said. She would worry for his safety all year long. Then she brightened. "Their father, my ex-husband, was abusive," she said casually, standing up and stretching out her back. "He beat them up. So now they want to show how tough they can be, too."

While the barracks teemed and roared with that year's new supply, Shannon stayed invisible. In the infirmary still, she found she could not keep her food down. Her energies were low. An intravenous tube was fitted to her arm. A quiet stream of people came and went. Officers from her company visited several times. One knelt down and prayed. The school chaplain visited. General Poole and others from Bond Hall came by. One girl among two thousand males. Outside her door, their world kept right on turning.

"I changed my mind about her," Beth Summerford said after watching Shannon for a week. "You know, I thought she was a smart aleck. But . . . I honest to God do not think she knew how far she was going to have to go. And I think she tried to get off that train." But the train had been on track for years, and still the journey wasn't done.

On campus as the week slipped by, the boys gradually began to think that they would get their school back after all. "I don't see how she can make it," John Volkmar mused, scratching at a bite on his tan forearm. "She only got halfway through the first day, so there are four days of training that she's missed since then. This whole thing is about class unity. She's missed the swearing in. She's missed learning how to brace. She missed Hell Night and all the rest of it. There have been two P.T. [physical training] tests, and we've had our first P.T. run. How can she get squared away? And how much are her classmates going to accept her after this? Any other knob who missed this much time, he'd be disqualified."

Ray Gerber, a junior, optimistically said her cadre could easily get her back to speed. They were trained, he said. The best. But a third cadet just waved his hand. "This is an intangible, people," he told them. "We don't know yet what will happen."

Gerber wanted her to make it. "They can teach her how to deal with an adversative environment," he said earnestly. "I think, if she can do it, same standards, same everything, then she should stay. That's what I think. I just wish she got the haircut."

Volkmar laughed, short and hard. "Everything for her is different," he said with some distaste. "There are only five people who are allowed to talk to or discipline her. Tell me where that's equal? The whole point is that anyone can get to a knob. That's the point. All the cadre. All the upper classes. You have to answer to everyone. So just look at that. That's preferred treatment for starters. Only five guys can talk to her. And you know they'll be careful or next she'll just be suing the school for sexual harassment. The whole thing is soft. Look at it. Private bathroom. Private bracing lessons. Video camera outside her room. Shannon's got special handling. It's all set up that way. This whole thing is a joke."

Terry Leedom was on the stairs again. "No," he announced wearily, "she still is not ready to join the rest of the corps. She's working on it. We are all working on it. But she's not there yet. It has been awfully hot here. We are doing our very best. We all want to help her along so we can get her back out there and right back on track."

Another day passed. The black flag was still flying.

In that first week, the basic outlines of the system became clear. There were riddles within riddles and intentionally contradictory commands. Contempt and punishment were daily fare. No one could avoid it. The system was designed to break boys down. Their failure was its goal. Submission was the driving purpose, suffering their due. And so they stood in front of shouting officers and kept their faces blank. "We are strong believers that our cadets should do what we call 'suck it up,'" Cliff Poole had said in a deposition months before. Now, a whole new class was learning. Warm spittle dribbled down their cheeks. They did not flinch. They did not move to wipe it off. They did not object. If they objected, life got worse.

Free time was "commander time" to be used at cadre's sole discretion. An administration memo offered bright suggestions. "Great time to show cadets how to fold clothes, shine shoes/brass," the commandant's office noted cheerily. But that was hardly how it was. More often, free time was hard time. The new boys learned that fast.

In Law Barracks on a sunny afternoon, a cadre officer made a fist and punched the hats off two knobs' heads as they stood with their jaws locked in place. The sophomore stomped the covers on the ground, then picked them up, shouted angrily and threw them down again, grinding the gray fabric into dusty concrete. The knobs stared out at nothing. Then the cadre member drew up close and pushed their soiled hats up to their noses.

"Why are your covers so filthy, knobs?" he screamed.

"Sir, no excuse *sir!*" the boys shouted back in tandem.

"Have you been careless, knobs?"

"Sir! No sir!"

"Well, if you weren't careless, knobs, then tell me how your covers got so dirty?"

"Sir! No excuse sir!" Their necks bulged as they shouted.

"You clean up, boys. You disgust me."

"Sir! Yes sir." They stooped to get their worried hats and then ran off to new ordeals.

Knobs did not argue or complain. When officers issued conflicting orders, they did not cry foul. At evidence of sabotage, they did not object. Open cruelty earned not a note of their displeasure. Instead they calculated risk and punishment and braced for the inevitable. When they were hurt, they did not cry. When they were humbled, they did not hang their heads. When they were frightened, they showed it only in the fluttering and reflexive widening of their eyes. Freaks. Next year would be their turn.

"How's it going, guys?" Trez would sometimes ask, looming into view.

"Sir," came the inevitable burst. "Just fine, sir."

"Are you glad to be here?"

"Sir, yes sir."

"Good day to be a Bulldog."

When Trez departed, cadre members smiled and whispered: "Good knobs," as though talking to a pack of panting Labradors.

Through all of it the cadre belittled and found fault. What they were going through, knobs were repeatedly informed, was nothing next to other years. The system was breaking down, the cadre sneered. It was stunted and misshapen by adult interventions. "You don't even deserve to be called knobs," the knobs were told. Their ordeals were laughable. They were lucky. Last year was worse. The year before that? Worse again. "We're taking it easy on you," cadre members taunted. New boys shouted agreement. "Sir, yes sir." There was no other answer. And a lot of them believed it.

In court, the system sounded almost tame. On May 25, 1994, Val Vojdik had called Dr. Alexander W. Astin to testify for the plaintiff. A professor of higher education and director of the Higher Education Research Institute at the University of California, Los Angeles, Astin described the environment as purposefully intense.

"The students, I am assuming, who apply to The Citadel and enroll there know about the adversative environment, the fourth class experience, the highly regimented and highly disciplined nature of that experience," he said in a brief preamble. "So you're going to have a peer group that is very special in certain ways. For example, they would tend to be very conservative politically. That would be one unique attribute. . . . They would tend to lean toward math, science and engineering and business in their career interests and field of study interests.

"Where they are subjected to some discomfort . . . and this is a shared experience, kind of like boot camp . . . there is a camaraderie formed and bonds formed, so it's a very unique environment. And one would be hard-pressed to find a similar, even remotely similar, environment outside of VMI and the military academies."

Vojdik pushed him on the point. "Dr. Astin," she said, approaching him, "based on your research and experience, do you have any reason to believe that women would not be interested in this type of education?"

He hardly paused. "No reason."

Yet under cross-examination by a Citadel lawyer named Bob Patterson, he modified his view.

"Now," asked Patterson, a disheveled, gray-haired old-timer from Richmond, Virginia, "in your study of higher education, which has been immense, have you ever come across a military school such as a Citadel for women?"

Astin said that he had not.

"And have you studied the adversative method, methodology, that's used at The Citadel and at VMI?"

The expert thought a moment and then gave a measured response. "I have familiarized myself with that, and I guess the closest I have come to studying it is in some of the early studies I did . . . [on] a lot of what I used to call hazing. I think we had some idea from those studies about what the effects of that method were," he said. "But nothing that really duplicates The Citadel or VMI as that adversative, that extreme, no."

Patterson smiled. The witness was heading exactly where he wanted. He would show that only males were strong enough to tolerate such stress. "Do you know of any educational authority that advocates the use of the adversative method for *women?*" he asked.

Astin shook his head. "I'm not sure I know of any authorities that advocate it for *anybody.*"

Patterson recoiled. That was not his question. "Do you know of any-body that's ever recommended the use of the adversative system for *women?*" he repeated.

There was no such institution. The witness had no answer.

Splendid. Patterson closed in again. "You have never recommended it yourself, have you?"

"No."

Point made.

But Astin was not finished. "I don't recommend it for men, either," he finished sourly.

Of course, that never was the issue. As Vojdik and Sara Mandelbaum would carefully show in court, the issue was unfair advantage. The Citadel had more books, more computers, more money per student than almost any other college in the state. It also had a network no other school could match. Why shouldn't Shannon want to go?

Craig had wanted that advantage once. He gave it up within a week. "I got out," he said excitedly. "I couldn't stand it in there." He told a rambling story. One day there was a confrontation. It gave him a bad scare. An upperclassman set the seeds of fear. On Friday, Craig called home.

There was a certain choreography to all departures. In Jenkins Hall, the colonels said weak spirits and soft parents were to blame. They said the boys who left were pampered and undisciplined. They made up stories when they quit. What they really could not stand, these colonels jeered, was that the barracks had no air-conditioning. Tales of misery were easily dismissed. Lies. Older men did not believe them. "They tell you that this thing or that thing happened," said Joe Trez. "They need an excuse. They look for it. And if they can't find it, they just make one up. It's always been that way. Otherwise they can't handle their sense of failure. They blame everyone except themselves. You can count on it."

Craig had a story. So did many other boys. In that school year, ninety-five knobs signed out by Christmas. Ninety-five stories to dis-count.

"The Citadel was the only place I ever wanted to go," Craig said after he was settled back at home. "But they lie about their traditions. And they lie about their honor and their codes of dignity. I hated it. I'll always hate it now. I'm going to burn everything I have from there. Maybe I'll sue them. I could do anything right now. I hate that place so much. Friday night when I left campus I was more afraid for my life than I've ever been."

"Outprocessing," as it was called, was a twenty-four-hour ritual of quarantine and reinforcement. Men at every level of the administration tried to keep the fourth class whole. There were kindly sessions full of respect and harsh lectures about growing up. But the colonels knew it was a losing battle. History told them so. Nonetheless, there was a pepped-up sense of urgency that year. The corps had not dipped below the seventeen hundred mark for decades. Now that bottom line was drawing near. Yet all the meetings and the hearty handshakes and heart-felt commiseration in the world could not keep a boy marching once he has resolved to go. That was how it was with Craig.

"When I left," he said, "there was this question about 'Had I been hazed?' I wrote down 'No.' I didn't want more trouble. You had to write down, 'No.' One night they had us down in the hellhole, down under-neath the stairwell and a couple of guys were there and they told us, 'In a few days, you're going to be asked if you've been hazed. I think you know the right answer, gentlemen. I think you know just what to say.'"

Craig's company had already lost seven knobs by then. The cadre members in charge called it disgusting. "They were telling us they were going to have this burning and burn all the knobs' stuff. This one guy kept saying, 'You guys are just a humiliation to me. We are going to have to deal with you.' He was real mean and sort of crazy looking. But then, when Colonel Trez came by he totally changed. Just like that, he looked at Trez and says, 'We got to take care of our knobs, sir. We need to make sure they all stay hydrated.' And Colonel Trez just smiled like they were doing everything just right. That's how they are. They switch. They say all this stuff about honor and discipline. But it's not honor. It's boys tak-ing boys and tearing them apart. It was like meat to wild dogs. We were just torn apart, and they enjoyed it."

Craig's friend had dropped out, too. He wanted only to forget the place. "My father told me to be careful," Craig's friend explained. "This whole town is heavy with Citadel men. We don't want to step on any-body's toes. My dad worries that I won't get any jobs. They run the banks. They run the construction company. They run the gas stations. It's not like we are worried about physical harm. Don't get me wrong. It's just that they can make your life hard without you even knowing it. And my dad isn't wanting any trouble."

That boy made it halfway through the week quite sure that he would stay. But he could not adjust to the atmosphere of violence. Every day, he explained, "you looked at people who you knew were going to torment you all year long. . . . That was hard." His first doubt came the day after he arrived, on Sunday after chapel. As knobs in his company walked across Summerall Field, several cadre members moved in close. "They walked right there beside us, and one of them said just loud enough so we could hear: 'Your momma and daddy are gone now, boys. Now you're ours. We own you. In seven hours, hell begins.'" They did not yell, he said. They spoke softly, almost gently, so that only those few knobs could hear.

For several nights, he weighed his fears. On Wednesday he was singled out for doing well. "I lay in bed that night and I thought about things and about the way that they were treating us. . . . If I stayed long enough, I knew I'd come to think the same way they thought. And that was more than I could take." It was a sensation he described as sliding down a hill, wanting to stop, but feeling more and more the speed and thrill of the descent, seductive, exhilarating and wild. "There's adrenaline pumping through you so hard, and they are marching around you so tight and fierce, and it has this kind of eerie other-dimension feeling to it. That other stuff . . . I understood the game. But there was something different, too." He struggled to explain it. That voice inside his head just never went away.

On Wednesday he told himself that he should leave that week or not at all. "I found that I had started to justify in my mind some of the hollering and the screaming. And that scared me more than anything, that I could be like them. . . . From my window you could see Second Battalion. And you could see the American flag flying there on top. And you could see the moon shining. And they played taps and you are looking at the moon and at the flag as it goes down, and it is the most lonely place on earth. And I started thinking about them and about what they called respect and the way they thought that they were teaching it."

Early Thursday, he signed into the infirmary. Shannon was there, too, "nasty as a dog. Like someone who had been rode hard and put up wet. She really looked like hell. I think she finally realized that, 'My God, I made the biggest mistake of my life.' She just looked real weak and drawn, and it couldn't have been through physical activity because she hadn't been through physical activity. But they treated her well. They called her Miss Faulkner. It was like she pretty much ran the place.

She was wearing her P.T.'s when I saw her pass by. All the nurses and some of the cadets were encouraging her. But there was no way on earth she could make it, not the way she looked."

He was wrestling with himself then, too. But that was different, he believed. He resented Shannon's special status. "If she'd come in and said: 'I want my head shaved. And I'm going to run with you and all that,' then, hey, I think that would have been cool. Only she wanted to do it but: 'Please don't give me a haircut. Please don't scream at me. Don't holler at me. I don't want none of that.'"

He objected to that style of leadership himself on both spiritual and ethical grounds. But when he spoke of Shannon, the distinction quickly blurred. She was just a whiner. Everybody said so.

Several hours after that encounter he was on his way. "I told my dad to come and get me. He said: 'Are you sure?' And I just said, 'Trust me, Dad.' I felt like a caged bird."

That fall, the administration watched the outflow with a mixture of alarm and resignation. The fourth class system was only for the few, the colonels said protectively. Any boy could tell a story. Attrition was inevitable. Every school had some of it. The Citadel probably came out better than most. The truth was, only the best cadets could make it through. The important thing was to prevent the ones who were leaving from infecting those who stayed. Nothing could be worse, said Tony Lackey, than letting someone who was wavering talk to someone who had quit.

"Once I told someone I was going to leave," said Craig, "they swept me out. That way, you can't contaminate the others. And I would have, you know. I would have contaminated all of them. I would have told them all to leave: 'Leave now, while you can.'"

Quad Surfing

E ARLY ON FRIDAY, August 18, there was bedlam in Bond Hall. The Board of Visitors had gathered. A special meeting was convened. Grim-faced men in uniform swept in and out of their closed conference room. When the door opened, a crowded table was jumping with activity. Men were arguing amid a chaos of Styrofoam cups and doughnuts, Coke cans and crumpled paper napkins. Several of them raised their voices and ran nervous fingers down the table edge. Others took notes, scribbling their thoughts on white legal pads with freshly sharpened pencils that were provided to record their thoughts. Bud Watts emerged. The door swung shut.

Peter Mailloux, the shaggy-haired English professor who years before had helped coordinate the faculty's protest against the termination of the veterans program, stopped his old hatchback outside a classroom building shortly after he first heard the news. He shook his head dejectedly. "It's a sad day for The Citadel," he said. "It's a sad, sad day."

At 11:30 that morning, Cliff Poole had told the faculty that Shannon would be gone after a final press conference. The general seemed unmoved by her departure, perhaps even relieved. But Mailloux felt deflated. "Now where do we go?" he asked. His voice trailed off and he stepped down hard on his accelerator. When his car streaked past the guardhouse next to Lesesne Gate a student sentry glumly waved him through. But Mailloux neither paused nor motioned in response. A rigorous student of Kafka and a fan of the iconoclastic feminist writer Djuna Barnes, he detested musty rituals of order and command.

In the wide central hallway in Bond Hall that day a school official could not hide his grin. "She's leaving," he whispered. "A police escort is being prepared. We are trying to figure out a way to sneak her out. We want to get her off the campus with as little trouble as possible."

Slowly, word of Shannon's decision drifted from one office to another. The response was overwhelming. Members of the staff shook hands and hugged. Here and there, the sound of laughter and occasional applause broke out. A woman in the finance office jumped out of her seat then scurried into the front lobby and tugged at a friend's sleeve.

"Oh, happy days! Happy days!" she cried, beaming. "Oh, I mean, happy days!"

Down the hall, a professor shouted to a friend, "Did you hear the news? She's leaving!"

As though a nagging fever finally broke, much of the staff erupted into relieved laughter and raucous cheers. Clusters of people gathered in the hallway, whispering and talking. Men slapped each other's backs, and women embraced or headed for the telephone. It was over. She was out, the battle won. A collective sigh of relief coursed through the building as though three years of tension suddenly had eased. Then the telephones lit up.

"This is the *best* day," a woman from the finance office said quite happily, turning on her heel. She poked her head into an office and shared the news with a slender young secretary who bounded to her feet then sat again and turned toward her ringing telephone. "Shannon Faulkner's gone," she said excitedly. "She's out of here."

It would be hours, still, before Ed Faulkner would arrive in Charleston in his van. Meanwhile, there were other problems to be tended to. Joe Trez was finishing a conversation with the football coach. "That's something you are going to have to solve," he advised gruffly. The coach nodded. "We've dealt with it," he reassured the commandant. "He was scared to death."

Knobs already had the hang of life at mess. They sat bolt upright in their metal chairs and served the upperclassmen. Plates of food moved up and down long tables. Knobs ate when they were told to eat. That day they ate quite well. A lot of school officials were in sight. The cadre was on best behavior.

At the far end of the hall, Sandra Thomas, beaming and nodding, gracious in a frilly suit, was moving primly through the chaos, bending occasionally to talk to young men in their uniforms. Blond and self-possessed, she was the heroine of the moment, a female godsend willing to agree that separate could be equal. She was criticized for it in some quarters, but on The Citadel's hard-baked campus on that morning Converse College's new president was introduced as visiting royalty.

Even the Charleston paper had provided its strong seal of approval. "We believe the decision to provide public funding to Converse—to be supplemented by as much as $8 million in private donations from Citadel supporters—reflects public sentiment in this state," the newspaper cheered shortly after the deal was struck. "It will help guarantee that both men and women who wish to be educated in a single-gender college in South Carolina will be able to do so."

Shannon, of course, was not so fond of that tall blonde. After Dawes Cooke's daughter was born, "Val suggested they name her Shannon," she said. Dawes replied "that her first word would be 'Converse.'" But Shannon did not laugh at that retort. Cooke fought hard in court, she explained, "but he will face his toughest [fight] ever on the day he has to explain to his daughter why he fought to keep [women] from going to a state-supported school." Shannon figured Thomas would have some things to answer for as well.

Thomas was well aware of critics' barbs. But she had made her choice and was content with it. In her office, on a side table, she kept a framed cartoon suggesting she had been bought off. In it, a girl in a plaid skirt and ponytails was pictured in a huff. "Five million? What kind of a girl do you think I am? I wouldn't *dream* of it for less than ten!" In her own defense, the former sorority president was clipped and to the point. "Rather than stamping out an opportunity for men," she said sternly, "why not create an opportunity for women?"

On that day, in her trim suit and steady smile, the Converse president looked out across a sea of shouting, gesticulating cadets and smiled. Joe Trez approached and hovered near. She laid her hand across his arm. "Well, yes, sir, colonel," she said brightly. "We are just delighted. And I am happy to tell you that everything is going well." Trez puffed his chest and nodded. Then he extended an invitation to the SCIL students to come on down to Charleston for a visit at homecoming. Thomas smiled back and happily agreed. Then she raised her voice above the din. "I think this whole thing is going to work out just fine," she nearly shouted.

In the barracks on that Friday afternoon, as word of Shannon's exit drifted through the corps, clusters of boys gathered to talk. In the guardroom of third barracks, Rush Limbaugh's voice drifted out of an old radio. Several cadets huddled close and quickly silenced anyone who tried to talk. Betty Friedan, announced Rush Limbaugh, had called The Citadel "the epitome of machismo." Limbaugh laughed. He thought she got that right. "The feminazis are demanding women in combat,"

he snorted. But now—after just one week, he informed the world—
Shannon Faulkner was dropping out.

Bond Hall was bubbling with the news just then, but it came as quite
a shock to most cadets. In the guardroom inside Law Barracks several
exchanged looks of astonishment and doubt. "This is the problem when
you come up with symbols," Limbaugh continued coldly. "This is not
the Cherry Avenue Little League, and this is not about girls playing second base because diamonds are a girl's best friend." A cadet slammed the
screen door and joined the group without a word. "That's why we have
respect for our men in the military," continued the voice drifting out
over the radio. "Because it is hard. Because it is tough." Several cadets
nodded silently. "Damn straight," said one. Rush was only saying what
they already knew. Limbaugh spoke their language. Shannon quit because
she was a girl.

"Has she quit?" A corporal stuck his head in through the door.

"We don't know," shot back a guard. "But that's what Rush Limbaugh is saying."

"Yeah. Everybody's talking about it."

A senior joined the group. "I have no information," he said, unprompted,
taking a seat.

"What's happening," came Limbaugh's voice, "is that you begin by
agitating women and getting them to infiltrate certain male bastions.
You get certain agitating women . . . and what it means to be a man is
being diluted and it's being watered down."

The cadets harumphed agreement, and when one of them began to
speak the others glared and told him to be quiet. They were part of this
strange history. And they hung on every word he said.

Outside of the infirmary, Terry Leedom was still trying to play coy.
"There remains a patient in the infirmary," he told a restless crowd.
"When she will be out, we are not sure. We will have another update for
you at three." There were rumors flying. He knew that. But he could not
confirm them. "She is still expected at some time to return to duty." Several reporters turned away. No one believed him anymore. The signs
were all too clear.

There was a rebel yell in fourth barracks as a local radio station put
out the news. At the same moment, Dawes Cooke bumped past the
infirmary seated on the back of an old golf cart, smiling, his feet dangling. When a cadet flashed him the thumbs-up sign Dawes grinned and
then elfishly returned it with a laugh and both hands raised.

A hollow-cheeked knob marched up the road, made a tight corner and walked up the stairs into the infirmary, looking fit and marching hard. Inside, the final act was playing out. Shannon's father had arrived.

Tourists from around the country gathered in a clump outside the building. "We're right in the middle of it," said a plump woman wearing glasses. "It's just so exciting." Then she tapped the shoulder of a man wearing a "1,952 Bulldogs and 1 Bitch" T-shirt. He recoiled as though stung, then sputtered it was only good news to him that Shannon had just quit.

"Oh, I'd sort of like to see her go ahead with it," sighed a tourist from Massachusetts. "Maybe if she'd been more fit . . ."

"It shouldn't even be in court!" replied a Texan who had just learned that The Citadel was a public school. "I can't imagine what they're thinking!"

Several feet to her right, a Citadel graduate wearing a Mickey Mouse cadet T-shirt adorned with a black ribbon glowered and shook his head. "We should have a right to single-gender education. Those girls have their women's colleges. We have The Citadel. That's what this is all about. *Our* rights."

Inside the infirmary just then, Shannon drifted toward the window and saw a mob of reporters on the lawn. Her stomach clutched. Her father and her brother hovered close.

In New York in those last hours, interrupted during a brief vacation on Long Island, Val Vojdik clutched her telephone. She was frantic and intense. On the line with Shannon, Vojdik urged her client to stay strong. There was still time to get back out there, Vojdik said. Shannon hadn't missed that much. She could do it. The important thing was to get back to the barracks. All she had to do was try. They had worked so hard and long, she pressed. Maybe they could get a medical waiver from the court. But Vojdik could feel her client drifting. "Shannon!" she cried out, as though her own passion could part a sea of teenage fear and loneliness. "Come on! I know you can make it." But while the lawyer coaxed and coached, Shannon set the telephone down and took a nervous step away from that harangue. The time for lawyers was behind her. Now she needed friends.

Suzanne Coe was in the room when that telephone call came in. After years of lawyers, judges, depositions and court dates, she was the only lawyer Shannon welcomed on that day. Shannon wanted her to come. They were friends by now, or friends of the sort that protracted legal cases make. So Coe had made one final trip south, driving with Shannon's father, Ed, and brother, Todd, down inland fields from Greenville to Charleston, that glinting confection by the sea, four hours and then some moving fast, just in time to catch the denouement. She tried her best to keep that sweet court victory intact. But Shannon had resolved to go, and nothing now could move her. Coe understood it. So she stepped aside and granted Shannon her sad blessing.

Vojdik could hardly find it in her heart to do the same. Jumpy and impatient and a world too far away to stop the crumbling, she kept talking into thin air until Coe finally plucked the telephone off the bed and told her it was done. Shannon was not listening, Coe said dully. No one was listening now. Vojdik might as well have talked into an empty can. She tried to fend off sickening waves of disbelief. She was no good at failure. Like a wrestler ever twisting and contorting, she could never quite believe in its last hold.

Down the hall, Beth Summerford was impatient for a resolution. Shannon had been going back and forth all week, she complained. It was time for a decision. "When I came and knocked on the door for something they were all here, in the bathroom," the nurse explained primly. Out the window, a horde of reporters shuffled in the shade. "There was just press all around. Vultures I call them. That's what I said to Suzanne Coe."

Coe gave her a sour look and said that the whole thing felt like some God-awful vigil—like waiting to see if someone was going to be executed or not. It had that feel, said Summerford. But now her ire shifted to the lawyers. "Suzanne Coe was wringing her hands and saying, 'What about other women?' That's what she was concerned about. The women was what she was interested in. I was surprised. . . . I felt like they had led Shannon down the garden path and then pushed her off the edge. And I thought, she's not a person to you all, she's a client and a case. . . . I wanted to get the telephone locked to keep the legal team from badgering her. She was fine when she made the decision, and then she was upset when they were trying to badger her."

All of a sudden, said Summerford, Shannon rallied. "I'm going home," she said. "She wanted to pack her stuff herself," explained the nurse. "She said that all day long . . . [but] I had no idea she'd be strong enough to go out that [front] door."

Across the campus in those last few hours Tony Lackey and Roger Popham had traded nervous updates. The rumors had been floating all day long: Shannon was leaving. Shannon was washing out. Shannon was heading home. All those courtroom antics came to nothing. Joe Trez had not confirmed it. Neither had Bud Watts. Lackey and Popham were out of the loop from where they sat but everyone could feel the mood. The great experiment was failing. Shannon would be dropping out.

The two retired colonels traded empty updates through the morning.

"Heard anything?"

Nothing. Only guesswork.

"Anything?"

Nothing.

The rumors swelled and increased and then fell away again giving an odd rhythm to the day. Both men had plenty of other work to do. Unhappy parents sat and shared their disappointments. Some tried to get their boys to stay. The two vice commandants, crisp and commanding in their Army uniforms, played good cop, bad cop, trying to get those kids to stick it out. Still, more and more kids kept dropping out. Some parents even made it easy, Lackey said with considerable contempt. They opened their arms wide and said that there was no disgrace to quitting. He watched those sad reunions with disgust. There was no better training ground, he told a dozen anguished parents. Four years marching would turn those teenagers into men. They should coach their boys to bend themselves to that new frame.

At midday, Popham leaned through Lackey's doorway with a slowly spreading grin. "What's your guess?" he prompted softly, gently pushing back his shock white hair. Lackey merely frowned. He was in no mood for games. He could not tolerate the exodus at hand. He looked up with a grunt. "Here I've got a father who blames himself," he said, waving a sheet of paper with frustration. After only one week at the school, the kid would rather turn and run than face that challenge squarely. "He hasn't even tried!" Lackey barked unhappily. "But here they are, tripping all over each other. Who should take the blame?" He mocked them. "The father blames himself. The mother blames herself. The boy blames himself. They all blame themselves." Nobody could change their minds. If only someone in that family had stood up and taken control. He slapped the papers with disgust, then sighed and tossed the file to one side. Popham watched him with a lonely smile. But Lackey just kept talking. "This kid is some New Jersey kid who always went to private schools. He's soft. Probably shouldn't have come here in the first place. So he's going. Let's see, that brings us to . . ."

Shortly before four o'clock, Popham appeared again, his expression quizzical and sad. When Lackey looked up from his duties, his colleague grimaced and moved his hand in a gesture both men knew from Vietnam: "The Summons," those old soldiers called it, palm down, thumb tucked close, nervous fingers wagging at the floor, come hither. "We got the word," Popham said without elaboration. "She's out."

Lackey clicked his tongue with a snap. "No kidding," he said distantly.

"No kidding," Popham said. "I've got to get over there. Her father's arrived. She told her mother around nine this morning that she wanted to go home. That's it. She's out. They've been on hold all day in there. They kept thinking she might change her mind."

Lackey made another click and shook his head. "That's too bad." He meant it. He believed that if Shannon put her mind to it, she could get along.

Popham turned to go, but Lackey caught him short before he vanished down the hall.

"Hey!" Lackey grinned, craning his neck. "You hear the song?"

Popham wheeled on one foot, still moving as he spoke. "Yeah, I heard it."

They smiled back and forth, then shared a joyless laugh.

"It's not too mean," Lackey said, suddenly defensive. "Well, maybe it's a little mean."

Popham waved and turned away. At The Citadel, mission orders were what mattered most, and he had an assignment.

Gray-faced and mild-mannered, Popham had a quiet way of walking. He drifted through the college as though he would rather not be seen. Even in his hard-soled shoes he could slip soundlessly along bare floors hardly stirring any air. His footfall was like snow. On that day he seemed to move more silently than usual, easing down the hall, drifting past confused cadets, ghosting down the stairwell and out into the parking lot. He pulled his new, white Jeep Cherokee out of its parking spot and turned a corner slowly. He was in no hurry for that ending. Driving in an arc, gliding around the close-cropped parade field and past the cannons and retired jets and rusty Army tanks that bristled as the school's only adornment, he set his mouth in a firm line and inhaled deeply through his nose like a man preparing for an underwater dive. The campus was his home both literally and figuratively. He knew its every acre well. Yet the place made him uncomfortable that day. So he drove slowly toward the end of it, dreading the last scene.

Okay, so it was true, he acknowledged, old traditions would survive. The corps would stay all-male for now. He shrugged. That was fine with him. He would pick up Shannon and her family and that woman lawyer who had come down, too, and drive them all off campus. It was a job like any other job. "Of course," he said stiffly, sounding utterly unconvinced, "I'm very pleased the school will stay all-male." He pulled his Jeep in front of the low white infirmary and eased it to a stop. The windshield wipers splashed in a sudden burst of rain. "I think the school should stay the same," he said. "Yes, sure, I'm happy about that. But I'm not happy for her." He left the engine running and turned the air-conditioning up high, then peered distractedly into a low kaleidoscope of clouds. "I'm sure this must be hard for her. I have daughters of my own."

As Popham spoke, Shannon bolted from the infirmary and headed toward her barracks. Suzanne Coe, bedraggled and in tears, followed in her wake. Stopping underneath a tree for shelter, Shannon's lawyer answered questions in her normal rush. "She has been in this fight for three years," Coe said shakily. "She's not up to this. She's all alone. She doesn't want to stay. She doesn't want to go through life like this. This was a hostile atmosphere."

There was a roar above her. The news was out. The only thing still missing was a quick drive off the campus. From one building to the next cadets began to yell. Coe looked up and wiped a stream of water from her face, then raised her voice above the uproar. "These are the people who testified against her in court," she said, fighting back her tears. "She has had death threats and constant harassment. She's upset. She's very tired. Nobody likes what we're doing here today. Nobody is happy. But it's been an emotional roller coaster for three years, and she wanted to step off."

Reporters peered in a side gate in Shannon's barracks, straining for a glimpse. A cadre member saw them and pushed a crowd of knobs up to the gate. He lined them up three deep and kept them huddled in a human wall. "Click," he said. Twenty boys locked into close attention, all eyes upon the corporal.

When Shannon reemerged she planted herself in front of a sodden huddle of reporters, choking back a surge of tears. Ed hovered in the background, ready for the end. "It's hard for me to leave," Shannon said with her voice cracking. Tears streamed down her cheeks. Her stomach heaved, her voice choked, a sudden downpour cascaded in thin rivulets down her brown hair and shaking legs. "This is something I have worked toward for so long."

A lot of people thought she should have skipped that sad last act. The Citadel had prepared a car and an easy escape route complete with a police escort. They expected her to slip out a back door, the picture of defeat. But that was never Shannon's style. And that was not her exit. Instead, she stopped out on the wet concrete and faced reporters with her hair in tangles and her cheeks drenched in salty tears and her clothes all soaked with seaside rain and sticky as she thanked a lot of people but haltingly admitted that, no, she could not do it. Three years in court had been too much. The toll of that long fight was more than she could bear. The isolation was too painful. The ordeal had been too long. She could not keep her food down now. She could not face the year alone. She would not break the barrier. The barrier had broken her. Now she was terrified. And she was sick. And she was quitting.

"I'm sorry," she told so many. "All I can say is I have to think about my own health right now."

The cameras clicked and spun.

Suzanne Coe stayed over to one side and cried. It was a bad last day. And it had come up fast. From the outside it looked as though Shannon had marched for barely half a day, then fallen ill and lost her nerve. Three years in court came down to that. Her breakdown was quite obvious. But the pieces of it hardly fit. One day she was laughing and triumphant. The next she was walking weakly toward the school infirmary while cadets snapped and marched at either side. Half a day of marching could hardly have done that. Only a few observers really grasped the choreography. They nodded while they watched the scene play out. The Citadel could break anyone, they said glumly. That was the school's tradition. Indeed, that was its point: order and control. Shannon was a magnet for that fate.

When Shannon finished speaking, Ed helped his daughter into Popham's waiting Jeep. Popham looked about him once to make sure all the doors were closed. Then he turned the wheel and laid his foot hard on the gas pedal.

On the road out near the college gates, three cadets in soaking uniforms danced as the Jeep passed by. *"Hey, hey, the witch is dead. The*

witch is dead, the witch is dead. Hey, hey, the witch is dead. . . ." They raised
their legs like showgirls.

Jeremy Wilson, the razor-faced senior who commanded Third Battalion, was staring hard into a camera. "I think it went well," he said
above the uproar. "I think the corps of cadets handled it well and so did
India Company. Everybody did what they had to do. She was going to
receive the same training as the rest of the cadets."

Behind him, a small group of boys marched past, shouting: "God
bless the all-male corps of cadets."

Another group ran behind them, following their wet and flapping
company flag, slamming their feet against the pavement in loud synco-
pated steps.

Moments later, the skies cleared. Just as suddenly as the rain had
come, the day abruptly brightened. The sun came back out burning and
left a veil of steam to rise above black asphalt in a dank perfume. Inside
the barracks all at once a roar gathered and gained volume. By the time
Popham and his famous cargo wheeled through the campus gates, that
college riot had found its wild crescendo. Barracks buildings exploded
with noise. Everywhere, cadets hugged and cheered and shouted. Shannon Faulkner was gone. The war was over. Their celebration was spontaneous and mean.

As Popham's Jeep slipped past a grim-faced sentry, young men in
matching shorts and T-shirts heaved mattresses from first-floor rooms
then ran, sliding, over rain-slicked ground. With awful whoops they
threw the plastic bedding out before them and climbed on board, "quad
surfing" over wet concrete. All four quadrangles roared with cheers and
laughter. Cadets ran and slipped and let out noisy whoops, swinging
sodden shirts over their heads. Bare chested, they tore at one another's
clothes and then leapt piggyback onto friends and classmates. Students
with their heads shaved nearly clean ripped off their hats and dropped
down to their knees to howl with delight. *Yeeeehaaaaa!* They gulped that
unexpected victory and splashed and slapped and punched each other
roughly in shared glee. Cadre sophomores doubled over laughing and
yowled nonsense syllables in crazy bursts. A lot of the new boys joined
in, too, caught up in that mass ecstasy.

Over in fourth barracks, the boys from one company set out on a stiff
march, holding their baby blue company flag out in front and chanting
as they flexed their muscles hard in unison. A small cluster of cadets sang
snippets from *The Wizard of Oz.* Every corner of the campus erupted in

waves of energy and thrill. Sophomores threw themselves onto the ground and slammed out push-ups in awkward pulses, heaving until they crumpled, laughing, to the ground. A metal wastebasket rattled down from an upstairs balcony. Metal struck metal. Flesh struck flesh. Upperclassmen rapped wood poles against the sally ports and banged on exposed pipes. The sound was sudden and tremendous, a prison riot in high gear. Then, suddenly it stilled. An order was repeated soberly over the public-address system. Everybody quieted. The celebration stilled.

Only one sound reverberated in the silence that ensued. It came from somewhere over in the Zoo. In a room almost directly across from the one Shannon had so briefly occupied, a cadet with a prickly Mohawk slapped a rifle hard across his naked, gleaming chest. Framed in silhouette, frowning against the darkness of the room behind, he cocked and recocked his rifle with loud metallic clicks. The motion was repetitive, threatening, frantic and intense.

Inside Popham's Jeep at that moment, Ed—seated in front and dressed for provocation in a T-shirt, socks and shorts painted with the mascot of the University of South Carolina, The Citadel's perennial rival—remarked laconically how it happened to be raining when Shannon first arrived and now it was raining again as she was leaving. Not another word was spoken on that awkward drive. Popham's tongue was frozen, though his mind was hard at work. He struggled to find something appropriate to say. As he wheeled through the college gate and turned right up near the football stadium, navigating standing pools of water and heading toward the Ashley River bridge, he weighed what note to strike, what tone to take, what soothing words to speak. Nothing came to him.

Police had stopped all traffic at the light beside the bridge. When Popham's Jeep pulled up, an officer smoothly signaled him to pass. No one wanted trouble. Popham pressed the Jeep ahead and listened to the slurp and splash of water pushed aside by his wide tires. He would get them safely to their van. There would be no final incident. His Jeep churned a muddy wake. His mouth stayed firmly closed. He flashed his blinker and turned south, moving across an old bridge above the Ashley River. Traffic was light. The rain had stopped. Popham spun the steering wheel and took a breath. But he was a shy man, and he stayed silent out of fear and indecision. Popham thought about his own daughter, now a lieutenant in the U.S. Army, just promoted, his great pride. In his heart, he said later, he wanted to tell Shannon about her. He wanted to tell her that there were other things she could accomplish in her life. He wanted to assure her that everything would turn out fine. He cleared his throat and stole a furtive look at the figure framed behind him in his rearview mirror.

Shannon's expression made his mind go blank. Her face was blotchy and still wet. Her hair was soaked and hanging limp. She looked bedraggled and half sick. He turned his eyes away and kept his focus on the road. Her pain unsettled him. Her disheveled ugliness embarrassed him. She was not the cocky radical he had assumed or the impishly attractive girl he had always seen in photographs. In that back seat, she was just someone with a broken heart. But there they were. All of it had come to this, and there was nothing he could do.

At the tall, round Holiday Inn on James Island where Ed had left the family's van, Popham finally struggled to say the words "Good luck." In the seat behind him, Shannon uncurled her legs and then was gone. One year later, she wouldn't even remember his name.

On the long trip home that afternoon as Ed drove away from that last stinging embarrassment, no one had much to say. Near Greenville, Ed stopped at a Wendy's and everyone piled out. Inside, girls tending to the counter giggled and said Shannon's name. Shannon Faulkner? Yes! That's Shannon Faulkner! Right here! Ain't you Shannon Faulkner? I seen you on TV. Shannon ordered a cheeseburger that she later threw away. She couldn't eat. But she smiled and said hello, then signed her name on several napkins. Her last moments in the spotlight would be bright but few. The lights on Times Square flashed. In London, the British Broadcasting Company ran a flash report at midnight. From Chile to Japan, her story was repeated. The message could not possibly have been clearer. The ancient order held. The girl was driven off. That country tune was right. It was folly for a girl to take those Bulldogs on. On campus, and in Charleston that night and in the next few days, a lot of people couldn't help but gloat. She was too fat, they said with mock concern. She was out of shape, they leered with undisguised delight. She wanted money for her story. She wanted fame for that brash attitude. Good riddance. Several women at The Citadel said they would have made it if they had tried. What a waste, they sneered. What vindication, others crowed. It was an American story. It was a story of the South. It could have happened nowhere else.

Late that day, a world away, the Shearman & Sterling team was fielding questions and taking telephone calls at Henry Weisburg's summer house. "We are very sorry that it didn't work out for Shannon," Weisburg said soberly, pacing the floorboards in a quiet spot in the Hamptons. "But there is a case about all women, now. No, I don't think it is moot. Our goal was to get Shannon admitted to The Citadel. We succeeded in our goal. This has nothing to do with any argument that women just can't hack it."

Val Vojdik put her glass of white wine down and took the telephone from Weisburg. "What I would hope is that people will recall that this is not about Shannon Faulkner, this is about discrimination," she said crisply. "Just think back to the battles over segregation. It was never just one individual. It took a lot of people fighting for justice for a long time to succeed. I also think we have to remember that at The Citadel, if they isolate you, you are out. It's not dishonorable to admit that you can't take it. Shannon has a lot she should be proud of."

Eventually the phone calls slowed, then stopped.

At midnight, The Citadel lay quiet as a stone. But one cadet was still too excited to retire. Having used masking tape to write the words "Bye Shannon" on his Honda hatchback, he was circling the campus time and time again. "It's over," he said, stopping to address a late-night visitor. "It's all over now. You can clear the area. It's done."

The corps had won. It held that sacred ground.

Echo Taps

For the next day, the sky swirled above the town in bursts like small explosions overhead. Winds that gathered on a wing beat far away gained strength over the sea and crashed to shore in howling, watery torrents. Hurricane season was a tumble of quixotic furies. Each one had its signature. In some years the worst storms played up and down the coast but left Charleston in a tranquilizing haze of might-have-beens and near misses, safe but ill at ease. In other years the storms all spent themselves at sea, exhausted over time and distance. Some hurricanes crashed to land elsewhere then curled up north in wind-whipped remnants. The rare one hit square on and left the city in a rotting mess. In 1995, a string of storms lined up along the coast, prepared to devastate those shores. But one by one they passed the Battery by.

In the years since Hurricane Hugo ripped the peninsula apart, Charleston met the season with heightened vigilance and renewed worry. That year, the rains came right on schedule. Shutters closed, air conditioners clanked, and all the tourists vanished. But it would be a mild season after all. The winds shrieked and the rain drove hard like tacks of ice. Yet there were breaks in all that wind and water. The Sunday after Hell Week dawned calm and clear. The sun glared, the temperature rose, and everybody rested.

The previous night, a hypnotist had entertained in Mark Clark Hall. One by one, boys already functioning deep inside a trance marched up and took their seats then fell beneath his spell. When the show was done the boys ran back to barracks, hardly waiting for a barked command. In the wool-thick dark, they moved in awkward steps. Near the Zoo, there came a noisy crack. Every new boy jumped as an older cadet in uniform snapped a bullwhip near his feet. The strap fell close but never touched. The boys ran on, their eyes locked straight, stifling their fear. A minor readjustment, a small miscalculation, a momentary lapse and that long whip would bring some blood. Yet the cadet who wielded it was skillful at his game.

By then, the knobs were grateful for that upperclassman's craft and self-restraint. They watched him furtively and moved their feet, frightened and yet awed by his control. New rules were taking shape for everyone who stayed. At first, they tangled in the mind, unintelligible and strange. Hidden traps and sudden shocks brought only terror. Slowly, though, a new vocabulary took shape. Routines began evolving. Old realities would fall away. "We must instill fear!" the soldier had told Joe Trez. How true that was, the new boys learned. And what exquisite expertise those upperclassmen could display.

Once, slavery was the theme. Now, the game was war. The transformation was complete. The shock and damage that they knew fit into old philosophies. War was good, soldiers brave. Only cowards crumpled. If they could just survive, The Citadel would make them whole.

Violence compels mythology. It always has. We look for lessons in its fury. A lifetime can go to pondering the deadly work of just one instant. Why me, and not the other? For what reason? At what cost? At The Citadel a new generation found old answers rubbed as smooth as creek stones. Hardship made for strength. Suffering built character. The followers would someday lead. The weak all fell away. To those who stayed, every action had its purpose, every bruise its rationale. The boy with the whip was teaching dominance and trust. The shouting corporals in their low-slung hats were stripping boys of childish arrogance. It was, the lawyers said in court, something studied and refined.

Power, crudely exercised, has always had that pull. Together, soldiers are a force, a tide, a power beyond reckoning. The sight can move some men to tears. Beside the Ashley, with the cannons booming and the sound of music drifting through a cordite fog, it always had.

On talk shows that Sunday, commentators gave their thoughts on Shannon's sorrowful last words. Many were not kind. "She has done a great disservice," Cokie Roberts said sharply on ABC's *This Week With David Brinkley.* "I mean, if you are going to be a pioneer, you have to get on the covered wagon and go across the country and be a pioneer."

G. Gordon Liddy described himself as "delighted" by that tearful exit. "The whale beached herself," he quipped, "and that's the end of that."

Freshmen had no time to steep themselves in aftermaths. Instead,

weak and limping from fresh blisters, they were awakened early, fed, cor-
ralled and herded out of town to the school's beach house on the Isle of
Palms. "Get up! Move it! What are you doing, knob? Let's get going."
On buses, exhausted boys scrambled for their seats, their eyes downcast.
The day was hot and windy, perfect for their outing. But they would
have gone in any case. Even recreation had its rules. Attendance was
mandatory. Physical training uniforms were required. There was no
room for personal choice. The Citadel was no place for individuals.
Lone wolves were always driven off. This was a marker, too. "If I can
make it this far . . ." And they had.

The outing was described as a reward and, indeed, knobs were offered
some much-needed rest. But like many things at The Citadel, the stated
purpose was not necessarily the most important one. Other dynamics
were in play. For while the dazed knobs ate and slept, the upper classes
signed back in. Most years, laughed Gunny Venable, some among them
showed up drunk. "The older guys," he explained with a broad wink,
"they've had their last couple beers." They ran the new boys down for
sport, he said. Life inside the barracks in those hours could get a little
out of hand.

Popham put it considerably more blandly. "The thing we have discovered is that everything goes down just a little bit easier if we have the
new guys at the beach. It calms things down, lets everyone adjust."

The cadre had long since warned the new boys that no matter how
hard Hell Week was, their real agony was yet to come. That week's training was just warm-up, some among the cadre said. "We are controlled,"
a short, chisel-faced corporal proudly informed his charges as they stood
in a stiff and blank-faced line waiting to board their bus. "We are your
friends. We are handpicked by the commandant. But there's no accounting what those other guys might do."

Some of the older boys were crazy, corporals said. Some of them were
mean. "Trust us," cadre said. They were better than the alternative.

By Sunday, the *Guidon*'s words were etched in every heart. "This will
be your way of life," it said. Cadre members were the masters. Anything
the cadre said was law. And any law they made was heeded. "When you
receive an order, carry it out," the *Guidon* ruled. "Never argue." Dissent
was unacceptable, suggestions out of place. "This is not in your best
interest." And so the new boys marched and suffered. They spoke when
spoken to and used only the forms allowed. Until October when train-

ing cadre ended and the upper classes got their chance, the knobs were cadre's alone. Two months later they would be fodder in a free-for-all, everybody's game.

First, they found much-needed rest. Fourteen buses lined up side to side in stubbly grass beside the road. At the beach house gate, several upperclassmen stood guard in their dark shorts and T-shirts, glinting sunglasses hiding their eyes. "Sorry . . . this event is closed," they announced with cool authority, waving visitors away. "No one is allowed inside. This event is closed. Those are our orders." Their attitude allowed no argument.

Hardly half a mile away, another world was turning. The window of a fancy real estate office beckoned with snapshots of expensive cottages. Vacationers with deep tans and shining skin drifted aimlessly from shop to shop. Beaches were white and broad and mobbed. Business was booming. Even in an August stupor, the island had a certain energy. Surfers and sunbathers, students and their families camped in steamy clusters by the sea. There, they drifted off to sleep or stood about half-naked in the broiling sun, smearing sunblock over sandy skin. On the roadway nearby, new arrivals parked their cars in the thick slam of mid-day heat. Clowning and preening, the occupants unpacked coolers and umbrellas and then settled into folding chairs that tilted at odd angles.

Not half a mile away, knobs moved stiffly through the same routines. But their faces were drawn and their spirits slack. A wedding party was under way when those buses pulled onto the beach house grounds. Freshmen were diverted to an open shed off to one side. There, dazed young boys shuffled forward toward huge tins of food. Shyly, they heaped their plates with hamburgers, potato salad, fried chicken and brownies made with butterscotch. Flawlessly polite and totally subdued, they ate in almost total silence while pitchers of lemonade, iced tea and watery juice were emptied and refilled. Most boys rose for seconds and politely asked for more. Once seated, they wolfed their food down wordlessly then drifted off into the day.

Tony Lackey, sipping a beer, watched them with approval and open pride. He had walked in those shoes, too, and wished each new boy well. As a soldier, he had proudly risked his life. Nothing meant more. Among that new crop of boys, there would be some others like him, hard and idealistic, patriotic to a fault. He felt a surge of warmth and even love for those young faces. In the harsh sun, his wrinkles ran brown and deep. "I know exactly how they feel," he said. He had been that nervous, once, that awkward and unsure. The Citadel would change them. It would teach them to be men.

Roger Popham stood alone, over to one side. As the sun drifted white against the sky he found a perch up on the beach house balcony where he could settle and survey the scene. He couldn't let that Friday go. "I have three daughters," he said. "So maybe I understand a little bit." He gazed out toward the water. Several knobs were body surfing, playing back and forth amid the waves. But hundreds more were slumped under the glaring sun, their shoulders drooped, their faces slack. Some talked quietly. Many others slept. A few gazed dully out to sea or walked the beach or played halfhearted volleyball down by the dunes. Several knobs found shade and were writing letters home. They cupped their pens and twisted their shoulders into odd contortions so that no one else could see. "Dear Mom and Dad . . ." But how could you explain it? Everything was fine, they said. There was no need to worry. Miss you. Love.

A tall knob with acne finished his correspondence and stepped stiffly up the stairs. He nodded grimly to the colonel and asked if there was any place to buy a stamp. There was not. The colonel pointed to a mailbox with a snarling bulldog painted across it and said that if he could find one, all letters went in there. Another knob slipped past and slid an envelope inside the box. Then he marched off toward the water and put his toes in the warm sea.

Popham watched them glide by and then continued with his reverie. "And I've got one daughter, my middle daughter, who was born in 1969. Her name is Paige. She's twenty-six. She's a second lieutenant in the Army now." He brought his arm up and checked his watch, then quickly corrected himself. "No . . . She's a first lieutenant now. She just got promoted. And she won't let you forget it. Because that promotion went through ahead of her husband's."

That daughter was an officer in the signal corps. She worked with high-tech gear. He smiled. It was Paige whom he had thought of most while driving Shannon out of town. "She called me," he said, getting ahead of himself, "and she said: 'Dad. It's a good thing it wasn't me. Because I would have made it.'"

Paige asked her father once what he would have done if she had applied. He answered glibly. She never would have gotten in, he joked, because there was no lawsuit then. It was more of an evasion than an answer, but they both let it go. Still, he wrestled with the question now.

"I look at my daughter, the first lieutenant, struggling with the idea that separate can be equal . . . He stopped abruptly and then shrugged. The whole thing was so confusing. And everything was changing fast. Not two days after Shannon left, most people on campus said they had no real objection to letting women march. The troubles of those years, they said, were simply Shannon's fault. It was Shannon who made things ugly. It was Shannon who had started it. She was abrasive and out of shape and seemed contemptuous of their whole world. They blamed Shannon for everything. She was the wrong person at the wrong time. Tony Lackey said so, too. "If it were someone else . . . ," began countless equivocations.

As the afternoon played out, the mailbox slowly filled. A freighter moved across the low horizon. Gunny Venable stood watching. Even without a cigar in his mouth he had the look of a man smoking. A knob approached and dodged quickly over to one side. He had flipped his college baseball cap around so that the visor faced his back. Gunny, who was short, pulled himself as straight as he could stand, then moved into that student's path. "Boy," he barked, blocking that knob's way. "If you are planning to wear a hat, then you wear it properly." The knob spun his hat around without ever making eye contact. Then he tucked a letter in the mailbox and darted down the stairs. Gunny smiled at his retreating form, and let out a contented sigh. "They're scared now," he cackled in a throaty voice, "because when they get home, the upperclassmen will be back."

Hussein Al-Majali, a 1981 graduate who stayed at the school in one job and another, described the new classes as weak. "It used to be, in the old days," he said easily, "that the cadre pressed cigarette butts in your forehead. They had those cigarette butt punishments and a lot of other stuff like knobby wands. They used the knobby wands to beat the new boys. Now, everything is going soft. The whole place is changing," he said, reflectively. "I guess that's good." He hardly seemed convinced.

In time, the buses started idling. The older boys were back in place, unpacking in the barracks. But the knobs were slow to gather. After the wedding party disbanded, many of them had drifted inside the air-conditioned hall. When the command was barked for them to go, more than one hundred boys lay sleeping in a tangled mass, like the victims of some grand catastrophe.

In time, that year, the new class would find its rhythm and its place. It had always been that way. Even those who mocked the city while they marched tended to drift back later to show their wives the dripping foliage and the perfectly kept gardens that happily confirmed that they were part of something grand. Like Popham, many would leave their college rings to slide smoothly over wedding bands. They swore their deepest loyalty upon that ground. Theirs was a club like other Charleston clubs, exclusive and self-important, "one great big fraternity," as both its members and its critics said, a closed set that had always played its part in a complex web of ascension, belonging, nostalgia and raw hope.

Most cadets saw in Charleston everything that they were not. She seduced them with the glimmer of her twining rivers and the heady, dark aroma of the sea. On randy adventures outside the campus gates, cadets peered into fecund gardens and walled estates and felt all the hardships of the barracks fall away. It was a city most would come to love. At sunset the river water turned to silver and the sky above it broke in long, fantastic streaks of color. Boats slid against the water's surface, suspended in a rippling haze. Etched in black against the brilliance to the west, those cruisers moved in silhouette. Around their hulls, dolphins splashed and broke the surface in cascading sprays, rising easily through that gray chop. Overhead, pelicans and seagulls, ibis and other marsh birds soared in strict formations or in hapless loopy lines, making charming crowds across the sky.

It was easy to forgive the city anything at that hour. Many cadets did. For four years, the city held them in her humid, long embrace. She promised rest and peace when they had so much suffering; she offered splendor and serenity when all they knew was pain. Once those boys were broken down, she offered gentle tokens of everything they lacked. From the hardship came the grace. It had always been that way. But now, that too was changing.

For generations, Charleston had always preened and flirted with her visitors. At last, the balance tipped. In 1995, the elite was losing ground to those it courted. Careful lines of power, so long held, were wearing thin. Newcomers had a growing voice and presence. Tourism, always irksome, barreled out of control. Old families groused that they were drowning in vast tides of roaming strangers. True, the city had sold her charm for profit for one hundred years or more. When roads were dirt and air travel mere fiction, almost fifty thousand visitors walked on the Battery each year. In the 1920s, the city earned $4 million from its tourists. "Nothing is more dreadful," commented one resident. "They will make Charleston rich and ruin her."

It was a bitter prophecy. By the time Shannon marched, the stampede was tremendous. Some outsiders came and stayed. Old houses were sold off. Antique deeds changed hands. Ancient houses were restored. New restaurants opened, and expensive boutiques multiplied. When the *Queen Elizabeth 2* docked off East Bay Street, spilling a transient population from decks that rose high above the city's rooftops in huge, ghostly plates of steel, one passenger confided: "Next year we're going to the Caribbean. But we wanted to come here before the tourist glut begins." For that, they were already much too late.

In every season, strangers peered and poked and pried. They strolled down narrow driveways and pressed their noses against glass. They jumped and pointed, moved in groups and by romantic pairs. On Meeting Street, they stopped frequently to knock at the trunk of an ancient wisteria vine that curled up and over an iron fence that marked off Bert Pruitt's handsome garden. Tap tap. "It's real!" they shouted, invariably with some surprise. On many weekends, rain or shine, a man and woman stood in the white gazebo by the Battery while someone read their vows. "We were married down in Charleston," they would later say.

The old guard tried in vain to protect its privacy. Elegant gardens warned visitors away with neatly painted signs that urged admiration at a distance. Respect for the owners' property, those signs politely advised, required that the lush displays be viewed from public ground. Almost nothing could control the flow. Real estate prices rose and kept on rising, bloating 800 and 900 percent in a decade and a half. City taxes followed suit. In rapid succession, many among the city's oldest houses—faded majesties sprawling over four floors with several living rooms, countless bathrooms and cascades of dripping chandeliers—started falling out of family hands. Grand old dwellings that once teemed with masters, mistresses, children and attending slaves became home to wealthy couples from New York, Chicago and California while inside musty mansions just next door the elderly descendants of true blue bloods ticked off their final days, marking time until the end of something surely bigger than themselves. They would not leave until they died. But death would be the end of it. The city's beating heart was slowly going, replaced now by a diorama of her history.

The Committee to Save the City resolved to intervene. In late 1995, it made a few demands: "Eliminate ALL tour buses from ALL residential neighborhoods," committee members urged. "Improve ENFORCEMENT of the tourism management plan, including enforcement of parking, carriage, tour bus, and walking tour regulations. LIMIT the number of people who can be on any one walking tour with a licensed guide. Improve residential parking. Manage non-residential traffic in ALL downtown neighborhoods."

Groups of up to seventy people at a time were now wandering through quaint back streets. The composition of those groups was changing too. Once the city attracted visiting garden clubs and old ladies wearing hats. Now it was just as likely that throngs of blacks would move along the sidewalks clutching pamphlets, eating ice cream, making noise. Teenagers swept by in hordes, dropping litter as they went. Swarms of gray-haired retirees in leisure wear pushed up to private gates. Tour buses idled belching fumes behind them in the heat. And huge clots of foreigners—chattering in French, in Japanese, in German—did not always part the seas for local residents.

On a hot Charleston night while a sharp wind blew in warm slaps from off the sea, a group of partygoers spilled out of a raucous party on East Bay Street. Stepping out in pairs and clusters, immaculate in party dresses and light summer suits, members of the old elite arrayed themselves along a balcony while balancing stiff drinks. "Just imagine the view," sighed an enraptured visitor who observed them from the street. But no one on that balcony looked out across the harbor. Their backs were turned, the landscape memorized.

One by one, old icons were transformed to accommodate the crowds. At Marion Square, the foreboding barracks building that once had housed cadets was utterly remade. Painted a bright Bermuda pink, freshly buffed and air-conditioned, the old Citadel reopened that same year as a hotel that welcomed visitors with stately palm trees standing sentry at the front. Now, anyone with a credit card could rent the thrill of history inside those halls.

In town, cadet uniforms began to feel quite out of place. Grim-faced boys moved in tight bands, buffered by their own. Mostly, they kept to haunts they knew, where drinks were cheap and conversations loud and a young man had only to run his hand along his stubbly head to win a rebel yell of admiration. Outside those last few enclaves, their welcome was no longer either automatic or particularly warm. For more than a century, military flourishes had held the city in thrall. But at last that dance was ending. Now, only 18 percent of the school's graduates pursued military careers. Military bases were closing around the South.

They closed in Charleston, too, making banner headlines. Meanwhile, a new generation poked fun at all that stiff-legged marching by the Ashley. "We're the freak show," said Harold Poston Jr., then the president of the junior class. "That's how I like to think of it."

Like a jilted lover slow to accept loss, the Military College of South Carolina still clung to old romances. And yet the courtship now was finished. The proof of it was everywhere. In town, expressions of contempt now alternated with well-worn murmurs of respect. "It's nothing but a sadistic cult," snapped one well-positioned socialite. "I think they should just shut it down." Hers was a minority opinion stated with unusual bitterness amid the hum and laughter of a cocktail party. But a decade earlier no one would have dared to share that sentiment aloud, nor in that company.

More common was a kind of hushed suspicion. "You heard about that shooting?" quizzed a heavy-set woman from back behind a drugstore counter. She clucked her tongue and clutched some change and kept the conversation going. "That black boy almost died!" she hissed. "But they never found who did it. Mmmmm-unhhh," she said, heaving her broad frame across the tan Formica. "They never do, down there." She waved her hand and pursed her lips and leaned in close. "That place scares me."

In Washington, the Pentagon was backing off as well. There, some top officials wondered if The Citadel's all-male environment might not be ill suited to the demands of a profession in which men and women labored side by side and women sometimes barked the orders. The Citadel's much-publicized (but later reversed) intention to shave Shannon's head had pushed the debate further. In private offices in Washington, grave discussions were held as to whether the school's ROTC program, the third-largest in the nation, should be closed. Frantic politicking staved off that powerful threat. But The Citadel's single-mindedness had come at a clear cost. And now that cost was growing. Instead of being revered as the West Point of the South, the school was ridiculed in military circles as a rusty vestige of another era. It did not keep up. In the *Navy Times* and other service newspapers a cartoonist drew a "Citadel Tree House" perched high up in the branches of an oak. Across its shoddily built entrance was the slogan WE HATE GIRLS!

Civilian artists and commentators were equally unsympathetic. As the Faulkner case dragged on, one publication after another had come to wonder if the school was just a hideout for the misogynist fringe. "The Louts of Discipline," rebuked a headline in *Time* magazine when Shannon left.

Even some of the school's faithful turned away. In Virginia that year, Ed Tivol watched with shame as his alma mater was ridiculed. Without fanfare one afternoon, he slipped his college ring off and hid it deep inside a drawer. The school that once had made him proud enough to almost float above the ground now triggered only vague discomfort.

There were glaring exceptions, of course, and stirring moments of new hope. A 1996 presidential candidate survey conducted by the conservative Center for Military Readiness showed that Lamar Alexander, Pat Buchanan, Robert Dole, Robert Dornan and Allan Keyes were all opposed to admitting women at either The Citadel or VMI. And in a political debate televised in South Carolina shortly after Shannon left the school, all the leading Republican candidates reiterated their belief that The Citadel should stay all-male. Tradition was at stake, those politicians all agreed.

Sandy Faulkner was so mad at them, she said, her head had almost burst.

Beside the Ashley, the toll of that long fight became increasingly clear. Six months after Shannon left, school officials rather ruefully announced that Citadel records showed a steady drop in applications. On campus, the exodus continued. In February that year, Joe Trez gave a bleak report regarding student withdrawals. In it, he included a breakdown of reasons why each cadet had left. Thirty different categories were listed to explain why students had dropped out. Most among them overlapped. The obvious and overriding fact was that the fourth class system drove them out. Perhaps the faithful had destroyed the school in their efforts to save it. Yet careful phrasings laid the blame on boys who quit:

> Does not care for military lifestyle.
> Unable to handle military/academic/athletics combination.
> Unable to handle academics/military combination.
> Lack of motivation.
> Dissatisfied with Fourth Class System.
> Couldn't handle stress.
> Deprivation of food/threats, verbal, cursing abuse (not
> substantiated).

Does not respond to counselling and The Citadel system.
Does not have mental ability to persevere.
Allegations of hazing.
Transferring to another college.
Lack of motivation/discipline.

Board members listened glumly. Then Cliff Poole gave an accounting of student academic performance. Thirty-six percent of the freshmen were falling below a 2.0 average.

Other problems were outlined as well. More and more boys left after Christmas break their senior year and never bothered to come back. They wore their rings, but earned their final credits elsewhere. The board was at a loss. "Things have changed," one board member commented dejectedly. "We have to start thinking of these students as customers."

A second report showed the corps' overall size contracting. Though full enrollment was placed at 2,000 cadets, projections showed that it might fall to 1,720 cadets that year and maybe lower. Bud Watts had earlier considered building enough new barracks space to accommodate a corps of up to 2,400 students. By then, he admitted it was wishful thinking. In reality, the school would be fortunate to remain at its present level. More likely, it would continue to contract. That fact, announced the chief financial officer, meant a negative impact in all areas of the budget. Fewer students meant less income. The corps was already functioning at 78 cadets under budget. That translated into a half-million-dollar shortfall for the fiscal year. Since the school had already spent its reserve fund, there was no emergency account to draw upon to make up the gap. To compensate, the college busily cut costs. Twenty-seven vacant staff positions went unfilled. Official policy required at least a twelve-week delay before new hirings were allowed.

Meanwhile, an expensive, badly needed expansion project was under way. The old barracks were out of date. Basic machinery often did not work. Bart Daniel, a younger member of the board, complained that two cadets had grumbled that they had not been able to take a hot shower since Thanksgiving. "It's February!" Daniel exploded, visibly shocked. "It's cold!"

Watts dismissed the charge as false. "I defy any cadet to come to me to tell me they haven't had a hot shower since before Thanksgiving," he said. "We are not uncaring or unfeeling. For a cadet to come to you and say he hasn't had a hot shower since Thanksgiving," he sputtered, "well, there are two sides to every story."

The bill from Shannon's long fight was due—and mounting. Not only had the school given Converse College a nonrefundable check for $5 million to set up its SCIL program, but Shearman & Sterling had asked for millions, too, as had The Citadel's own legal team. While the state insurance fund would pass most of those costs on to taxpayers, the tally was enormous and hard to justify in the state capital. Meanwhile, the issue was still open. Following Shannon's departure, a new female candidate appeared. Judge Houck allowed Nancy Mellette's name to be substituted in the case but declined to expand the matter into a class action suit. In the end, Mellette would sidestep The Citadel in favor of West Point. But still the matter wasn't finished.

In Charleston, meanwhile, the boys kept right on marching. Yet their discipline was oddly lax. It was a paradox that Joe Trez struggled to correct. During a surprise visit in the barracks made by Trez and Watts that year, dozens of cadets were found relaxing in their rooms in flagrant violation of school rules. "We were either watching soap operas, we were playing Nintendo, or we were sleeping," said Trez, using the patronizing tone of a disgruntled schoolmarm in a "free fire" meeting designed to explore barracks problems. "That was in virtually every—not all—but virtually every room we went into. That's what the general found." There were other problems, too. "We go into the barracks and find fifteen people—and every one of them has written a false report" about his whereabouts, Trez complained. His solution was more adult intervention. But the cadets reacted in an angry outburst. The corps ran the corps, they said. Trez paled and pursed his lips.

On Corps Day that spring, cadets gathered in the shadow of the old Citadel at Marion Square to march in their best uniforms. Behind them, construction workers put the finishing touches on the new Embassy Suites hotel. As cadets took their places underneath those towering pink walls, a handful of men in T-shirts and hard hats took up seats along the roof. For almost an hour, they lingered there to watch. Few others in the city bothered. On Meeting Street, rush hour traffic crawled and surged with every changing light.

The head of the Association of Citadel Men addressed the sparse crowd that year with cautious words of change. "It has been a difficult and long struggle," he said wearily. "But I recall Einstein. From every difficulty, there comes an opportunity." He paused. The buzz saws screamed. "Let us put aside our defensive mode. . . . Let us refocus our thinking and our efforts and our time and our energies on recruiting, training and educating the current and future corps of cadets." Half a dozen college administrators clapped listlessly. "I hope everyone has a wonderful time," the association president said with a salute. On cue, a cadet who had taken up a position among construction workers on the roof played taps. It was a lonely sound above the din of traffic. Soon another trumpet followed. Together they played echo taps, the haunting sound of loss.

It was the end of something old. But nobody took notice. Several teenagers chatted and whispered in the shade. A middle-aged couple held hands, and a small group of tourists stopped and stared at the cadets. When The Citadel's band played the national anthem, Watts and Poole and several other college administrators stood and held their hands above their hearts. Then a bagpipe played, and many in the crowd began dispersing. "Must be all freshmen," one man observed. "They have no hair." In the hazy springtime air, American flags fluttered and rolled, flapping lazily in the warmth. Cadets snapped sharply back and forth. But they seemed lost in that large field. One onlooker gently steered his wife away. "Shall we head back?" he offered. She nodded, and they were out of sight before the marching finished.

In May, the board met once again. After their meeting, it was announced that Watts would soon be leaving. "This divorce is not amicable," commented a former board member. "The level of discontent grew enough to force the board to do something. . . . Tribal drums say that there has been considerable concern regarding the post-Christmas drop in enrollment. Especially unusual was the number of upperclassmen not returning. It is rare for a cadet to make it through the Fourth Class year and then decide to drop out. At last count there are well over two hundred empty beds in the barracks. I am told there has been little attempt to learn why. In the meantime Bud [Watts] is sending Spearman about the state with a 'Don't Worry' speech."

Not long after that, the Supreme Court ruled. The Virginia Military Institute, justices of the court agreed, could no longer legally exclude women from its ranks. Citadel officials rushed to hold a press conference. Women were now welcome, they proclaimed. The change was swift and final.

In Washington, D.C., that summer, Petra Lovetinska, the blond, big-boned daughter of a driver at the Czech Republic Embassy, received an acceptance letter from The Citadel. Though she did not have the financial means to enroll, alumni from the Washington area pledged to come up with whatever she might need.

In Charlotte, North Carolina, around that same time, Jeanie Mentavlos, the daughter of a former Secret Service agent, decided to follow in her brother's footsteps. Though she competed in the Miss Citadel contest in Shannon's year, a shako would now replace a tiara as her quest upon that ground.

Elsewhere, Kim Messer, the daughter of a retired Army sergeant from Clover, South Carolina, let out a whoop. She had already settled on a military career. Charleston would be her proving ground.

In a suburb of Charleston, too, that summer, the comely daughter of a retired Army general signed her forms and started planning. Her father, Brigadier General James Emory Mace, wore a Citadel ring marked 1963. A hard-driving, cigar-smoking, self-proclaimed tough guy with a reputation for pushing his underlings to vivid extremes, Mace would soon replace Joe Trez as commandant.

Epilogue:
Fear Is like a Tree

IT COULD HAVE BEEN a time for nothing but success. It almost was. Everybody wanted easy answers, happy endings. But too much lay behind, and hidden, for anything so simple. On the same day that four women stood and took their oath as new cadets, a Charleston lawyer from the class of 1968 walked into the offices of the *Post and Courier* to deliver a letter intended for the general public. It was written by a graduate of the class of 1994. In that letter, George F. Cormeny III confessed to something that had gnawed at him for years. It was he who shot and nearly killed a black cadet on that old campus. He described the moment in detail.

"I am writing this letter to bring to a conclusion the incident of the shooting of Cadet Berra Byrd on The Citadel campus, March 12, 1992—the worst day of my life," he wrote. "The last four and a half years of living with this secret and the pain I caused Berra, his family, and The Citadel have been unbearable.

"The day before the shooting, as a sophomore cadet, I took a 9mm pistol into the barracks where I lived with other cadets. . . .

"At approximately 5:30 p.m., I was handling the pistol in my fourth floor, corner room. I unknowingly and unintentionally chambered a round by not first checking to see if the pistol held a clip. Pointing the pistol out the window and thinking it unloaded, I pulled the trigger. To my indescribable horror, the pistol fired. . . .

"I panicked," wrote Cormeny. "I have no excuse, only an explanation. That panic led me to make the most foolish decision yet in a long line of foolish decisions. . . ."

During a four-year investigation, the FBI had drawn closed an ever tightening net. Finally, somebody talked. In exchange for a promise of immunity from prosecution, David Alan Burdock Jr., Cormeny's former roommate and a witness to the shooting, said that Cormeny had fired the shot. When FBI agents came calling, Cormeny confessed. In the months that followed, law enforcement officials explained that investigators had been purposefully misled by those two students. In an effort to obscure any evidence of crime, they did away with the empty shell casing, cut holes in the window screen and disposed of the weapon. They washed their room thoroughly to remove trace elements of gunpowder and used fans to dissipate the smell. As a final touch, they moved about the barracks poking random pencil holes in window screens to throw off the police.

Soon, Cormeny would stand before the Board of Visitors to ask for their forgiveness. They granted it, respectfully.

"We don't sit in judgment," Jimmie Jones assured him. "The compassion you have shown speaks well of your integrity."

Bart Daniel, himself a former U.S. attorney, nodded and agreed. "Mr. Cormeny," he said gravely, "everyone makes mistakes. . . . As far as I am concerned, you are absolved."

Late that October, Cormeny was assigned four hundred hours of community service and sentenced to thirty days in jail. He had pleaded guilty to illegally possessing a handgun under the age of twenty-one, a misdemeanor. A second charge, a felony, accused him of illegally carrying a firearm into a public building. He pleaded guilty to that, too. There was no charge to indicate that the gun was ever fired, nor that it had hit a human target. The FBI concluded that the shooting was an accident. The shock soon fell away. The light of public scrutiny was dimmed. Old routines repeated.

Throughout that fall, Terry Leedom announced that The Citadel's four female cadets were doing well. Yet in messages that flashed across the Internet, someone who carefully obscured his own identity painted a far different picture. At first, the author spoke only of danger facing two of the four female students who had arrived at The Citadel that year. Eventually, he told a broader tale about the trials of many, including, at last, himself. Always, he spoke with anger and with sadness. He loved The Citadel, he claimed. And yet he was afraid of what it had become. In daring to say that, he feared retribution against himself and members of his family. Still, he continued. Over the course of nearly a year, he would write almost daily in an eloquent soliloquy consuming many hundreds of pages, each examining an environment of violence and fear. Boys always have their stories. This was his.

V watched Shannon Faulkner come and go. He saw the institution twist and change as a new team sat down in Jenkins Hall. Abuses in the barracks were decreasing. Reforms were having some effect. But on the day that Shannon dropped away, V watched at a distance as cadre members started dancing in the rain. And as he watched, he cried. He did not cry for Shannon, he explained. He cried for his whole school, perhaps even for himself.

"I have done much soul searching these past two weeks," he said at the outset of his correspondence. "I not only want to do what is right, but I want to make a difference. If coming forth would change anything I would do so no matter what the consequences. I would do it for The Citadel, which you may not understand."

Instead, he would struggle and stay hidden, slowly letting go of his last innocence.

Through November and the first two weeks of December, at a time when Citadel officials were reporting that all was well with their four female cadets, V wrote with increasing anguish of another reality playing out behind the barracks walls. Jeanie Mentavlos and Kim Messer, he said, were exhausted, blank and disoriented, breaking into pieces. Day after day, he watched them drowning in a system that he knew in every detail. Yet there was silence from the school and silence from the women, too. By all outward accounts, all was well inside those gates. Still, V's messages flashed once or twice a day, growing in urgency, gaining force and credibility. He was frightened and preoccupied. Yet there was nothing he could prove. "How can I explain?" he wondered. And so he looked backward, at Shannon's passage through those gates.

"The official story was that Shannon succumbed to the heat," he wrote. "The truth of the matter was that she was terrified to the point she could not keep anything in her stomach. It was battle stress. Simply put, it is when a person's fear becomes so overwhelming their bodies physically rebel. The school officials provided her an easy way out, affording her the sanctuary of the Infirmary. . . .

"The truth was right in front of everyone, but never mentioned because it didn't fit the popular theme. There is no doubt Shannon was overweight. But did anyone bother to investigate how many other knobs came to The Citadel overweight as well even in that very class? Did anyone bother to find out that it was no big deal even if she didn't meet the fitness tests? Did anyone bother to find out that you can graduate from The Citadel and *never* meet those requirements? Did anyone bother to ask her parents or friends if she could have in fact met those requirements which were pretty minimal? Did anyone bother to take notice that all she did that morning was just knob stuff at the bookstore? Certainly not. The truth would have detracted from the clarity of the story being put forth."

He spoke in riddles and drew eloquent analogies. He suspected something far more intricate.

"Fear is like a tree," he said. "You can water a piece of ground until the end of Creation and no tree will spontaneously spring from it. On the other hand, you can plant a seed but without water it will never grow. To have a tree you must first plant the seed below the ground and then water it from above. Do you understand what I am saying?"

V spoke of two Citadels. One worked above the ground, with crisp salutes and gracious smiles. One worked in total secrecy with threats of violence and pain. He went back to Shannon, using recent history to outline his beliefs.

"The legal and public relations battle to keep Shannon out of The Citadel had to be waged in the open and conducted in a proper respectable manner by those with enough financial resources and influence to pursue it," V said, elaborating carefully. "That is the right arm of those in official positions of power. However, what that right arm could do in the open was not enough to achieve the objective by itself. This is why the left arm came in with threats and intimidation."

V worked the details out with ever finer brush strokes. "No actual physical force could have been used against her," he advised. "There were U.S. Marshals protecting her. If someone did harm her, Shannon was too visible. Such action would have evoked forces far beyond the control of those in South Carolina. . . . That is not what the powers wanted, but they wanted Shannon gone. They had to exploit her fear which was a challenge given that Shannon is a person of courage and fortitude, given the resources that were protecting her and the intense public scrutiny of her progress at The Citadel."

V feared the same tactics were now being used to drive Kim Messer and Jeanie Mentavlos from the barracks. He made his case at a time when no one was complaining. Yet day by day, his fears increased, and the tone of his letters grew more insistent. "Hazing isn't about hurting someone, at least in a physical sense," he lectured. "It's about submission. It's far more akin to a theft than an assault, as one is robbed of dignity and worth. . . . With a hazing, you give in. That's the part that eats your soul. You come to blame yourself for whatever it was they did." Serious physical harm was generally avoided. It left unwelcome evidence and long avenues for repercussion. "The process has been adapted to the times, with the threat of harm taking the place of the harm itself," he explained. "It is a psychological exercise."

Yet there were real terrors, too, and real injuries as well that sometimes landed freshmen in the hospital. He wrote around them at the start, as though they did not matter much. Then he conceded that those hurts were just as real. "I am not for a minute dismissing the issue of physical abuse," he corrected. "Yes, it exists." On another day he worried: "What happens when those women show up with the crap beat out of them and the officials at The Citadel say they were fighting with each other? Do you honestly think it will stop there? Then what do you think comes next?"

He stared into a puzzle. There were questions he could never ask. And answers he would never get. He had learned those lessons, too. The system overwhelmed him.

"Under the Honor Code there is something called an 'Improper Question,'" he explained in one of four messages that flashed on November 21, 1997. "It is like the Fifth Amendment for cadets for lack of a better explanation. But unlike the Fifth Amendment which gives a person the right to decline to answer a question because it may be incriminating, it is a prohibition against *asking* incriminating questions and applies even to administrators like General Poole. It is taken very seriously."

Under the Improper Question rule, honor was assumed. Cadets were unassailable. That was the tradition. While all of America convulsed, The Citadel had quietly reversed a modern axiom. On that ground, as a matter of strictest policy, authority was *never* questioned. Instead, it was assumed that an honorable man would come forward with transgressions of his own accord.

V examined the results with anguished concentration. Always, he focused his attention on Messer and Mentavlos. Nancy Mace and Petra Lovetinska seemed to thrive. He had a theory for that, too. Mace was the daughter of a general, a man who wore the ring and would protect her. She was primed and ready for that environment. Lovetinska was a good candidate, too, V surmised. Because of her financial indebtedness to alumni and "her Old World acceptance of authority . . . [she is] certainly not someone who is going to blow any whistles.'

Mace's father and Lovetinska's primary benefactor, Langhorne A. "Tony" Motley, were in fact powerful well beyond the school's confines. General Mace, a veteran of several tours in Vietnam and a proud wearer of the Distinguished Service Medal, had served at Fort Benning as chief of the Ranger Task Force at the United States Army Infantry School, then as the commander of the Ranger Training Brigade. In 1989, he was made brigadier general. In 1991, he retired, leaving behind him a reputation as a ruthless and abrasive commander who led by intimidation and by bullying. Lovetinska's benefactor's connections crisscrossed military and political realms. A former Air Force officer who had served as ambassador to Brazil, Motley was appointed assistant secretary of state of inter-American affairs under Ronald Reagan, a role in which he served as "the architect and the general contractor and chief mason of our policy in Central America," in the words of George P. Shultz. It was a hard time to occupy that seat. Political conflict over policy hastened his exit. Motley, opined the *National Journal,* was "a casualty of the bureaucratic sniping generated by the highly contentious debate over Central America."

Messer and Mentavlos had no such powerful figures at their backs. That, V believed, left them vulnerable.

"The goal is quite simple and is what it has always been," V said. "That is to keep The Citadel the way it is. To put the issue in clearer, although perhaps too narrow terms, to keep the school de facto nearly all male while at the same time putting forth a barrage of disingenuous window dressing."

By then, the Supreme Court had spoken. Outside interest in the school had dissipated. Only on homecoming weekend did it briefly reignite. As alumni gathered to cheer the struggling Bulldogs on the football field, Messer, Mentavlos and Lovetinska reported to their classes with their heads shaved nearly clean. Those self-inflicted "barracks haircuts" were an ugly botch. The barber did repairs and left all three with knob cuts, indistinguishable from the men's. Outside the gates, the world was laughing softly. The Citadel, having backed off its much-pilloried intent to shave Shannon's head, could now boast three female cadets shorn nearly to the skin. It made a perfect circle. The school had its scalps after all, though the women did the cutting. Their forlorn images appeared from coast to coast and dominated the front page of the Charleston paper on the very day that thousands of alumni converged on that old ground.

At the infirmary that fall, Pat Locklair, a member of the nursing staff, shared many of V's concerns. More and more cadets, she said, were showing signs of trauma. Quietly, she struggled with a rising sense of helplessness and shame. Knobs that year seemed slack and dazed. Many wandered in with injuries that did not fit neat explanations. She soothed and salved each one. "I'm the patients' advocate," she said. "I stay because I love these boys." Yet by then she thought of leaving. The corps that year appeared to be almost as brutal as any she had ever seen. She was discouraged and depressed. "There's part of me, you know, I don't want to know what's going on here," she said, tears streaming down her face. All around her, loyal Citadel men and respected institutions underscored that basic instinct. Administrators dismissed her fears as motherly overprotectiveness. Nor did she want to involve the police. The one time she called 911 on a private matter (suspecting that a burglar was lingering outside her house), a former cadet appeared at her door grinning with his new badge.

Another fact made reporting almost impossible. Most cadets vehemently denied that they had ever been abused. Life was easier that way.

"I heard of another Citadel once," V wrote wistfully while home for his Thanksgiving break. "It was a noble place of honor and distinction where people entered as equals and were given the opportunity to make what they could of themselves. . . . That Citadel only existed in the heart of a day student from Powdersville."

Over subsequent weeks, as the weather in Charleston cooled and darkness took the campus earlier each night, V's tone turned hopeless and morose. There was nothing he could prove, he said. All he knew, he knew by instinct and experience. It was not enough. If he spoke out, he felt convinced, the corps would turn against him. Everything he had worked for and all the tuition that his parents paid would come to nothing.

By early December, V's messages became fragmented. At times he was hostile, at other times resigned. Increasingly, he struggled with insomnia and rage. Repeatedly, he called himself a coward and wondered what to do. "I don't sleep much anymore," he said dejectedly one day. "I am afraid." He didn't know exactly why.

On December 13, V's fears took public form. Mentavlos and Messer sought refuge in the school's infirmary. A new scandal soon erupted. The story that they told matched many that had come before. In long sessions with lawyers, school officials, police, reporters, FBI investigators, Justice Department representatives and old friends, the two girls described a vicious and sometimes horrifying ordeal that had intensified throughout the fall. Toward the end of that long cycle, at a time when their exhaustion peaked and their wills were seriously corroded, several upperclassmen took the girls aside, poured flammable liquid on their clothing near their breasts and then approached with licks of flame. At last, the girls came forward.

V broke a brief silence three days after they went public. "I am so scared right now I don't know what to do or where to go," he wrote. He was ashamed and full of sorrow. "I've let the women down. I've let myself down. I'm a coward. . . . Damn me. Damn us all."

In Bond Hall that winter, old grooves of contempt were carefully retraced. Those girls were washing out, the faithful said. Their grades were poor, their wills were weak. They needed an excuse. Terry Leedom suggested that perhaps upcoming final examinations had triggered their complaints. "The timing is interesting," he told reporters. "Usually people come up with these things around this time of year—at finals." When pressed, Leedom said he was not accusing those students of lying. Yet his insinuations set the seeds of doubt. He suggested that the girls were sexually loose, drank too much and behaved deceitfully. On national television he barked that they were caught eating popcorn in a place where they were not authorized to be. Deep inside The Citadel, the faithful nodded glumly as petty transgressions gained the force of major flaws.

Cliff Poole and Jimmie Jones moved quickly to soothe any disturbance. In a letter to "The Citadel Family" written on December 20, they defended the administration's actions. "We have constantly and actively provided oversight and made inquiries in an effort to identify any difficulties, problems or misconduct," they informed alumni. When school officials did learn of the harassment, they said, immediate action followed.

On campus, some cadets laughed openly at the unfolding drama. When Harvey Messer escorted his daughter to her final exams, several cadets stood by and loudly mocked the hazing charges. "Oh, they doused her with lighter fluid and set her on fire!" one of them hissed. "Oh, they *drowned* her in lighter fluid," came an echo. Harvey did not hide his rage. "I didn't send her down there to get hurt, beaten and set on fire," he snapped. He called the school a "torture camp" and said his daughter sometimes cried hysterically when she called home. But she pleaded with her father not to call the school. If he complained, his daughter cautioned, her life would just get worse.

Many cadets laughed and said "the fire thing" was nothing but a joke. If those two girls were burned, they asked, where were their scars to prove it? If they were hurt or terrorized, why didn't they report it at the time?

When Kim Messer explained to Dawes Cooke why she chose to leave the school she was concise and to the point. "First, the setting us on fire, being hit and punched by the company commander, the company XO, getting shoved with a rifle by my cadre sergeant, being interrupted while I was sleeping, having people come in—upperclassmen come in—during study periods, not eating, not getting enough sleep, having food thrown on my clothes—food like mustard and ketchup thrown on my clothes during lunch—[ordered to drink] tea until I threw up."

The Justice Department depositions, the victims' statements to the school, The Citadel's own commandant's board hearings and the FBI and South Carolina Law Enforcement Division studies all moved through their sad paces. What they discovered was a pattern long familiar to the school. The two girls were diagnosed with pelvic stress fractures early in the fall. Once the diagnosis was made, they were singled out as slackers in the corps. New difficulties followed.

As the story filtered out into the newspapers, Jim Bradin's temper rose. Though he had marched in Charlie Company with Cliff Poole and Tony Motley, had worked as a tac officer and commandant and had been a member of the board, he felt a lifetime of unquestioning loyalty come to a sudden end. "The sounds you hear coming from Charleston are the familiar sounds of wagons being circled," he wrote testily in an e-mail as the school prepared for its defense. "The Brotherhood is gathering; digging in; stringing razor wire; planting mines and planning final defensive fires. . . . What is this all about? Hell, I don't know. Every time I begin to get comfortable with that damn place, they haul off and do something catastrophically stupid. Apparently, two of the girls have been subjected to a living hell for the last few months. They have been on 'light duty' as the result of pelvic stress fractures, and in E Company to boot."

Stalag Echo, it was called. Since the 1960s E Company had carefully maintained a reputation as among the most "military" in the school. Cadets used the term as a euphemism for its particularly virulent forms of discipline. Echo Company was well known, too, for the prevalence of Nazi lore and memorabilia within its circle.

In correspondences that spring, Bradin signed off as "the old cavalryman" and said he had put his boots of war back on. Once he started speaking out, he discovered other alumni who agreed. Tentatively at first, then with increasing confidence, those men prepared to make their distress public. For each among them the simple act of speaking out meant breaking years of ingrained loyalty and a tendency to "keep things in the family." When Jim decided to become involved, his wife, Jervey, retreated with migraines, afraid of retribution and frightened of the couple's vulnerabilities. In the Bradins' hometown of Beaufort, The Citadel's network was pervasive. Still, Jim Bradin forced the issue. "The alleged fire incident is not being denied," he noted with disgust. "It alone is so far outside the box even I have trouble understanding it. If nothing else proves correct or true, this one stupid act ought to be enough to send shivers down spines; it has done so to mine. Like many similar incidents in the past, my guess is that this is but the proverbial 'tip of the iceberg.'"

Two cadets spoke out, meanwhile, suggesting there had been a cover-up orchestrated by the administration. Citadel officials denied it and traveled to newspapers around the state to make their case. "A spear went through my heart," said Joe Trez.

V broke a short silence after Christmas. Calling from home, he introduced himself by his e-mail code name, then talked for nearly five hours, carefully reviewing every charge that the two girls made and adding insight from the vantage point of a cadet. The fire incident, he said, seemed to have stemmed from a common "parlor trick" played in many companies. The trick was performed with an alcohol-based nail polish remover used to strip new brass of its protective finish. The game was fairly simple. A knob was ordered to brace and cup his hands in front of him while an upperclassman poured a cool liquid into his palm. A match was lit. A fire leapt and sizzled. "The vapors burn," V explained. "The liquid doesn't. That's the trick. It all burns harmlessly away. I could do it all day long. But if somebody panics and turns their hand upside down or tries to wipe it off, then you've got flaming liquid everywhere." It was, he said, a means of teaching loyalty. The purpose was to show new cadets that they must entrust themselves to the system. The lesson was straightforward: Follow us, and you'll be fine. Rebel, and you will feel our heat. Knobs who lost control were sometimes hurt. But then, of

course, the victims were to blame. "Nobody hurts you," V explained. "If
you move, you hurt yourself. That's the way it works." Of course, with
the two girls, he pointed out, the liquid was poured not into their open
palms but straight onto their clothing.

In a deposition, Cliff Poole described what he had come to believe
was a serious miscalculation on his own part. He tried too hard to get
those girls to stay, he said. "I think if I had to do it over, I would probably step back from that and just let the system work its will." That way,
he concluded, those girls would have been long gone before the difficulties of that fall.

It was spring in Charleston as Poole said those words. And in that
radiantly beautiful month of April, while the Holy City was heady with
sweet fragrances and softened by a blanket of fresh flowers, Bradin and
his band called fellow graduates to action. "Today," those alumni said in
a letter mailed to every graduate, "cadets live in an abominable system . . . [one that] tolerates physical abuse, extortion of money, denial
of food, interruption of study time, and deprivation of sleep."

Richard Lovelace, the Conway lawyer who had been peppering the
administration with critiques ever since the Faulkner case began, counted
himself a member of "that merry band of renegades" and pledged a million dollars to its cause. He wanted broad reforms within the barracks
and vowed to push and press until he felt assured they were in place.
"Phase Two is trench knife and piano wire time," Bradin reported with
some glee. He called Lovelace "our junkyard dog" and said that he
would stop at nothing. Lovelace agreed, smiling, saying he had waited
thirty years to wage that fight.

Throughout that spring, V's anger increased and his disaffection
deepened. Slowly, he pulled back a curtain that had long hung heavily
across the sally ports. That curtain was The Citadel's essential paradox: a
screen to all the world, invisible and yet opaque, a mystery in plain sight.
It closed those walls to all but its initiates. He would be a surreptitious
guide behind that drape, breaking every code of cultish loyalty he had
been trained to honor. The world that he described was a boys' world
nearly devoid of supervision. In it, the childish merged seamlessly with
the obscene.

In classrooms that spring, professors tried to keep their wits and continue with their course work. But it was difficult. Watts had been correct. The college sat in the eye of a hurricane one year before. Now it felt
the backwind, and it was more intense. Cadets showed the strain of it in

class, sometimes snapping at each other and lashing out with threats of violence. Professor Peter Mailloux watched sadly as that last safe haven was destroyed. There was a pattern to those students' misery, he explained. "Boys cry with me all the time when there's some kind of sympathy. They just crack. But they're okay if you yell."

Mailloux was as shocked as anyone about the revelations of that season. And though he was hardly naive about the ordeals inside the barracks, he was taken aback by some things he heard that year. One student told him that tradition in his company dictated that on Ring Night a single student should be tied to a chair and left where everyone could get to him. Mailloux told the student that if someone ever tried to tie him up, he would still be fighting when the sun came up. But the boy just frowned dejectedly. "You don't understand, sir," the student answered glumly. "If you did fight back, your life would be miserable for the whole rest of the year."

V confirmed the practice but dismissed the rope as a redundancy. "Are you really of the belief that the designated knob would otherwise run away or fight back?" he asked. "Do you think upperclassmen need a special occasion like Ring Night to abuse a particular knob?" On the telephone, he elaborated. The ropes used on Ring Night were not strictly necessary, he explained. But they were an important part of the stress induced by that experience. "The rope provides the terror, the helplessness, the lack of control and fear, the vulnerability," V said. "Without the rope the knob can say, 'I am here, I am taking this by choice. If I want to, I can leave. I can always leave.' That provides a false sense of security and of strength. It's that sense of a total loss of control with the rope that is what does the emotional harm. . . . They pick somebody who is different. From New York, short, wears thick glasses, anything." In fact, the emotional dynamics were more complex than at first appeared. "There's this duality," V cautioned. "If you do it, there's always an inducement. The guys say, 'Here is your opportunity to earn grace. You'd like to be *In* and you are not *In* now, and we are going to give you the opportunity.' So there's almost an element where they passively comply."

V found it easier, at the start, to talk about ordeals that he had never suffered. Smoothly critiquing from a distance, he described drills and routines with the dispassion of a lawyer. Knobs were always "set up to fuck up," he explained. The game took many forms. "Some unseen hand swipes your brass or trashes your rack just before an unannounced inspection. Upperclassmen know the gag. . . . Or your textbook and

notes disappear the night before a big test only to have some upperclassmen jump your shit later for leaving the stuff in the latrine. Calculators
disappear only to turn up later when some upperclassman who wouldn't
pee on you if you were on fire generously offers to help you find it and
then you get a ration for misplacing it. An upperclassman would come
in to personally check a big assignment right before it's due. Somehow
the thing catches on fire and you catch hell from the prof because it's
turned in late."

Tentatively at first and then with rising passion, he described his own
worst suffering. "It is not all that rare for upperclassmen to shave down a
knob," he noted casually one day. Generally, the ritual started at the toes
and stopped just at the neck. He described it as a "prank" and made a
sharp distinction based on sex. A group of fully clothed men who huddled around a naked woman and shaved her head to toe would be considered rapists, he felt sure. "No one is going to take on that kind of
liability." Among men, the practice was easier to dismiss as nothing but
a joke. "What brings on shaving down a knob? What brings anything on
a knob? Nothing besides being a knob. Yes, it is a full body shave, when
the knob is naked and braced. Depending on the charity of the upperclassmen involved, it may be a dry shave and/or with rubbing alcohol
applied afterwards." The practice, he admitted, had led to ugly scenes
and some sad endings.

V had been shaved, too. At first he described the experience as no
worse than his knob haircut. But shortly after that admission, a new
tone of bitterness crept into his messages. Why had no one stopped it?
he wondered. Why did no one care? "Nobody said a word about it even
though the other knobs and I showered with other cadets all the time.
None of the so-called adults, including the tac officers, ever questioned
why male knobs had shaved legs which showed in exercise shorts. Everybody knows the routines. That is exactly why Jeanie could go around
with a hole burned in her exercise uniform and not get called on it."

Pat Locklair sometimes asked cadets why they would shave their legs.
Their answers embodied barracks logic. To keep their shirts tucked
tight, they said, they ran elastic stays along their legs down to their feet.
Sometimes those stays caught and chafed against their legs. Shaving
helped. Shaved arms were harder to explain. She did not ask. Nor did
she press those boys for answers when she found that all their hair was
shaved. They did not want to tell. She did not want to know. It made
a ginger balance. She let her mind close off and concentrated most on

treating injuries that she could reach, like that of a boy who arrived at the infirmary with chemical burns on his penis and his testicles, or that of the black cadet who had reached for his eyedrops only to find them laced with bleach, or the countless other cases of boys suffering from hysteria who were carried to the infirmary "with their arms and legs drawn up . . . unable to tell you what is wrong."

Throughout the spring, V tapped urgent messages saying that some cadets were thinking of speaking out against the system. Through fathers and friends, those students had learned that a group of alumni was preparing to criticize the school. The news encouraged them. But they did not wholly trust it. Was it a ruse, a way to flush out the unfaithful? Would there be "another Byrd case—someone hurt, nothing done?" V looked back upon his freshman year with growing nostalgia for the boy that he had been. "The tragedy of war is that one becomes the same as their adversary in the end," he said. "There is a real feeling of despair, fear, and hopelessness now. The sense of shame we all feel is overwhelming. No one wants to talk about that."

Eventually, he shared his hardest stories. As a freshman V was constantly harassed and several times injured during hazing episodes in the barracks. He stayed silent. The trauma only increased. It culminated in an act of obscene violence. "I still have nightmares about what happened . . . ," V said. "You would not imagine what some of the guys that year were capable of."

In retrospect, he rued his silence and perceived it as a form of cowardice. "The difference between Shannon and myself was not our ideals, which we shared, but our courage to protect them," he concluded sadly. Shannon left and faced the shame the world heaped on her for that failure. "I chose to abandon The Citadel of my ideals to remain in its ugly and hollow namesake. I had become a part of the system which was no more than the aggregate of its ugly parts." To survive, he leaned on friends and held his secrets close and dreamed that someday he might be a hero. Meanwhile, every awful detail that he knew nagged at him that spring.

Late one night in March, Richard Lovelace leaped from his bed and scribbled several phrases hastily across an envelope: "501-C, civil conspiracy, RICO, breach of fiduciary duty, unfair practices." Together, they made a careful shorthand of his strategy, one he jovially described as modeled on the federal government's in its long war against the Mafia.

"If you're going to really cripple somebody, hit them in the pocket-book," Lovelace said with a broad grin. The problem with the Faulkner case, he decided, was South Carolina's taxpayers paid most of the bills. He wanted to reverse the weight of risk, calling individual board members to task and forcing them to hire networks of new lawyers at their own expense. In a terse letter to Jimmie Jones, Lovelace laid out his objectives, his assets and his allies. If reform was not forthcoming, he threatened, "we shall launch our missiles, and the war is on."

In Charleston that May, weary veterans of the Faulkner case met for one last time. The Justice Department had prepared to use the treatment of Messer and Mentavlos as a way to attack the school's plans for the integration of women in the corps. Yet just before the court convened, a new stack of papers was delivered to Judge Houck's chambers. Those papers detailed a new assimilation plan with new guidelines and controls. Court hearings were suspended as lawyers worked behind closed doors. After several days of haggling, both sides declared a victory. A new stack of papers would be added to the pile.

Val Vojdik had no place in those negotiations and no reason to be in Charleston that week. But she could not resist those final days of conflict. Paperwork and gentlemanly assurances meant nothing to her now. "They're blowing it," she exploded when she heard the details of that backstage deal. "They are blowing this whole case." She wanted nothing short of revolution. Just as Cliff Poole feared, she wanted the entire corps to change.

During that last courtroom scene, as The Citadel's new assimilation plan was about to be embraced, Lovelace slid along a worn wooden bench to settle down beside the Board of Visitors' vice president, the gentlemanly author of the Mood Report. Frank Mood smiled and gestured a smooth welcome. But Lovelace, Bradin's "junkyard dog," leaned in close and spoke softly, almost whispering his plans. While he talked, Mood's face paled, then flushed under his crown of perfectly white hair.

"Let's talk," Mood mouthed as the gavel sounded and the judge settled down into his seat.

On the witness stand, Poole declared that a new day had now dawned. The Citadel promised to be the best coeducational military college in the nation. It was the same speech he had given to newspaper editors around the South. Before the day was done, however, Judge Houck turned toward Vojdik and asked if she would like to speak. Dawes

Cooke shot to his feet with an objection. The judge just waved him off. "I don't know anybody that has spent more time on this case than Valorie Vojdik," the judge interrupted. "I want to hear what she has to say."

She was brief. She whittled three years of frustration into a single lean suggestion. Why not require all cadets to sign a statement once a week noting whether they knew of any hazing or harassment that had taken place? Judge Houck leaned forward. If a cadet signed a false statement, she advised, that student would be expelled for a violation of the honor code. It was not a perfect solution, she admitted, but it would provide an avenue for strict accountability.

There was an angry murmur from the back. Lewis Spearman, Watts's loyal right-hand man, shook his head. Poole flushed and cleared his throat. Vojdik continued, unperturbed. Such a rule, she said, would break the "code of silence" that had long enveloped that old school.

When she sat down, Cooke asked for a short break. Over to one side, Spearman laughed derisively. Vojdik knew nothing of the school, he scoffed. Her suggestion only confirmed it. A written form like that, he said, would only "bureaucratize right and wrong, integrity and whatever. It will give the cadets the idea that by merely filling out a form, they've met their moral obligations." They would no longer have to search their souls to find integrity. It defied every sacred principle the school stood for.

When court was reconvened, Poole was called to the witness stand. He provided a more scholarly objection. The shift in policy suggested by opposing counsel, he said sourly, would undermine The Citadel's "Improper Question" rule. Under that rule, it was expected that cadets would volunteer any knowledge of abuse. It was a matter of honor. It was a question of history. Vojdik could not have understood that, the interim president said disdainfully; she did not understand his school.

For Vojdik that week, bitter endings met her everywhere. The city's charm had ebbed. During a walk through town one day, she flinched as someone leaned out a truck window screaming ugly obscenities. "Cocksucker!" a stranger boomed, leaning on his horn. She knew the word was meant for her.

The 1995–96 yearbook showed Junior Sword Drill on its cover. There, in a childish drawing, fourteen cadets stood in their formal uniforms, shakos standing tall, their arms aloft to make an arc of steel. Inside, a misty photograph showed the Summerall Chapel underneath a glinting moon. A cross glowed ghostly white. Among the yearbook's images were several showing boys tied down in chairs and smeared with boot black and with shaving cream. A cap in another photograph was marked with a phrase from the 1960s: "Mike Reich." Swastikas were scribbled elsewhere.

It fell to Poole that year to write the school's response to fresh allegations that The Citadel was hiding a dark subculture. He did so with his usual precision. "The Citadel categorically denies that it now condones or ever has condoned the display of Nazi emblems or regalia anywhere on campus," he protested. General Mace, the commandant assigned to replace Trez after the debacle of that autumn, was ordered to conduct an extensive investigation. It was designed to stretch throughout that summer—while all cadets were gone.

"They are blind," said Will Hiley, a junior who would return that fall to lead Golf Company. "They do not want to see." Hiley thought the school should close. Only by shutting it down for at least four years, he said, could The Citadel again become what it was meant to be. Painstakingly, over a dinner out of town, Hiley compared the men in Bond and Jenkins Halls to women who survived Cambodia's killing fields. Doctors, he explained, found nothing wrong with those women physiologically. And yet those war survivors could not see.

Vojdik was finally ready to retreat. After her last day in court, while The Citadel's new assimilation plan was being signed and finalized, she and a former colleague from Shearman & Sterling went to a Charleston restaurant to relax. "It's time for the next team," Vojdik said, quickly draining a half-filled wineglass. "I'm tired."

"That's the problem," her colleague replied dejectedly. "This whole thing wears people out. That's how they win. They wear you down."

"We need a tag team," Vojdik responded. "I'm ready to pass this on." She stirred her she-crab soup and bent to take in its rich smell. She took a spoonful and smiled with satisfaction. Then her face fell. "They know," she said distractedly. "They all know what goes on. They just want to protect their little clubs and live in their little world."

That night, a television crew that had been on the campus on and off for several months—ferried about by Terry Leedom and a handpicked crew of upperclassmen—produced a report showing the college as a fierce protector of old values and stern discipline. Leedom was beside himself with pleasure the next day. He arranged a press conference for the morning. Petra Lovetinska and Nancy Mace, both of whom had remained silent that whole year, would finally speak. Each had passed through Recognition Day and earned her place as a rising sophomore. They held the same opinions. In jovial, even tones, they indicated that the other women simply could not handle stress.

Was there ever any hazing?

None, came the answer. Neither Mace nor Lovetinska would have stood for it.

"Someone said something to me that I didn't appreciate," Mace said calmly. "But the gentleman apologized."

Supportive laughter surged around the room.

Lovetinska said that she once had a minor problem, too. "A senior was asking me out, which is against school regulations," she told reporters with a grin. "He ended up walking sixty tours on the quad."

Laughter rang again.

Was there some sort of Nazi underground, someone wanted to know.

No, that was not true, both girls said calmly.

"I haven't seen any Nazi signs," Lovetinska added. "If there are any, I haven't seen them. Sometimes we would say Stalag Echo, which symbolizes that Echo Company is sometimes difficult."

"Yes," said Nancy Mace, "it's sort of like a prison."

"Yes, like a prison," echoed Lovetinska. "That's what some people say it's like."

Back in his office, Leedom beamed and moved his hand through the air to imitate a jet at take-off. "They were great," he gushed. "Fantastic. They just did fantastic." He grinned and shook his head and moved his hand abruptly skyward. Pursing his lips, he imitated the whining roar of engines.

Over in Jenkins Hall, Tony Lackey and Roger Popham sat at a round table. They had piles of paper to attend to. There were new orders to follow and new plans to integrate into the workings of the corps. Things were changing. Lackey was hopeful. New faces would be coming in the fall. Women would soon play a greater role both in the corps and in Jenkins Hall. The summer would be busy. "It's going to take a lot of work," Lackey said, shaking his head stiffly, "but we're moving in the right direction. We really are. It's a fine school. You've got to remember that. It's a fine school. We'll change. We are going to make a success of it."

He would do his best. He always did. But he looked older and more wary at the end of that long year. None of it had been easy. The hot lights were still on. Yet always, he would be a loyal graduate. The agony of change would fade away. His alma mater would survive. He put a lot of stock in the new president. "So far the signs are all good," Lackey said with confidence. "We are working hard, believe we will have a good year. Remember the school is a good school with good values and ethics. People from time to time mess these things up, but the institution marches on."

A new time of reform began. That summer, a retired Marine would move into Bond Hall. When he did so, Major General John Grinalds asked that the broad wooden desk used by many presidents before him be removed. In its place, he set up a small field desk as a signal of the seriousness of his intention to clean house. Six months earlier, he had announced that he believed there were three systems operating at The Citadel. There was a written system, outlined in the *Blue Book,* he said. There was a "permitted" system through which school officials winked off any problems. And there was a secret, "unseen" system that functioned late at night. He vowed to make them one, and worthy of the school. He had some different ideas about leadership. Leaders, he believed, should *serve* those whom they led.

It was hot that May when Grinalds came. The sun already bore down hard. The case was finally closed. When Judge Houck adjourned his court, dozens of men and women emerged from that dim room laughing and relieved. At last, it was over. In small clusters, they filed past an oil painting in the hall, preoccupied with the banalities of endings, details to attend to, bags to pack, planes to catch. Above their heads, Fritz Hollings, a member of the United States Senate and former South Carolina governor and a graduate of the Citadel class of 1942, gazed down upon the scene, his hair white, his expression quite intense, his garb somber and elegant. In that artist's pose, the senator's hands were cupped before him as though to hold an invisible orb, an orb of power, an orb of wisdom, a circle of tradition. Against that palest flesh there flashed a band of gold, his sole adornment.

Acknowledgments

While this book is not a work of history in any traditional sense, I owe a great debt to many historians who have written ably and with passion of The Citadel and of the South and of the growth of America as a nation. I have benefited, too, from the thoughtful scholarship of others who have written on themes and subjects that course throughout this tale. Walter J. Fraser Jr.'s fine volume *Charleston! Charleston!* managed to do exactly what all my favorite English professors used to urge, which was to both instruct and delight. It is a pleasure and a treasure trove, and I drew much of my understanding of that complex city from his work. Walter Edgar's *South Carolina: A History* provided a welcome rounding out. Taken together, John Peyre Thomas's *The History of the South Carolina Military Academy,* Oliver J. Bond's *The Story of The Citadel,* and D. D. Nicholson Jr.'s *A History of The Citadel: The Years of Summerall and Clark* provided solid ground from which to spring.

College officials opened the doors to the school's Museum and Archives, from which I pulled a clearer understanding of the school's internal workings, particularly from Mark Clark's time forward. Several members of the staff at The Citadel's Daniel Library proved particularly helpful guiding me to back issues of the *Brigadier* and the college's full collection of yearbooks. They also helped me find obscure and out-of-print books from other sources in the region. I was always grateful for their assistance. John W. Meffert, then the executive director of the Preservation Society of Charleston, set me early on my way, pointing me to books and sharing his own insights. Because of his help, I was spared much frustration. Charleston is a fascinating city and has been much written about. Yet for my own purposes, several books proved particularly illuminating. *The Shadow of a Dream,* Peter A. Coclanis's very thorough study of the low country's economic life from 1670 to 1920, provided a concise yet detailed examination of Charleston's cycles of boom and bust. *Black Charlestonians: A Social History, 1822–1885* by Bernard E. Powers Jr., was another work of rich detail that opened windows to an era long since gone. *Days of Defiance: Sumter, Secession, and the Coming of the Civil War* provided a fine account of that most crucial time. James M. McPherson's *Battle Cry of*

Freedom moved the clock hands forward. For an understanding of the history of women in the South I relied most upon Margaret Ripley Wolfe's *Daughters of Canaan: A Saga of Southern Women* and Catherine Clinton's *The Plantation Mistress.* Those books and many others inevitably led me to a fascination with the Grimké sisters, who, to our good fortune, left behind original writings of their own.

Though I have read about the Vietnam War most of my life, I found myself going back again to several classics from that era. Of these, *Vietnam: A History* by Stanley Karnow and *A Bright Shining Lie* by Neil Sheehan proved just as fresh and insightful as the day they were published. I leaned on both. Taylor Branch's *Parting the Waters: America in the King Years 1954–1963* and Leon F. Litwack's *Trouble in Mind: Black Southerners in the Age of Jim Crow* provided details from the nation's bitter struggles over civil rights and supplied context for material from The Citadel's own files and history. Other books that influenced my thinking on the social evolution of this century were David McCullough's biography *Truman* and Alan Brinkley's marvelously readable textbook *The Unfinished Nation: A Concise History of the American People.*

Several books on war, warriors and the trauma of soldiering stand side by side on my bookshelves with works on trauma in the civilian sphere. That placement is no accident. As different as those realms are, the terror and damage each can produce are equally real and equally deserving of respectful study and deep thought. Perhaps the most important of these books to me was Judith Lewis Herman's *Trauma and Recovery: The Aftermath of Violence—From Domestic Abuse to Political Terror.* Susan Griffin's *A Chorus of Stones* provides an improbably lyrical and profoundly disturbing look at the legacy of violence in ways that cross seamlessly over the usually opaque borders separating warfare, education and home. Taken together, these books offer powerful testimony. *The Harmony of Illusions* by Allan Young, though it diverges somewhat in its theoretical approach, provided a sound history of medical and psychological theories about trauma.

I owe a genuine debt to many at The Citadel. Difficult as the subject of my interviews often was, many men and women there gave unstintingly of their time, their insights and their own experience to help me understand their institution. The college administration allowed me open access to the campus (excluding classrooms and barracks) for nearly one year. During that time, I spoke with hundreds of cadets, administrators, employees and faculty—sometimes formally, sometimes less so—and observed almost every aspect of their life at The Citadel. On Hell Night, 1996, I sat in the infirmary watching trembling and hysterical boys breathing into paper bags. In May 1996, a college employee appeared at my house ready to talk and lugging a small collection of Tupperware. As I opened one container after the next to discover roasted turkey, mashed potatoes, candied yams and an array of other homemade delicacies I commented that she had brought us a Thanksgiving dinner. "Yes," she said on that warm spring evening. "I have. It is my Thanksgiving to speak freely." That moment and many others moved me more deeply than I can say.

Some among my sources appear nowhere in these pages and, at their request, cannot be acknowledged publicly. I thank them anyway. Others appear as central figures in the tale. Some of those have become valued friends. Two cadets appear under names changed at their request. Craig and his friend who dropped out at the same time Shannon Faulkner did were fearful of retribution and asked that their identities be obscured. I have done so. Every other individual in the book but one spoke for the record or appeared in the court case speaking under oath. Yet the cadet whom I call V remains anonymous even to me. In the course of a year, we spoke on the telephone once and exchanged enough e-mail messages to fill more than one computer disk—a correspondence that is, incredibly, actually longer than this book. Much of that dialogue contained material that I confirmed elsewhere and knit into the text using those other sources. Some details, however, were too personal to verify beyond his own account. Other matters involved the abuse of fellow cadets whose struggles I confirmed but whose privacy I had no wish and perhaps no right to disturb. As for V himself, I leave it to readers to determine whether his comments and his accounts of his own treatment should be dismissed as "stories" told by a cowardly adolescent or legitimate observations shared by an anguished soul. That ambiguity is necessary because as many Citadel men understand so well, belief is something different than proof, and proof can be exquisitely elusive in that environment.

Generations of the Faulkner family opened their doors and their hearts to me. I wish to thank them all. Their lawyers, too, were generous with their time and their materials. The American Civil Liberties Union allowed me open access to their files, a detail that spared me hours in a dimly lit courthouse. Shearman & Sterling likewise proved generous in both time and access, as did Dawes Cooke, The Citadel's lead lawyer. His flawlessly courteous staff copied computer disks and shared their time as well.

In Charleston, Bert and Helen Pruitt offered bounteous warmth and welcome doses of true Charleston hospitality—often washed down with bushels of laughter and glasses of something a bit stronger. For the friendship, humor and soulful insights of Alexandra Lehmann through much of this time, I am indebted. Stephen Crowley, a gifted colleague and dear friend at the *New York Times,* gave me invaluable help with photographs. Johanna Lambert shared quiet but crucial encouragement—prologue to epilogue. My editor at Knopf, Jonathan Segal, steered me firmly across the rockiest of shoals and won my respect and fondness while keeping me from an ugly shipwreck. Other friends know who they are and how much I have valued and needed their support. To all of the above, my gratitude runs deep.

Index

A NOTE ABOUT THE AUTHOR

Catherine S. Manegold covered the litigation between Shannon Faulkner and The Citadel as a reporter with the *New York Times*. Prior to joining that newspaper's staff, she worked as a foreign correspondent for the *Philadelphia Inquirer* and *Newsweek* magazine, reporting on military and civilian matters throughout Southeast Asia, Korea and Japan. In 1991 she covered the Gulf War. While at the *Times*, which she joined in 1992, she reported on cultural issues, the U.S. military intervention in Haiti, the terrorist attack on the World Trade Center and the bombing of the federal building in Oklahoma City. While working on this book she lived in Washington, D.C., and Charleston.

A NOTE ON THE TYPE

This book was set in Adobe Garamond. Designed for the Adobe Corporation by Robert Slimbach, the fonts are based on types first cut by Claude Garamond (c. 1480–1561). Garamond was a pupil of Geoffroy Tory and is believed to have followed the Venetian models, although he introduced a number of important differences, and it is to him that we owe the letter we now know as "old style." He gave to his letters a certain elegance and feeling of movement that won their creator an immediate reputation and the patronage of Francis I of France.

Composed by NK Graphics, Keene, New Hampshire
Printed and bound by Quebecor Printing, Martinsburg, West Virginia
Designed by Robert C. Olsson